THE *AGAMEMNON* OF AESCHYLUS

The *Agamemnon* of Aeschylus

A Commentary for Students

by

DAVID RAEBURN and OLIVER THOMAS

OXFORD
UNIVERSITY PRESS

OXFORD

UNIVERSITY PRESS

Great Clarendon Street, Oxford OX2 6DP

Oxford University Press is a department of the University of Oxford.
It furthers the University's objective of excellence in research, scholarship,
and education by publishing worldwide in

Oxford New York

Auckland Cape Town Dar es Salaam Hong Kong Karachi
Kuala Lumpur Madrid Melbourne Mexico City Nairobi
New Delhi Shanghai Taipei Toronto

With offices in

Argentina Austria Brazil Chile Czech Republic France Greece
Guatemala Hungary Italy Japan Poland Portugal Singapore
South Korea Switzerland Thailand Turkey Ukraine Vietnam

Oxford is a registered trade mark of Oxford University Press
in the UK and in certain other countries

Published in the United States
by Oxford University Press Inc., New York

© David Raeburn and Oliver Thomas 2011

The moral rights of the authors have been asserted
Database right Oxford University Press (maker)

First published 2011

British Library Cataloguing in Publication Data
Data available

Library of Congress Cataloging in Publication Data
Data available

Typeset by RefineCatch Limited, Bungay, Suffolk
Printed in Great Britain
on acid-free paper by
MPG Books Group, Bodmin and King's Lynn

ISBN 978–0–19–959560–0 (hbk)
978–0–19–959561–7 (pbk)

1 3 5 7 9 10 8 6 4 2

Preface

The *Agamemnon*, and the *Oresteia* of which it is the first part, rank among the masterpieces of European drama. To be able to study this play in the original is one of the richest rewards for the effort of learning ancient Greek. However, the text is extremely challenging, and existing commentaries in English are not a suitable help for first-time readers of Aeschylus today.

Eduard Fraenkel's massive three-volume edition, though an outstanding work of scholarship, contains more material than almost all undergraduate students will have time to absorb; nor does Fraenkel's presentation make it easy to extract quickly the central points from his longer notes. The more commonly used edition by J. D. Denniston and D. L. Page is now rather dated; although the commentary skilfully and forcefully illuminates much of Aeschylus' difficult language, it shows less appreciation of his dramaturgy, imagery, and style.

This book is aimed at students who are approaching the play for the first time. Writing for this audience had various consequences for our presentation. The book had to be affordable and digestible, and at every turn we had to omit interesting material. We have assumed that students tackling *Agamemnon* will have already read a few plays by Euripides or Sophocles in Greek, and some Homer, but we have cited parallels from other authors only rarely. One of our primary concerns was to guide students through the bold, dense language—explaining the more confusing constructions, and elucidating the imagery. But we have not removed the need to consult the large Liddell & Scott frequently, since browsing through the lexicon is so important for learning Greek.

Difficulties of meaning are often complicated by problems of text, many of which make a significant impact on interpretation. Students should not be shielded from these; but a full analysis of every issue would be distracting and unwieldy, and so counter-productive. We have started from and reprinted Page's Oxford Classical Text, which is the edition on which students are currently most likely to be examined. In many passages where total confidence would be foolhardy, we have mentioned alternative construes and left the student to decide between them.

Similarly, we have been selective in our references to the wealth of scholarship on the play, though our particular debt to the work of Martin West and Alan Sommerstein will be evident throughout. In view of our audience we have almost exclusively cited scholarship in English, and so with some reluctance omitted reference to the huge French commentary of Bollack and Judet de la Combe (1981–2, 2001), or to various recent German and Italian monographs such as Gruber (2009). Nevertheless, the Introduction draws a good deal of attention towards secondary literature, which we hope will encourage further study.[1]

Though one can reconstruct only a few details of the play's original performance, we have encouraged students to imagine the staging, and to appreciate the text as a dramatic organism, given its peculiar movement and tension on stage by the power attributed to ominous language. Our commentary also tries to stimulate an appreciation of Aeschylus' poetry, as rich in original vocabulary and in imagery as the tragedies of Shakespeare. Besides the content of the verse, we would stress its sound and rhythm. Hence the appendix on 'Sound and Rhythm' by D.A.R., which he has supplemented with a recording available separately.[2]

Finally, we hope that, after studying *Agamemnon* in the original, our readers will feel confident enough to explore the other two plays of the *Oresteia* in Greek.

This book is very much the product of a joint effort. Initial drafts of the commentary by D.A.R. were developed by O.R.H.T. towards their final form. We discussed the whole commentary together several times over, and by the powers of $\pi\epsilon\iota\theta\dot{\omega}$ reached agreement on almost all points. As indicated by the initials at the end of each section, we divided the introduction between us, though here too we have benefited from each other's comments. The appendix reflects D.A.R.'s particular interest and experience in the live delivery of Greek tragic verse, and he is responsible for the rhythmical analysis supplied there.

[1] It is worth mentioning here Goward (2005), a useful survey of modern approaches to the play.
[2] 'The Agamemnon of Aeschylus recorded in ancient Greek' [CD].

We would like to acknowledge: Hilary O'Shea, Kathleen Fearn, and other staff at the Press for their invaluable assistance; James Morwood for constructive criticism; the staff of Fondation Hardt, where we benefited from a fortnight of intensive study in 2009; colleagues at New College and Christ Church for their encouragement; Henry Mason and Robert Colborn for their typing; and the students on whom earlier versions of our work were tested.

D.A.R., O.R.H.T.

Oxford
2011

Contents

Abbreviations

This list supplements the widely used abbreviations laid out in LSJ and *L'Année philologique*.

CHO   A. Heubeck et al., *A Commentary on Homer's Odyssey*, 3 vols. (Oxford: Clarendon, 1988–92)

Denniston   J. D. Denniston, *The Greek Particles*, 2nd edn. (Oxford: Clarendon, 1954).

D–P   J. D. Denniston and D. L. Page, *Aeschylus: Agamemnon* (Oxford: Clarendon, 1957).

Fraenkel   E. Fraenkel, *Aeschylus: Agamemnon*, 3 vols. (Oxford: Clarendon, 1950).

LIMC   L. Kahil (ed.), *Lexicon iconographicum mythologiae classicae*, 8 vols. (Zurich: Artemis, 1981–99).

LSJ   H. G. Liddell, R. Scott., and H. S. Jones, *A Greek–English Lexicon, with a Revised Supplement*, 9th edn. (Oxford: Clarendon, 1996).

MacNeice   L. MacNeice, *The Agamemnon of Aeschylus* (London: Faber & Faber, 1936).

NP   H. Cancik (ed.), *Brill's New Pauly: Encyclopaedia of the Ancient World: Antiquity*, 15 vols. (Leiden: Brill, 2002–9).

OCD   S. Hornblower and A. Spawforth (eds.), *The Oxford Classical Dictionary*, 3rd edn. (Oxford: Oxford University Press, 1996).

OCT   Oxford Classical Text (= Page, unless stated).

Page   D. L. Page, *Aeschyli tragoediae* (Oxford: Clarendon, 1972).

PMG   D. L. Page, *Poetae melici graeci* (Oxford: Clarendon, 1962).

Smyth   H. W. Smyth, *A Greek Grammar for Colleges* (New York: American Book Co., 1920).

Sommerstein	A. H. Sommerstein, *Aeschylus II: The Oresteia*, Loeb Classical Library (Cambridge, Mass.: Harvard University Press, 2008).
TrGF	B. Snell, S. L. Radt, and R. Kannicht, *Tragicorum graecorum fragmenta*, 5 vols. (Göttingen: Vandenhoeck & Ruprecht, 1971–2004).
West	M. L. West, *Aeschyli tragoediae cum incerti poetae Prometheo*, 2nd edn. (Stuttgart: Teubner, 1998).

Fragments by ancient authors are cited from the following editions:

Alcaeus, Sappho	E. Lobel, E. and D. L. Page, *Poetarum lesbiorum fragmenta* (Oxford: Clarendon, 1955).
Anaximander	H. Diels and W. Kranz, *Die Fragmente der Vorsokratiker*, i, 6th edn. (Berlin: Weidmann, 1951).
Aristophanes, Cratinus	R. Kassel and C. A. Austin, *Poetae comici graeci* (Berlin: De Gruyter, 1983–).
Hesiod	R. Merkelbach and M. L. West, *Fragmenta Hesiodea* (Oxford: Clarendon, 1967).
Pherecydes	R. L. Fowler, *Early Greek Mythography*, i (Oxford: Oxford University Press, 2000).
Solon	M. L. West, *Iambi et elegi graeci ante Alexandrum cantati*, ii, 2nd edn. (Oxford: Oxford University Press, 1992).
Sophocles	*TrGF* iv.

Introduction

Introduction

1. *AGAMEMNON* AND THE *ORESTEIA*

Agamemnon was composed not as an independent work, but as the first movement of a connected tetralogy. Of this, the first three tragedies survive as the *Oresteia* (*Agamemnon, Choephoroe* or *Libation-Bearers, Eumenides*), while the concluding satyr-play (*Proteus*) is almost entirely lost. Exactly what it contained, and how it affected the audience's perception of the preceding trilogy, can only be conjectured. Nevertheless, the trilogy in itself does have a convincing unity both of dramatic shape and of thought, which is essential to any consideration of its parts.[1] When Aeschylus directed and probably acted in the *Oresteia*, at the City Dionysia festival during the month of Elaphebolion 458 BC, he was nearing seventy (born 525/4; died 456/5), and was the dominant Attic tragedian—a master of his art. According to ancient sources, who used early festival records, his career had begun without any victories in its first fifteen years (499–485). But from the death of Phrynichus (473?) to his own death, Aeschylus was nearly unbeatable. The *Oresteia* tetralogy, like those containing *Persae, Septem*, and *Supplices*, won first prize.[2]

We now give a short overview of the story of the trilogy, in chronological order. This offers no more than a bare skeleton of the trilogy; the flesh consists in numerous ideas, themes, and images, and in the handling of the theatrical space and characterization, for which see §§ 4–9 below.

Prior events recalled in the trilogy: In a quarrel between the brothers Atreus and Thyestes over the sovereignty of Argos, Thyestes

---

[1] Although Aeschylus in particular composed several connected tetralogies, the *Oresteia* is our only instance of connected plays surviving. We therefore cannot know how typical its use of the form was. For the normal guess that *Proteus* dealt with Menelaus' return, see e.g. Griffith (2002), 238–9. Aristarchus (a scholar of the second century BC) interestingly described the *Oresteia* as a trilogy rather than a tetralogy: Schol. Ar. *Ran.* 1124.

[2] The string of victories suggests not only the brilliance of the author (which we can sense on the page), but also good directing and high production values.

seduced Atreus' wife Aerope.[3] Thyestes was exiled, then returned as a suppliant, upon which Atreus welcomed him to a feast, but killed his young children (except Aegisthus) and served them to their father. Thyestes cursed the joint family, then left Argos again with Aegisthus. Besides human motives, Aeschylus grounds this series of crimes in a chorus of Erinyes or a δαίμων, which has haunted the palace since the seduction of Aerope.

A subsequent chain of crime and punishment was initiated by Paris, who abused Menelaus' hospitality by seducing Helen and eloping with her. The consequence was the Greek expedition to Troy, led by Agamemnon and Menelaus. This entailed the suffering of innocent Greek soldiers and Trojan citizens, for which (in Aeschylus) Agamemnon was required to pay in advance by sacrificing his innocent daughter Iphigenia to Artemis, so as to calm the contrary winds. The Chorus's account of this in the parodos forebodes the vengeance of Clytemnestra, who has ruled Argos in her husband's absence. She is now living in an adulterous relationship with Aegisthus, who is also bent on revenge, and has sent away her son Orestes.

Agamemnon: A beacon-chain brings the news that the Greeks have captured Troy. Agamemnon's fleet is largely destroyed by a storm during its return, but his own ship survives. Clytemnestra welcomes her husband and tempts him to enter his palace over rich fabrics, in what he knows is an act liable to excite the gods' anger. Agamemnon has brought home among his booty Cassandra, a daughter of Priam with prophetic powers, who describes both previous and future disasters in the family's story. Clytemnestra then kills Agamemnon and Cassandra, and she and Aegisthus exult in their revenge, in the face of the Chorus's challenges. By the end of the play, Clytemnestra at least is aware of the retribution which threatens them in their turn.

Choephoroe: Some years later, Orestes returns from exile on the command of Apollo, to avenge his father. A nightmare prompts Clytemnestra to send her daughter Electra with female slaves to placate Agamemnon's spirit, and it is at his tomb that Electra meets her brother. Together, they call on Agamemnon's spirit to assist Orestes. He tricks Clytemnestra into letting him into the palace, by disguising himself as a traveller with news of Orestes' death. He goes

---

[3] Aeschylus does not describe Thyestes' motive, which one naturally takes to be lust. For the alternative story, see Gantz (1993), 545–7.

on to kill Aegisthus, followed, after an anguished altercation, by his mother Clytemnestra. As he triumphs over their bodies, he sights the Erinyes who are bent on avenging Clytemnestra, and flees in terror.

Eumenides: The Erinyes have pursued Orestes to Delphi, where he has taken sanctuary. While they sleep Apollo directs Orestes to escape to Athens and appeal to its patron goddess Athena. She refuses to judge such an important case herself, but sets up a court of Athenian citizens which listens to the arguments on either side. Eventually, Orestes is acquitted only by the deciding vote of Athena herself. The indignant Erinyes threaten Athens, but Athena wins them round by offering them a place of worship and a new function of sustaining Athenian families. The play ends with them being escorted to this new position.

As this basic summary suggests, for all the richness and complexity which must have been a factor in its success, the *Oresteia* is unified and shaped by a central preoccupation with justice, and with the advance from a system of punishment through mere tit-for-tat revenge (in this case depicted in the traditional mythology of the ven-dettas within a single family) to the collective justice of the Athenian *polis*.[4] The first two plays of the trilogy have parallel endings where exultant agents of justice come to anticipate the price she or he must eventually pay. The problem is only resolved when a new kind of justice, based on a new social order, is established in *Eumenides*. Aeschylus' treatment in *Agamemnon* and *Choephoroe* of the self-perpetuating futility and horror of violent retribution was pertinent to contemporary Athenian politics (see § 2), and is still pertinent today, when the ideas of international cooperation, law, and justice developed in the wake of two world wars sometimes struggle to make themselves felt in practice.

Situating *Agamemnon* within the context of the whole trilogy also shows that it is not primarily a personal tragedy of character (as is more typical of Sophocles). Agamemnon's character and responsi-bility are explored, but Aeschylus embeds his predicament within a longer series, with violent antecedents and the even more horrific matricidal 'justice' which follows. Furthermore, one sees that what

---

[4] On the theme of justice see § 4.1; on the mythical background see § 3. In what follows, we will also refer to the system of tit-for-tat revenge by its Roman name, the *lex talionis*.

might appear as a disproportionate build-up to Agamemnon's death is fully justified as an introduction to the key motifs of the trilogy as a whole.

D.A.R., O.R.H.T.

2. THE HISTORICAL CONTEXT OF THE *ORESTEIA*

The relationship of tragedies to their specific social and historical context has been one of the most debated topics in Greek literature during the last twenty-five years.[5] Some research has been addressed to tragedy as a whole rather than to specific tragedies. Did tragedians aim to please the audience and judges (and who were they?) by challenging their views or by reinforcing them? What does the ancient truism that poets were teachers mean, in a genre where every utterance comes from a character and almost all refer to a society of the legendary past? How does the audience find its way between judging behaviour within the play by their own standards, by standards traditionally attributed to legendary society (especially in Homer), or by values expressed within the play? How did the overtly political parts of the Dionysia festival colour the audience's perception of the tragedies? Was tragedy part of a ritual to which a social function (such as group cohesion) was fundamental? What might tragedy have been like outside the Dionysia, or outside democratic Athens?

Other research has concentrated on how particular passages can engage with their socio-political context. Any use of language is embedded in but can react against the ways of thought (*mentalité*) characteristic of its society. Tragedies constantly bring up issues of general interest to a *polis*, such as tyranny, gender-relationships, persuasion, rhetoric, and the nature of the gods; but a whole play rarely offers a straightforward 'line' on any of them. Finally, some tragedies (in particular Aeschylus' *Persae*) directly mention particular contemporary political events and institutions. However, specifying a passage's engagement with a contemporary context is fraught with

---

[5] It is far beyond our scope to review the matter in detail. The 'Suggested Reading' at the end of this section, and throughout the Introduction, gives some particularly useful points of orientation on the general topics addressed.

difficulties. Our understanding of the development of and variations within 'Athenian ideology' in the fifth century is far from complete, and we almost never know the extent to which an aspect of it, or a given mode of thought, was *specifically* 'Athenian', rather than characteristic of Greek *poleis*, or Greeks generally. Furthermore, scholars regularly disagree about whether a particular play affirms a point of ideology (for example), or opens it up for contemplation, or questions it outright. And finally, one must keep apart scholars' varying conceptions of 'ideology' and 'the political'.[6]

We do not propose to take on these large and rather diffuse questions directly, though points relevant to each can be found throughout this book (especially § 4 below) and the scholarship we cite. However, the influence of certain contemporary political events on Aeschylus' design can be identified with confidence, and the following discussion focuses on these.

One goal of the *Oresteia*'s examination of retributive and juridical justice is to engage with policy concerns of Athens's recent past. At the resolution of *Eumenides* stands an innovative foundation-myth for the Areopagus, the body comprising retired archons which was normally said to have been formed well before Orestes' time (cf. also 1595 ἀνδρακάς with n.). We also hear Athena's own charter for this (*Eum.* 690–706: the best citizens, guarding the state and judging murder cases), Orestes' grateful declaration that Argos will always be allied with Athens, and the foundation of the cult of the Semnai Theai. In each case, duration into the future occupied by Aeschylus' audience is mentioned. The second and third points were particularly topical, in the tense aftermath of 462–1 BC.

In the 470s and 460s, Cimon had led a strategy of cooperation with Sparta against Persia, while others such as Themistocles were suggesting that Sparta itself was the threat. Events of 462–1 BC brought the impetus for Cimon's opponents to overturn his policies and ostracize him. Sparta had called in Athenian help to quell a Messenian rebellion, but the Athenians were uneasy at being used to attack fellow Greeks, and the Spartans lost trust and sent them away.[7] The alliance with Sparta was ended, and pointedly replaced by one

---

[6] The general trend has been to broaden the sense of 'political', from questions of contemporary policy to any questions pertinent to the identity of a *polis* or citizen.

[7] This chronology is contested. Some scholars argue (on the basis of Plutarch's *Cimon*) that Ephialtes' reforms happened while the troops were away, and caused Sparta's jitters. See e.g. Badian (1988), 309–10, 316 versus Rhodes (1992), 69.

with Sparta's enemy Argos, which was now resurgent after three troubled decades, and Thessaly (whose prince was intriguingly called 'Orestes': Thuc. 1. 111).

In internal affairs, Ephialtes now successfully proposed a reform of the Areopagus, which transferred some of its powers that were alleged to be ἐπίθετα ('add-ons') to the public courts and the Council; the Areopagus was left with jurisdiction over murder trials and a few religious trials. Further details of the reform and its motivations are disputed.[8]

Both reforms were divisive. Ephialtes was soon murdered. By Thucydides' time people thought that the Battle of Tanagra (summer 458 or 457: soon after the *Oresteia*) had been hastened by conservative Athenian aristocrats calling on Spartan troops to help 'put an end to the *dēmos*' (Thuc. 1. 107. 4). Immediately after the battle the Athenians offered their Argive allies burial in the Kerameikos with a public monument, a sign of their gratitude remarkable for its size and workmanship (*IG* I[3] 1149).

Aeschylus' desire to engage with this situation in *Eumenides* explains why he moved Agamemnon and Menelaus to Argos (from Sparta or Amyclae, or Mycenae which Argos had recently devastated).[9] He presents the recent Argive alliance very positively. Regarding Ephialtes' reforms he is studiedly open, but his characters make repeated calls to avoid civil strife, and the whole trilogy valorizes the justice of the courtroom over retribution, i.e. an anti-extremist position. Athena's description of the Areopagus admits alternative readings. Are the Areopagites supposed to be 'guardians' *in addition to* judging murder trials, or *by* doing so?[10] When Athena talks of it potentially being sullied by ἐπιρροαί ('influxes'), does Aeschylus support Ephialtes' claims about ἐπίθετα, or oppose the

---

[8] Possibly, Ephialtes wanted to reform a court most of whose cases were sent to public courts anyway on appeal, or to resolve friction between the Areopagus and the Generals. The 'add-ons' may have included the rights to judge the particularly serious prosecutions brought by *eisangelia*, and to vet magistrates as they entered office (*dokimasia*: emphasized by Rihll 1995). See also n. 10, and e.g. Wallace (1989), 77–93 for a survey.

[9] Conversely, Spartan generals had used their claim on Agamemnon's homeland to further their position during the Persian Wars: Hdt. 7. 159. Homer located Agamemnon at Mycenae but at the head of 'Argive' troops; Stesichorus' *Oresteia* put him in Sparta, and Pindar at nearby Amyclae where Agamemnon received hero-cult. Xanthus (a lyric poet, *c*.600 BC) placed him at Argos, like Aeschylus.

[10] It is unclear whether it was Ephialtes or someone later who moved the Areopagus' duty of 'guarding the laws' to a new board of Νομοφύλακες.

idea that the archonship and so the Areopagus might be opened to 'middle-class' *zeugitae*, as they were in 457 BC?

The most pertinent aspect of contemporary policy against which to view *Agamemnon* specifically is Athens's vigorous military policy after the break with Sparta. The Athenians allied with Megara against Corinth, which was Sparta's strongest ally, and also besieged Aegina. Meanwhile, they sent a large fleet to Cyprus against the Persians; it eventually diverted to help a revolt in Egypt. Athens was thus fighting multiple campaigns around 460, and in 460 or 459 we know that one of the ten tribes lost a staggering 177 men in action (*IG* I³ 1147; Fornara 1983, no. 78). This—as well as Aeschylus' personal experience of fighting and losing his brother Cynegeirus at Marathon (Hdt. 6. 114)—must colour the bitterness which those remaining in Argos feel at the losses in the Trojan war (*Ag.* 437–51), and the Herald's description of the hardships of campaign (555–66). The same strophe refers to the practice of sending home the ashes of the war-dead rather than burying them on the battlefield, which is only attested in Athens from 468 BC onwards (Pritchett 1985, 249–51). Thirdly, Agamemnon's power as an *admiral* is emphasized, at a time when Athens relied heavily on its navy for its imperial ambitions.[11] In 212 the word λιπόναυς, which alludes to an Athenian legal term (λιποναυτίου γραφή, 'prosecution for naval desertion': Pollux 8. 43), encourages us to see this aspect of Agamemnon's character in fifth-century Athenian terms.

Suggested reading:
Tragic texts and their socio-historical context: Carter (2007) is a basic guide to important issues. Particularly influential older articles include Vernant (1981) on the relationship between the worlds of legend and Athens during a tragedy, and Goldhill (1990) on the relationship between the tragedies and the overtly political ceremonies of the Dionysia. Goldhill (2000) reviews the debate generated by the latter; M. Heath (2006) responds, and makes a valuable call for precision of terminology. Pelling (1997), particularly the editor's concluding chapter, has a range of useful analysis. Contextual

---

[11] See Rosenbloom (1995), who pushes the point rather further than we would. See also 944–9 n. for the possible similarity of Agamemnon to the Spartan general Pausanias.

material about the festival and its place in society can be found in
e.g. Csapo & Slater (1994), Wilson (2000).

Political references of Eumenides: Carter (2007), ch. 2 gives a survey.
The most useful contributions are: Podlecki (1966), ch. 5 (with a
dated attempt to infer Aeschylus' political agenda); Dodds (1973),
ch. 3; Macleod (1982), who urges that some passages are better
explained in dramatic rather than political terms; Pelling (2000),
167–77; Sommerstein (2010), § 12.1.

O.R.H.T.

3. AESCHYLUS AND PREVIOUS VERSIONS OF THE MYTH

Comparative material about how other writers and artists treated the
story can help us to assess Aeschylus' dramaturgical skill, and to
consider what his audience might have found remarkable. However,
both the literary and artistic background is very fragmented. The
influence of some lost texts, such as Pherecydes' mythographical
compendium, written in Athens a few decades before the *Oresteia*,
must remain a matter of pure speculation. Throughout this section,
we focus on Agamemnon's return from Troy and the murders of
Agamemnon and Cassandra.[12]

3.1. The *Odyssey* and the *Nostoi*

The most detailed earlier treatment of the story to survive is that of
the *Odyssey*, where it is introduced in the opening divine conversation, and is an important foil for Odysseus' successful homecoming.
Agamemnon and Clytemnestra contrast with Odysseus and
Penelope; Aegisthus is in a similar position to Penelope's suitors,
and the banquet where he kills Agamemnon resembles the suitors'
final banquet; Orestes is generally a positive model of filial loyalty for
Telemachus. The different characters fashion their recollections with
different nuances, but a consistent sequence emerges.[13]

[12] For Aeschylus' handling of other details, see Index s.v. 'myth'.
[13] The passages are: 1. 35–43, 298–300, 3. 130–83, 193–8, 234–5, 248–312, 4. 91–2,
499–537, 546–7, 11. 383–9, 409–39, 452–3, 13. 383–4, 24. 20–2, 96–7, 199–200. See
Olson (1995), 24–42.

In Agamemnon's absence, Aegisthus optimistically began flirting
with Clytemnestra; his motivation is left unclear. For a while she
resisted, since Agamemnon had charged a singer with exhorting her
to fidelity. However, eventually Aegisthus had him abandoned on a
desert island, and Clytemnestra lapsed into willing compliance, to
Aegisthus' surprise and delight (so Nestor, 3. 263–75). Hermes had
warned Aegisthus that he would be avenged by Orestes if he attacked
Agamemnon or wooed Clytemnestra, but he went ahead anyway,
even against fate (Zeus, 1. 35–43). Presumably it was around now
that Orestes left.[14] Athena caused the Greeks a difficult voyage back
from Troy, beginning with a rowdy assembly at which Menelaus
called for immediate departure whereas Agamemnon advocated
staying to placate Athena. Among the first to leave was Menelaus;
the party reached Euboea smoothly but were then delayed at Sunium
and blown off course to Egypt (Nestor, 3. 130–83, 276–302).
Agamemnon sailed later, along with Locrian Ajax; Hera saved him
from the storm sent to kill the latter near Myconos. Near home
Agamemnon was briefly blown slightly off course, towards
Aegisthus' house where his unexpected arrival would have saved
him.[15] But having brought him so near to salvation the gods blew
him back to harbour, from where Aegisthus' spy announced his
arrival. Aegisthus organized an ambush, and went immediately in a
chariot to invite Agamemnon for a banquet. Agamemnon came,
apparently before stopping at his own palace, and was slaughtered at
dinner, along with his men and the henchmen of Aegisthus who had
attacked them.[16] Agamemnon was stabbed, and Clytemnestra killed
Cassandra over him. After the murders, Clytemnestra did not tend
Agamemnon's corpse (Agamemnon's shade, 11. 421–6). Aegisthus
oppressed Mycenae for seven years until Orestes returned, killed him
and Clytemnestra, and buried them; it was during the funeral feast
that Menelaus eventually returned (Nestor, 3. 304–12).

---

[14] Agamemnon's ghost complains that he did not get to see Orestes on his return:
11. 452–3. At 3. 307 Nestor says that Orestes returned from Athens; S. West in *CHO* i
suspects the text.
[15] The storm happens near Cape Malea, which is too far south. S. West in *CHO*
i considers 4. 514–20 interpolated from a version where Agamemnon lived
in Sparta.
[16] All these details come from Menelaus, who cites the 'unerring' Proteus (4. 499–
537). Agamemnon's ghost understandably presents the fight as a one-sided massacre
(11. 409–20).

Clytemnestra's part in Agamemnon's death provokes the largest discrepancies, though on the whole the epic suggests that Clytemnestra conspires, and kills Cassandra, whereas Aegisthus kills Agamemnon. Sometimes Clytemnestra's involvement is not mentioned, but there is always a simple explanation of the ellipse: Zeus (1. 36) mentions Agamemnon's death just as an abbreviated example; Athena (disguised as Mentes, 1. 298–300) suppresses Clytemnestra because she is presenting Orestes as a model of filial duty to Telemachus, who has a good mother; similarly Nestor (3. 193–8, 305) seems to be fostering Telemachus' empathy with Orestes, given how he clearly downplays Orestes' matricide (3. 306–10). By contrast, Clytemnestra is a conspirator according to Athena-as-Mentor (3. 234–5), Menelaus (4. 92), and Agamemnon's shade (11. 409–11). The last even suggests Clytemnestra's active involvement in the murder (11. 430, 24. 97; more explicitly 24. 200). But this seems tendentious: he is understandably bitter, and in both underworld scenes he markedly contrasts Clytemnestra with the faithful Penelope.

The *Odyssey* drew on pre-existing traditions about Agamemnon's return and death which also influenced the Cyclic *Nostoi* (or *Returns of the Greeks*), a poem in five books which Aeschylus must have known. This poem treated Agamemnon's return more sequentially than the *Odyssey*, but very largely corresponds. Perhaps the most notable divergence is that Achilles' ghost appeared to Agamemnon as he was setting out from Troy, to warn him about what awaited him at home.[17]

3.2 Lyric Poetry

The first lyric treatments of the myth of which we have any record come from the sixth century. Probably the most influential for Aeschylus was Stesichorus' *Oresteia*, in two books (*c*.550 BC), but little information survives about it. Stesichorus set the action at Sparta, perhaps under the influence of his patrons at the time. He described the sacrifice of Iphigenia. Clytemnestra played some role in

---

[17] For the fragments see M. West (2003), 152–63, and *LIMC* Agamemnon 93, a Hellenistic bowl from Thebes which claims to illustrate the banquet where Aegisthus and Clytemnestra kill Agamemnon and Cassandra respectively. Another divergence, relevant to *Cho.*, is the appearance in *Nostoi* of Pylades as Orestes' helper.

Agamemnon's death, since she was troubled by a dream of a snake portending vengeance (rather as at *Cho.* 527–33).[18]

We have more to work with in the case of Pindar's *Pythian* 11 (474 BC).[19] This ode was initially performed in Thebes to celebrate a boy sprinter, and seems to bring in Orestes as a prominent example of a youth acting successfully on his filial duties; it may be relevant that Orestes had, like the victor, received support from Apollo at Delphi, though Pindar leaves this implicit. Pindar's compressed account (vv. 17–37) begins with a statement that the 'pitiless' Clytemnestra sent Agamemnon and Cassandra to Hades 'with grey steel', while Orestes' nurse stole him away. The narrator asks whether Clytemnestra was motivated by Iphigenia's sacrifice or by her adultery with Aegisthus, before returning to the murders with slightly more detail and context: Agamemnon is presented as a Spartan from Amyclae (where he received local hero-cult); the sack of Troy to recover Helen is mentioned. Agamemnon ὄλεσσε ('lost' or 'destroyed') Cassandra, and the choice of verb may put some responsibility on him. Finally, we hear how Orestes reached Strophius, who raised him until he returned to exact vengeance on Clytemnestra and Aegisthus. The marked focus on Clytemnestra adds a disturbing touch to Orestes' value as a role model: contrast the *Odyssey*, where in such contexts Clytemnestra and the unpleasant matricide were put into the background.

3.3. Art before Aeschylus

Although artistic sources treat only specific moments from the narrative, and often stylize them to include only the central figures in a recognizable configuration, they can suggest how Greeks envisaged the murders of Agamemnon and Cassandra, and throw light on a wider range of communities than the literary sources.

There are two possible images of Agamemnon's murder from seventh-century Crete. A seal from the beginning of the century

---

[18] For the fragments, see Campbell (1991), 126–33. As in *Cho.*, Orestes' nurse was a character (see 877–86 n.), and Electra recognized Orestes by a lock of hair. Apollo also protected Orestes against the Erinyes, rather as in *Eumenides*. Stesichorus was apparently influenced by Xanthus (*c.*600 BC), about whose poem we know practically nothing except that he set the scene at Argos, and (unlike Homer) included Electra's role: Campbell (1991), 26–7.

[19] See Finglass (2007), who argues for this dating.

depicts a standing, clothed woman thrusting something in her right hand towards a naked man who seems to be falling backwards from his seat; a large vessel (a bath?) is visible in the corner (*LIMC* Agamemnon 94). The second image is a *pinax* with three figures (ibid. 91; *c.*625 BC). A clothed and armed king sits on a stool. A woman approaches, and with her right arm clutches one of the king's arms. Behind the king is a second man, gripping the king's spear to stop him retaliating, and apparently pressing down on the king's head. Poor production means that further crucial details are unclear. Prag (1985), 1–2 suggests that Clytemnestra is stabbing Agamemnon in the back with her concealed left hand, but admits that it would be odd if the focal event was invisible.

Argive workmanship of the seventh and sixth centuries offers probable images of Agamemnon's and Cassandra's deaths. Perhaps Argos, as one of Agamemnon's possible homes, was particularly interested in the story. Earliest is a bronze plaque on which one woman stabs another; scholars have not found a plausible identification other than Clytemnestra stabbing Cassandra.[20] From the sixth century come two bronze shield-bands with mythical decorations.[21] In each, a central man is visibly stabbed in the back by a woman on the left of the image, while he collapses to the right towards another man who restrains him from reaching a spear (compare the Cretan *pinax*). Agamemnon's death seems the most likely identification. There is also an Argive connection with the north-facing metope frieze from the temple of Argive Hera at Foce del Sele in Italy (*c.*560 BC), which depicts the Trojan war and (probably) its aftermath. In the eleventh metope a woman wielding a hatchet, which was Clytemnestra's attribute in later art, is hindered by another woman (perhaps Electra or Orestes' nurse). In the tenth, a man sits in a vessel on a tripod, with an arm raised. Unfortunately half the surface is lost, but given the neighbouring scene the identification of Agamemnon being attacked in the bath (as in Aeschylus) is plausible.[22]

---

[20] *LIMC* (vol. vii) Kassandra I 199; *c.*650 BC. The identification of the figures in *LIMC* Kassandra I 200 (Attic column crater; 470–60 BC) is based on the same reasoning.

[21] *LIMC* Agamemnon 92 (and see perhaps 95). Others may depict Orestes' vengeance: *LIMC* Aigisthos 2, 19.

[22] The twelfth, fourteenth, and fifteenth metopes (the thirteenth is lost) are more speculatively linked to the *Oresteia* story: see Van Keuren (1989), 110–31, pl. 4.

So far we have only one depiction of Agamemnon's murder from Attica before Aeschylus wrote.[23] This is a calyx crater by the Dokimasia Painter, whose reverse shows a mirroring scene of Aegisthus' death (*LIMC* Agamemnon 89; 470–60 BC). An unarmed Agamemnon, whose straggly beard appears still damp from a bath, struggles to extricate himself from an armless robe under which he is naked. Aegisthus prepares to stab him in the chest for the second time. Behind Aegisthus is Clytemnestra, carrying her hatchet (a motif transferred from the iconography of Aegisthus' death), and another woman in shock. Balancing them behind Agamemnon are two anxious women. The painter situates the event within a broader context by adding spectators and by constructing a relationship with the death of Aegisthus on the other side of the vase. He makes Aegisthus, rather than Clytemnestra, the wielder of the sword, and offers the first clear depiction of Agamemnon's death-robe.

3.4. Aeschylus' Treatment

Aeschylus naturally retained the traditional focus on Agamemnon's homecoming and its consequences.[24] One major decision was to situate his play outside Agamemnon's palace, in opposition to the version of the *Odyssey*.[25] This decision has several ramifications. Throughout *Agamemnon* and *Choephoroe* Aeschylus uses the looming presence of the house with its resident δαίμων to focus on the internecine nature of the cycles of vengeance. Secondly, Aegisthus does not belong in the palace, so he has to hide until Clytemnestra has entrapped Agamemnon.[26] Aegisthus' need for secrecy is connected to the oppressive atmosphere in Argos throughout the earlier part of the play, where the Watchman and Chorus repeatedly express anxiety but shy away from speaking freely about Clytemnestra's

---

[23] Indeed, no Attic art can be identified with much certainty as dealing with the Atreid house until *c.*510 BC (though cf. *LIMC* Agamemnon 88, Iphigenia 2, Aegisthus 39 for possibilities). Then in *c.*510–470 nine Attic vases depict Orestes stabbing Aegisthus. All have similar compositions, which suggests a public model such as a wall-painting in a civic building. See also n. 20 for an Attic depiction of Cassandra's death.

[24] Several other tragedies treat homecomings, and show the flexibility which the motif affords: e.g. *Persae*, Soph. *Trachiniae*, Eur. *Bacchae*.

[25] For the location of the palace at Argos rather than Mycenae, see § 2.

[26] This is rationalized at 1637, where Aegisthus points out that Agamemnon would have treated him with suspicion given their family history.

relationship. Then Agamemnon arrives by choice and seems to be on comfortable 'home turf'; Aeschylus omits the warning which Achilles' ghost had offered in the *Nostoi*. Agamemnon's reversal of fortune (his '*peripeteia*', to use Aristotle's term) is thereby enhanced.

The choice of location offers several possible methods of assassination. A further important plot decision is that Clytemnestra commits both murders on her own. Pindar hinted at a similar scenario, whereas in the epic accounts and the Dokimasia Painter's depiction Aegisthus killed Agamemnon, and in the Cretan *pinax* (possibly) and Argive shield-grips was at least present to help. Aeschylus' choice increases Clytemnestra's dominance, suggests Aegisthus' cravenness, and adds pathos to Agamemnon's death at his own wife's hands. Moreover, the precise way in which Clytemnestra stage-manages the whole situation is important. She first gives a public display of her ability to manipulate her husband, by persuading him to enter the palace over rich garments in an act which he appreciates is hubristic. She then arranges a particularly undignified death which again emphasizes Agamemnon's *peripeteia*: from the intimate and invigorating welcome of a bath, he is abruptly killed while nearly naked and struggling with a robe; instead of preparing himself for a sacrifice, he is being 'sacrificed'. This sequence is unlikely to be wholly new to the audience, since Cassandra's oblique description of it (1100–35) is designed to elicit dramatic irony, where the audience understands but the Chorus does not.[27] Finally, Aeschylus achieves a further effect by delaying Aegisthus' entrance. After Clytemnestra has committed the murders she appears in person, and through an argument with the Chorus reaches a certain objective distance from her actions and begins to think of her future requital. Only now does Aegisthus enter. Aeschylus has dropped the idea that the gods have warned him of his come-uppance (as in *Od.* 1. 35–43), and made him exult with undeserved self-confidence, and so give a taste of the tyranny to come (cf. *Od.* 3. 305, 'the populace was broken under his rule'). His exultation seems the more hollow given what Clytemnestra has begun to realize.

---

[27] Nevertheless, Seaford (1984) rightly emphasizes that *until* Cassandra's visions we may well expect Agamemnon to die at a feast. The Dokimasia Painter's crater shows Agamemnon wet from the bath, but Clytemnestra only assists Aegisthus. The Cretan seal and metope from Foce del Sele also involve the bath but are not securely linked to our characters.

Aeschylus' handling of the earlier part of the play is characterized by a relentless build-up of foreboding, discussed further in § 6. The Watchman has been instructed by Clytemnestra to look out for the first sign of Agamemnon's return, which comes after a year; he evidently corresponds to Aegisthus' spy watching for Agamemnon's ship in the *Odyssey*, who also waits for a year (4. 526).[28] But his fidelity to Agamemnon (34–5) and anxiety at the current government (19) introduce the oppressive atmosphere, and the repeated technique whereby Agamemnon's supporters descend from moments of optimism back to despair. The decision to make the sign a military telegraph rather than the straightforward return of Agamemnon's ship enables Aeschylus to show Clytemnestra's mastery of signalling in her first appearance, as the background to her crucial mastery of language (see § 6). The Chorus (see further § 7) in the parodos and first two stasima gives a back-story which raises questions of Agamemnon's judgement: were Iphigenia's sacrifice and the war-effort justified? And we may add a third question: was the treatment of Troy justified? Interspersed with this are general reflections on wealth, greed, and sin which bode ill for Agamemnon, though he is not the conscious object of the Chorus's thoughts. The Herald's episode also creates foreboding. His account of Troy's sack unwittingly suggests a level of bloodthirstiness which is liable to retribution, and the account of the storm (familiar from epic) has to be dragged from him, forcing him to 'defile' the day (637).[29] Aeschylus elides the traditional fractious departure, so that a single herald can account for Menelaus, but with the further effects that Menelaus' situation turns more suddenly from triumph to calamity, and that Agamemnon's contrastive 'luck' brings a strong sense of dramatic irony, since we know that he has been saved only for a more grisly demise. In other words, this detail emphasizes the *peripeteiai* of both brothers. Furthermore Aeschylus avoids mention of Locrian Ajax, who was the traditional target of such a violent storm: the blame for sacking Troy's shrines is spread over all the chieftains, including their commander. Finally, even after Agamemnon's entrance Aeschylus brilliantly suspends the expected dénouement

[28] The comparison was already made in antiquity (Schol. *Ag.* 1).
[29] Aeschylus may have been influenced on this point by *Od.* 3, where Nestor's speech about his and Diomedes' easy returns leaves a gaping hole about the fate of Menelaus, which Telemachus perceives and forces Nestor to fill.

with Cassandra's long episode. The seeress is able not only to challenge Clytemnestra's dominance, but also to situate the murder we are about to hear in the broader context of the Thyestean banquet and Aegisthus' vengeance of it, and the future revenge of Orestes.

In this outline we have focused on plotting. How the fragmentary literary works treated questions of motivation and responsibility (see below, § 4.3) is difficult to judge: at least the *Nostoi* and Stesichorus had probably offered subtle depictions. Only Pindar offers material for comparison. He considers as the main possibilities for Clytemnestra's motivation Iphigenia's sacrifice and her own adultery; he passes entirely over Aegisthus' interests and the concept of a palace δαίμων.

Suggested reading:
Prag (1985); Gantz (1993), 545–56, 582–8, 664–86.
For similar discussions of *Cho.* and *Eum.* see Garvie (1986), pp. ix–xxvi and Sommerstein (1989), 1–6 respectively.

O.R.H.T.

4. THE IDEAS IN *AGAMEMNON*

The main subject-matter of the *Oresteia* has been summarily stated in § 1 above. It needs, however, to be seen against a background of legal, religious, moral, and social ideas which were current in Aeschylus' time, but which the dramatist integrated and interpreted in his own way. It is beyond the compass of this introduction to discuss all these ideas in depth. The following paragraphs are designed to draw attention to some particularly salient topics and the passages of greatest importance for each, and to suggest further scholarship which the student may wish to pursue after a careful reading of the text.

4.1. Forms of Justice

Central to the *Oresteia* are δίκη and the development in how it is enacted. The first two plays show retributive justice to be self-perpetuating and thus self-defeating, and also horrendous. It is therefore progress when in *Eumenides* Orestes escapes the cycle through Athena's institution of a homicide court.[30]

Already in *Agamemnon,* the word δίκη and its cognates can refer to general upright behaviour, and also to either specific form of justice—the retributive or the juridical.[31] However, juridical language is repeatedly co-opted to describe the retributive mission of the Atridae against Troy—by the Chorus at 41 and 451, the Herald at 532–7, and Agamemnon at 813–17. Furthermore, in the latter part of the play Δίκη herself and the adjective δίκαιος are always directly associated with retributive acts, for example when Clytemnestra and Aegisthus claim justification and the broader values that Δίκη represents.[32] These two facts indicate the central position within 'justice' which the characters in *Agamemnon* ascribe to violent self-help after a personal grievance.

After Agamemnon's murder, the Chorus forcefully states the code of revenge to Clytemnestra at 1429–30 'You must yet pay back blow with blow' and 1562–4 'The ravager is ravaged; the killer pays in full; there remains the law ... that the doer suffers'; the resounding summary there—παθεῖν τὸν ἔρξαντα—is repeated in *Cho.* 312–14, which ends with the saying δράσαντι παθεῖν, 'that it is for the doer to suffer'.[33] These passages imply the retributive principle that homicide is answered by homicide, which is stated repeatedly in *Choephoroe* (121–3, 142–4, 400–4). However, other serious crimes such as Paris' abduction of Helen or Thyestes' adultery with Aerope are also avenged by homicide.

A few passages suggest the possibility of a public punishment rather than a personal revenge. This may involve stoning (1118, 1616) or exile (1410–21). As the Atridae's vengeance on Troy is described using juridical metaphors, so Clytemnestra at 1412 and 1421 describes the Chorus as a 'judge' of her actions when it threatens her with exile. But Aeschylus gives the impression that

---

[30] For other types of 'progress', whereby aspects of social order are restored in *Eum.,* see Macleod (1982). However, some scholars have been too blithe in idealizing the Athens of *Eumenides,* as explained by e.g. Goldhill (1986), ch. 2.

[31] A δίκη can also be an individual claim on justice: 813, or, with more striking personification, *Cho.* 461, 'Ares will clash with Ares, Δίκη with Δίκη', i.e. Orestes' claim, pursued violently, will clash with that of Clytemnestra and Aegisthus. For Aeschylus' use of δίκην + genitive, 'in the manner of', see 3 n.

[32] Δίκη: 911, 1432, 1535, 1607, 1611. δίκαιος: 812, 1406, 1604. Also δικαίως and ὑπερδίκως in 1396; ξυνδίκως in 1601; δικηφόρος in 525 and 1577.

[33] See also *Ag.* 533, 1318–19, 1338–40 for the balance of action and suffering.

Argos has no institutions for a public trial of its rulers: exile will be imposed, if at all, after a revolt.[34] Indeed, by the end of the play the Chorus's thoughts have turned towards Orestes' return and vengeance as their only viable hope (1646–8, 1667).[35]

Besides the prevailing code of revenge, and these vain threats of public punishment, Clytemnestra at one point (1568–76) hopes to put down blood-money to bargain with the δαίμων of the house. This response to homicide is mentioned in the *Iliad* (9. 632–6, 18. 497–500), but there blood-money is paid to the victim's family rather than to an implacable δαίμων. Even as Clytemnestra utters her idea we perceive its futility, and at *Cho.* 48 the Chorus asserts explicitly that there can be no λύτρον (money given in atonement) for blood that has fallen on the ground.

As the *Iliad*'s recourse to blood-money pointedly clashes with the prevailing values of the play, so *Agamemnon*'s focus on life-for-life revenge contrasts expressively with the civic procedure in classical Athens for dealing with homicides, which is ushered in by the new justice system of *Eumenides*. If an Athenian citizen was suspected of committing homicide, it was the duty of the victim's kinsmen (or owner, in the case of a slave) to initiate a prosecution. Someone convicted of killing a citizen while intending to harm them, or of planning such a killing, received the death penalty; the executioner was, of course, not liable for homicide.[36] In *Agamemnon* and *Choephoroe*, however, the victim's kinsmen are to kill in their turn, after which they will themselves be liable.

The situation is particularly horrific when, as in our case, a first crime between kinsmen leads to a seemingly infinite chain of homicides within the family, which is 'glued fast to ruin' (*Ag.* 1566). For Clytemnestra, it involves a kind of demonic possession, and even an intense joy at the moment of retribution (1388–92; see also

---

[34] The idea of a general assembly is mooted at 844–6, but there is no implication that it is regular, or that the people will get a vote as well as a voice. See also 450–1, 883–5 for threats of public violence; in the latter passage (see n.) Clytemnestra may mention a council, but there is no sign that it has been active recently.

[35] The idea of a trial arises in passing at *Cho.* 120 δικαστήν ('judge'). In the Athens of *Eumenides*, the idea of single judges for minor cases is available (470–1), but Athena's foundation of a court of jurors to try a murder case is new.

[36] See MacDowell (1978), ch. 7. Self-help was confined to other cases, such as responding to highwaymen. Forced exile is also mentioned as a threat at *Ag.* 1410. It was the sentence for accidental homicide in Athens, and a citizen who feared conviction for deliberate homicide could volunteer to go into exile at any time until the middle of his trial.

Aegisthus at 1610–11). And it is, as she movingly comes to realize, a vicious circle which she rues and longs to break if possible (1568–76, 1654–61); similarly Orestes leads his mother to her death with the stark words 'You killed the man you should not have, and so suffer what you should not' (*Cho.* 930).

Suggested reading:
δίκη *in the Oresteia*: Goldhill (1986), ch. 2; Mitchell-Boyask (2009), ch. 5; Sommerstein (2010), §§ 7.9, 13.3.
Greek ideas of revenge: McHardy (2008), chs. 1, 2, and 5.

4.2. The Religious Dimension of Justice

The underpinning of human activity by what occurs at the divine level is fundamental to the *Oresteia* (as to many other Greek texts). In particular, the changing relationships among the gods complement the development of justice outlined in § 4.1.[37] *Agamemnon* 89 refers to two types of deity, ὕπατοι and χθόνιοι. This reflects the broad distinction in Greek religion between gods who were thought to dwell on Olympus or in heaven, and the 'chthonians' in the earth or underworld whose functions were associated particularly with death and fertility.[38] The most important chthonians in the *Oresteia* are the Erinyes or Furies, who ensure that serious crimes do not go unpunished.[39] It is the relationship of these figures to Zeus and subsequently to Apollo and Athena—in other words between the guarantors of justice in its various forms—which is of particular interest here.

In *Agamemnon*, a number of Olympians are mentioned in passing, including some groups whose identity is obscure to us (513, 519 nn.). Of somewhat greater importance are Apollo, as the god who both inspires and destroys Cassandra (1081–2, 1202–13, 1269–76), and his sister Artemis, who demands the sacrifice of Iphigenia if the Greeks

---

[37] See also § 4.3.1, where the relationship between human and divine dimensions is discussed with respect to human responsibility.

[38] Artemis may be identified with the 'chthonian' Hecate at *Ag.* 140. Nevertheless, in the *Oresteia* the categories of Olympians and chthonians are distinguished in a more thoroughgoing way than in Greek religion as a whole. See in general on that distinction Scullion (1994*b*).

[39] Various other figures of a similar conception appear in passing: the ἀλάστωρ at 1501, 1508; Μῆνις at 701; Στάσις at 1117. The idea of a chorus of Erinyes at the palace is also related to the idea of an unfriendly δαίμων there, on which see § 4. 3. 4.

are to sail to Troy.[40] But above and behind all these stands Zeus, the supreme god whose hand the characters see in so many of the play's events, and whom the Chorus describes as the 'cause of all, worker of all' (1486); the Chorus's Hymn to Zeus at 160–83 is one of the cornerstones of the trilogy's theology, as described in § 4.4. In *Eumenides*, Zeus recedes slightly in favour of his children Apollo and Athena, both of whom appear on stage. Both, however, declare their intimate connection to their father (e.g. *Eum.* 616–18, 736).

The Erinyes also appear in *Eumenides*, as the chorus. They had already featured in Greek epic, avenging serious crimes such as murder and perjury, or implementing a victim's curse (especially a parent's).[41] In the *Oresteia* they are terrifying and implacable hellhounds who implement the code of revenge, and who latterly personify Clytemnestra's dying curses against Orestes.[42] They may appear individually or as a collective. They owe their authority to Μοῖρα or the Μοῖραι.[43] The Erinyes sometimes inspire human agents to the violence of retribution, or when no kinsmen of the victim are left with a grudge (as at the end of *Choephoroe*), they pursue the criminal themselves.

In the first two plays Olympians and Erinyes are perceived to work together towards justice. The Olympians watch over events which require vengeance, and three times in *Agamemnon* we hear that they send Erinyes to bring this about (55–9, 461–7, 748–9). However, after Orestes has killed his mother a conflict arises between Apollo, who instructed him that he would be free of liability (*Cho.* 1031–2) and would otherwise suffer (*Cho.* 271–96, *Eum.* 465–7), and the Erinyes who relentlessly seek vengeance on Clytemnestra's behalf and at the urging of her ghost. In *Eumenides* the parties are in open conflict, and the Erinyes indignantly protest that the younger gods (Apollo and Athena) have ridden roughshod over their more ancient and venerable system of justice (*Eum.* 162–3, 778–9).

---

[40] For Apollo in the *Oresteia* see Roberts (1984), ch. 3.

[41] On the Erinyes and their background, see Sewell-Rutter (2007), ch. 4.

[42] In *Eum.* the Erinyes apply a broader range of punishments (186–90) to a narrower range of crimes, though the latter is not defined consistently. At 210–12, 336, 355–6 they imply that they pursue only those who have killed a relative, and they are not concerned for Aegisthus' claim against Orestes. But at 316–20, 421 they avenge homicide in general.

[43] *Eum.* 335, 392, and cf. 173, 961–2. See also the comments on *Ag.* 130, 1025–9, 1535–6, and Fraenkel 728–30.

But Athena, with the help of Peitho (970–2), prevails upon the Erinyes to accept a cult in the new order. She finds common ground in the view that the justice system should include deterrents against homicide, such as the Erinyes are (517–25), and she welcomes their ability to pursue criminals who evade detection by humans. But she persuades them to combine these points with a more constructive civic role under the name of Σεμναὶ Θεαί. Aeschylus thus provides a foundation-myth ('aetiology') of the cult of the Semnai just below the Acropolis, and of their constructive and terrifying aspects, via the important Athenian contribution to social development which is the institution of a homicide court.[44]

Almost the last words of the trilogy are Ζεὺς παντόπτας οὕτω Μοῖρά τε συγκατέβα ('All-seeing Zeus and Moira [the Erinyes' patron] have thus come down together', *Eum.* 1045–6). The trilogy therefore, as well as tracing the futility of retributive justice and its replacement by a homicide court, on the divine level traces a conflict and subsequent reconciliation among the different gods concerned with justice. The Erinyes gain a civilizing aspect, which again suggests that we are to see the situation in Athens at the end of *Eumenides* as an advance on the situation in the previous plays.

Suggested reading:
R. Parker (2009); Winnington-Ingram (1983), ch. 8.
Particularly useful works dealing with Greek religion in broader contexts: Burkert (1985); R. Parker (1997) on tragedy.

4.3. Causation and Responsibility

In purely human terms, Aeschylus' characters have complex motivations.[45] Agamemnon sails to Troy to help his brother retrieve Helen, but also to increase his own κλέος; when instructed to sacrifice Iphigenia, he is moved by conflicting obligations to his family and to his allies. Clytemnestra is concerned to avenge Iphigenia's death, but also has her relationship with Aegisthus, and feels a subtly

---

[44] For recent treatments of what may have been an innovative aetiology, see Mitchell-Boyask (2009), 23–33; R. Parker (2009), 145–51. The euphemistic name 'Eumenides' ('Kindly Ones') does not occur until after Aeschylus, and was probably not the original title of the play.
[45] Contrast Sommerstein (2010), 311, who asserts that the only purpose of vengeance in *Agamemnon* is to slake anger.

portrayed anger at Agamemnon's own adulteries. Aegisthus wants to avenge his siblings, but also appears to thirst for the wealth and power of a tyrant. Orestes is concerned to recover his patrimony from the usurpers (*Cho.* 299–305) as well as to avenge Agamemnon with bloodshed. However, it is in the complementarity of human motivation and responsibility with superhuman forces that Aeschylus' presentation is particularly complex. This section aims to tease out the various strands of this topic, and how Aeschylus places each within the developing drama.

4.3.1. *The Coexistence of Human and Divine Causes*

Aeschylus presents the gods as closely involved in earthly justice, so that their changing relationships complement the changes which are taking place in human society (§ 4.2). This divine involvement also has implications for questions of human responsibility. Aeschylus adopts a principle of 'multiple determination', whereby a god may cause an action while also allowing that the human agent has motivations, acts deliberately, and subsequently carries responsibility. As Sommerstein (2010, 263) encapsulates it, 'The involvement of divine hands does not relieve human ones of their responsibility.'

Though events may be describable in purely human terms, the gods are steering them (cf. 781, Justice 'guides all to its end'). The Atridae are motivated to sail against Paris by the pursuit of revenge and glory, but Zeus Xenios oversees the process (61–2), as the guarantor of the sacred rules of hospitality which Paris breached. The latter description is not merely a symbol or metaphor for the former, nor does it absolve the Atridae of responsibility for the war they wage. Zeus steers the war to completion (355–66, 581–2), which does not undermine the human efforts of the Greek soldiers (their 'many limb-tiring wrestlings', 63), or their responsibility for the brutal and sacrilegious treatment of Troy;[46] Agamemnon in his opening lines says that the local gods 'share with me in responsibility'

---

[46] The Chorus imagines that Paris' kinsmen actively performed at his marriage to Helen (704–8). But the war undoubtedly incurs the suffering of innocent Trojans, as Zeus' eagle-and-hare omen signifies (148–55 n.). At 359 the Chorus welcomes the fact that no young Trojan escaped. Clytemnestra warns that the victors should exercise restraint (338–47), but annihilation is emphasized in 525–8 and 824. The Herald seems to recognize that the storm sent upon the returning fleet is divine punishment for their misdeeds (e.g. 649), as it was traditionally presented.

for the justice he has exacted (810–13). But the divine viewpoint may be disconcertingly at odds with the human one, as in the second stasimon regarding Helen's arrival at Troy (717–49). To the Trojans, a delightful woman seems to arrive, but in time they recognize the complementary arrival of an Erinys from Zeus, to punish them for accepting Helen's abduction. Similarly, a man tries to raise a lion cub as a pet, while a god is raising it as a 'priest of Atē' which will eventually wreak havoc. In neither case does the divine hand diminish the responsibility of the human (Paris, the lion-owner) who removed something (Helen, the cub) from its rightful place in the world.

In the case of Clytemnestra's murder of Agamemnon, the relationship between its human and divine motivations is confronted with greater detail. Both the Chorus and Clytemnestra see the influence of the palace's δαίμων (1468–80), and the Chorus go on to identify Zeus' hand behind that (1485–8). But these divine forces do not stop them from denouncing the murder as 'impious' (1493). Clytemnestra then brings in a second strand of divine motivation, partly from a sense that she is recovering from being possessed. She was not involved 'herself'; rather, an ἀλάστωρ demanding revenge for Thyestes acted in Clytemnestra's body. But the Chorus rejects the suggestion that divine motivation has entirely supplanted her personal responsibility: nobody would consider her ἀναίτιος (1505), though the ἀλάστωρ may have been her 'accomplice'. Indeed, Clytemnestra has clearly operated in large part from very human motivations.

4.3.2. Necessity and Fate

Although the Greeks had a sense of fate, its effects are normally limited to determining a few crucial moments in one's life, especially birth and death.[47] Thus the word μοῖρα (literally one's 'portion') occurs in the play, but this portion is generally only invoked as determining one's point of death (except at 1588). Similarly 1171 χρή, and τὸ πεπρωμένον ('what has been offered') in 68, 684, and 1657, refer to the ends of Troy and Agamemnon.[48] Personified

---

[47] See e.g. Dietrich (1965), ch. 7 for the *Iliad*'s influential presentation of fate, and *OCD* s.v. fate.

[48] If the text is right at 766–7, the date of hubristic acts is κύριον, which could mean that these too are fated. cf. also Cassandra's ἥξει τὸ μέλλον in 1240, with 1246–7 n.

Moira is mentioned twice: as noted above (at n. 43) she figures in Aeschylus especially as a guarantor of retribution. Thus both μοῖρα and Μοῖρα are associated primarily with death, though only the latter is closely tied to retribution.

A rather different conception of μοῖρα seems to occur at 1026. According to our interpretation of this very difficult passage (1025–9 n.), μοῖρα here denotes a human's portion of prosperity at *any* moment, and is preordained (τεταγμένᾱ); these portions constrain each other and their boundaries are constantly policed (probably by Justice), so that at no point during life can one secure more prosperity than one's initial allotment. Human beings are still regarded as fully responsible for their avarice.

The word ἀνάγκη is often translated 'necessity', and it or its cognates appear at 218 (Agamemnon 'put on the halter of ἀνάγκη' when he decided to sacrifice his daughter), 726, [902], 1042, 1071. In each case the word applies to a force beyond the control of an individual, but it is never necessary to understand it as pre-destination.[49] In 1042 and 1071, for example, ἀνάγκη is the Greek *force majeure* which has condemned Cassandra to slavery. In 218, ἀνάγκας ἔδυ λέπαδνον suggests that Agamemnon actively, after consideration, chooses to submit to the obligations imposed externally by an network of alliances, which he perceives to be overriding: he 'bows to the inevitable'.

4.3.3. Folly and Psychological Determination

Immediately after describing how Agamemnon 'put on the halter of ἀνάγκη', the Chorus generalizes on the sort of mindset which brought him to kill his daughter (222–3): βροτοὺς θρασύνει γὰρ αἰσχρόμητις τάλαινα παρακοπὰ πρωτοπήμων, 'For shameful-counselling, brazen derangement, first cause of woe, *emboldens* mortals.' παρακοπή, literally 'a sideways knock', is an external force which shakes its victims from their senses. It makes them susceptible to shameful and rash ideas, which when acted upon lead to woe.

The Chorus returns to this theme at 376–86, 461–8, and 757–71. In the first of these, we hear that excessive *wealth* may lead a man to injustices, which will be exposed; Folly (Ἄτη rather than παρακοπή, but still an external agent) makes him susceptible to be persuaded or

---

[49] Compare e.g. Ostwald (1988), 18–19 on Thucydides' sense of ἀνάγκη.

tempted into sinful action.[50] At 461–8, the Erinyes overthrow the man who has achieved fortune without justice (such as a πολυκτόνος). In the second stasimon (757–71), the Chorus believes that one act of hubris and impiety leads in time to another, and to folly characterized by rashness; immediately before and after, they are speaking particularly of the wealthy (752, 776). These latter two passages thus again suggest the sequence 'wealth may lead to folly, then susceptibility to be persuaded into rash sin', but the Chorus expands its focus to suggest that a prior injustice is the initial cause. These ideas are crucial to interpreting the end of the third episode, where Agamemnon (wealthy and with sins in his past) is susceptible to be tempted by Clytemnestra, against his strongly held better judgement, to trample on precious fabric which should belong to the gods.[51]

A second analysis without reference to justice or wicked decisions also appears on the Chorus's lips: a high degree of prosperity often leads straight to misfortune, probably through the envy of the gods. The Chorus mentions this idea at 467–71 (paired with the alternative analysis), then explicitly distances itself from the 'old saying' at 750–7. It appears to readopt it in the third stasimon (1005–13), where it adds that the rich man can save himself by sacrificing some of his wealth before it is ruined; however, humans are never sated with their wealth (1331–4). The idea also lies behind Clytemnestra's malevolent attempt to inspire divine φθόνος against Agamemnon by using an excess of laudatory appellations (895–905).

4.3.4. Inherited Liability

Agamemnon's murder unites two chains of events, one centred on the Trojan war (including the sacrifice of Iphigenia), and the other on previous events within the family. Central to the latter is that Aegisthus avenges the banquet at which his siblings were served up to their father by Atreus. The idea that persons might escape paying for

---

[50] For ἄτη as a force in Homer and Aeschylus, see e.g. Padel (1995), 174–87, 249–53.

[51] See also Helm (2004). On this 'hubris syndrome' in earlier authors, see 750–62 n.; the main variation is whether hubris breeds excess (κόρος) or vice versa. At 1407–8 the Chorus suggests a quite different origin of the criminal's derangement: perhaps Clytemnestra's madness was caused physiologically, by poisonous food or a salt-water drink.

their sins, but their descendants would then be liable, was stated before Aeschylus notably by Solon fr. 13. 25–32. Solon explicitly remarks that the descendants may be guiltless. Agamemnon certainly is not entirely guiltless, though he had no hand in Atreus' crime.

In *Agamemnon* the principle of inherited liability comes to the fore towards the end of the play, when Cassandra sets Agamemnon's death within the broad series of crimes in the palace (she mentions the Thyestean banquet at 1095–7 and adds Aegisthus' plotting at 1217–26), and in the final episode where Aegisthus appears.[52] At 1600–2 Aegisthus asserts that his vengeance is divinely grounded in a curse by Thyestes, that all the descendants of Pleisthenes (which with Aeschylus' genealogy must include Aegisthus himself) should perish utterly.[53]

As well as inherited liability, pursued by human agents and the divine powers (such as Erinyes) who guarantee curses, the residents of the palace inherit the malign influence of nameless gods who haunt it. The 'agency' of the house is already hinted at by the Watchman at 37–8, but again the theme only comes to the fore during Cassandra's prophecies. She speaks at 1117 of a 'spirit of insatiable discord for the family' (which the Chorus interprets as an Erinys), and at 1186–93 of a 'revelling band of kindred Erinyes' which abides in the palace, commemorating the $\pi\rho\dot\omega\tau\alpha\rho\chi\sigma\varsigma$ $\check\alpha\tau\eta$ that was the adultery between Thyestes and Aerope. Later the Chorus speaks rather of a spirit of strife working through Helen ($^{\prime}E\rho\iota\varsigma$, 1461), and then of the $\delta\alpha\acute\iota\mu\omega\nu$ of the palace or family working through both Clytemnestra and Helen (1468). Clytemnestra immediately accepts this, 'for it is from him that the desire to lap blood is fostered in the belly; before the old pain fades, new pus comes' (1477–9, if the text is right). And the $\delta\alpha\acute\iota\mu\omega\nu$ haunts her final thoughts in the play, at 1569 and 1660.

Suggested reading:
For 4.3.1: Lesky (1983); Williams (1993), ch. 3; also Sommerstein (2010), §§ 11.1–11.3; Winnington-Ingram (1983), ch. 5.
For 4.3.4: R. Parker (1983), 198–206; Sewell-Rutter (2007).

---

[52] For possible earlier appearances of the motif see 83–4, 148–55, 374–8 (corrupt), 783–4 nn.
[53] Sewell-Rutter (2007), 71–6 discusses the importance of this curse.

4.4. Enlightenment

We have seen above that a positive development in Δίκη is crucial to the trajectory of the *Oresteia*, in contrast to myths such as that of the five generations (Hesiod *Op.* 106–201) where the Greeks imagined social deterioration from a pristine golden age. Progress more generally comes through the divine dispensation of good sense—τὸ φρονεῖν (*Ag.* 176) or τὸ σωφρονεῖν (181)—towards which Zeus set mortals on the path according to the Hymn to Zeus in the parodos, by ordaining πάθει μάθος, that from suffering one can attain learning. That passage is picked up at *Eum.* 1000, where the Athenians, with their new order of justice, are σωφρονοῦντες ἐν χρόνωι. Mortals, first in Athens and later elsewhere, learn this order from Athena, who responds to the πάθη of the Argive royal family. So too, if tragedy 'teaches', Aeschylus teaches his audiences through these πάθη (cf. 176–8 n.). At first, the Chorus envisages rather more direct mechanisms of learning: good sense can come through nights of contemplating one's woes (*Ag.* 179–81). But in fact, the characters do not gain from their own πάθη.[54] Some learn too late, such as the aged Troy which through suffering 'learns afresh' to lament Helen rather than sing her wedding-hymn (709–11), shortly before its utter destruction. And the elders face a debased form of 'learning through suffering' when Aegisthus threatens that prison will teach them to kow-tow.[55]

In the form of learning through suffering seen in the trilogy as a whole, learning brings a release from πόνος, and the trilogy begins within a prayer for precisely that. The phrase ἀπαλλαγὴ πόνων (*Ag.* 1 with n.) is associated with the Eleusinian Mysteries and, as at the climax of the Mysteries, the Watchman gains his release through the appearance of torchlight—the beacon announcing the fall of Troy. The house of Atreus, and human society broadly, must wait much longer for their release, but that too is signalled by the return of torchlight in the procession which leads the Erinyes, now Semnai Theai, out of the theatre to their new cult at the end of *Eumenides*.

Suggested reading:
Dodds (1973), chs. 1 (on Greek ideas of progress in general) and 3.

---

[54] Except possibly Orestes, though this point is not driven home.
[55] 1619–23; cf. 1639–42, and 584, 1425 for other appearances of the motif of 'the elderly learning'.

Introduction

4.5. Men and Women

The relationship between the sexes had captured Aeschylus'
imagination in the Danaid tetralogy from which *Supplices* (dated to
the 460s) survives. The importance of the male/female antithesis for
the *Oresteia* as well is already suggested at *Ag.* 11 by the Watchman's
striking description of Clytemnestra's heart, the γυναικὸς ἀνδρόβουλον . . . κέαρ—belonging to a woman but planning like a man.
The antithesis goes on to be an important frame for Clytemnestra's
characterization. She is in a male position of power, and speaks
freely in public.[56] She 'conquers' her husband in the third episode
(940–3, 956), in part by playing the role of the submissive wife
(600–10, 855–905; and in bathing him). She shows self-assertion as
a woman (348, 592 nn.; and cf. 1661 n.) while the Chorus displays
the normal patronizing assumption of women's limitations (e.g. 351,
483–7, 1251; cf. 592 n.).

Aeschylus' plot emphasizes the close familial nature of the acts
of retribution (contrast the *Odyssey*: § 3.1). Clytemnestra's role in
Agamemnon's death is more important than Aegisthus'; her murder
by Orestes is more important than her lover's. Given this decision,
Aeschylus constructs Clytemnestra's character in *Agamemnon*
against traditional gender roles, to make her 'unnatural' trans-
gression plausible.[57] But although for much of the play she threatens
normal Greek ideas of masculinity, towards the end a more vulnerable woman emerges, in preparation for the character who at the
start of *Choephoroe* dispatches libations to Agamemnon's tomb to
placate her dead husband's ghost.[58]

Besides Clytemnestra, Helen also wields metaphorical power
(esp. 415, 688–9, 1470–1); conversely, Aegisthus is called a 'woman'
(1625).[59] In the palace, relations between men and women are

---

[56] Some scholars attach special importance to the idea that the outside is a
masculine space, whereas the dark interior of the *skēnē* is 'feminine' (e.g. Wiles 1997,
84; Goward 2005, 26, 89–90). However, one should keep in mind the tragic convention whereby women have greater liberty to speak in public, and the internal
subdivisions of Greek houses into male and female spaces (which are represented by
separate *skēnē*-doors in *Cho.*). Furthermore, the *skēnē* was still a recent invention in
458 BC, designed to extend the mechanics of theatrical presentation.

[57] See § 8 for the general subordination of characterization to broad design, rather
than character-study being an end in itself.

[58] Only briefly in *Choephoroe* does she revert to her former character, when she
calls for an axe with which to meet Orestes (889–90); it does not arrive in time.

[59] Again, see also § 8 below, especially n. 90.

dysfunctional—Thyestes, Helen, and Aegisthus commit adultery; Iphigenia, Agamemnon, and Clytemnestra are killed. The relative status of the sexes returns to the fore at the trial of Orestes. Male Apollo advances the claims of the father, and the female Erinyes defend those of the mother; the role of the mother in reproduction is debated (*Eum.* 605–8, 658–66). These claims appear to be equally balanced, until Athena casts her vote for Orestes' acquittal on the arbitrary grounds that she herself sprang from Zeus' head and is 'for the male' (736–8). The final part of the trilogy emphasizes that the Erinyes will in future promote proper familial relationships in Athens.

Scholars have reached very divergent interpretations of whether a particular agenda underlies this motif.[60] For example, Zeitlin even claimed that '*the basic issue* of the trilogy is the establishment, in the face of female resistance, of the binding nature of patriarchal marriage in which wifely subordination and patrilineal succession are reaffirmed' (1996, 87; our italics). By contrast, Winnington-Ingram (1983), ch. 6 argued that Aeschylus was criticizing the unequal status of women in Athenian marriages. In our view, the audience would have welcomed the support for 'normal' Athenian families secured at the end of *Eumenides*, but perhaps have questioned the belittlement of motherhood that is voiced during the trial, given Apollo's strong rhetoric and Athena's special status as a 'masculine' goddess. Unlike Zeitlin, we would see gender dynamics not as 'the basic issue' of the *Oresteia*, but as one important strand in Aeschylus' complex dramatization of oppositions among humans and gods, and the striking of an appropriate balance between them to preserve domestic and civic order. According to some Greek sources, this is the province of none other than Δίκη.[61]

Suggested reading:
Useful starting-points are Conacher (1987), 206–12 and Sommerstein (2010), § 7.8, with further bibliography. As mentioned, Zeitlin (1996), ch. 3 and Winnington-Ingram (1983), ch. 6 are worth reading for contrasting general interpretations.

---

[60] Goldhill (1986), 55 gives a stimulating summary of several.
[61] Cf. 1025–9 n. for a possible allusion to this idea. See also Seaford (2003) for a related argument about the 'unity of opposites' in the *Oresteia*, which treats the topic in much broader terms.

4.6. Summary

Aeschylus' powerful and moving drama is given intellectual depth by a wealth of ideas. He presents in dramatic form philosophical issues about politics, ethics, and theology. Retaliatory violence is shown in its futility. But the suffering which characterizes the life of mortals can be qualified by an ability to learn and to progress—towards civic law, for example, and reasoned use of persuasion for diplomatic ends. A solution to retaliation is eventually located in a contemporary Athenian institution, the Areopagus court. This exploration of justice needed, for a Greek, to be viewed in the perspective of polytheistic religion and the elusive guiding hands of the gods. This second level of action also provokes an engagement with the various factors which determine human decisions and responsibility. Human will and the freedom to get things right or wrong coexist with external forces including gods, fate, inherited liability, overriding circumstance, and the recurring behavioural patterns of human nature. In the first play of the trilogy, the retaliatory action notably brings with it Clytemnestra's challenge to stereotypes of female behaviour. None of these fundamental ideas is simple; hence, in good measure, the trilogy's enduring interest and challenge.

D.A.R., O.R.H.T.

5. AESCHYLUS' USE OF HIS MEDIUM

Agamemnon should be read as a dramatic artefact, as well as for other reasons such as its historical and intellectual interest. To picture the action in the mind's eye, however roughly, is an invaluable aid to the work's appreciation. This section highlights how Aeschylus used the resources of his theatre in this play, and exploited the conventions within which he was working.[62]

5.1. Theatrical Space and Material Features

Some details of the layout of Aeschylus' theatre are disputed. We envisage that the *orchēstra* was basically circular with a central *thymelē*,

[62] Aeschylus' use of the Chorus is discussed at greater length in § 7. The Appendix explores the musical aspect of *Agamemnon*.

and that there was already a low platform with steps in front of the central door of the stage-building (the wooden σκηνή).[63] We would not assume other features such as statues by the *skēnē*-door, which are known in plays of a later date (see 519, 1072–81 nn.). In most of *Agamemnon*, Aeschylus uses the *skēnē*, stage, and *orchēstra* as a unified space.[64] The principal characters (except the Watchman) all communicate with the Chorus through its leader. Agamemnon, on his wagon, enters into the *orchēstra*, and his confrontation with Clytemnestra is played out there, as the lyric dialogues of the Chorus with Cassandra and Clytemnestra would have been. With the spectators seated along roughly two thirds of the periphery of the *orchēstra*, these movements would have been performed in close relationship with the audience, in an atmosphere of intense concentration.

Aeschylus' surviving plays prior to the *Oresteia* do not require a stage-building. But in this trilogy he made it much more than a convenient dressing-room screen. Aeschylus' theatrical surprises probably start right at the beginning of the play with the Watchman speaking from the roof of this building (see 1–39 n.). More significant is the building's interior, and the royal palace is an important part of *Agamemnon* and *Choephoroe*, a brooding physical sign of the connection between the crimes in successive generations of a single family, and the home of a 'revel of kindred Erinyes' (*Ag.* 1189–90) or a *daimōn* which also embodies the inherited nature of the family's disasters (§ 4.3.4). The Watchman's prologue already puts the audience in a firm relationship with the οἶκος in its ill management (18–19) and dark secrets (37–8).

The stage-building also provides a central entrance with its double doors, to go with the two *eisodoi* at the sides which lead respectively to the port (whence enter the Herald and Agamemnon) and the rest of Argos (whence Aegisthus).[65] These doors in the *skēnē* are used

---

[63] For the slight archaeological evidence for the shape of the *orchēstra*, see Scullion (1994*a*), 3–66 versus Goette (2007). Wiles (1997), 70–2 questions the usual view of the *thymelē* as simply an altar. Stage: see e.g. Sommerstein (2010), 22.

[64] Contrast *Cho.* and *Eum.*, where the stage helps to articulate the changes of setting from Agamemnon's tomb (at the *thymelē*) to the palace, then from Apollo's temple at Delphi (the *skēnē*) to Athens.

[65] *Choephoroe*, in another example of Aeschylus' flexible use of the *skēnē* at this early date, employs (probably) three doors, which allow for an exciting flurry of entrances and exits at 875–92. *Eumenides* also uses the main *skēnē*-door remarkably: the Priestess re-enters on hands and knees (34), and some of the chorus of Erinyes enter through it on the *ekkyklēma* asleep, rather than conventionally processing down an *eisodos*.

with great significance within the play. Clytemnestra alone crosses and 'guards' this threshold until Agamemnon is swallowed up in the murky interior; she halts the Herald's path inside at 587, and stage-manages Agamemnon's at 908–74. But Clytemnestra fails to control how Cassandra enters (1035–68): the latter's eventual departure to the death which she can foresee, through what she calls the 'gates of Hades' (1291), is no less striking. Probably, the doors were opened inwards by stagehands behind the *skēnē*. This invisible action would add to their sinister impressiveness.

The *skēnē* also allows for Agamemnon's offstage cries as he is murdered (1343–5), and the—possibly innovative—power of the offstage cry was subsequently also harnessed by both Sophocles and Euripides (S. *Electra* 1415–16 alludes to Aeschylus; also e.g. *Ajax* 333–43, E. *Medea* 96–167). Next, at 1372, as the elders advance on the palace, the doors open and in contrary motion a tableau is wheeled out, displaying the bodies of Agamemnon and Cassandra with Clytemnestra standing over them in gloating triumph, sword in hand. This *coup de théâtre*—also used at *Cho.* 973 and after *Eum.* 63—would have been even more powerful if the wheeled trolley used (the *ekkyklēma*) was itself a very recent or even brand-new invention.

5.2. Performers

Aeschylus worked with a chorus of twelve young male citizens (as opposed to the later fifteen) whom he trained personally, though perhaps with an assistant. They were amateurs, though all—especially their leader, the 'Coryphaeus'—are likely to have had relevant experience in (for example) boys' dithyrambs. Training them successively to perform long roles as elders, female libation-bearers, Erinyes, and finally satyrs must have occupied months of intensive rehearsal.[66]

Aeschylus also makes use of three male actors, who were at least semi-professional and probably included himself.[67] Aristotle (*Poet.* 4 1449a 15–19) states that he had introduced the second actor and Sophocles the third. However, for the bulk of *Agamemnon* a single

---

[66] Aeschylus is recorded as having been inventive in his choreography: *TrGF* iii test. 103. See Wilson (2000) for the practicalities of producing a tragedy (e.g. 81–6 on training a chorus), as well as its social history.

[67] Sophocles was supposedly the first tragedian not to act: *TrGF* iv test. 1 ll. 20–5.

character is engaged with the Chorus on his or her own, as in tragedy's earliest, one-actor form. This makes the unique and crucial passage of conversation between actors, centred on the thirteen lines of stichomythia when Clytemnestra tempts Agamemnon to walk over crimson garments into the palace (931–43), all the more telling.[68] Also, Aeschylus creates an effect by giving no hint during the third episode that Cassandra will speak, and making a point of her muteness at the beginning of the fourth. Only when she suddenly breaks into her series of cries at 1072 does he indicate his use of a third actor.[69]

The roles of Clytemnestra, Agamemnon, and Cassandra (who has to sing) must have been played by different actors, since all are onstage simultaneously. It is a fair assumption that the same actor played all four male roles.[70] Aeschylus also employed κωφὰ πρόσωπα, mute extras, for the attendants who bring on Agamemnon's and Cassandra's wagons, the handmaidens who carry out the crimson garments, and Aegisthus' bodyguards. Some scholars (e.g. Sommerstein) believe that a few silent attendants entered with actors as a matter of course, even if they have no dramatic function.

5.3. Spectacle

Rich costumes and imposing masks and wigs would have made their own impact, but *Agamemnon* contains several special moments of visual spectacle. The interesting opening position of the Watchman has been mentioned (§ 5.1). Agamemnon's arrival in a wagon with (we argue: 783–974 n.) a further wagon of spoils behind, has a grandeur which seems empty because of the emphasis on his losses and on the dangers of excessive wealth in the preceding episode and stasimon. Subsequently Clytemnestra's maids (six or eight, perhaps) process in from the house to lay down and then to line the symbolic

---

[68] Clytemnestra tries to reason with Aegisthus and the Chorus at 1654, but her intervention is soon swept aside; her next comment to Aegisthus ends the play.

[69] Compare the effect when Pylades breaks his silence at *Cho.* 900–2 to reaffirm Apollo's command to Orestes. Indeed, Pylades is probably a *fourth* actor (along with those playing Orestes, Clytemnestra, and the servant who was onstage until 889). For Aeschylus' famous use of silences see Taplin (1972).

[70] Marshall (2003) speculates that roles in *Ag.* could have been related to those in *Cho.* and *Eum.* by being performed in the recognizable voice of the same actor.

route of crimson garments, stretching up to the threshold like a stream of blood. Cassandra's divesting herself of her prophetic garments would have made another memorable moment (1264–8; it influenced Eur. *Tro.* 451–4). The revelation of Clytemnestra with the bath and corpses has been described above; this spectacle is an important part of the dramatic structure, since it is pointedly paralleled by the tableau of Orestes and corpses at *Cho.* 973. The play's ending also relies for its effect on the visual, as the Chorus squares up against Aegisthus' bodyguards, with staffs drawn against swords, and is perhaps forced out of the theatre by them, in lieu of the choral coda which seems to have been conventional (see the final n. of the commentary).

The choral songs and exchanges, and Cassandra's agitated singing, also offered scope for visual interest, whose nature cannot be determined. Given the character of the Chorus as old men, the style of choreography was probably more processional than animated.[71] Their staves (75) would presumably have been a conspicuous feature of their concerted movement, and at least the narrative of Iphigenia's sacrifice provided a good opportunity for the illustrative mime which was a central part of Greek dance.

5.4. Formal Structure

Aeschylus uses the conventional sequence of discrete alternating movements for chorus and soloists to create a powerfully mounting tide of suspense. One factor is that each of the choral songs until the murder is shorter than the last.[72] These are skilfully integrated with the prologue and first two episodes, so that the long exposition in 1–781 builds up different notes of foreboding in different voices. This leads to the central 'contest' between Agamemnon and Clytemnestra. After Agamemnon has passed indoors, we expect a report of his murder, but the event is held in suspense for fifteen to twenty minutes during Cassandra's scene, which locates it in a broader perspective. Here Aeschylus makes moving use of the *kommos* form with intricate shifts from speech towards song and

---

[71] The first half of *Eumenides* calls for animated dancing. For Aeschylus' choreography see n. 66 above.

[72] This is beautifully balanced in *Eumenides* where the lyrics grow longer towards the trilogy's harmonious conclusion.

vice versa.[73] The second *epirrhēma*, when the Chorus calls Clytemnestra to account, is powerfully constructed to chart the change in her attitude as she recovers from her frenzy and recognizes the threat of vengeance. The exodos reinforces this anticipation of *Choephoroe.*

Aeschylus' use of recited anapaests and song is explored in the Appendix, but his handling of spoken iambic sections also repays attention. Though the text is unusually long for a Greek tragedy, and especially for Aeschylus, no words are wasted. The long speeches (*rhēseis*) each have a carefully constructed logic and internal variety, to enable a skilful actor to draw the audience's interest on. The dialogue passages, though less extended and (for the most part) less adversarial than those found in Sophocles and Euripides, provide skilful transitions and develop the argument with a telling economy.

Suggested reading:
The Ancient Theatre: Simon (1982) is still a useful guide; see also n. 63 above.
Performers: Wiles (2000), ch. 6; Easterling and Hall (2002).
Staging: Taplin (1977) is still fundamental; see also Ewans (1995) for a serious though conjectural attempt to reconstruct the staging of the *Oresteia* in detail. Davidson (2005) gives a general survey. Ley (2007), ch. 1 and Wiles (2000), ch. 5 are stimulating discussions of the theatrical space, from very different perspectives.
Pickard-Cambridge (1988) assembles a very wide range of evidence touching on all these topics.

D.A.R.

6. DRAMATIC TECHNIQUE: THE POWER OF WORDS

Aeschylus' dramaturgy may strike a modern audience as extremely static, with many words and little action. During the first 781 lines of *Agamemnon*—about an hour in performance—very little 'happens'

---

[73] 1035–1330 n. For our purposes, a *kommos* is an *epirrhēma* with a strong element of lament, and an *epirrhēma* is a partly or wholly sung exchange between the chorus and an actor. Aeschylus became famous for composing laments (*TrGF* iii test. 138).

onstage. Yet when Agamemnon enters, expectation has been steadily built up in such a way that his doom is sealed. The play's compulsive dynamic lies in the accumulation of ominous words, which should be perceived as a *form* of action, with power to influence what happens. This idea is not totally unfamiliar today, but figured rather differently in Aeschylus' culture.[74]

Although the origins of tragedy are obscure, it plausibly arose from a fusion of some genres of choral lyric with solo performance of narrative poetry.[75] The goal of much choral lyric was to inspire the favour of a god or hero, in whose honour the chorus was singing and dancing at a religious occasion, and so of ensuring the future prosperity of the local community. Few if any of Aeschylus' choruses were formally hymns to Dionysus Eleuthereus, during whose festival they were performed, but they play a larger role in the drama and more often adopt openly ritual forms than choruses in Sophocles or Euripides, and they partly inherit the verbal efficacy of their ritual cousins. Particularly striking examples of 'active' Aeschylean odes are the incantation at *Pers.* 623–80 which summons Darius' ghost; the *kommos* at *Cho.* 308–478 which rouses Agamemnon's spirit and other underworld powers, and hardens Orestes' resolve; and the Erinyes' 'binding song' against Orestes at *Eum.* 307–96.

Verbal efficacy in Aeschylus extends well beyond the choral odes, however, though their ritual background seems to reinforce the following considerations. The power of words to persuade or tempt a hearer into action is an issue in *Agamemnon*, where Peitho acts on sinners even against their reason (§ 4.3.3), and in the trial and reconciliation of *Eumenides*. Prayers and curses aim to determine the future: we hear of an instance of the latter in Thyestes' curse on the house of Atreus (1600–2), while desperate prayers for the general good are a recurrent feature of the play.[76] Words can also be the

---

[74] The seminal discussion of 'speech-acts' as a part of natural English is J. L. Austin (1962). cf. also the popular superstition of 'jinxing' something by praising it excessively.

[75] In the later sixth century, Homer was being recited in Athens at the Panathenaea. On the general question of tragedy's origins, see e.g. Herington (1985), Scullion (2002).

[76] Lines 20, 121, 217, 255, 349, 674, 998–1000, 1249. Schenker (1999), 649–57 adopts a similar position to us on these passages.

material for prophecy. Names in particular were regarded as potential signs of the bearer's destiny, as in the case of Helen (681–90), or even as determining it.[77]

More generally, in the popular Greek form of divination by κληδόνες a chance remark could be interpreted as an omen, whether intended as such or not. Aegisthus invokes the principle at 1652–3:

Χο.   ἀλλὰ κἀγὼ μὴν πρόκωπος, οὐδ' ἀναίνομαι θανεῖν.
Αι.   δεχομένοις λέγεις θανεῖν γε·

CORYPH.   I too have my hilt forward and do not refuse to die.
AEGISTH.   *This* word, 'to die', you speak to men who welcome the omen.[78]

In all Aeschylus' plays (excluding *PV*), the risk that any utterance may affect events, either favourably or adversely, is a recurrent concern. εὐφημία (well-omened speech) is correspondingly important. In Greek ritual *euphēmia* generally implied silence, to avoid any word which might impair or invalidate proceedings. In Aeschylus it may entail speaking, but with reticence (euphemism in the modern sense) or careful avoidance of potentially damaging language.

In *Agamemnon*, the practical issue until 1343 is Agamemnon's safe return to his household. The Watchman, the Chorus, and the Herald are loyally concerned to utter the propitious word which will determine the return favourably. Repeatedly, however, and whether the speakers are conscious of it or not, Aeschylus leads their thoughts and utterances to a dismal, unpropitious conclusion. Foreboding punctures the Watchman's joy, so that he hopes just to shake Agamemnon's hand, and refuses to speak further (34–9). The Chorus ends its account of Iphigenia's sacrifice reticently, expressing very vague thoughts about what it implies for the future (248–55); its pronouncements on wealthy sinners such as Paris are uncannily apt for Agamemnon; it begs Cassandra not to declare Agamemnon's death (1246). The Herald accidentally betrays the brutality of Troy's

---

[77] Regarding Helen's name, cf. Soph. *Aj.* 430–2 on 'Ajax', Eur. *Bacch.* 368–70 on 'Pentheus'. Stanford (1942), 72–5 asserts that Aeschylus uses such 'paronomasia' more than other Greek authors. The hope that a name could *determine* destiny is reflected in the many transparently positive Greek personal names. Evidently Sophocles' father hoped his son would win 'fame for wisdom', as he did.

[78] For γε and the specific sense of δέχομαι see 1653 n.

sack, and is forced to 'pollute' his good news with his account of the storm (525–8, 635–6).

Clytemnestra, by contrast, deliberately employs language malevolently, though often in an auspicious guise; sinister ambiguity is one of her chief weapons. A particularly telling example is her double use of the phrase 'malignant κληδόνες' during her address to the Chorus in Agamemnon's presence (863, 874). Here κληδόνες is itself a malignant word; behind its superficial sense in the context— 'rumours'—lurks the sense 'ominous words'. Clytemnestra is inventing rumours about Agamemnon's extreme suffering, in the knowledge that by stating them she is ominously spelling his actual death.[79] All these words have their practical result onstage when Agamemnon hubristically enters his palace over crimson garments, then offstage when he is murdered.

Drama of this kind presupposes the audience's sensitivity and close attention to the spoken word, perhaps more characteristic of an essentially oral society than of our literary culture. But even as the fifth century proceeded, the intellectual climate of Sophocles and Euripides became less receptive to the *klēdōn*, whose ambiguities become the source of dramatic irony, particularly in Sophocles.[80]

Aeschylus' interest in word-power as a dramatic device means that the power of Clytemnestra is largely expressed through her mastery of language. Aeschylus has, more generally, given Clytemnestra a mastery of non-verbal symbols as well, namely the chain of beacons whose workings she proudly and marvellously describes in her first *rhēsis*, and the symbolism of the carpet of garments (cf. 926–7 ποικίλων κληδών with n.). A good deal is made of whether the beacons are reliable compared to a human message.[81] Clytemnestra's control meets its match in Cassandra, whom she fails to engage in speech or sign-language, and who has access to a quite different kind of sign which, however, she is unable to communicate because of Apollo's curse on her. Several characters emphasize the 'clarity' of an utterance, often when it is *not* clear (e.g. 26, 615–16, 1047, 1087–8,

[79] 855–913 n. See also 281–316, 334–7, 338–47, 605, 611–12, 904, 958–74, 1372 with nn.
[80] See e.g. Soph. *El.* 59–61, *Phil.* 64–7 for rationalizing statements that fictions cannot harm one, as Clytemnestra's *klēdones* do. Sophocles' and Euripides' plays of course retain an interest in other sorts of word-power, such as that of prophecies, and the rhetorical power of persuasion.
[81] Lines 352, 475–97, 583–4, 587–93; cf. the metaphor of the torch 'talking' in 9–10. See also 1366–7 n.

1584; cf. 268–9, 1366–71). Thus language, signs, and interpretation are a major motif of the play, and one whose importance is in our view best seen as rooted in the assumed power of words to determine events.[82]

Suggested reading:
Power of words: Peradotto (1969).
Theme of language and interpretation: Goldhill (1984*a*), 8–98—a dense, but rewarding and important study.

D.A.R.

7. THE CHORUS

The chorus certainly brings metrical, musical, and choreographical variety to a tragic performance, and often intensifies the poetic texture with rich imagery. But it is not easy to pin down its further functions in the artistic design. The danced song is a cultural form visibly related to the genres of choral lyric and their ritual performances; § 6 has emphasized the relevance of this sacral background and the way Aeschylus seems to have adapted choral 'efficacy' to his dramatic context. But at the same time the tragic chorus is a group with some defined identity (e.g. 'Argive elders'), taking part in and witnessing the play's action. Various theories about the nature of choral identity have been put forward, of which the most general are unsatisfactory, for example that the chorus's identity is less important than a function of representing 'ideal spectators' or 'the common man', or conversely that the chorus has as full a character as the solo roles.[83] Often, however, the communal nature of the chorus, its physical proximity to the audience, and its tendency to observe and survive the tragic crisis, suggest a role of mediating between the audience and the characters who are fully caught in the action, a role of guiding our responses and sympathies.[84] All in all, the chorus was

---

[82] This is rather different from Goldhill (1984*a*), whose emphasis is on Aeschylus' presentation of the inherent impossibilities of adequate communication. Conacher (2000), 338–44 has down-to-earth criticisms of some details of Goldhill's argument.

[83] The nature of characterization in the solo roles is itself debated: see § 8.

[84] *Eumenides*, however, is one exception: there, the chorus is fully involved, and its identity alienates the audience.

a resource which the tragedians employed flexibly, and each ode needs to be examined in relation to its particular context within the drama. At different points, the stylized utterances can move somewhat 'out of character', and various links to the background of choral lyric move in and out of focus. What follows tries to draw together some threads from the more detailed material in the commentary on each ode, beginning with the Chorus's 'character'.

In *Agamemnon*, Aeschylus presents his choreuts in bearded masks with grey wigs, 'plying a childlike strength on staves' (74–5); they are elders of Argos. They are too old to have joined the Trojan expedition, and reflect the political and personal concerns of the men and women left behind. Their loyalty to Agamemnon is indicated particularly in their anxiety during the parodos (99–104, 165–6), the Coryphaeus' tears at the news that Troy has fallen (270), and their lament after the murder (1489–96). They do, however, acknowledge that Agamemnon is not faultless (implicitly in the parodos; 799–806, 1560–1). To Clytemnestra they show a rather patronizing respect until the murder (e.g. 258–60), but warily. They are conscious of sinister goings-on in the palace, but willing only to hint at them (543–50, 615–16, 807–9), and unable to conjecture the precise plot.[85] Their sympathy for the vulnerable figure of Cassandra is touching by contrast to Clytemnestra's attitude.

The Chorus's physical infirmity anticipates the extraordinary moment that follows Agamemnon's death-cries, when the chorus's 'ritual' role as a united body is temporarily shattered (1343–71 n.). It also motivates its unequal struggle in the exodos, and its silent retreat from the theatre in the face of Aegisthus' guards (see final n. of commentary). However, the Chorus's opening line of song contrasts this physical weakness with 'sovereign authority' to declare what has happened (104–7). In these opening words one perceives, behind its identity, the background of tragic and sacred choruses, which gave it the longest role in *Agamemnon* and other Aeschylean plays.

The Chorus is κύριος . . . θροεῖν (104) in that its utterances have the word-power described in § 6, to affect the issue at a given point, for better or worse. However, it proves unable to harness this power for its aspirations. At first, it is concerned to foster the chances of Agamemnon's safe return by auspicious language. But in both the parodos and the first stasimon, after a positive start, it finds itself

---

[85] This fallibility of the Chorus is emphasized to the extreme in Gantz (1983).

reaching gloomy conclusions and ominous words.[86] The second
stasimon already begins with thoughts of destruction, and the juxtaposition of Agamemnon's entrance with its closing reflections on
justice and the wealthy sinner only intensifies the gloom. After
Agamemnon's shocking exit, the third stasimon expresses fear, and
the expectation that no words from the Chorus can help. After
Cassandra's exit it confronts Agamemnon's imminent death and its
implications head-on (1331–42). Similarly, in his iambic speeches,
the Coryphaeus' questions during the first two episodes elicit
responses from the actors which on the whole damage Agamemnon.
In their scene with Cassandra the elders lack authority in a different
sense, since their inability to understand the prophetess's riddles is
being emphasized. And after Agamemnon's death-cries the members
of the Chorus can only argue with each other ineffectually.

From then on, however, in the *epirrhēma* with Clytemnestra and
in the exodos with Aegisthus, it recovers its initiative. It gradually
breaks down the queen's triumphant confidence and illuminates
the predicament of the house with growing insight. Its final cry of
despair for the family is importantly invested by Clytemnestra with
the truth and power of a χρησμός ('oracle': 1567–8).

Besides this feature of efficacy, Aeschylus gives his Chorus two
functions which also appear throughout choral lyric. The first is
narrative; this features notably in the remains of Stesichorus
and Pindar, and in hymns. Aeschylus can thus trace the antecedents
of Agamemnon's murder: the parodos describes the departure of
the Trojan expedition, culminating with pathos in the sacrifice of
Iphigenia; the first and second stasima elaborate on the parts played
in the story by Paris and Helen. In this way former events are
recounted, and perhaps enacted in the Chorus's stylized dancing,
within the compass of the drama.

The second element familiar from earlier sacred lyric is γνῶμαι.
Aeschylus largely uses the Chorus to articulate the religious and
moral ideas which underpin his dramatic treatment of the mytho-
logical material (see § 4). All three stasima explore the dangers
of excessive wealth and the 'hubris-syndrome' (381–7, 750–80,
1005–17; also 1331–4). Other passages refer to the wrath of the gods

---

[86] See Calchas' prophecy about the abiding wrath in the palace, followed by 159
αἴλινον, and their anxious appeal to Zeus, then 445–60 where they quote the Argives'
resentment at the expedition.

(69–71), the punishment of the wrongdoer (369–75, 385–98, 461–70), the balance in nature (1001–4, 1025–7), and the irremediability of murder (1018–21). Above all, the Chorus gives optimistic expression to the central doctrine of πάθει μάθος (§ 4.4). It is they who make most of the references to Zeus, through which the play acquires its profoundly religious atmosphere.[87] Aeschylus integrates these reflections plausibly within the dramatic structure: although their philosophizing is not wholly naturalistic, the elders turn to contemplation in their struggle to find a meaning in the story which they describe or witness (165–7, 681–5, 975–83); their reflections do not merely expound the poet's thinking.

In summary, crucial to understanding the Chorus in *Agamemnon* is the fusion of its dramatic characterization with the 'efficacious', narrative, and gnomic choral functions which tragedy derived from pre-existing lyric. Through the last of these, it serves as the dominant voice, alongside Cassandra, in setting the events of the drama within Aeschylus' universal vision.

Suggested reading:
Among basic surveys Rehm (1992), 51–60 is particularly useful on 78–92 he discusses the Chorus of *Agamemnon*. Foley (2003) discusses the importance of the identity of tragic choruses. The pair of chapters by Gould and Goldhill in Silk (1996) discuss how a chorus differs from an 'ideal spectator', but may still have an authoritative voice. Swift (2010) discusses the interaction between tragic choruses and particular lyric genres (see esp. 26–31, 367–76). Owen (1952), 2–4, 62–87 argues that this background gives choral utterances a particular power.

D.A.R.

8. THE SOLO CHARACTERS

The precise nature of characterization in Greek tragedy is contentious. Tragedies are stylized in form and language; actors wore masks

---

[87] Seventeen of the twenty-seven uses of Ζεύς come from the Chorus, which speaks rather fewer than half the words of the play.

and special theatrical costumes. Characters behave artificially towards each other, and deal with crises rather than everyday situations. The cues by which we judge personality in normal human interaction are radically altered. Furthermore, there is the difficult question of how Greek conceptions of 'personality' differed from our own. Rounded portraiture, psychological 'depth' (such as the unconscious) and personal idiosyncrasies are hardly ever to be found. Agamemnon and Clytemnestra are designed, in the first instance, to accord with and to exemplify the main themes Aeschylus wished to represent in his trilogy, rather than those themes being fitted to a character-study. Each of the other roles also has a clear function within the design of the drama. Nevertheless each is vested—selectively and economically—with enough features and enough continuity to become a dramatically convincing and vital individual, rather than a stock character or stereotype, and we are given enough material to judge their reasons for acting as they do.[88]

In what follows, the characters are discussed in the light of these two perspectives—their function within the broad design of the play, and the humanity in which that function is clothed.

What has been said in § 1 and § 4 shows that *Agamemnon* is not to be seen primarily as the tragedy of an individual who comes to grief because of his own inadequacies or misfortune. Rather, Agamemnon's fate is part of a chain of retribution, and illustrates ideas which are applicable to other cases. It illustrates how a person may be driven under the auspices of justice to commit sin and incur punishment, the self-perpetuating futility of the *lex talionis*, and the relationship between personal responsibility and external forces. The third episode stages the 'hubris syndrome', whereby past hubris, combined with excessive prosperity and glory, generates foolish pride which, with the forceful aid of Peitho, prompts Agamemnon to his last act of excess—trampling on the purple garments. In the exodos,

[88] A useful principle is advanced by Winnington-Ingram (1983), 96: 'Character enters into Aeschylean tragedy in so far as there is an action to be performed that needs such-and-such a person, acting from such-and-such motives, to perform it.' Seidensticker (2009)—a useful study for those with German—argues that the characterization in *Agamemnon* is more detailed than in some of Aeschylus' earlier work.

through the motivation of Aegisthus, he can finally be seen as a man also made to suffer for the sins of his father.

While Agamemnon can be seen in these thematic terms, he is fleshed out in a compelling way. During the parodos the Chorus explores his complex emotions during the agonized decision before the sacrifice of Iphigenia. And although he is only onstage for the third episode, Aeschylus succeeds in making him vivid and memorable. The king's grandiloquent language suggests a magnificent conquering hero, a lion who has tasted blood (827–8), with the arrogance and blood-guilt attendant on being a sacker of cities. He demonstrates sufficient piety and public spirit to arouse some compassion (844–50 n.), and to justify the affection which the Watchman, Herald, and Chorus feels towards him. However, he is subtly accorded the lack of discernment which prevents his seeing through Clytemnestra's insincerity (see esp. 830–7, 841–4 nn.). These qualities ensure that his resistance to stepping on the embroidered garments is all too easily overcome by Clytemnestra's superior intelligence.[89]

Clytemnestra, in terms of the broad design, is repeatedly presented as the incarnation of destructive forces which work against Agamemnon. She is the child-avenging Wrath (155), a force like the family δαίμων (but female) who is waiting to punish Agamemnon's sacrifice of their daughter. In the third episode she embodies Persuasion, the child of Atē (385–6), which impels her husband towards his ruin. Cassandra relates her to a 'spirit of discord' at 1117–18 (see n.). After the murder, she is the incarnation of the family daimōn, or the alastōr seeking vengeance for Thyestes (1468–74, 1500–4). Indeed, in her speech of triumph after the murder, Aeschylus presents her as 'demonically' (in our sense) possessed; but, under the Chorus's pressure, the daimōn gradually appears to leave her and she is revealed more as a human being, frightened by the retribution which awaits her in turn (see the commentary on 1407–1576, passim).

Aeschylus' portrayal of Clytemnestra as a convincing human being is unusually elaborate, though he has still picked out certain crucial traits for particular emphasis. To murder her husband she must be extremely formidable and unfeminine; and Aeschylus arranged the

---

[89] See 944–9 n. for the sense in which this process characterizes Agamemnon.

story so that she rules Argos, rather than power having devolved to a male. Clytemnestra is first mentioned in the words ὧδε γὰρ κρατεῖ | γυναικὸς ἀνδρόβουλον ... κέαρ (10–11): she is a woman, but with power and masculine initiative. Her queenly authority continues to be stressed after she appears onstage at 251, and she combines it with an interesting self-assertion as a woman in a man's world (348, 592 nn.); at 351 the Chorus naively acknowledges that she has spoken 'like a man'.[90] Throughout the first three episodes a central aspect of her authority is her rhetorical power. Not only is she given tremendous imagination (especially in describing the beacon-chain, the scene at Troy's capture, and her 'fears' while Agamemnon was away), but like a sorceress she is the mistress of damaging language, particularly through ambiguities whose ominous meanings are largely lost on her male interlocutors.[91] We can also understand Clytemnestra's personal motivations, though these are left implicit until after Agamemnon's murder. Unlike in the *Odyssey* or Euripides' *Electra* (1030–40), Aeschylus does not emphasize her adultery with Aegisthus as a motivation, or her jealousy of Agamemnon's concubines.[92] Cassandra suggests (1260–3) only that Clytemnestra is partly angry at Agamemnon for bringing a concubine home and publicly parading her as his special prize (at 954–5). More important, and implicit at least from 155, if not from the start, is Clytemnestra's anger at the sacrifice of her daughter. She articulates this only late on in the play, at 1415–18 and—more poignantly still—at 1525–30 and 1555–9. By then, she is gaining a clearer perspective on what she has done, and beginning to fear what lies ahead. Here the audience is invited to feel some compassion towards her, rather than terror. There is a moving pathos in her plea to Aegisthus to avoid further bloodshed (1654–61); 1661 recalls her ealier feminine self-assertiveness, but now sounds markedly deflated.

Cassandra's function within the trilogy is, at the moment when Agamemnon's death finally seems inescapable, to use her prophetic vision to present this imminent catastrophe as one of a series

[90] Compare § 4.5. For the relationship between Clytemnestra's masculine and feminine qualities, especially in her ways of speaking, see Betensky (1978), Podlecki (1983), 32–5, McClure (1999), 70–100; also, more generally, Rosenmeyer (1984), 235–41.

[91] See § 6, particularly n. 79.

[92] See 611–12, 1431–47 nn. Her feeling towards Cassandra is more scorn than jealousy.

governed by divine forces, typical of a problem which goes beyond the immediate event. Secondarily, she introduces the importance of Apollo. But like Clytemnestra, she is a striking dramatic creation whose depiction is more detailed than the plot requires. The young concubine is at first unresponsive to Clytemnestra, and offers the first obstacle to the latter's powers of deception and persuasion, and control over the palace threshold. Her access to signs of the past and future and her inability to persuade, which we see after she memorably comes to life at 1072, also contrast interestingly with Clytemnestra's authoritative language.[93] Her part begins and ends with pity (1069, 1330), a quality noticed by the ancient précis of the play (*hyp.* 11–12). There is particular pathos in her inability to communicate with the Chorus, her realization that the god who desired her has now led her to her death because of her 'error' (1212), and her perspective on the suffering of the Trojans. She shows nobility as she exits willingly into the palace, dignified but resigned, lamenting the precariousness of all human life.[94]

Aegisthus arrives in the exodos to emphasize that Atreus' crimes have played a part in Agamemnon's death, and to confirm that that will inevitably lead to a fresh situation of a similar kind. His character is that of a tyrant, and (surely deliberately) rather more stereotyped than the others. Vindictive, craven, complacent, and bullying, he arouses no sympathy. But this portrayal contrives the right discordant mood for the ending of Aeschylus' first act: the audience is left with an appropriate feeling of unease, and eager anticipation of Orestes' revenge in the next play.

The functions of the Watchman and the Herald overlap. Both announce apparently happy news (the fall of Troy; Agamemnon's return) whose enjoyment is soon supplanted by anxiety. They therefore contribute to our foreboding in the build-up to Agamemnon's entrance, and both suggest the power of words to determine events (as described in § 6). Both, also, are interesting and vivid characters in their own right. One can identify with the Watchman's tedium

[93] Her iambics are further characterized linguistically by a high frequency of very rare words (§ 9.1). These show her inspired state, but also feed into the contrast between her and Clytemnestra, whose persuasiveness in the third episode was conducted in simpler terms.

[94] For Cassandra see Knox (1972), Morgan (1994); Mitchell-Boyask (2006), 269–88 follows quite different lines from us, but includes a number of interesting ideas.

and fear for the future, through the circumstantial details of how he watches the stars, paces up and down, and tries in vain to hum cheerfully. We thus share his excitement at the beacon's appearance, and are touched by the loyalty which looks forward to his master's return but is overclouded by the secret fear to which he dare not give full expression. Human emotions equally render the Herald more characterful than the messengers of many tragedies who remain non-descript despite their graphic narratives. The Herald's relief and disbelief at eventually being home are convincing, as is the way in which his pride to be the official bearer of glad tidings turns to deep distress at having to spoil it all by bad news. His dejected exit is in powerful contrast with his joyful entrance.

Suggested reading:
Tragic characterization: Easterling (1973) focuses particularly on Agamemnon; Gould (1978); Pelling (1990), particularly the contributions of Easterling and Goldhill (esp. pp. 100–14, 122–4), and the editor's conclusion.
Individual characters: see footnotes 90, 94 above.

D.A.R.

9. LANGUAGE, IMAGERY, AND THEMES

9.1. Linguistic Style

Aeschylus' distinctive poetic style already interested the ancients. Aristophanes caricatures it in *Frogs*, mostly in the polemical mouth of Euripides. Aeschylus is prone to uncontrollable anger, like a giant, a storm, or a river breaching its dam. His speech is also uncontrolled and he frequently roars inarticulately, or suppresses himself in silence. His words are like monsters, hailstones, boulders, towers, mountains, or the warriors whose ethic his plays instil; the words are weighty, like his subject-matter, and swollen, and come in bundles. They are pegged together, his mind does carpentry on them, and his utterances are marked by compounds. Both words and concepts are unfamiliar to the audience, and his characters terrify them. His prologues are jumbled any-old-how; his choral songs are long. Euripides charges him with haughtiness both for his silences and for

Introduction

his grand language. Overall, Dionysus finds his advice σοφός but not σαφής.[95]

The next detailed appreciation comes from Dionysius of Halicarnassus (first century BC). At *Imit.* 2. 10 Aeschylus 'is lofty and cleaves to magnificence, and knows what is suitable in character and emotion. He is exceptionally artistic in his use of both figurative and common language, and often creates special words and concepts of his own.' Aeschylus represents the 'austere' style in Dionysius' schematic theory (*Comp.* 22): this style is slow and weighty, lacking in 'polish' and balance, focuses on emotions, and sounds old-fashioned. Somewhat similarly the ancient *Vita Aeschyli* comments that 'In his composition he aims at a continuous weightiness of form, using neologisms, adjectives, metaphors, and everything which can lend grandeur to language' (13–15).[96]

All these early readers noticed Aeschylus' boldness in using compounds, and especially new coinages. Among the extant plays, this means of escaping the vernacular is especially prominent in *Agamemnon*.[97] Such words are much more frequent in lyric and *epirrhēma* than in the trimeter *rhēseis*, and are rare in stichomythia.[98] Individually an unfamiliar word such as 51 στροφοδινοῦνται, 116 δοριπάλτου, or 563 οἰωνοκτόνος arrests the listener's attention and conjures a vivid mental image. But Aeschylus regularly enhances the effect by contrasting clusters of such words with patches of simpler language. Thus Calchas' prophecy climaxes with dense language including the unusual ἄδαιτον, δεισήνορα, παλίνορτος, and τεκνόποινος (151–5), whereas in the following Hymn to Zeus (160–83) the interpretative difficulties—though numerous—are

<hr/>

[95] See Ar. *Ran.* 814–1434 *passim*, usefully surveyed at Stanford (1942), 2–3. Ar. fr. 663 calls Aeschylus 'sinewy'. The *reductio ad absurdum* of Aeschylus' supposed lack of control is the story that he wrote while drunk (*TrGF* iii test. 117a).

[96] Ancient comments about Aeschylus, including these, are gathered in *TrGF* iii 31–108.

[97] So Citti (1994), 19, who finds eighty-nine words (mostly compounds) not extant elsewhere, except in Aeschylus or contexts which betray his influence. Given the loss of the epic Cycle, most lyric, and early tragedy, we cannot be sure whether a particular word was absolutely new, or just unusual. Aristophanes parodies Aeschylus' compounds and three-word trimeters (*Ag.* 262, 1113, 1127, 1208; Stanford 1940 gives lists) in lines such as *Ran.* 839 ἀπεριλάλητον κομποφακελορρήμονα 'unchatterboxy bundle-of-pomp-declaring', 966 σαλπιγγολογχυπηνάδαι σαρκασμοπιτυοκάμπται 'bugled-speared-and-bearded flesh-rippers-by-pine-bending'.

[98] The exception in *Agamemnon* is their frequency in Cassandra's speeches, where they characterize her inspired state.

not caused by unusual vocabulary. Similarly the third episode and stasimon are left comparatively simple in this particular respect.[99]

As well as this general contrastive effect, compounds (whether newly coined or more familiar) are deployed in a variety of ways, and rarely fall into frigid pomposity.[100] Sometimes, compounds are used with a certain superfluity to reinforce a single concept (e.g. 56–7 οἰωνόθροον γόον ὀξυβόαν). A more common effect is rich scene-painting where several adjectives qualify a single substantive, as in 148–55, 193–5; the former passage combines several sentences' worth of concepts into a dense nucleus of meaning.[101] Such adjectives in particular are frequently metaphorical, or transferred rather than strictly applying to the referent (e.g. 193, 412–13 n.). Since a Greek compound often does not imply the precise relationship between its first and second half, it can open possible ambiguities and demand interpretative work. Examples would include Calchas' phrase κτήνη δημιοπληθῆ (129: δημιο- is superficially 'belonging to the public', but the prophet's actual sense is 'consisting of the public'), and the brilliant ambiguities of 136–7 (see n.).

Coining new compound words was—to a lesser degree—a traditional feature of the main literary genres which influenced Aeschylus' style, namely epic hexameter and choral lyric. Most of the latter is lost, so Aeschylus' debt is hard to describe: the first odes in *Agamemnon* might be compared with the fragments of Stesichorus in terms of extended choral narrative technique, whereas Aeschylus' use of metaphor (§ 9.2) is often compared to that of Pindar.[102]

Regarding epic, we have seen something of Aeschylus' engagement with Homer in § 3, in terms of plot. Linguistically, Aeschylus' plays 'contain many distinctly "Homeric" . . . words, and a fair sprinkling of epic dialect forms and expressions as well', though 'Aeschylus does not make any sustained attempt to replicate Homeric dialect . . . and there is almost no direct citing or usage of epic formulae as such;

---

[99] Other notable instances of this 'clustering' are 653–7 (see 653 n.), 1090–2, 1168–72, 1292–9.

[100] 'Frigid' series of compounds are a charge levelled by old comedy against dithyramb. Those dithyrambs are largely lost, so we cannot compare Aeschylus' practice.

[101] See Stanford (1942), 133–5 on this trait. Aeschylus' descriptive richness extends to his use of adverbs, more varied than those of Sophocles or Euripides (Griffith 1977, 150–1).

[102] See Griffith (2009), 14–18 for a summary.

even relatively few specific mannerisms of epic narrative technique.'[103] Examples of epicisms in *Agamemnon* include:

features of epic morphology, e.g. 723 πολέα for πολλά, 892 ὑπαί for ὑπό;

epic words, e.g. 783 πτολίπορθος, 975 τίπτε, 1496 βέλεμνον;

words used in an epic sense, e.g. 257 ἕρκος metaphorically of a person;

epic words used with a non-epic twist, e.g. 141 μαλερός of lions rather than (as in epic) fire; 653 ὠρώρει of a night-time storm, whereas at *Od.* 5.293 night ὀρώρει during a storm;

epic formulas, e.g. 1606 τυτθὸν ὄντ' (τυτθὸν ἐόντα occurs eleven times in epic);

remodelling of longer epic phrases, e.g. 1299 οὐκ ἔστ' ἄλυξις ~ *Il.* 22.270 οὔ τοι ἔτ' ἔσθ' ὑπάλυξις, 66–7 θήσων Δαναοῖσιν Τρωσί θ' ~ *Il.* 2.39–40 θήσειν ... Τρωσί τε καὶ Δαναοῖσι, 1559 περὶ χεῖρε βαλοῦσα ~ *Od.* 11.211 περὶ χεῖρε βαλόντε (both situated in the underworld).

Lines 49–59 offer an extended simile in the Homeric manner, unique in Aeschylus, which expands on a simile in the *Odyssey* (see n.).

Despite Aeschylus' elevation, his ability to vary register is equally important. We have already mentioned the distinctive 'prophetic register' of Calchas and Cassandra, though the latter herself varies between fits of inspiration and the brutal clarity of 1246 Ἀγαμέμνονός σέ φημ' ἐπόψεσθαι μόρον. Aeschylus makes sparing use of more colloquial language.[104] Besides exclamations such as 22 ὦ χαῖρε, 25 ἰού, 1125 ἰδού, and 1650 εἶα δή, possible examples include the speech-ending tags 582 πάντ' ἔχεις λόγον and 1406 τάδ' ὡς ἔχει, the use of χαίρειν in 574 (if correct: see n.), and 1239 and 1404 ὅμοιον 'It's all the same ... '. Perhaps the most striking variations in register come from Clytemnestra's deliberate flouting of the bounds of feminine decorum, at 605 ἐράσμιον, 1443 ἱστοτρίβης, and 1447 εὐνῆς παροψώνημα ... χλιδῆι. A different kind of variation is in the syntax of long sentences, where Aeschylus appears to characterize his

---

[103] Ibid. 7–9 gives a useful survey; the quotations are from p. 8. The classic study is Sideras (1971), in German; see also Stanford (1942), 18–32, Earp (1948), 52.

[104] On colloquialism see M. West (1990*b*), Collard (2005). Griffith (2009), 1–38 emphasizes the more general point that Aeschylus' style embraces variation; see also 36–9 n.

humbler minor characters by more straggling structures including anacolutha. Both the Watchman and Herald of *Agamemnon* offer instances of this: in the former, it suggests the associative thinking of a person left on their own at night, and in the latter it expresses unease (555–66 n.).

9.2. Imagery and Motifs

Whereas Greek epic is striking in its similes but generally unobtrusive in its metaphors, Aeschylus is the other way round. *Agamemnon* is rather exceptional in having several short similes introduced by δίκην 'in the manner of', since the word δίκη must be constantly in our minds (see 3 n.); it also contains an extended simile at 49–59, and the extended analogy of the lion-cub (717–36, though this is not typical of epic either). Nevertheless, it is the metaphors which demand further analysis as a feature of Aeschylus' style.

Metaphors can have various effects. All language contains 'dead' metaphors which are hardly noticed (such as the 'length' of time); then there is the stock of metaphors such as the 'ship of state' to which Greek poetry returns time and again (and a corresponding stock of prosaic clichés); then there are metaphors which strike the audience as a bold novelty.[105] Aeschylus' practice varies. In the first half of *Septem*, for example, the 'ship of state' recurs, along with a small set of related metaphors (war as storm, governor as helmsman). In the *Oresteia*, and particularly *Agamemnon*, metaphors again return significantly, but a much larger and broader set of them are interwoven, often in quick succession ('mixed' metaphor). As with his compound adjectives, Aeschylus' metaphors are almost never 'ornamental'. In particular, the topics of the recurrent metaphors frequently occur literally in the trilogy as well. The imagery of light (~ salvation) and dark is introduced immediately alongside a real light appearing in the darkness. The metaphor of Agamemnon's 'puffing' a change of mind (187, 219) interacts with the adverse winds which are affecting him at that moment. The hunting images are realized when the Erinyes track Orestes from Delphi to Athens

---

[105] Earp (1948), ch. 5 attempts a rough categorization of Aeschylus' metaphors along these lines, and argues that those of the *Oresteia* are particularly often bold, and particularly often 'visualize' invisible qualities.

by sniffing out the blood on his hands. Perhaps most importantly, the courtroom metaphors of *Ag.* are realized in Orestes' trial in *Eumenides* (see § 4.1).

A list of the motifs which are carefully placed throughout the trilogy, in images or in the plot, might include sacrifice and libation, birds, snakes, lions, dogs, other domesticated animals, agriculture, hunting and nets, illness and medicine, fire, light and dark, sleep, winds, music, drawings, sets of three, etc. Readers must explore this network for themselves, and there is no 'right' way of interpreting every connection. A single example here—appearances of dogs—may suggest how the study can be pursued.

Greek views about dogs differed slightly from our own.[106] Dogs were used for hunting, for working with livestock, for guarding houses and livestock, occasionally as pets, and rarely as food; Homer also refers to wild, scavenging dogs. They could be pre-eminently faithful animals, but females in particular could also be thought of as pre-eminently shameless. As work-animals they may be 'servile'. The range of breeds and shapes was quite different from today.[107]

The Watchman compares himself to a dog in the first striking image of *Agamemnon* (3): both his posture and function are similar to that of a dog who guards a house at night. His φρουρά is ordered by Clytemnestra, whose connection to guarding the house is strengthened during the first episode (257 μονόφρουρον, 301 her beacon-watchers are φρουραί). This culminates in the second episode with her boast that she is a good guard-dog for Agamemnon (607–9), who in the third episode does call her the φύλαξ of his house (914). Conversely the Chorus has alluded to 'him of the citizens who has been an unsuitable house-guard of the city' (808–9), and Clytemnestra has described Agamemnon himself as a guard-dog for a farmstead (896—in a series of images for a saviour). Slightly more complex is the Chorus's warning against sycophants who 'fawn' (798 σαίνω, fundamentally of dogs) on Agamemnon like a trusty pet, but are really unreliable: this seems to allude to the dangers of Clytemnestra, so that there is a brief crossing between her

---

[106] A much greater cultural adjustment is needed in assessing the sense in which (for example) ritual or medical terms, or 'personifications' of abstract qualities, were felt as metaphorical.

[107] For this background see e.g. *NP* s.v. Dog.

as guard-dog and as pet.[108] Finally in the exodos, Aegisthus and Clytemnestra cast the Chorus's threatening language as 'yapping' (1631, 1672); this is meant to refer derogatively to the servility of dogs, as well as their inarticulacy, but the Coryphaeus accepts it, saying 'It would not be Argive to fawn on a bad man' (1665: σαίνειν).[109] In other words, it is the Chorus who are Argos' faithful guard-dogs, 'yapping' at the intruders despite their inferior status. Dog-imagery therefore illuminates the motif of guarding, and in particular the question of who has guardianship of the royal palace and of Argos.[110]

Meanwhile *Ag.* 135 introduces dogs as hunting animals. Zeus' eagles are 'winged dogs' when they 'sacrifice' the hare. The eagles represent the Atridae, and in the second stasimon the Greek chieftains hunt Helen to Troy (694 κυναγοί). Hunting with hounds is here an image of vengeance against Troy, as hunting with nets is at 357–61; the latter also figures Clytemnestra's pursuit of vengeance against Agamemnon and (less markedly) Orestes' against Clytemnestra. In the final round of vengeance, the Erinyes are repeatedly hounds on the bloody trail of Orestes (from *Cho.* 924 to *Eum.* 247). However, the correlation of hunting (including with dogs) and vengeance is complicated by Cassandra. She is also a hound on the scent of past bloodshed (1093, 1185), but unlike the Erinyes she is tracking information about the palace's history.[111] Tracking-as-learning also makes notable appearances when the Chorus detects the ἴχνος of Zeus' punishment in Troy's sack (368), when it fails to learn from Cassandra's prophecies (1245), or when Electra recognizes Orestes by his footprints (*Cho.* 205–10, 228). Hunting thus appears both as an image of retributive πάθος, and as one of μάθος.

---

[108] When σαίνω is used of the lion-cub at 725, it emphasizes its unnatural domestication, by implicitly opposing lions to pet dogs.

[109] The idea of 'yapping' also recalls 449, where the Chorus used βαΰζω 'snarl like a dog' of public threats against the Atridae's régime. And in 1228–30 (see below) Clytemnestra's 'bitchiness' is related to her tongue.

[110] The motif of guarding resurfaces particularly in *Eumenides*: Apollo and Hermes guard Orestes (64, 90); Justice guards a marriage-bed (217–18); the Areopagus guards Attica (706, 949); Attica guards the gods (919). But these guards are no longer imagined as dogs.

[111] On a different axis, this image must be viewed as part of a chain of animal-imagery for Cassandra (see 1050–2 n.), which economically charts her changing fortunes.

Thirdly, Clytemnestra is dog-like in her brazenness. This is only brought out explicitly by Cassandra at 1228–33.[112] However, especially against the background of Clytemnestra's self-declared 'lack of shame' at 856 (and cf. 1373), already during the third episode one feels this aspect supplanting her claim to be a female 'guard-dog'.

This analysis of one of the *Oresteia*'s more circumscribed motifs hopefully gives a sense of how suggestive Aeschylus' imagery is. Dogs provide a focal point at which several broader ideas intersect—guarding the city/house, hunting for vengeance/learning, ways of speaking before authority. These images could also be explored in relation to the broader class of animal imagery. As mentioned (n. 111), two passages should simultaneously be seen in the perspective of a chain of animal images for Cassandra. Several passages combine dog-imagery with other important motifs, such as that of sacrifice at 135–7.

This kind of analysis rests on treating the repetition of certain motifs in the trilogy as significant, and it can be productively extended to the repetition of some 'theme-words' which Aeschylus includes particularly frequently. Among these one might class καιρός, νίκη, πείθω, τέλος, τλάω, φρονέω, etc., and of course δίκη, in each case including cognates.[113] It is perhaps worth dwelling on a less clear interpretative tool, namely treating the repetition of very unusual words as significant. In some cases this hypothesis is rewarded. There is a clear point in relating *Ag.* 1277, where Cassandra foresees the ἐπίξηνον 'butcher's block' which awaits her, and *Cho.* 883 where a slave (probably) foresees the ἐπίξηνον which awaits Clytemnestra. The word stands apart from normal tragic vocabulary, and occurs otherwise only in Aristophanes' *Acharnians* and dictionaries; its long-range repetition is therefore noticed, and signals that Clytemnestra's come-uppance is imminent. However, subconscious reuse of unusual words is a well-documented phenomenon, and we at least do not see significance in many other

---

[112] Here Clytemnestra is compared to the monster Scylla, who is partly a bitch. At *Cho.* 613–22 Clytemnestra is implicitly compared to the woman Scylla, who is κυνόφρων. Aeschylus was probably inspired by the description of Clytemnestra as κυνῶπις at *Od.* 11. 424–7.

[113] For δίκη see § 4.1; for τέλος-words, Goldhill (1984a); for νίκη, Moritz (1979), 200–4, Goldhill (1986), 43–5. Study of these word-groups overlaps with the study of motifs which appear in imagery: it is the latter which seems more characteristic to the *Oresteia*, which is why it has received more attention here.

similar cases in the *Oresteia*, such as the two uses of Aeschylus' probable coinage δεμνιοτήρης (53, 1449), or the three of the rare word ψύθος (478, 999, 1089). Each case must be judged on its merits.

Suggested reading:
Rutherford (2010) gives a good survey of tragic language. Stanford (1942) is still the most useful study in English of Aeschylus' style, if one ignores its many biographical fallacies.
On the *Oresteia*'s imagery in general see Fowler (1967), Lebeck (1971), Porter (1986). Particularly interesting treatments of individual metaphors include Zeitlin (1965) on sacrifice, Goldhill (1984a), *passim* on light, and J. Heath (1999) on animals; Harriot (1982) discusses canine imagery, with similar results to those above. On repeated motifs other than the metaphorical, see also Yarkho (1997).

O.R.H.T.

10. THE TRANSMISSION OF *AGAMEMNON*

The *Agamemnon* was first performed in spring 458 BC, at which point there were perhaps a handful of copies of the text, used in preparing the production. The story of this libretto's survival is interesting, and also central to understanding Aeschylus' influence, and textual problems.

We know little about the book trade in fifth-century Athens, but we can imagine certain limited groups of collectors. One comprises later dramatists including Euripides, Aristophanes, and Aeschylus' descendants; Aristophanes was able to allude to at least twenty-five plays by Aeschylus, including *Agamemnon* (e.g. at *Ran.* 1276–89, 1431–2). A second group would be schoolmasters and the scholars who began work on tragedy at least by the fourth century.[114] However, *Agamemnon*'s early fame rested more on reperformance than reading.

---

[114] Unfortunately their works are almost wholly lost. They include *On Aeschylus' Myths* by a 'Glaucus' whose identity is unclear; then, from Aristotle's school, books entitled *On Aeschylus* by Theophrastus and Chamaeleon, and Heraclides' *On the Three Tragedians*. Much later, Draco's *On Satyr-plays* (second century AD) still presupposes extensive first-hand knowledge.

The engagement with *Agamemnon* by Aristophanes and later tragedians sometimes implies an appreciative public who knew the play. One example is the reworking of Agamemnon's offstage death-cries by Sophocles (*Electra* 1415–16, where Clytemnestra is murdered). In Euripides' *Electra*, at 988–1146, Clytemnestra enters in a wagon, to be greeted by choral anapaests then tempted indoors (though not before a characteristically Euripidean *agōn*) to a 'sacrifice'; Electra has an ambiguous speech during and after Clytemnestra's exit. The episode's structure is therefore similar to that of Agamemnon's return in the third episode of *Agamemnon*, with Electra as it were 'playing her mother' in revenge.[115]

Revivals, although we have no firm evidence, may well have taken place at the smaller dramatic festivals held throughout Attica, or indeed elsewhere. In 426 BC someone (admittedly dimwitted) might expect an Aeschylean revival at the City Dionysia (see Ar. *Acharn.* 9–11); such revivals were allowed there from 386 BC.[116] Our evidence about fourth-century reperformances suggests that Aeschylus was comparatively unpopular.[117] It is doubtful that the whole tetralogy would have been performed, since connected tetralogies were no longer the norm. That *Agamemnon*, unlike *Choephoroe* or *Eumenides*, had almost no discernible influence on the visual arts (Knoepfler 1993, ch. 5), perhaps suggests that its early history was separate.

It was as a response to revivals that Lycurgus commissioned an official edition of the works of Aeschylus, Sophocles, and Euripides (*c.*330 BC); thereafter, it was illegal for actors to depart from these texts (Ps.-Plutarch *Mor.* 841–2). This was probably not a 'critical edition', but just a state copy of whichever books could be found, with (if necessary) changes to the familiar alphabet, which had only

[115] For some passing allusions in later drama, see the nn. on 943, 1264–7, 1280–1, 1292–4, 1389–90, 1580; also, more fully, Garner (1990) s.v. 'Aeschylus *Agamemnon*'; Thalmann (1993). Euripides *Electra* 518–44 is a particularly prominent example of allusion to *Choephoroe*.

[116] An inscription records a title beginning Ἀγα- for the Lenaea of 419: *TrGF* i 27. Bain (1977) discusses the hypothesis that *Agamemnon* was revived shortly before Euripides' *Electra*. See also, more sceptically, Biles (2006–7).

[117] This largely saved his texts from later adaptation (contrast those of Euripides). The only lengthy interpolation extant is the end of *Septem*: Hutchinson (1984), 209–11. When at Ar. *Nub.* 1365 Pheidippides considers Aeschylus very old-fashioned, it says more about his newfangled thinking than about Aeschylus, but equally cannot be without a grain of truth.

become standard in Athens in the late fifth century BC. Some time around 240 BC Ptolemy III Euergetes bought these texts at great expense and with some sleight of hand, to improve the library in the ascendant cultural centre of Alexandria (according to Galen: see Csapo and Slater 1994, 11). Around fifty years later, Aristophanes of Byzantium produced the first critical edition of the three canonical tragedians. He added a prose summary ('hypothesis') to each play, and marginal symbols to mark changes of speaker, ends of choral stanzas, and remarkable usages; he took an early step towards arranging the choral odes into cola as we do today, and he probably made some conjectures and compared other copies in the Alexandrian library. This influential edition became the text on which the first running commentaries were based, and from where ancient lexicographers excerpted Aeschylus' rich vocabulary for their literary dictionaries.[118]

Outside the philological world, Aeschylus' impact after the fifth century is much harder to trace than that of Homer, Hesiod, Sophocles, Euripides, and Aristophanes. Plato, Aristotle, and later Philodemus seem to know a range of plays first-hand. Dionysius of Halicarnassus gives a thumbnail sketch of Aeschylus' qualities which does not seem to be entirely stereotyped (§ 9.1). But at Rome comparatively few Republican tragedies, fragmentary as they are, seem to have used Aeschylus as a source. Other Roman authors offer only the odd reference, and even Seneca's *Agamemnon* rarely overlaps with Aeschylus (see Tarrant 1976, 8–23; Lavery 2004*c*); Quintilian 10. 1. 67 declares that Sophocles and Euripides 'far outshone' Aeschylus in writing tragedy. If we jump forwards momentarily, the only texts after the third century AD to preserve a significant number of citations of Aeschylus are Stobaeus' *Anthology* (derived mostly from previous anthologies rather than his own reading), and the *Christus Patiens*—a tragedy on the Passion, much of which is modelled on the lines of Euripides, Lycophron, *Agamemnon*, and *Prometheus Vinctus*.

The evidence is slightly richer for the period from Plutarch, who cites at least a dozen lost plays, to Athenaeus' *Deipnosophistae* (*c*.AD 230), which cites at least twenty-three. In each case, some

---

[118] Who wrote the first important commentaries is unknown. Whereas Didymus' works on Sophocles and Euripides (*c*.AD 1) became fundamental, no citations remain of any commentary he did on Aeschylus.

references may be second-hand, but the authors surely knew more plays than the ones they happen to have cited. For example, Plutarch never cites the *Oresteia*. Besides these masters of erudition, interest in classical poetry was a general intellectual trend. An unexpected example of this comes from Oxyrhynchus where, against the general dearth of papyri of Aeschylus, we have found fragments of a set of Aeschylus' works including *Agamemnon*, *Septem*, and at least seven lost plays, carefully written by one scribe, presumably for a single patron. If this range of plays was available in Oxyrhynchus, libraries in major cultural centres probably preserved many more. *P.Oxy.* xviii 2178 contains parts of *Ag.* 7–17, 20–30, and is denoted **P. Oxy.** in the *apparatus criticus* (and Π_5 by West).[119]

Themistius lists the authors he read at school in c.AD 330: he includes Sophocles, Euripides, and even Sappho, but not Aeschylus (*Epit.* 236c). However, Aeschylus was certainly read in some major schools, because at one of these, at an uncertain date, a teacher put together the selection of seven plays which came down to us. The plays were recopied into a single large codex with broad margins, which were gradually filled with pre-existing and new comments, some of which survive as the *scholia vetera* (O. Smith 1976). Meanwhile without this nurture Aeschylus' other eighty or so plays, prey to time, accident, and perhaps Christian book-burnings, were lost. Fortunately, a copy of the seven plays with their scholia reached Constantinople. Possibly, it was there by c.AD 500, when Eugenius wrote a study of the lyric metres of fifteen tragedies.[120] In any case, the tradition survived to c.900 when a new copy was made from which all our medieval manuscripts of *Agamemnon* derive.

Whereas *Persae*, *Septem*, and *Prometheus* were part of the Byzantine curriculum from the thirteenth century, and are represented in scores of manuscipts, Aeschylus' other plays were less popular. The *Agamemnon* survives in just five related manuscripts, and their copies.

M: Florence, Biblioteca Medicea Laurenziana, Plutei 32.9; written in Constantinople c.960–1000. The oldest and most reliable

---

[119] Image available from www.papyrology.ox.ac.uk/POxy (accessed 29 November 2010). Sigla for the manuscripts are given here in bold, for ease of reference.
[120] Suda ε 3394. Hall (2005), 56 notes a possible allusion to Aeschylus' Clytemnestra in Theodora's speech at Procopius *Bell.* 1. 24. 33–7, written in Constantinople c.AD 545.

manuscript, and the only one to contain all seven plays, M also contains many ancient scholia. Several folios covering *Ag.* 311–1066 and 1160 to *Cho.* '9' were lost by the fourteenth century.[121]

V: Venice, Biblioteca Nazionale Marciana, Z gr. 468 (653); written in Constantinople *c.*1270. Now contains only the first 348 lines of *Ag.*

The other manuscripts all descend from a lost book, denoted *τ* by West. The famous scholar Demetrius Triclinius acquired this in Thessaloniki *c.*1320, and made a few corrections. It must have been an exciting find, since it contained *Agamemnon, Eumenides,* and ancient scholia, which were hardly known at the time. The following copies were made at Triclinius' scriptorium:

G: Venice, Biblioteca Nazionale Marciana, Z gr. 616 (663); written *c.*1325. Has lost the pages containing *Ag.* 46–1094.

Tr: Naples, Biblioteca Nazionale, II F 31. Triclinius himself wrote this *c.*1330, and included many further corrections and comments.

F: Florence, Biblioteca Medicea Laurenziana, Plutei 31.8; written before 1348. Draws on both *τ* and Tr.

The relationships of the manuscripts can be represented thus:[122]

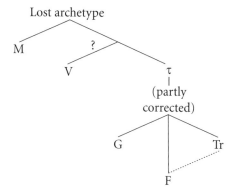

---

[121] Readers may be interested in the rather grainy online facsimile: from <http://teca.bmlonline.it>, search for 'Plut.32.09' without spaces (accessed 20 April 2010). The surviving sections of *Agamemnon* can be found on pages 131ʳ–135ᵛ. For images of F, search for 'Plut.31.08', pp. 71ʳ–106ᵛ.

[122] The affiliation of V is unclear: M. West (1990*a*), 352–3.

From the early fifteenth century, as Constantinople and Greece were threatened by Ottoman incursions, Greek-speaking scholars and some Greek manuscripts came to Western Europe. M, for example, was bought in 1423 by Giovanni Aurispa for the Maecenas of contemporary Florence, Niccolò de' Niccoli.[123] It became the basis for the first printed editions—the Aldine of 1518, then those of Adrian Turnebus and Francesco Robortello in 1552. These could therefore only print 400 or so lines of *Agamemnon*. The first complete edition came from Pier Vettori ('Victorius') in 1552/3, but unfortunately the most popular Latin translation of Aeschylus in the early modern period (by Jean Saint-Ravy, or 'Sanravius'; 1555) was based on Turnebus' edition. Outside scholarly circles, therefore, awareness of *Agamemnon* long remained very limited, and Seneca's play had greater prominence. Aeschylus' *Agamemnon* was in fact not translated into English until the 1770s, and from the middle of that century his style was gaining favour against the neo-Aristotelian fashion. Performances, as of most other Greek tragedies, began in the second half of the nineteenth century.[124]

Suggested reading:
Ancient Transmission: A slightly broader treatment is Kovacs (2005). The only detailed discussion is Wartelle (1971), in French. West's edition refers to most of the ancient authors who quote from *Agamemnon*, in the register between text and app. crit.
Manuscripts: M. West (1990*a*), ch. 11 (especially 321–3, 350–3).
Examples of modern reception: Macintosh et al. (2005); Van Steen (2008); Macintosh (2009).

O.R.H.T.

---

[123] The latter bequeathed it to Florence's public library at the convent of San Marco, which was subsequently absorbed into the Medici library, where it remains.

[124] The history of modern philology on the one hand, and of adaptations of the play to contemporary sensibilities on the other, both form burgeoning fields of study, and are far too diverse to admit of a summary here.

ΑΓΑΜΕΜΝΩΝ

ΑΓΑΜΕΜΝΩΝ

ΦΥΛΑΞ

θεοὺς μὲν αἰτῶ τῶνδ' ἀπαλλαγὴν πόνων,
φρουρᾶς ἐτείας μῆκος, ἣν κοιμώμενος
στέγαις Ἀτρειδῶν ἄγκαθεν, κυνὸς δίκην,
ἄστρων κάτοιδα νυκτέρων ὁμήγυριν
καὶ τοὺς φέροντας χεῖμα καὶ θέρος βροτοῖς   5
λαμπροὺς δυνάστας, ἐμπρέποντας αἰθέρι
ἀστέρας, ὅταν φθίνωσιν ἀντολαῖς τε τῶν·
καὶ νῦν φυλάσσω λαμπάδος τὸ σύμβολον,
αὐγὴν πυρὸς φέρουσαν ἐκ Τροίας φάτιν
ἁλώσιμόν τε βάξιν· ὧδε γὰρ κρατεῖ   10
γυναικὸς ἀνδρόβουλον ἐλπίζον κέαρ·
εὖτ' ἂν δὲ νυκτίπλαγκτον ἔνδροσόν τ' ἔχω
εὐνὴν ὀνείροις οὐκ ἐπισκοπουμένην
ἐμήν· φόβος γὰρ ἀνθ' ὕπνου παραστατεῖ,
τὸ μὴ βεβαίως βλέφαρα συμβαλεῖν ὕπνωι·   15
ὅταν δ' ἀείδειν ἢ μινύρεσθαι δοκῶ,
ὕπνου τόδ' ἀντίμολπον ἐντέμνων ἄκος,
κλαίω τότ' οἴκου τοῦδε συμφορὰν στένων
οὐχ ὡς τὰ πρόσθ' ἄριστα διαπονουμένου.
νῦν δ' εὐτυχὴς γένοιτ' ἀπαλλαγὴ πόνων   20
εὐαγγέλου φανέντος ὀρφναίου πυρός.

ὢ χαῖρε λαμπτὴρ νυκτός, ἡμερήσιον
φάος πιφαύσκων καὶ χορῶν κατάστασιν
πολλῶν ἐν Ἄργει τῆσδε συμφορᾶς χάριν.

2 ἦν FGTr: δ' ἦν MV   4–6 Achill. in Arat. p. 28 Maass
5 βροτοῖς θέρος FGTr   6 αἰθέρι: ἐν θέρει V et Achill. cod. Vat.
7–30 initia exstant in P. Oxy. 2178   7 versus multis suspectus;
habuit P. Oxy.   ἀντολαῖς Margoliouth: -λάς codd.   11 Io. Sice-
liota, schol. ad Hermog. π. ἰδ. 6. 225 Walz   ἐλπίζων, sscr. ο, MV
17 ἐκτέμνων F(sscr. εν)G   23 φάος MV P. Oxy.: νῦν φῶς FGTr

ἰοὺ ἰού·   25
Ἀγαμέμνονος γυναικὶ σημαίνω τορῶς
εὐνῆς ἐπαντείλασαν ὡς τάχος δόμοις
ὀλολυγμὸν εὐφημοῦντα τῇδε λαμπάδι
ἐπορθιάζειν, εἴπερ Ἰλίου πόλις
ἑάλωκεν, ὡς ὁ φρυκτὸς ἀγγέλλων πρέπει·   30
αὐτός τ’ ἔγωγε φροίμιον χορεύσομαι,
τὰ δεσποτῶν γὰρ εὖ πεσόντα θήσομαι
τρὶς ἓξ βαλούσης τῆσδέ μοι φρυκτωρίας·
γένοιτο δ’ οὖν μολόντος εὐφιλῆ χέρα
ἄνακτος οἴκων τῇδε βαστάσαι χερί.   35
τὰ δ’ ἄλλα σιγῶ· βοῦς ἐπὶ γλώσσῃ μέγας
βέβηκεν· οἶκος δ’ αὐτός, εἰ φθογγὴν λάβοι,
σαφέστατ’ ἂν λέξειεν· ὡς ἑκὼν ἐγὼ
μαθοῦσιν αὐδῶ κοὐ μαθοῦσι λήθομαι.

ΧΟΡΟΣ

δέκατον μὲν ἔτος τόδ’ ἐπεὶ Πριάμου   40
μέγας ἀντίδικος
Μενέλαος ἄναξ ἠδ’ Ἀγαμέμνων,
διθρόνου Διόθεν καὶ δισκήπτρου
τιμῆς ὀχυρὸν ζεῦγος Ἀτρειδᾶν,
στόλον Ἀργείων χιλιοναύτην   45
τῆσδ’ ἀπὸ χώρας
ἦραν, στρατιῶτιν ἀρωγήν,
μεγάλ’ ἐκ θυμοῦ κλάζοντες Ἄρη,
τρόπον αἰγυπιῶν οἵτ’ ἐκπατίοις
ἄλγεσι παίδων ὕπατοι λεχέων   50
στροφοδινοῦνται
πτερύγων ἐρετμοῖσιν ἐρεσσόμενοι,

---

26 σημαίνω M : σημανῶ rell.   29 ἐπορθρι- MV   30 πέ[πτωκεν ut vid. P. Oxy.   ἀγγέλλων GTr : ἀγγέλων MVF   31 τ’ : δ’ Blaydes   39 αὐδῶν οὐ V   40 Πριάμω MV   44 -δῶν Ald.   45 χιλιοναύτην M^{s}Tr^{sscr} : -ταν MTr rell. ; Ἴλιον αὐτὰν M^{syp}F^{yp} post h.v. deficit G   47 ἀρωγὴν M^{s}Tr^{sscr} : -γὰν MTrVF   48 μεγάλ’ Page : μέγαν codd.   κλάγξαντες FTr

δεμνιοτήρη
πόνον ὀρταλίχων ὀλέcαντεc·
ὕπατος δ' ἀίων ἤ τις Ἀπόλλων   55
ἢ Πὰν ἢ Ζεὺς οἰωνόθροον
γόον ὀξυβόαν τῶνδε μετοίκων,
ὑστερόποινον
πέμπει παραβᾶcιν Ἐρινύν·
οὕτω δ' Ἀτρέως παῖδας ὁ κρείccων   60
ἐπ' Ἀλεξάνδρωι πέμπει ξένιος
Ζεὺς πολυάνορος ἀμφὶ γυναικός,
πολλὰ παλαίcματα καὶ γυιοβαρῆ,
γόνατος κονίαιcιν ἐρειδομένου
διακναιομένης τ' ἐν προτελείοιc   65
κάμακος, θήcων Δαναοῖcιν
Τρωcί θ' ὁμοίωc. ἔcτι δ' ὅπηι νῦν
ἔcτι, τελεῖται δ' ἐc τὸ πεπρωμένον·
οὔθ' ὑποκαίων οὔτ' ἀπολείβων
ἀπύρων ἱερῶν   70
ὀργὰc ἀτενεῖc παραθέλξει.
ἡμεῖς δ' ἀτίται cαρκὶ παλαιᾶι
τῆς τότ' ἀρωγῆς ὑπολειφθέντες
μίμνομεν ἰcχὺν
ἰcόπαιδα νέμοντες ἐπὶ cκήπτροιc·   75
ὅ τε γὰρ νεαρὸς μυελὸς cτέρνων
ἐντὸς ἀνάιccων
ἰcόπρεcβυc, Ἄρης δ' οὐκ ἐνὶ χώραι·
τό θ' ὑπέργηρων φυλλάδος ἤδη
κατακαρφομένης τρίποδας μὲν ὁδοὺς   80
cτείχει, παιδὸς δ' οὐδὲν ἀρείων
ὄναρ ἡμερόφαντον ἀλαίνει.

---

64 ἐρειδο- VF^{sscr}: ἐριδο- M, ἐρειπο- FTr   69 ὑποκαίων Casaubon: -κλαίων codd.   οὔτ' ἀπολείβων Bothe: οὔθ' ὑπο- codd.   70 ante ἀπύρων habent οὔτε δακρύων codd., del. Bamberger   72 ἀτίται FTr: ἀτίτᾱι M^{pc}, ἀτίτ* M^{ac}, ἀτίταια V   77 ἀνάιccων Hermann: ἀνάcc- codd.   78 ἐνὶ V, ἐνι M, ἔνι FTr   79 τό θ' ὑπέργηρων Tr: τίθιπερ γήρως M, τόθιπερ γήρως VF   80 τρίποδος FTr   82 ἡμερόφατον MV

6 AICXYΛOY

cὺ δέ, Τυνδάρεω
θύγατερ, βασίλεια Κλυταιμήςτρα,
τί χρέος; τί νέον; τί δ' ἐπαιcθομένη,				85
τίνος ἀγγελίας
πειθοῖ περίπεμπτα θυοσκεῖς;
πάντων δὲ θεῶν τῶν ἀστυνόμων,
ὑπάτων, χθονίων, τῶν τε θυραίων
τῶν τ' ἀγοραίων .						90
βωμοὶ δώροιcι φλέγονται·
ἄλλη δ' ἄλλοθεν οὐρανομήκης
λαμπὰc ἀνίcχει
φαρμαccομένη χρίματος ἁγνοῦ
μαλακαῖc ἀδόλοιcι παρηγορίαιc			95
πελανῶι μυχόθεν βασιλείωι.
τούτων λέξας' ὅ τι καὶ δυνατὸν
καὶ θέμις, αἴνει παιών τε γενοῦ
τῆcδε μερίμνης,
ἢ νῦν τοτὲ μὲν κακόφρων τελέθει,			100
τοτὲ δ' ἐκ θυcιῶν ἃc ἀναφαίνεις
ἐλπὶc ἀμύνει φροντίδ' ἄπληστον
†τὴν θυμοφθόρον λύπης φρένα†.

κύριός εἰμι θροεῖν ὅδιον κράτος αἴcιον ἀνδρῶν	[cτρ. α
ἐκτελέων· ἔτι γὰρ θεόθεν καταπνείει		105
Πειθώ, †μολπὰν ἀλκὰν† cύμφυτος αἰών·

83 Τυνδάρεω: -ρέου et -ρέα Mⁱⁿˢᶜʳ   84 Κλυταιμήςτρα M (ut solet):
-μνήςτρα rell. (ut solent); non amplius notatur   87 πυθοῖ F;
πευθοῖ Scaliger   θυοσκεῖς Turnebus: θυοσκινεῖς MVFTr, θυοσκοεῖς
var. lect. in schol. vet. Tr   89 τε θυραίων Enger: τ' οὐρανίων codd.
91 δώροιcι Tr: -οις rell.   94 χρίμ- M: χρήμ- V, χρίcμ- FTr
98 αἴνει Wieseler: αἰνεῖν MV, εἰπεῖν FTr   101 ἃc ἀναφαίνεις
H. L. Ahrens: ἀγανὰ φαίνεις M, ἀγανὰ φαίνει V, ἀγανὰ φαίνουc' FTr
102 ἄπλειστον M   103 θυμοβόρον FTr (cf. MΣ ἥτις ἐςτὶ θυμοβόρος
λύπη τῆς φρενός)   λύπης φρένα MVF: λυπόφρενα Tr; λύπης φρένα
θυμοβορούcης Diggle   104 ὅcιον κράτος Ar. Ran. 1276 codd.
excepto R ὃc δῖον   105 ἐντελέων Auratus   καταπνείει Aldina:
-πνέ*ει M, -πνεύει rell. et fort. Mᵃᶜ   106 μολπὰν Mᵃᶜ; fort. μολπᾶι
δ' ἀλκᾶν

ὅπως Ἀχαιῶν δίθρονον κράτος, Ἑλλάδος ἥβας
ξύμφρονα ταγάν, 110
πέμπει ξὺν δορὶ καὶ χερὶ πράκτορι
θούριος ὄρνις Τευκρίδ' ἐπ' αἶαν,
οἰωνῶν βασιλεὺς βασιλεῦσι νεῶν, ὁ κελαινὸς ὅ τ' ἐξόπιν ἀργᾶς, 115
φανέντες ἴκταρ μελάθρων χερὸς ἐκ δοριπάλτου
παμπρέποις ἐν ἕδραισιν,
βοσκομένω λαγίναν ἐρικύμονα φέρματι γένναν,
βλάψαντε λοισθίων δρόμων· 120
αἴλινον αἴλινον εἰπέ, τὸ δ' εὖ νικάτω.

κεδνὸς δὲ στρατόμαντις ἰδὼν δύο λήμασι διςςοὺς [ἀντ. α
Ἀτρεΐδας μαχίμους ἐδάη λαγοδαίτας,
πομποὺς ἀρχᾶς, οὕτω δ' εἶπε τεράιζων· 125
"χρόνωι μὲν ἀγρεῖ Πριάμου πόλιν ἅδε κέλευθος,
πάντα δὲ πύργων
κτήνη πρόσθετα δημιοπληθῆ
Μοῖρα λαπάξει πρὸς τὸ βίαιον· 130
οἷον μή τις ἄγα θεόθεν κνεφά-
σηι προτυπὲν στόμιον μέγα Τροίας
στρατωθέν· οἴκτωι γὰρ ἐπίφθονος Ἄρτεμις ἁγνὰ
πτανοῖσιν κυσὶ πατρὸς 135
αὐτότοκον πρὸ λόχου μογερὰν πτάκα θυομένοισιν·
στυγεῖ δὲ δεῖπνον αἰετῶν."
αἴλινον αἴλινον εἰπέ, τὸ δ' εὖ νικάτω.

109 ἥβας Ar. l.c.: -αν codd. 110 σύμ- VFTr ταγάν
VFTr: τὰν γᾶν M⁵ in spat. vac. 111 καὶ χερὶ Ar. Ran. 1280:
δίκας codd. 115 ἀργᾶς Blomfield: ἀργίας codd. 116 δορι-
Turnebus: δορυ- codd. 118 παμπρέπτοις ἐν ἕδραισιν MV: παμ-
πρέποιςιν ἕδραις F, παμπρέπεσιν ἕδραις Tr 119 βοσκομένω Page:
-νοι MVF, -νην Tr ἐρικύματα M φέρματι MV: φέρβοντο FTr
120 βλάψαντε Page: βλαβέντα codd. 122 δύω M λήμμασι FTr
123 λαγοδ- MV 125 πομποὺς ἀρχᾶς Rauchenstein: πομπούς τ'
ἀρχὰς MV, πομπούς τ' ἀρχοὺς FTr δ' οὖν εἶπε F 129 lectio
incerta; προσθετὰ M, πρόσθε τὰ VFTr 130 μοῖρ' ἀλαπ- codd.
131-2 ἄγα Hermann: ἄτα codd. κνεφάσειε προτυφθὲν Tr 134 οἴκτωι Scaliger: οἴκωι codd. 136 πτάωνκα V, πτῶκα FTr

"τόσον περ εὔφρων ἁ καλὰ   [ἐπωιδ.

δρόσοις ἀέπτοις μαλερῶν λεόντων   141

πάντων τ' ἀγρονόμων φιλομάστοις

θηρῶν ὀβρικάλοισι τερπνά,

τούτων αἰτεῖ ξύμβολα κρᾶναι,

δεξιὰ μὲν κατάμομφα δὲ φάσματα·   145

ἰήιον δὲ καλέω Παιᾶνα,

μή τινας ἀντιπνόους Δαναοῖς χρονί-

    ας ἐχενῆιδας ἀπλοίας

τεύξηι σπευδομένα θυσίαν ἑτέραν ἄνομόν τιν' ἄδαιτον,   150

νεικέων τέκτονα σύμφυτον, οὐ δει-

    σήνορα· μίμνει γὰρ φοβερὰ παλίνορτος

οἰκονόμος δολία, μνάμων Μῆνις τεκνόποινος."   155

τοιάδε Κάλχας ξὺν μεγάλοις ἀγαθοῖς ἀπέκλαγξεν

μόρσιμ' ἀπ' ὀρνίθων ὁδίων οἴκοις βασιλείοις·

τοῖς δ' ὁμόφωνον

αἴλινον αἴλινον εἰπέ, τὸ δ' εὖ νικάτω.

Ζεὺς ὅστις ποτ' ἐστίν, εἰ τόδ' αὐ-   [στρ. β

    τῶι φίλον κεκλημένωι,   161

τοῦτό νιν προσεννέπω·

οὐκ ἔχω προσεικάσαι

    πάντ' ἐπισταθμώμενος

πλὴν Διός, εἰ τὸ μάταν ἀπὸ φροντίδος ἄχθος   165

χρὴ βαλεῖν ἐτητύμως·

οὐδ' ὅστις πάροιθεν ἦν μέγας,   [ἀντ. β

    παμμάχωι θράσει βρύων,

οὐδὲ λέξεται πρὶν ὤν·   170

140 τόσσων M   ἁ om. MV   141 δρόσοισιν MVF   ἀέπτοις VFTr (-σι) et ut vid. M^Σ: ἀέλπτοις M   λεόντων Et. Mag. 377. 37: ὄντων MV, om. FTr   143 -κάλοις FTr   145 φάσματα στρουθῶν MV, φ. τῶν στρ. FTr; gloss. del. Porson; siquid supplendum, e.g. ⟨κρίνω⟩ 149 ἀπλοΐδας FTr   151 σύμφυτον MFTr: συμμενεῖ φυτόν V 154 γὰρ om. FTr   163 προσηκάσαι M^{ac}   165 εἰ τὸ Pauw: εἰ τόδε MVF, εἴ γε Tr   170 οὐδὲ λέξεται H. L. Ahrens: οὐδὲν λέξαι MVF, οὐδέν τι λέξαι Tr

ὃς δ' ἔπειτ' ἔφυ, τρια-
κτῆρος οἴχεται τυχών·
Ζῆνα δέ τις προφρόνωc ἐπινίκια κλάζων
τεύξεται φρενῶν τὸ πᾶν,   175

τὸν φρονεῖν βροτοὺc ὁδώ-   [cτρ. γ
cαντα, τὸν πάθει μάθος
θέντα κυρίωc ἔχειν·
cτάζει δ' ἔν γ' ὕπνωι πρὸ καρδίαc
μνηcιπήμων πόνοc· καὶ παρ' ἄ-   180
κονταc ἦλθε cωφρονεῖν·
δαιμόνων δέ που χάριc βίαιοc
cέλμα cεμνὸν ἡμένων.

καὶ τόθ' ἡγεμὼν ὁ πρέ-   [ἀντ. γ
cβυc νεῶν Ἀχαιικῶν,   185
μάντιν οὔτινα ψέγων,
ἐμπαίοιc τύχαιcι cυμπνέων,
εὖτ' ἀπλοίαι κεναγγεῖ βαρύνοντ' Ἀχαιικὸc λεώc,
Χαλκίδοc πέραν ἔχων παλιρρό-   190
χθοιc ἐν Αὐλίδοc τόποιc·

πνοαὶ δ' ἀπὸ Cτρυμόνοc μολοῦcαι   [cτρ. δ
κακόcχολοι, νήcτιδεc, δύcορμοι,
βροτῶν ἄλαι,
ναῶν ⟨τε⟩ καὶ πειcμάτων ἀφειδεῖc,   195
παλιμμήκη χρόνον τιθεῖcαι
τρίβωι κατέξαινον ἄνθοc Ἀργεί-
ων· ἐπεὶ δὲ καὶ πικροῦ

---

177 τὸν Schütz : τῶι codd.   179 ἔν γ' Page : ἔν θ' codd. ; ἀνθ' ὕπνου
Emperius, sed sensus est 'etiam dum dormit, vexatur'; ἔν γε sicut πρόc
γε Cho. 419; ἔν γε etiam Cho. 223 aliter usurpatum   182 βίαιοc
Turnebus : βιαίωc codd.   187 cυμπνέει Tr   190 seq. παλιρ-
ρόχθοιc H. L. Ahrens : παλιρρόθοιc codd.   195 τε suppl. Porson
198 κατέξαινον MᵃFTr : κατέξενον M, κατάξενον V

χείματος ἄλλο μῆχαρ
βριθύτερον πρόμοισιν　　　　　　　　　　　　　200
μάντις ἔκλαγξεν προφέρων
　　Ἄρτεμιν, ὥστε χθόνα βάκ-
　　τροις ἐπικρούσαντας Ἀτρεί-
δας δάκρυ μὴ κατασχεῖν·

ἄναξ δ' ὁ πρέσβυς τόδ' εἶπε φωνῶν·　　　　[ἀντ. δ
"βαρεῖα μὲν κὴρ τὸ μὴ πιθέσθαι,　　　　　206
βαρεῖα δ' εἰ
　　τέκνον δαΐξω, δόμων ἄγαλμα,
μιαίνων παρθενοσφάγοισιν
ῥείθροις πατρῴους χέρας πέλας βω-　　　210
　　μοῦ· τί τῶνδ' ἄνευ κακῶν;
πῶς λιπόναυς γένωμαι
ξυμμαχίας ἁμαρτών;
παυσανέμου γὰρ θυσίας
　　παρθενίου θ' αἵματος ὀρ-　　　　　　215
　　γᾷ περιόργωι σφ' ἐπιθυ-
μεῖν θέμις. εὖ γὰρ εἴη."

ἐπεὶ δ' ἀνάγκας ἔδυ λέπαδνον　　　　　[στρ. ε
φρενὸς πνέων δυσσεβῆ τροπαίαν
ἄναγνον ἀνίερον, τόθεν　　　　　　　　220
τὸ παντότολμον φρονεῖν μετέγνω·
βροτοὺς θρασύνει γὰρ αἰσχρόμητις
τάλαινα παρακοπὰ πρωτοπήμων·
ἔτλα δ' οὖν θυτὴρ γενέ-
　　σθαι θυγατρός, γυναικοποί-　　　　225
νων πολέμων ἀρωγὰν
καὶ προτέλεια ναῶν.

---

206 πειθ- codd.　　　210 ῥείθ- Tr: ῥεέθ- rell.　　　πέλας βωμοῦ Blomfield: βωμοῦ πέλας codd.　　　212 πῶς λιπόναυς Tr: τί πῶς λιπόναυς τε
rell.　　　215 ὀργᾷ MVF: αὐδᾷ Tr (cf. M^Σ τῶι τρόπωι γὰρ αὐδᾶι, ὁ
μάντις δῆλον ὅτι)　　　216 περιόργωι σφ' Bamberger: περιόργως codd.
217 θέμις γὰρ εὖ FTr　　　222 βροτοὺς Spanheim: βροτοῖς codd.

λιτὰς δὲ καὶ κληδόνας πατρώιους   [ἀντ. ε
παρ' οὐδὲν αἰῶνα παρθένειόν τ'
ἔθεντο φιλόμαχοι βραβῆς·   230
φράςεν δ' ἀόζοις πατὴρ μετ' εὐχὰν
δίκαν χιμαίρας ὕπερθε βωμοῦ
πέπλοισι περιπετῆ παντὶ θυμῶι
προνωπῆ λαβεῖν ἀέρ-
δην στόματός τε καλλιπρώι-   235
ρου φυλακᾶι κατασχεῖν
φθόγγον ἀραῖον οἴκοις,

βίαι χαλινῶν τ' ἀναύδωι μένει·   [στρ. ζ
κρόκου βαφὰς δ' ἐς πέδον χέουσα
ἔβαλλ' ἕκαστον θυτή-   240
ρων ἀπ' ὄμματος βέλει φιλοίκτωι,
πρέπουσά θ' ὡς ἐν γραφαῖς, προσεννέπειν
θέλους', ἐπεὶ πολλάκις
πατρὸς κατ' ἀνδρῶνας εὐτραπέζους
ἔμελψεν, ἁγνᾶι δ' ἀταύρωτος αὐδᾶι πατρὸς   245
φίλου τριτόσπονδον εὔποτμον παι-
ῶνα φίλως ἐτίμα.

τὰ δ' ἔνθεν οὔτ' εἶδον οὔτ' ἐννέπω·   [ἀντ. ζ
τέχναι δὲ Κάλχαντος οὐκ ἄκραντοι.
Δίκα δὲ τοῖς μὲν παθοῦ-   250
σιν μαθεῖν ἐπιρρέπει· τὸ μέλλον δ'
ἐπεὶ γένοιτ' ἂν κλύοις· πρὸ χαιρέτω·

229 παρθένειόν τ' Elmsley: παρθένειον FTr, παρθένιον MV; αἰῶ τε παρθ. O. Müller   230 βραβεῖς VFTr   236 φυλακᾶι Blomfield: -κᾶν codd.   238 δ' ἀναύδωι Tr   239 δ' om. Tr   241 βέλει ἀπ' ὀμμάτων φιλ. Tr   245 ἁγνᾶι Tr: ἁγνὰ MVF   αὐδᾶι FTr: αὐδὰ MV   246 εὔποτμον M^pc: εὐπόταμον M^acVF, εὔποτον Tr 246-7 παιῶνα Hartung: αἰῶνα codd.; παιᾶνα exspectasses (cf. 645, Cho. 151, ScT, 635, 870, Pe. 393, et fere semper in Soph. et Eur.; sed variasse videtur noster, vid. Ag. 99, 1248, Cho. 343)   251 μέλλον δ' Elmsley: μέλον codd., post quod τὸ δὲ προκλύειν habent M^sVF (om. Tr) 251 ἐπιγένοιτ' M   προχαιρέτω codd.

ἴςον δὲ τῶι προςτένειν·
τορὸν γὰρ ἥξει ςύνορθρον αὐγαῖς.
πέλοιτο δ' οὖν τἀπὶ τούτοιςιν εὖ πρᾶξις, ὡς   255
θέλει τόδ' ἄγχιςτον Ἀπίας γαί-
ας μονόφρουρον ἕρκος.

ἥκω ςεβίζων ςόν, Κλυταιμήςτρα, κράτος·
δίκη γάρ ἐςτι φωτὸς ἀρχηγοῦ τίειν
γυναῖκ', ἐρημωθέντος ἄρςενος θρόνου.   260
ςὺ δ' εἴ τι κεδνὸν εἴτε μὴ πεπυςμένη
εὐαγγέλοιςιν ἐλπίςιν θυηπολεῖς,
κλύοιμ' ἂν εὔφρων· οὐδὲ ςιγώςηι φθόνος.

ΚΛΥΤΑΙΜΗΣΤΡΑ
    εὐάγγελος μέν, ὥςπερ ἡ παροιμία,
    ἕως γένοιτο μητρὸς εὐφρόνης πάρα·   265
    πεύςηι δὲ χάρμα μεῖζον ἐλπίδος κλύειν·
    Πριάμου γὰρ ἡιρήκαςιν Ἀργεῖοι πόλιν.
Χο. πῶς φήις; πέφευγε τοὔπος ἐξ ἀπιςτίας.
Κλ. Τροίαν Ἀχαιῶν οὖςαν· ἦ τορῶς λέγω;
Χο. χαρά μ' ὑφέρπει δάκρυον ἐκκαλουμένη.   270
Κλ. εὖ γὰρ φρονοῦντος ὄμμα ςοῦ κατηγορεῖ.
Χο. τί γὰρ τὸ πιςτόν; ἔςτι τῶνδέ ςοι τέκμαρ;
Κλ. ἔςτιν, τί δ' οὐχί; μὴ δολώςαντος θεοῦ.
Χο. πότερα δ' ὀνείρων φάςματ' εὐπιθῆ ςέβεις;
Κλ. οὐ δόξαν ἂν λάβοιμι βριζούςης φρενός.   275
Χο. ἀλλ' ἦ ς' ἐπίανέν τις ἄπτερος φάτις;
Κλ. παιδὸς νέας ὡς κάρτ' ἐμωμήςω φρένας.

Χο. ποίου χρόνου δὲ καὶ πεπόρθηται πόλις;
Κλ. τῆς νῦν τεκούςης φῶς τόδ' εὐφρόνης λέγω.
Χο. καὶ τίς τόδ' ἐξίκοιτ' ἂν ἀγγέλων τάχος;   280
Κλ. Ἥφαιστος, Ἴδης λαμπρὸν ἐκπέμπων cέλαc·
   φρυκτὸς δὲ φρυκτὸν δεῦρ' ἀπ' ἀγγάρου πυ οὸς
   ἔπεμπεν. Ἴδη μὲν πρὸς Ἑρμαῖον λέπαc
   Λήμνου, μέγαν δὲ πανὸν ἐκ νήcου τρίτον
   Ἀθῶιον αἶπος Ζηνὸς ἐξεδέξατο·   285
   ὑπερτελὴς δὲ πόντον ὥcτε νωτίcαι
   ἰcχὺς πορευτοῦ λαμπάδος πρὸς ἡδονὴν
   ‹   ›
   πεύκη τὸ χρυcοφεγγὲc ὥc τιc ἥλιος
   cέλαc παραγγείλαcα Μακίcτου cκοπαῖc.
   ὁ δ' οὔτι μέλλων οὐδ' ἀφραcμόνωc ὕπνωι   290
   νικώμενος παρῆκεν ἀγγέλου μέρος,
   ἑκὰς δὲ φρυκτοῦ φῶc ἐπ' Εὐρίπου ῥοὰc
   Μεccαπίου φύλαξι cημαίνει μολόν.
   οἱ δ' ἀντέλαμψαν καὶ παρήγγειλαν πρόcω
   γραίαc ἐρείκηc θωμὸν ἅψαντες πυρί·   295
   cθένουcα λαμπὰc δ' οὐδέ πω μαυρουμένη,
   ὑπερθοροῦcα πεδίον Ἀcωποῦ, δίκην
   φαιδρᾶc cελήνηc, πρὸς Κιθαιρῶνος λέπαc
   ἤγειρεν ἄλλην ἐκδοχὴν πομποῦ πυρός.
   φάοc δὲ τηλέπομπον οὐκ ἠναίνετο   300
   φρουρά, πλέον καίουcα τῶν εἰρημένων·
   λίμνην δ' ὑπὲρ γοργῶπιν ἔcκηψεν φάοc,
   ὄρος τ' ἐπ' αἰγίπλαγκτον ἐξικνούμενον
   ὤτρυνε θεcμὸν †μὴ χαρίζεcθαι† πυρός·
   πέμπουcι δ' ἀνδαίοντεc ἀφθόνωι μένει   305

280 καὶ πῶc τόδ' Tr   281 Clyt. tribuit M, nuntio Mˢ rell.
282 ἀγγάρου Phot. 10. 22, Et. Mag. 7. 18, Suid. s.v. ἄγγαροι, Eust.
Od. 1854. 27: ἀγγέλου codd.   284 πανὸν Phot., Athen. 15. 700e:
φανὸν codd.   286 ὑπερτελὴς MV: ὑπεὶρ ἕληc FTr et schol. vet. Tr
δὲ Blaydes: τε codd.   287 post h.v. lacunam statuit Paley
289 cκοπαῖc Turnebus: -ὰc codd.   293 μολών F   297 πεδίον
Ἀcωποῦ FTr: παιδίον ὠποῦ MV   304 μὴ: δὴ Tr   χρονίζεcθαι
Casaubon

φλογὸς μέγαν πώγωνα †καὶ Cαρωνικοῦ
πορθμοῦ κάτοπτον πρῶν' ὑπερβάλλειν πρόσω
φλέγουσαν†· εἶτ' ἔσκηψεν, εἶτ' ἀφίκετο
Ἀραχναῖον αἶπος, ἀστυγείτονας σκοπάς,
κἄπειτ' Ἀτρειδῶν ἐς τόδε σκήπτει στέγος   310
φάος τόδ' οὐκ ἄπαππον Ἰδαίου πυρός.
τοιοίδε τοί μοι λαμπαδηφόρων νόμοι,
ἄλλος παρ' ἄλλου διαδοχαῖς πληρούμενοι·
νικᾶι δ' ὁ πρῶτος καὶ τελευταῖος δραμών.
τέκμαρ τοιοῦτον σύμβολόν τέ σοι λέγω   315
ἀνδρὸς παραγγείλαντος ἐκ Τροίας ἐμοί.

Χο.   θεοῖς μὲν αὖθις, ὦ γύναι, προσεύξομαι·
      λόγους δ' ἀκοῦσαι τούσδε κἀποθαυμάσαι
      διηνεκῶς θέλοιμ' ἄν, ὡς λέγοις πάλιν.

Κλ.   Τροίαν Ἀχαιοὶ τῆιδ' ἔχουσ' ἐν ἡμέραι.   320
      οἶμαι βοὴν ἄμεικτον ἐν πόλει πρέπειν·
      ὄξος τ' ἄλειφά τ' ἐγχέας ταὐτῶι κύτει
      διχοστατοῦντ' ἂν οὐ φίλω προσεννέποις·
      καὶ τῶν ἁλόντων καὶ κρατησάντων δίχα
      φθογγὰς ἀκούειν ἔστι, συμφορᾶς διπλῆς·   325
      οἱ μὲν γὰρ ἀμφὶ σώμασιν πεπτωκότες
      ἀνδρῶν κασιγνήτων τε καὶ †φυταλμίων
      παῖδες γερόντων† οὐκέτ' ἐξ ἐλευθέρου
      δέρης ἀποιμώζουσι φιλτάτων μόρον·
      τοὺς δ' αὖτε νυκτίπλαγκτος ἐκ μάχης πόνος   330
      νήστεις πρὸς ἀρίστοισιν ὧν ἔχει πόλις
      τάσσει, πρὸς οὐδὲν ἐν μέρει τεκμήριον,
      ἀλλ' ὡς ἕκαστος ἔσπασεν τύχης πάλον.
      ἐν ⟨δ'⟩ αἰχμαλώτοις Τρωϊκοῖς οἰκήμασιν

306–8 fort. sani, si lacuna post 307 statuitur (Blomfield)   307 κάτοπτον Canter: -οπτρον codd.   310 τόδε σκήπτει FTr: τόγε σκήπτει
M, τόδ' ἐνσκήπτει V; post h.v. deficit M usque ad v. 1067   312 τοιοίδε τοί μοι Schütz: τοιοίδ' ἔτοιμοι VF(ἔτυμοι)Tr   νομοί Lowinski
317 nulla personae nota   319 λέγεις V   320 Κλ. hic Casaubon,
ante 321 codd.   322 ἐγχέας Canter: ἐκχέας codd.   323 φίλω
Stanley: -ως codd.   327 seq. φυτάλμιοι παίδων γέροντες Weil
331 νῆστις F, νήστισι V   334 δ' suppl. Pauw

ναίουϲιν ἤδη, τῶν ὑπαιθρίων πάγων 335
δρόϲων τ' ἀπαλλαχθέντεϲ, ὡϲ δ' εὐδαίμονεϲ
ἀφύλακτον εὑδήϲουϲι πᾶϲαν εὐφρόνην.
εἰ δ' εὐϲεβοῦϲι τοὺϲ πολιϲϲούχουϲ θεοὺϲ
τοὺϲ τῆϲ ἁλούϲηϲ γῆϲ θεῶν θ' ἱδρύματα,
οὔ τἂν ἑλόντεϲ αὖθιϲ ἀνθαλοῖεν ἄν· 340
ἔρωϲ δὲ μή τιϲ πρότερον ἐμπίπτηι ϲτρατῶι
πορθεῖν ἃ μὴ χρή, κέρδεϲιν νικωμένουϲ·
δεῖ γὰρ πρὸϲ οἴκουϲ νοϲτίμου ϲωτηρίαϲ,
κάμψαι διαύλου θάτερον κῶλον πάλιν.
θεοῖϲ δ' ἀναμπλάκητοϲ εἰ μόλοι ϲτρατόϲ, 345
ἐγρηγορὸϲ τὸ πῆμα τῶν ὀλωλότων
γένοιτ' ἄν, εἰ πρόϲπαια μὴ τύχοι κακά.
τοιαῦτά τοι γυναικὸϲ ἐξ ἐμοῦ κλύειϲ·
τὸ δ' εὖ κρατοίη μὴ διχορρόπωϲ ἰδεῖν·
πολλῶν γὰρ ἐϲθλῶν τὴν ὄνηϲιν εἱλόμην. 350
Χο. γύναι, κατ' ἄνδρα ϲώφρον' εὐφρόνωϲ λέγειϲ·
ἐγὼ δ' ἀκούϲαϲ πιϲτά ϲου τεκμήρια
θεοὺϲ προϲειπεῖν εὖ παραϲκευάζομαι·
χάριϲ γὰρ οὐκ ἄτιμοϲ εἴργαϲται πόνων.

ὦ Ζεῦ βαϲιλεῦ καὶ Νὺξ φιλία 355
μεγάλων κόϲμων κτεάτειρα,
ἥτ' ἐπὶ Τροίαϲ πύργοιϲ ἔβαλεϲ
ϲτεγανὸν δίκτυον, ὡϲ μήτε μέγαν
μήτ' οὖν νεαρῶν τιν' ὑπερτελέϲαι
μέγα δουλείαϲ 360
γάγγαμον ἄτηϲ παναλώτου·
Δία τοι ξένιον μέγαν αἰδοῦμαι
τὸν τάδε πράξαντ', ἐπ' Ἀλεξάνδρωι

---

336 ἀπαλλαγέντεϲ FTr   δ' εὐδαίμονεϲ Casaubon : δυϲδαίμονεϲ codd. et
schol. vet. Tr   340 οὔ τἂν ἑλόντεϲ Hermann : οὐκ ἀνελόντεϲ V, οὐκ
ἄν γ' ἑλόντεϲ FTr   ἀνθαλοῖεν Auratus : ἂν θάνοιεν V, αὖ θάνοιεν FTr
341 πρῶτον V   ἐμπίπτηι F : -τει V, -τοι FˢˢᶜʳTr   342 τὰ μὴ V
346 ἐγρηγορὸϲ Askew : -ρον codd.   347 τύχηι Tr   348 κλύοιϲ
FTr; post h.v. deficit V   351-4 nuntio, 355 choro tribuunt
codd.   356 τῶν μεγάλων Tr

τείνοντα πάλαι τόξον, ὅπως ἂν
μήτε πρὸ καιροῦ μήθ᾽ ὑπὲρ ἄστρων   365
βέλος ἠλίθιον σκήψειεν.

Διὸς πλαγὰν ἔχουσιν εἰπεῖν,   [cτρ. α
πάρεστιν τοῦτό γ᾽ ἐξιχνεῦcαι·
ἔπραξεν ὡς ἔκρανεν· οὐκ ἔφα τις
θεοὺς βροτῶν ἀξιοῦcθαι μέλειν   370
ὅcοιc ἀθίκτων χάρις
πατοῖθ᾽· ὁ δ᾽ οὐκ εὐcεβής·
πέφανται δ᾽ ἐγγόνοιc
†ἀτολμήτων ἄρη†   375
πνεόντων μεῖζον ἢ δικαίωc,
φλεόντων δωμάτων ὑπέρφευ
ὑπὲρ τὸ βέλτιστον· ἔcτω δ᾽ ἀπή-
μαντον, ὥcτ᾽ ἀπαρκεῖν
εὖ πραπίδων λαχόντι.   380
οὐ γὰρ ἔcτιν ἔπαλξις
πλούτου πρὸς Κόρον ἀνδρὶ
λακτίcαντι μέγαν Δίκαc
βωμὸν εἰς ἀφάνειαν.

βιᾶται δ᾽ ἁ τάλαινα Πειθώ,   [ἀντ. α
προβούλου παῖς ἄφερτος Ἄταc·   386
ἄκος δὲ πᾶν μάταιον· οὐκ ἐκρύφθη,
πρέπει δέ, φῶc αἰνολαμπέc, cίνοc·
κακοῦ δὲ χαλκοῦ τρόπον   390
τρίβωι τε καὶ προσβολαῖc
μελαμπαγὴc πέλει

367 ἔχουcαν Fᵃᶜ, ἔχους᾽ Fᵖᶜ   368 τοῦτ᾽ ἐξιχν- F   369 ἔπραξεν
ὡc Hermann : ὡc ἔπραξεν ὡc codd. ; ἔπραξαν ὡc Franz   374 ἐγγόνοιc
Casaubon : ἐγγόνουc FTr, ἐκγόνουc Trˢˢᶜʳ   375 ἀτολμήτων ἀρή
Headlam   379 ὥcτε κἀπαρκεῖν Tr   380 λαχόντι Auratus :
-τα codd.   383 ἐκλακτ- Tr   μέγαν Canter : μεγάλα codd.
386 προβούλου παῖc Hartung : προβουλόπαιc codd.   387 ὡc ἄκος
Tr   παμμάταιον codd.   389 cίνοc FTr : cέλαc Trˢˢᶜʳ et schol. vet.
Tr   391 τε om. F   προcβ- Casaubon : προβ- codd.

δικαιωθείς, ἐπεὶ
διώκει παῖς ποτανὸν ὄρνιν,
πόλει πρόστριμμα θεὶς ἄφερτον.　　　395
λιτᾶν δ' ἀκούει μὲν οὔτις θεῶν,
　τὸν δ' ἐπίστροφον τῶν
φῶτ' ἄδικον καθαιρεῖ·
οἷος καὶ Πάρις ἐλθὼν
ἐς δόμον τὸν Ἀτρειδᾶν　　　400
ἤισχυνε ξενίαν τράπε-
ζαν κλοπαῖσι γυναικός.

λιποῦσα δ' ἀστοῖσιν ἀσπίστορας　　　[στρ. β
κλόνους λοχισμούς τε καὶ
　ναυβάτας ὁπλισμούς,　　　405
ἄγουσά τ' ἀντίφερνον Ἰλίωι φθοράν,
βέβακει ῥίμφα διὰ
　πυλᾶν ἄτλητα τλᾶσα. πολὺ δ' ἀνέστενον
τόδ' ἐννέποντες δόμων προφῆται·
"ἰὼ ἰὼ δῶμα δῶμα καὶ πρόμοι,　　　410
ἰὼ λέχος καὶ στίβοι φιλάνορες·
πάρεστι †σιγᾶς ἄτιμος ἀλοίδορος
ἄδιστος ἀφεμένων† ἰδεῖν·
πόθωι δ' ὑπερποντίας
φάσμα δόξει δόμων ἀνάσσειν·　　　415
εὐμόρφων δὲ κολοσσῶν
ἔχθεται χάρις ἀνδρί,
ὀμμάτων δ' ἐν ἀχηνίαις
ἔρρει πᾶσ' Ἀφροδίτα.

394 ποτανὸν Schütz: πτανὸν F, πτανόν τιν' Tr　　395 θεὶς ἄφερτον Wilamowitz: ἄφερτον θεὶς F, ἄφερτον ἐνθεὶς Tr　397 τῶν Klausen: τῶνδε codd.　400 ἐς δόμον F: εἰς οἶκον Tr　τὸν Tr: τῶν F　401 τὴν ξενίαν Tr　402 κλοπαῖς F　404 λοχισμούς Heyse: λογχίμους codd.　407 βέβακει Keck: -κε F, -κεν Tr　408 πολλὰ δ' ἔστενον Tr　410 ἰὼ et δῶμα semel F　412–13 πάρεστιν F σιγᾶς ἀτίμους ἀλοιδόρους Hermann, σιγᾶς ἀτίμους ἀλοιδόρως . . . ἀφημένων Dindorf; fort. σιγᾶς ἀτίμους ἀλοιδόρως ἀλίστως ἀφημ.　416 δὲ F: γὰρ Tr　417 τἀνδρὶ Tr　419 Ἀφροδίτη FTrsscr

ὀνειρόφαντοι δὲ πενθήμονες   [ἀντ. β
πάρεισι δόξαι φέρου-   421
 σαι χάριν ματαίαν·
μάταν γάρ, εὖτ' ἂν ἐcθλά τιc δοκοῦνθ' ὁρᾶι,
παραλλάξαcα διὰ
 χερῶν βέβακεν ὄψιc, οὐ μεθύcτερον   425
πτεροῖc ὀπαδοῦc' ὕπνου κελεύθοιc."
τὰ μὲν κατ' οἴκουc ἐφ' ἑcτίαc ἄχη
τάδ' ἐcτὶ καὶ τῶνδ' ὑπερβατώτερα·
τὸ πᾶν δ' ἀφ' Ἑλλανοc αἴαc cυνορμένοιcι πένθεια τληcικάρδιοc   430
δόμωι 'ν ἑκάcτου πρέπει.
πολλὰ γοῦν θιγγάνει πρὸc ἧπαρ·
οὓc μὲν γάρ ⟨τιc⟩ ἔπεμψεν
οἶδεν, ἀντὶ δὲ φωτῶν
τεύχη καὶ cποδὸc εἰc ἑκά-   435
 cτου δόμουc ἀφικνεῖται.

ὁ χρυcαμοιβὸc δ' Ἄρηc cωμάτων   [cτρ. γ
καὶ ταλαντοῦχοc ἐν μάχηι δορὸc
πυρωθὲν ἐξ Ἰλίου   440
φίλοιcι πέμπει βαρὺ
ψῆγμα δυcδάκρυτον ἀντ-
 ήνοροc cποδοῦ γεμί-
 ζων λέβηταc εὐθέτου.
cτένουcι δ' εὖ λέγοντεc ἄν-   445
 δρα τὸν μὲν ὡc μάχηc ἴδριc,
τὸν δ' ἐν φοναῖc καλῶc πεcόντ',
 ἀλλοτρίαc διαὶ γυναι-

423 δοκοῦνθ' ὁρᾶι Salzmann: δοκῶν ὁρᾶν codd. 425 χειρῶν F
426 ὀπαδοῦc' Dobree: -δοῖc codd. 429 Ἑλλανοc Bamberger: Ἑλ-
λάδοc codd. cυνορμένοιc codd. 431 δόμωι 'ν Dobree: δόμων codd.;
δόμοιc Auratus 433 τιc suppl. Porson πέμψεν Tr 434 φωτῶν
F: βροτῶν Tr 435 seq. πρὸc ἑκάcτου τοὺc δόμουc εἰcαφικνεῖται Tr
441 βραχὺ Schütz 443-4 γεμίξων F^{pc} τοὺc λέβηταc Tr εὐθέτουc
Auratus 448 διαὶ An. Ox. Cramer 1. 119. 10 seqq.: διὰ F, γε
διὰ Tr

κός· τάδε σῖγά τις βαΰ-
ζει, φθονερὸν δ᾽ ὑπ᾽ ἄλγος ἕρ-   450
πει προδίκοις Ἀτρείδαις.
οἱ δ᾽ αὐτοῦ περὶ τεῖχος
θήκας Ἰλιάδος γᾶς
εὔμορφοι κατέχουσιν, ἐχ-
θρὰ δ᾽ ἔχοντας ἔκρυψεν.   455

βαρεῖα δ᾽ ἀστῶν φάτις σὺν κότωι,   [ἀντ. γ
δημοκράντου δ᾽ ἀρᾶς τίνει χρέος·
μένει δ᾽ ἀκοῦσαί τί μου
μέριμνα νυκτηρεφές·   460
τῶν πολυκτόνων γὰρ οὐκ
ἄσκοποι θεοί, κελαι-
ναὶ δ᾽ Ἐρινύες χρόνωι
τυχηρὸν ὄντ᾽ ἄνευ δίκας
παλιντυχεῖ τριβᾶι βίου   465
τιθεῖσ᾽ ἀμαυρόν, ἐν δ᾽ ἀί-
στοις τελέθοντος οὔτις ἀλ-
κά· τὸ δ᾽ ὑπερκόπως κλύειν
εὖ βαρύ· βάλλεται γὰρ οἴ-
κοις Διόθεν κεραυνός.   470
κρίνω δ᾽ ἄφθονον ὄλβον·
μήτ᾽ εἴην πτολιπόρθης,
μήτ᾽ οὖν αὐτὸς ἁλοὺς ὑπ᾽ ἄλλωι βίον κατίδοιμι.

πυρὸς δ᾽ ὑπ᾽ εὐαγγέλου   [ἐπωιδ.
πόλιν διήκει θοὰ   476
βάξις· εἰ δ᾽ ἐτήτυμος,

449 σιγᾶι F   451 προδίκοισιν F   452 οἶδ᾽ codd.   454 seq. ἐχθρῶς Tr
457 -κράντου Porson : -κράτου codd.   459 μοι Karsten   462 ἀπό-
σκοποι F   463 δ᾽ F : δ᾽ οὖν Tr   465 παλιντυχεῖ Scaliger : -τυχῆι
codd.   468 ὑπερκόπως Casaubon : -κότως codd.   469 seq.
οἴκοις Weil : ὄσσοις codd.   472 μὴ δ᾽ F   -πόρθις F   473 seq.
ἄλλωι Karsten : -ων codd.   476 τὴν πόλιν Tr   477 ἐτήτυμος
Auratus : -μως codd.

τίς οἶδεν, ἤ τι θεῖόν ἐστί πηι ψύθος;
τίς ὧδε παιδνὸς ἢ φρενῶν κεκομμένος,
φλογὸς παραγγέλμασιν   480
νέοις πυρωθέντα καρδίαν, ἔπειτ'
ἀλλαγᾶι λόγου καμεῖν;
γυναικὸς αἰχμᾶι πρέπει
πρὸ τοῦ φανέντος χάριν ξυναινέσαι·
πιθανὸς ἄγαν ὁ θῆλυς ὅρος ἐπινέμεται   485
ταχύπορος· ἀλλὰ ταχύμορον
γυναικογήρυτον ὄλλυται κλέος.

Κλ. τάχ' εἰσόμεσθα λαμπάδων φαεσφόρων
φρυκτωριῶν τε καὶ πυρὸς παραλλαγάς,   490
εἴτ' οὖν ἀληθεῖς εἴτ' ὀνειράτων δίκην
τερπνὸν τόδ' ἐλθὸν φῶς ἐφήλωσεν φρένας·
κῆρυκ' ἀπ' ἀκτῆς τόνδ' ὁρῶ κατάσκιον
κλάδοις ἐλαίας· μαρτυρεῖ δέ μοι κάσις
πηλοῦ ξύνουρος διψία κόνις τάδε,   495
ὡς οὔτ' ἄναυδος οὔτε σοι δαίων φλόγα
ὕλης ὀρείας σημανεῖ καπνῶι πυρός·
ἀλλ' ἢ τὸ χαίρειν μᾶλλον ἐκβάξει λέγων·
τὸν ἀντίον δὲ τοῖσδ' ἀποστέργω λόγον·
εὖ γὰρ πρὸς εὖ φανεῖσι προσθήκη πέλοι.   500
Χο. ὅστις τάδ' ἄλλως τῆιδ' ἐπεύχεται πόλει,
αὐτὸς φρενῶν καρποῖτο τὴν ἁμαρτίαν.

ΚΗΡΥΞ
ἰὼ πατρῶιον οὖδας Ἀργείας χθονός,
δεκάτου σε φέγγει τῶιδ' ἀφικόμην ἔτους,

478 ἤ τι θεῖόν ἐστί πηι ψύθος H. L. Ahrens: ἤ τοι FTr, εἴ τοι F^sscr, mox
ἐςτιν μὴ F, ἔςτι μὴ Tr   481 seq. καρδίαν ἔπει / ἔπειτ' ἀλλαγᾶι F   482 λό-
γους F   483 γυναικὸς Scaliger: ἐν γυν- codd.   αἰχμᾶι suspectum
485 obscurus; ἔρος H. L. Ahrens   489 Clyt. tribuunt codd., choro
edd. plurimi   490 φρυκτωρίας Wilamowitz   496 οὗτος, οὐ
δαίων Wilamowitz   501-2 choro tribuunt codd., Clyt. edd. plurimi qui 489-500 choro tribuunt   504 δεκάτου Iacob: -τωι codd.

πολλῶν ῥαγεισῶν ἐλπίδων μιᾶς τυχών·   505
οὐ γάρ ποτ᾽ ηὔχουν τῆιδ᾽ ἐν Ἀργείαι χθονὶ
θανὼν μεθέξειν φιλτάτου τάφου μέρος.
νῦν χαῖρε μὲν χθών, χαῖρε δ᾽ ἡλίου φάος,
ὕπατός τε χώρας Ζεὺς ὁ Πύθιός τ᾽ ἄναξ,
τόξοις ἰάπτων μηκέτ᾽ εἰς ἡμᾶς βέλη·   510
ἅλις παρὰ Σκάμανδρον ἦσθ᾽ ἀνάρσιος·
νῦν δ᾽ αὖτε σωτὴρ ἴσθι καὶ παιώνιος,
ἄναξ Ἄπολλον· τούς τ᾽ ἀγωνίους θεοὺς
πάντας προσαυδῶ τόν τ᾽ ἐμὸν τιμάορον
Ἑρμῆν, φίλον κήρυκα, κηρύκων σέβας,   515
ἥρως τε τοὺς πέμψαντας, εὐμενεῖς πάλιν
στρατὸν δέχεσθαι τὸν λελειμμένον δορός.
ἰὼ μέλαθρα βασιλέων, φίλαι στέγαι,
σεμνοί τε θᾶκοι δαίμονές τ᾽ ἀντήλιοι,
εἴ που πάλαι, φαιδροῖσι τοισίδ᾽ ὄμμασιν   520
δέξασθε κόσμωι βασιλέα πολλῶι χρόνωι·
ἥκει γὰρ ὑμῖν φῶς ἐν εὐφρόνηι φέρων
καὶ τοῖσδ᾽ ἅπασι κοινὸν Ἀγαμέμνων ἄναξ.
ἀλλ᾽ εὖ νιν ἀσπάσασθε, καὶ γὰρ οὖν πρέπει,
Τροίαν κατασκάψαντα τοῦ δικηφόρου   525
Διὸς μακέλληι, τῆι κατείργασται πέδον.
βωμοὶ δ᾽ ἄιστοι καὶ θεῶν ἱδρύματα,
καὶ σπέρμα πάσης ἐξαπόλλυται χθονός·
τοιόνδε Τροίαι περιβαλὼν ζευκτήριον
ἄναξ Ἀτρείδης πρέσβυς εὐδαίμων ἀνὴρ   530
ἥκει· τίεσθαι δ᾽ ἀξιώτατος βροτῶν
τῶν νῦν· Πάρις γὰρ οὔτε συντελὴς πόλις
ἐξεύχεται τὸ δρᾶμα τοῦ πάθους πλέον·
ὀφλὼν γὰρ ἁρπαγῆς τε καὶ κλοπῆς δίκην
τοῦ ῥυσίου θ᾽ ἥμαρτε καὶ πανώλεθρον   535
αὐτόχθονον πατρῶιον ἔθρισεν δόμον·

---

511 ἦσθ᾽ Needham : ἦλθ᾽ F, ἦλθες FˢˢᶜʳTr   512 καὶ παιώνιος
Dobree : καὶ παγώνιος F, κἀπαγώνιος Tr   520 εἴ Auratus : ἢ codd.
πω Headlam   τοῖσιν Tr   521 δέξαισθε Tr   522 ἡμῖν F
529 τοιοῦδε F

διπλᾶ δ' ἔτεισαν Πριαμίδαι θάμαρτια.

Χο.   κῆρυξ Ἀχαιῶν χαῖρε τῶν ἀπὸ cτρατοῦ.

Κη.   χαίρω· τὸ τεθνάναι δ' οὐκέτ' ἀντερῶ θεοῖc.

Χο.   ἔρωc πατρώιαc τῆcδε γῆc c' ἐγύμναcεν;   540

Κη.   ὥcτ' ἐνδακρύειν γ' ὄμμαcιν χαρᾶc ὕπο.

Χο.   τερπνῆc ἄρ' ἦτε τῆcδ' ἐπήβολοι νόcου.

Κη.   πῶc δή; διδαχθεὶc τοῦδε δεcπόcω λόγου.

Χο.   τῶν ἀντερώντων ἱμέρωι πεπληγμένοι.

Κη.   ποθεῖν ποθοῦντα τήνδε γῆν cτρατὸν λέγειc;   545

Χο.   ὡc πόλλ' ἀμαυρᾶc ἐκ φρενόc ⟨μ'⟩ ἀναcτένειν.

Κη.   πόθεν τὸ δύcφρον τοῦτ' ἐπῆν cτύγοc †cτρατῶι†;

Χο.   πάλαι τὸ cιγᾶν φάρμακον βλάβηc ἔχω.

Κη.   καὶ πῶc; ἀπόντων κοιράνων ἔτρειc τινάc;

Χο.   ὡc νῦν, τὸ cὸν δή, καὶ θανεῖν πολλὴ χάριc.   550

Κη.   εὖ γὰρ πέπρακται. ταῦτὰ δ' ἐν πολλῶι χρόνωι
      τὰ μέν τιc ἂν λέξειεν εὐπετῶc ἔχειν,
      τὰ δ' αὖτε κἀπίμομφα. τίc δὲ πλὴν θεῶν
      ἅπαντ' ἀπήμων τὸν δι' αἰῶνοc χρόνον;
      μόχθουc γὰρ εἰ λέγοιμι καὶ δυcαυλίαc,   555
      cπαρνὰc παρήξειc καὶ κακοcτρώτουc, τί δ' οὐ
      cτένοντεc, οὐ λαχόντεc ἤματοc μέροc;
      τὰ δ' αὖτε χέρcωι καὶ προcῆν πλέον cτύγοc·
      εὐναὶ γὰρ ἦcαν δαΐων πρὸc τείχεcιν,
      ἐξ οὐρανοῦ δὲ κἀπὸ γῆc λειμώνιαι   560
      δρόcοι κατεψάκαζον, ἔμπεδον cίνοc,
      ἐcθημάτων τιθέντεc ἔνθηρον τρίχα.

538, 540, et cett.: alternos versus choro tribuit Heath; Clyt. codd.
539 τὸ τεθνάναι Schneidewin: τεθνᾶναι codd.   οὐκέτ' Tr: οὐκ F
541 ἐκδακρ- Tr   542 ἦτε Tr: ἴcτε F; ἦcτε H. L. Ahrens, fort. recte
544 πεπληγμένοι Tyrwhitt: -νοc codd.   546 μ' suppl. Scaliger   547 cτρατῶι: λεῶι Heimsoeth   549 κοιράνων Tr: τυράννων
F   550 ὡc Auratus: ὧν codd.   551 ταὐτὰ Haupt: ταῦτα codd.
552 ἂν Auratus: εὖ codd.   556 κακοτρ- F   558 καὶ πλέον
προcῆν Blaydes   559 δαΐων Dindorf: δηΐων codd.   560 δὲ
I. Pearson: γὰρ codd.   561 -ψάκαζον Dindorf: -ψέκαζον codd.
562 τιθέντεc (sc. δρόcοι) suspectum; fort. cίνοc / ἐcθημάτων, τιθεῖcι δ'
ἔνθ.

χειμῶνα δ' εἰ λέγοι τις οἰωνοκτόνον,
οἷον παρεῖχ' ἄφερτον Ἰδαία χιών,
ἢ θάλπος, εὖτε πόντος ἐν μεσημβριναῖς   565
κοίταις ἀκύμων νηνέμοις εὖδοι πεσών·
τί ταῦτα πενθεῖν δεῖ; παροίχεται πόνος·
παροίχεται δέ, τοῖσι μὲν τεθνηκόσιν
τὸ μήποτ' αὖθις μηδ' ἀναστῆναι μέλειν,
ἡμῖν δὲ τοῖς λοιποῖσιν Ἀργείων στρατοῦ   [573] 570
νικᾶι τὸ κέρδος, πῆμα δ' οὐκ ἀντιρρέπει.   [574]
τί τοὺς ἀναλωθέντας ἐν ψήφωι λέγειν,   [570]
τὸν ζῶντα δ' ἀλγεῖν χρὴ τύχης παλιγκότου;   [571]
καὶ πολλὰ χαίρειν συμφοραῖς καταξιῶ,   [572]
ὡς κομπάσαι τῶιδ' εἰκὸς ἡλίου φάει   575
ὑπὲρ θαλάσσης καὶ χθονὸς ποτωμένοις
"Τροίαν ἑλόντες δή ποτ' Ἀργείων στόλος
θεοῖς λάφυρα ταῦτα τοῖς καθ' Ἑλλάδα
δόμοις ἐπασσάλευσαν ἀρχαῖον γάνος".
τοιαῦτα χρὴ κλύοντας εὐλογεῖν πόλιν   580
καὶ τοὺς στρατηγούς· καὶ χάρις τιμήσεται
Διὸς τάδ' ἐκπράξασα. πάντ' ἔχεις λόγον.
Χο. νικώμενος λόγοισιν οὐκ ἀναίνομαι,
ἀεὶ γὰρ ἡβᾶι τοῖς γέρουσιν εὐμαθεῖν.
δόμοις δὲ ταῦτα καὶ Κλυταιμήστραι μέλειν   585
εἰκὸς μάλιστα, σὺν δὲ πλουτίζειν ἐμέ.
Κλ. ἀνωλόλυξα μὲν πάλαι χαρᾶς ὕπο,
ὅτ' ἦλθ' ὁ πρῶτος νύχιος ἄγγελος πυρὸς
φράζων ἅλωσιν Ἰλίου τ' ἀνάστασιν·
καὶ τίς μ' ἐνίπτων εἶπε "φρυκτωρῶν διὰ   590
πεισθεῖσα Τροίαν νῦν πεπορθῆσθαι δοκεῖς;
ἦ κάρτα πρὸς γυναικὸς αἴρεσθαι κέαρ."
λόγοις τοιούτοις πλαγκτὸς οὖσ' ἐφαινόμην·
ὅμως δ' ἔθυον, καὶ γυναικείωι νόμωι

563 λέγει Tr   570 seqq. ordo versuum incertus; [573-4] huc trai.
Elberling   574 συμφοράς Blomfield   577 Τροίην F   584 ἥβη
Margoliouth   εὖ μαθεῖν ‛codd.   587 ἀνωλολύξαμεν codd.
590 ἐνίπτων F   593 πλακτὸς Tr

ὀλολυγμὸν ἄλλος ἄλλοθεν κατὰ πτόλιν   595
ἔλασκον εὐφημοῦντες, ἐν θεῶν ἕδραις
θυηφάγον κοιμῶντες εὐώδη φλόγα.
καὶ νῦν τὰ μάccω μὲν τί δεῖ c' ἐμοὶ λέγειν;
ἄνακτος αὐτοῦ πάντα πεύcομαι λόγον.
ὅπως δ' ἄριcτα τὸν ἐμὸν αἰδοῖον πόcιν   600
cπεύcω πάλιν μολόντα δέξαcθαι· τί γὰρ
γυναικὶ τούτου φέγγος ἥδιον δρακεῖν,
ἀπὸ cτρατείας ἄνδρα cώcαντος θεοῦ
πύλας ἀνοῖξαι; ταῦτ' ἀπάγγειλον πόcει,
ἥκειν ὅπως τάχιcτ' ἐράcμιον πόλει·   605
γυναῖκα πιcτὴν δ' ἐν δόμοις εὕροι μολὼν
οἵανπερ οὖν ἔλειπε, δωμάτων κύνα
ἐcθλὴν ἐκείνωι, πολεμίαν τοῖς δύcφροcιν,
καὶ τἄλλ' ὁμοίαν πάντα, cημαντήριον
οὐδὲν διαφθείραcαν ἐν μήκει χρόνου·   610
οὐδ' οἶδα τέρψιν οὐδ' ἐπίψογον φάτιν
ἄλλου πρὸς ἀνδρὸς μᾶλλον ἢ χαλκοῦ βαφάς.
τοιόcδ' ὁ κόμπος, τῆς ἀληθείας γέμων,
οὐκ αἰcχρὸς ὡς γυναικὶ γενναίαι λακεῖν.
Χο.   αὕτη μὲν οὕτως † εἶπε μανθάνοντί cοι,   615
τοροῖcιν ἑρμηνεῦcιν εὐπρεπῶς † λόγον.
cὺ δ' εἰπέ, κῆρυξ, Μενέλεων δὲ πεύθομαι,
εἰ νόcτιμός τε καὶ cεcωμένος πάλιν
ἥκει cὺν ὑμῖν, τῆcδε γῆς φίλον κράτος.
Κη.   οὐκ ἔcθ' ὅπως λέξαιμι τὰ ψευδῆ καλά,   620
ἐς τὸν πολὺν φίλοιcι καρποῦcθαι χρόνον.
Χο.   πῶς δῆτ' ἂν εἰπὼν κεδνὰ τἀληθῆ τύχοις;
cχιcθέντα δ' οὐκ εὔκρυπτα γίγνεται τάδε.
Κη.   ἀνὴρ ἄφαντος ἐξ Ἀχαιικοῦ cτρατοῦ,
αὐτός τε καὶ τὸ πλοῖον· οὐ ψευδῆ λέγω.   625
Χο.   πότερον ἀναχθεὶς †ἐμφανῶς† ἐξ Ἰλίου,

615–16 lectio dubia; fort. εἶπεν ἀνδάνοντά cοι (Bothe), τοροῖcι δ'
(Metzger) ἑρμηνεῦcι δυcτερπῆ (Dawe)   618 τε Hermann : γε codd.
619 ἥκει Karsten : ἥξει codd.   622, 626, 630, 634 Clyt. tribuunt codd.
622 τύχοις Porson : -χης codd.   626 ἐμφανοῦς ἐξ ἡλίου Dawe

ἢ χεῖμα, κοινὸν ἄχθος, ἥρπασε στρατοῦ;
Κη. ἔκυρςας ὥςτε τοξότης ἄκρος σκοποῦ,
μακρὸν δὲ πῆμα συντόμως ἐφημίςω.
Χο. πότερα γὰρ αὐτοῦ ζῶντος ἢ τεθνηκότος   630
φάτις πρὸς ἄλλων ναυτίλων ἐκλήιζετο;
Κη. οὐκ οἶδεν οὐδεὶς ὥςτ᾽ ἀπαγγεῖλαι τορῶς
πλὴν τοῦ τρέφοντος Ἡλίου χθονὸς φύσιν.
Χο. πῶς γὰρ λέγεις χειμῶνα ναυτικῶι στρατῶι
ἐλθεῖν τελευτῆσαί τε δαιμόνων κότωι;   635
Κη. εὔφημον ἦμαρ οὐ πρέπει κακαγγέλωι
γλώςσηι μιαίνειν· χωρὶς ἡ τιμὴ θεῶν.
ὅταν δ᾽ ἀπευκτὰ πήματ᾽ ἄγγελος πόλει
στυγνῶι προσώπωι πτωςίμου στρατοῦ φέρηι,
πόλει μὲν ἕλκος ἓν τὸ δήμιον τυχεῖν,   640
πολλοὺς δὲ πολλῶν ἐξαγιςθέντας δόμων
ἄνδρας διπλῆι μάςτιγι, τὴν Ἄρης φιλεῖ,
δίλογχον ἄτην, φοινίαν ξυνωρίδα·
τοιῶνδε μέντοι πημάτων σεσαγμένον
πρέπει λέγειν παιᾶνα τόνδ᾽ Ἐρινύων·   645
σωτηρίων δὲ πραγμάτων εὐάγγελον
ἥκοντα πρὸς χαίρουσαν εὐεστοῖ πόλιν,
πῶς κεδνὰ τοῖς κακοῖς συμμείξω, λέγων
χειμῶν᾽ †Ἀχαιῶν οὐκ ἀμήνιτον θεοῖς†;
ξυνώμοσαν γάρ, ὄντες ἔχθιστοι τὸ πρίν,   650
πῦρ καὶ θάλασσα, καὶ τὰ πίστ᾽ ἐδειξάτην
φθείροντε τὸν δύστηνον Ἀργείων στρατόν.
ἐν νυκτὶ δυσκύμαντα δ᾽ ὠρώρει κακά·
ναῦς γὰρ πρὸς ἀλλήλησι Θρήικιαι πνοαὶ
ἤρεικον, αἱ δὲ κεροτυπούμεναι βίαι   655
χειμῶνι τυφῶ σὺν ζάληι τ᾽ ὀμβροκτύπωι
ὤιχοντ᾽ ἄφαντοι ποιμένος κακοῦ στρόβωι.
ἐπεὶ δ᾽ ἀνῆλθε λαμπρὸν ἡλίου φάος,
ὁρῶμεν ἀνθοῦν πέλαγος Αἰγαῖον νεκροῖς

639 ςμοιῶι προςώπωι ex Hesych. s.v. M. Schmidt   644 ςε-
ςαγμένον Schütz: -νων codd.   649 Ἀχαιοῖς . . . θεῶν Blomfield
654 -λαιςι Tr   655 ἤρειπον Tr   κερωτ- codd.

ἀνδρῶν Ἀχαιῶν ναυτικοῖc τ' ἐρειπίοιc.   660
ἡμᾶc γε μὲν δὴ ναῦν τ' ἀκήρατον cκάφοc
ἤτοι τιc ἐξέκλεψεν ἢ 'ξηιτήcατο
θεόc τιc, οὐκ ἄνθρωποc, οἴακοc θιγών,
Τύχη δὲ cωτὴρ ναῦν θέλουc' ἐφέζετο
ὡc μήτ' ἐν ὅρμωι κύματοc ζάλην ἔχειν   665
μήτ' ἐξοκεῖλαι πρὸc κραταίλεων χθόνα.
ἔπειτα δ' Ἅιδην πόντιον πεφευγότεc
λευκὸν κατ' ἦμαρ, οὐ πεποιθότεc τύχηι,
ἐβουκολοῦμεν φροντίcιν νέον πάθοc
cτρατοῦ καμόντοc καὶ κακῶc cποδουμένου.   670
καὶ νῦν ἐκείνων εἴ τιc ἐcτὶν ἐμπνέων,
λέγουcιν ἡμᾶc ὡc ὀλωλόταc· τί μήν;
ἡμεῖc τ' ἐκείνουc ταῦτ' ἔχειν δοξάζομεν.
γένοιτο δ' ὡc ἄριcτα. Μενέλεων γὰρ οὖν
πρῶτόν τε καὶ μάλιcτα προcδόκα μολεῖν·   675
εἰ δ' οὖν τιc ἀκτὶc ἡλίου νιν ἱcτορεῖ
καὶ ζῶντα καὶ βλέποντα, μηχαναῖc Διὸc
οὔπω θέλοντοc ἐξαναλῶcαι γένοc,
ἐλπίc τιc αὐτὸν πρὸc δόμουc ἥξειν πάλιν.
τοcαῦτ' ἀκούcαc ἴcθι τἀληθῆ κλύων.   680

Χο.   τίc ποτ' ὠνόμαζεν ὧδ'   [cτρ. α
             ἐc τὸ πᾶν ἐτητύμωc,
        μή τιc ὅντιν' οὐχ ὁρῶμεν προνοί-
             αιcι τοῦ πεπρωμένου
        γλῶccαν ἐν τύχαι νέμων,   685
        τὰν δορίγαμβρον ἀμφινει-
             κῆ θ' Ἑλέναν; ἐπεὶ πρεπόντωc
        ἑλένac ἕλανδροc ἑλέ-
             πτολιc ἐκ τῶν ἀβροτίμων   690

660 ναυτικοῖc τ' ἐρειπίοιc Auratus: -κῶν τ' ἐριπίων codd.   672 τί
μήν Linwood: τί μή codd.   673 ταῦτ' Casaubon: ταῦτ' codd.
674 γὰρ ἂν Bothe   677 χλωρόν τε καὶ βλέποντα ex Hesych. s.v.
Toup   680 κλύων F: κλύειν F^{sscr}Tr   681 ὠνόμαξεν F
683 προνοίαιc codd.   688 ἑλέναυc Blomfield   690 ἀβροπήνων
Salmasius

προκαλυμμάτων ἔπλευcεν
Ζεφύρου γίγαντος αὖραι,
πολύανδροί τε φεράcπιδες κυναγοὶ
κατ' ἴχνος πλατᾶν ἄφαντον   695
κέλcαν τὰς Cιμόεντος ἀ-
κτὰς ἐπ' ἀεξιφύλλους
δι' Ἔριν αἱματόεccαν.

Ἰλίωι δὲ κῆδος ὀρ-   [ἀντ. α
θώνυμον τελεccίφρων   700
Μῆνις ἤλαcεν, τραπέζας ἀτίμωcιν ὑcτέρωι χρόνωι
καὶ ξυνεcτίου Διὸς
πραccομένα τὸ νυμφότι-   705
μον μέλος ἐκφάτωc τίοντας,
ὑμέναιον ὃc τότ' ἐπέρ-
ρεπε γαμβροῖcιν ἀείδειν.
μεταμανθάνουcα δ' ὕμνον
Πριάμου πόλις γεραιὰ   710
πολύθρηνον μέγα που cτένει, κικλήcκου-
cα Πάριν τὸν αἰνόλεκτρον
†παμπρόcθη πολύθρηνον
αἰῶν' ἀμφὶ πολιτᾶν†   715
μέλεον αἷμ' ἀνατλᾶcα.

ἔθρεψεν δὲ λέοντος ἷ-   [cτρ. β
νιν δόμοις ἀγάλακτον οὔ-
τωc ἀνὴρ φιλόμαcτον,
ἐν βιότου προτελείοις   720
ἄμερον, εὐφιλόπαιδα,

696 seq. κέλcαν τὰς Auratus (ἔκελcαν) : κελcάντων codd.   ἀκτᾶc F
ἐπ' F: εἰc Tr   ἀεξι- Tr: ἄξι- F   700 τελεcί- F   701 seq.
ἀτίμωcιν Canter: ἀτίμωc ἵν' F, ἀτίμωc Tr   707 seq. ἐπέπρεπεν Tr
710 γεραιοῦ Auratus   714 seq. fort. παμπορθῆ (Seidler) πολύθρηνον
αἰῶνα διαὶ (Emperius)   πολίταν codd.   717–18 λέοντος ἶνιν
Conington : λέοντα cίνιν codd.   718–19 οὔτωc Fsscr Tr : οὗτος F

καὶ γεραροῖς ἐπίχαρτον·
πολέα δ᾽ ἔσχ᾽ ἐν ἀγκάλαις
νεοτρόφου τέκνου δίκαν,
φαιδρωπὸς ποτὶ χεῖρα σαί-   725
νων τε γαστρὸς ἀνάγκαις.

χρονισθεὶς δ᾽ ἀπέδειξεν ἦ-   [ἀντ. β
θος τὸ πρὸς τοκέων· χάριν
γὰρ τροφεῦσιν ἀμείβων
μηλοφόνοισι σὺν ἄταις   730
δαῖτ᾽ ἀκέλευστος ἔτευξεν·
αἵματι δ᾽ οἶκος ἐφύρθη,
ἄμαχον ἄλγος οἰκέταις,
μέγα σίνος πολυκτόνον·
ἐκ θεοῦ δ᾽ ἱερεύς τις Ἄ-   735
τας δόμοις προσεθρέφθη.

πάραυτα δ᾽ ἐλθεῖν ἐς Ἰλίου πόλιν   [στρ. γ
λέγοιμ᾽ ἂν φρόνημα μὲν
νηνέμου γαλάνας,
ἀκασκαῖον ⟨δ᾽⟩ ἄγαλμα πλούτου,   740
μαλθακὸν ὀμμάτων βέλος,
δηξίθυμον ἔρωτος ἄνθος.
παρακλίνασ᾽ ἐπέκρανεν
δὲ γάμου πικρὰς τελευτάς,   745
δύσεδρος καὶ δυσόμιλος
συμένα Πριαμίδαισιν,
πομπᾷ Διὸς ξενίου
νυμφόκλαυτος Ἐρινύς.

παλαίφατος δ᾽ ἐν βροτοῖς γέρων λόγος [ἀντ. γ

723 ἔσκ᾽ Casaubon   727–8 ἦθος Conington : ἔθος codd.
728 τοκήων F   729 τροφεῦσιν Tr : τροφᾶς F   730 -φόνοισι σὺν
Fix : -φόνοισιν codd. ; -φόνοισιν ἐν Bothe   ἄταισιν Tr   733 δ᾽ ἄλγος
F   736 προσεθρέφθη Heath : προσετράφη codd.   738 πάραυτα
δ᾽ F : πάραυτα δ᾽ οὖν Tr   741 δ᾽ suppl. Porson ; τ᾽ ἄγαλμα Hermann   744 -κλίνουσ᾽ Tr   745 πικρὰς F^sscrTr : -ροῦ F
750 ἐν τοῖς βροτοῖς Tr

τέτυκται, μέγαν τελε-
cθέντα φωτὸς ὄλβον· 751
τεκνοῦcθαι μηδ᾽ ἄπαιδα θνῄcκειν,
ἐκ δ᾽ ἀγαθᾶς τύχας γένει 755
βλαστάνειν ἀκόρεcτον οἰζύν.
δίχα δ᾽ ἄλλων μονόφρων εἰ-
μί· τὸ δυccεβὲc γὰρ ἔργον
μετὰ μὲν πλείονα τίκτει,
cφετέραι δ᾽ εἰκότα γένναι· 760
οἴκων γὰρ εὐθυδίκων
καλλίπαιc πότμοc αἰεί.

φιλεῖ δὲ τίκτειν ὕβριc [cτρ. δ
μὲν παλαιὰ νεά-
ζουcαν ἐν κακοῖc βροτῶν 765
ὕβριν τότ᾽ ἢ τόθ᾽, ὅτε τὸ κύριον μόληι φάοc τόκου,
δαίμονά τε τὰν ἄμαχον ἀπόλεμον, ἀνίερον θράcοc μελαί-
νας μελάθροιcιν ἄταc, 770
εἰδομέναc τοκεῦcιν.

Δίκα δὲ λάμπει μὲν ἐν [ἀντ. δ
δυcκάπνοιc δώμαcιν,
τὸν δ᾽ ἐναίcιμον τίει· 775
τὰ χρυcόπαcτα δ᾽ ἔδεθλα cὺν
πίνωι χερῶν παλιντρόποιc
ὄμμαcι λιποῦc᾽ ὅcια †προcέβα
τοῦ†, δύναμιν οὐ cέβουcα πλούτου παράcημον αἴνωι· 780

758 δυccεβὲc γὰρ Pauw: γὰρ δυccεβὲc codd.   766 ὅτε Klausen:
ὅταν codd.   767 μόληι φάοc τόκου H. L. Ahrens: μόληι νεαϝὰ
φάουc κότον codd.   768 τε τὰν Hermann: τε τὸν codd.; τίταν
Heimsoeth   ἄμαχον om. Tr   770 μελάθροιc F   771 εἰδομέναc Casaubon: -ναν codd.   775 τίει H. L. Ahrens: τίει βίον
codd.   776 -παcτα δ᾽ ἔδεθλα Auratus: -παcτα δ᾽ ἐcθλὰ F, -παcτ᾽ ἐcθλὰ Tr
777 παλίντροπ᾽ Tr   778-9 προcέβα τοῦ codd.: προcέμολε Hermann, προcέβατο Verrall

πᾶν δ' ἐπὶ τέρμα νωμᾷ.

ἄγε δὴ βασιλεῦ, Τροίας πτολίπορθ',
Ἀτρέως γένεθλον,
πῶς σε προσείπω; πῶς σε σεβίξω   785
μήθ' ὑπεράρας μήθ' ὑποκάμψας
καιρὸν χάριτος;
πολλοὶ δὲ βροτῶν τὸ δοκεῖν εἶναι
προτίουσι δίκην παραβάντες·
τῶι δυσπραγοῦντι δ' ἐπιστενάχειν   790
πᾶς τις ἕτοιμος, δῆγμα δὲ λύπης
οὐδὲν ἐφ' ἧπαρ προσικνεῖται.
καὶ ξυγχαίρουσιν ὁμοιοπρεπεῖς
ἀγέλαστα πρόσωπα βιαζόμενοι
⟨   ⟩
ὅστις δ' ἀγαθὸς προβατογνώμων,   795
οὐκ ἔστι λαθεῖν ὄμματα φωτὸς
τὰ δοκοῦντ' εὔφρονος ἐκ διανοίας
ὑδαρεῖ σαίνειν φιλότητι.
σὺ δέ μοι τότε μὲν στέλλων στρατιὰν
Ἑλένης ἕνεκ', οὐκ ἐπικεύσω,   800
κάρτ' ἀπομούσως ἦσθα γεγραμμένος
οὐδ' εὖ πραπίδων οἴακα νέμων,
θράσος ἐκ θυσιῶν
ἀνδράσι θνήισκουσι κομίζων·
νῦν δ' οὐκ ἀπ' ἄκρας φρενὸς οὐδ' ἀφίλως   805
εὔφρων πόνον εὖ τελέσασιν ⟨ἐγώ·⟩
γνώσηι δὲ χρόνωι διαπευθόμενος
τόν τε δικαίως καὶ τὸν ἀκαίρως
πόλιν οἰκουροῦντα πολιτῶν.

---

783 πτολί- Blomfield: πολί- codd.   785 σεβίξω Γᵖᶜ: -ίζω FᵃᶜTr
789 -βαίνοντες Tr   791 δῆγμα Tr et Stob. ecl. 4. 48. 12: δεῖγμα F
792 προσεφικν- Tr   793 καὶ νυκτὶ δὲ χαίρουσιν Stob.   794 post
h.v. lacunam indicavit Hermann   800 οὐκ codd.: οὐ γὰρ
codd.   803 θάρσος Tr   ἐκ θυσιῶν H. L. Ahrens: ἑκούσιον codd.
804 ἀνδράσιν εὖ θν. Tr   806 εὔφρων τις Tr   πόνον Auratus: πόνος
codd.   ἐγώ suppl. Wilamowitz

ΑΓΑΜΕΜΝΩΝ

πρῶτον μὲν Ἄργος καὶ θεοὺς ἐγχωρίους   810
δίκη προσειπεῖν, τοὺς ἐμοὶ μεταιτίους
νόστου δικαίων θ' ὧν ἐπραξάμην πόλιν
Πριάμου· δίκας γὰρ οὐκ ἀπὸ γλώccης θεοὶ
κλύοντες ἀνδροθνῆτας Ἰλιοφθόρους
ἐc αἱματηρὸν τεῦχος οὐ διχορρόπως   815
ψήφους ἔθεντο, τῶι δ' ἐναντίωι κύτει
ἐλπὶc προcήιει χειρὸς οὐ πληρουμένωι.
καπνῶι δ' ἁλοῦcα νῦν ἔτ' εὔcημος πόλις·
ἄτης θύελλαι ζῶcι, δυcθνήιcκουcα δὲ
cποδὸc προπέμπει πίονας πλούτου πνοάς.   820
τούτων θεοῖcι χρὴ πολύμνηcτον χάριν
τίνειν, ἐπείπερ χάρπαγὰc ὑπερκόπους
ἐπραξάμεcθα, καὶ γυναικὸς οὕνεκα
πόλιν διημάθυνεν Ἀργεῖον δάκος,
ἵππου νεοccός, ἀcπιδηφόρος λεώς,   825
πήδημ' ὀρούcας ἀμφὶ Πλειάδων δύcιν·
ὑπερθορὼν δὲ πύργον ὠμηcτὴς λέων
ἅδην ἔλειξεν αἵματος τυραννικοῦ.
θεοῖc μὲν ἐξέτεινα φροίμιον τόδε·
τὰ δ' ἐc τὸ cὸν φρόνημα, μέμνημαι κλύων   830
καὶ φημὶ ταὐτὰ καὶ cυνήγορόν μ' ἔχεις·
παύροιc γὰρ ἀνδρῶν ἐcτι cυγγενὲς τόδε,
φίλον τὸν εὐτυχοῦντ' ἄνευ φθόνων cέβειν·
δύcφρων γὰρ ἰὸς καρδίαν προcήμενος
ἄχθος διπλοίζει τῶι πεπαμένωι νόcον·   835
τοῖc τ' αὐτὸς αὐτοῦ πήμαcιν βαρύνεται
καὶ τὸν θυραῖον ὄλβον εἰcορῶν cτένει.
εἰδὼς λέγοιμ' ἄν, εὖ γὰρ ἐξεπίcταμαι

814 Ἰλιοφθόρους Karsten : Ἰλίου φθορὰς codd.   819 δυcθνήιcκουcα
Enger : cυνθν- codd.   822 χάρπαγὰc Tyrwhitt : καὶ παγὰς codd.
-κόπους Heath : -κότους codd.   823 (πάγας ...) ἐφραξάμεcθα Francken
825 -ηφόρος Blomfield : -ηcτρόφος F, -οcτρόφος Tr   828 ἅδδην Tr
831 ταὐτὰ Auratus : ταῦτα codd.   833 φθόνων F : φθόνου Tr, ψόγου
Stob. ecl. 3. 38. 28   834 καρδίαι Casaubon   835 πεπαμμένωι
codd.

ὁμιλίας κάτοπτρον, εἴδωλον σκιᾶς,
δοκοῦντας εἶναι κάρτα πρευμενεῖς ἐμοί· 840
μόνος δ' Ὀδυσσεύς, ὅσπερ οὐχ ἑκὼν ἔπλει,
ζευχθεὶς ἑτοῖμος ἦν ἐμοὶ σειραφόρος·
εἴτ' οὖν θανόντος εἴτε καὶ ζῶντος πέρι
λέγω. τὰ δ' ἄλλα πρὸς πόλιν τε καὶ θεοὺς
κοινοὺς ἀγῶνας θέντες ἐν πανηγύρει 845
βουλευσόμεσθα· καὶ τὸ μὲν καλῶς ἔχον
ὅπως χρονίζον εὖ μενεῖ βουλευτέον,
ὅτωι δὲ καὶ δεῖ φαρμάκων παιωνίων,
ἤτοι κέαντες ἢ τεμόντες εὐφρόνως
πειρασόμεσθα πῆμ' ἀποστρέψαι νόσου. 850
νῦν δ' ἐς μέλαθρα καὶ δόμους ἐφέστιος
ἐλθὼν θεοῖσι πρῶτα δεξιώσομαι,
οἵπερ πρόσω πέμψαντες ἤγαγον πάλιν.
νίκη δ', ἐπείπερ ἕσπετ', ἐμπέδως μένοι.
Κλ. ἄνδρες πολῖται, πρέσβος Ἀργείων τόδε, 855
οὐκ αἰσχυνοῦμαι τοὺς φιλάνορας τρόπους
λέξαι πρὸς ὑμᾶς. ἐν χρόνωι δ' ἀποφθίνει
τὸ τάρβος ἀνθρώποισιν. οὐκ ἄλλων πάρα
μαθοῦσ' ἐμαυτῆς δύσφορον λέξω βίον
τοσόνδ' ὅσονπερ οὗτος ἦν ὑπ' Ἰλίωι. 860
τὸ μὲν γυναῖκα πρῶτον ἄρσενος δίχα
ἧσθαι δόμοις ἔρημον ἔκπαγλον κακόν,
πολλὰς κλύουσαν κληδόνας παλιγκότους,
καὶ τὸν μὲν ἥκειν, τὸν δ' ἐπεισφέρειν κακοῦ
κάκιον ἄλλο πῆμα, λάσκοντας δόμοις· 865
καὶ τραυμάτων μὲν εἰ τόσων ἐτύγχανεν
ἀνὴρ ὅδ' ὡς πρὸς οἶκον ὠχετεύετο
φάτις, τέτρηται δικτύου πλέω λέγειν.
εἰ δ' ἦν τεθνηκὼς ὡς ἐπλήθυον λόγοι,

---

839 post h.v. lacunam statuit Dawe   850 πῆμ' ἀποστρέψαι νόσου
Porson: πήματος τρέψαι νόσον codd.   851 ἐφέστιος Karsten: -ιους
codd.   860 ἐπ' Ἰλίωι Tr   863 κληδόνας Auratus: ἡδονὰς codd.
868 τέτρηται H. L. Ahrens: τέτρωται codd.   869 ἐπλήθυον Porson: -θυνον codd.

τρισώματός ταν Γηρυων ὁ δεύτερος 870
[πολλὴν ἄνωθεν, τὴν κάτω γὰρ οὐ λέγω,]
χθονὸς τρίμοιρον χλαῖναν ἐξηύχει λαβών,
ἅπαξ ἑκάστωι κατθανὼν μορφώματι.
τοιῶνδ' ἕκατι κληδόνων παλιγκότων
πολλὰς ἄνωθεν ἀρτάνας ἐμῆς δέρης 875
ἔλυσαν ἄλλοι πρὸς βίαν λελημμένης.
ἐκ τῶνδέ τοι παῖς ἐνθάδ' οὐ παραστατεῖ,
ἐμῶν τε καὶ σῶν κύριος πιστωμάτων,
ὡς χρῆν, Ὀρέστης· μηδὲ θαυμάσηις τόδε·
τρέφει γὰρ αὐτὸν εὐμενὴς δορύξενος 880
Στροφίος ὁ Φωκεύς, ἀμφίλεκτα πήματα
ἐμοὶ προφωνῶν, τόν θ' ὑπ' Ἰλίωι σέθεν
κίνδυνον, εἴ τε δημόθρους ἀναρχία
βουλὴν καταρρίψειεν, ὥς τι σύγγονον
βροτοῖσι τὸν πεσόντα λακτίσαι πλέον. 885
τοιάδε μέντοι σκῆψις οὐ δόλον φέρει.
ἔμοιγε μὲν δὴ κλαυμάτων ἐπίσσυτοι
πηγαὶ κατεσβήκασιν, οὐδ' ἔνι σταγών·
ἐν ὀψικοίτοις δ' ὄμμασιν βλάβας ἔχω
τὰς ἀμφί σοι κλαίουσα λαμπτηρουχίας 890
ἀτημελήτους αἰέν· ἐν δ' ὀνείρασιν
λεπταῖς ὑπαὶ κώνωπος ἐξηγειρόμην
ῥιπαῖσι θωύσσοντος, ἀμφί σοι πάθη
ὁρῶσα πλείω τοῦ ξυνεύδοντος χρόνου.
νῦν, ταῦτα πάντα τλᾶσ', ἀπενθήτωι φρενὶ 895
λέγοιμ' ἂν ἄνδρα τόνδε τῶν σταθμῶν κύνα,
σωτῆρα ναὸς πρότονον, ὑψηλῆς στέγης
στῦλον ποδήρη, μονογενὲς τέκνον πατρί,
ὁδοιπόρωι διψῶντι πηγαῖον ῥέος, [901]
καὶ γῆν φανεῖσαν ναυτίλοις παρ' ἐλπίδα, 900
κάλλιστον ἦμαρ εἰσιδεῖν ἐκ χείματος.

---

871 versum miserrimum eiecit Schütz   878 πιστωμάτων Spanheim: πιστευμ- codd.   882 θ' F: τ' Tr   884 τι Hartung: τε codd.
888 καθεστήκασιν Fsscr   898 στόλον F   899 huc traiecit Bothe;
post 901 codd.   900 καὶ γῆν: γαῖαν Blomfield

[τερπνὸν δὲ τἀναγκαῖον ἐκφυγεῖν ἅπαν].
τοιοῖςδέ τοί νιν ἀξιῶ προσφθέγμασιν,
φθόνος δ᾽ ἀπέστω· πολλὰ γὰρ τὰ πρὶν κακὰ
ἠνειχόμεςθα. νῦν δέ μοι, φίλον κάρα,　　　　　905
ἔκβαιν᾽ ἀπήνης τῆςδε, μὴ χαμαὶ τιθεὶς
τὸν ςὸν πόδ᾽, ὦναξ, Ἰλίου πορθήτορα.
δμωιαί, τί μέλλεθ᾽, αἷς ἐπέςταλται τέλος
πέδον κελεύθου ςτορνύναι πετάςμαςιν;
εὐθὺς γενέςθω πορφυρόςτρωτος πόρος,　　　910
ἐς δῶμ᾽ ἄελπτον ὡς ἂν ἡγῆται Δίκη·
τὰ δ᾽ ἄλλα φροντὶς οὐχ ὕπνωι νικωμένη
θήςει δικαίως ςὺν θεοῖς εἱμαρμένα.
Αγ.　Λήδας γένεθλον, δωμάτων ἐμῶν φύλαξ,
ἀπουςίαι μὲν εἶπας εἰκότως ἐμῆι·　　　　915
μακρὰν γὰρ ἐξέτεινας. ἀλλ᾽ ἐναιςίμως
αἰνεῖν, παρ᾽ ἄλλων χρὴ τόδ᾽ ἔρχεςθαι γέρας.
καὶ τἄλλα μὴ γυναικὸς ἐν τρόποις ἐμὲ
ἅβρυνε, μηδὲ βαρβάρου φωτὸς δίκην
χαμαιπετὲς βόαμα προςχάνηις ἐμοί,　　　920
μηδ᾽ εἵμαςι ςτρώςας᾽ ἐπίφθονον πόρον
τίθει· θεούς τοι τοῖςδε τιμαλφεῖν χρεών,
ἐν ποικίλοις δὲ θνητὸν ὄντα κάλλεςιν
βαίνειν ἐμοὶ μὲν οὐδαμῶς ἄνευ φόβου.
λέγω κατ᾽ ἄνδρα, μὴ θεόν, ςέβειν ἐμέ.　　　925
χωρὶς ποδοψήςτρων τε καὶ τῶν ποικίλων
κληδὼν ἀυτεῖ· καὶ τὸ μὴ κακῶς φρονεῖν
θεοῦ μέγιςτον δῶρον. ὀλβίςαι δὲ χρὴ
βίον τελευτήςαντ᾽ ἐν εὐεςτοῖ φίληι.
εἰ πάντα δ᾽ ὡς πράςςοιμ᾽ ἄν, εὐθαρςὴς ἐγώ.　930
Κλ.　καὶ μὴν τόδ᾽ εἰπὲ μὴ παρὰ γνώμην ἐμοί.
Αγ.　γνώμην μὲν ἴςθι μὴ διαφθεροῦντ᾽ ἐμέ.
Κλ.　ηὔξω θεοῖς δείςας ἂν ὧδ᾽ ἔρδειν τάδε;

---

902 del. Blomfield　　903 τοί νιν Schütz: τοίνυν codd.　　905 δ᾽
ἐμοὶ codd.　　907 ἄναξ F　　908 τέλος F: τάδε Tr　　909 ςτορνύναι Elmsley: ςτρωννύναι codd.　　920 βόημα F^sscr^Tr　　930 πράς-
ςοιμεν Dindorf　　933 interpretatio dubia; ἔρξειν Headlam

Αγ. εἴπερ τις εἰδώς γ' εὖ τόδ' ἐξεῖπεν τέλος.

Κλ. τί δ' ἂν δοκεῖ σοι Πρίαμος, εἰ τάδ' ἤνυσεν; 935

Αγ. ἐν ποικίλοις ἂν κάρτα μοι βῆναι δοκεῖ.

Κλ. μή νυν τὸν ἀνθρώπειον αἰδεσθῆις ψόγον.

Αγ. φήμη γε μέντοι δημόθρους μέγα σθένει.

Κλ. ὁ δ' ἀφθόνητός γ' οὐκ ἐπίζηλος πέλει.

Αγ. οὔτοι γυναικός ἐστιν ἱμείρειν μάχης. 940

Κλ. τοῖς δ' ὀλβίοις γε καὶ τὸ νικᾶσθαι πρέπει.

Αγ. ἦ καὶ σὺ νίκην τῆσδε δήριος τίεις;

Κλ. πιθοῦ, †κράτος μέντοι πάρες γ'† ἑκὼν ἐμοί.

Αγ. ἀλλ' εἰ δοκεῖ σοι ταῦθ', ὑπαί τις ἀρβύλας
λύοι τάχος, πρόδουλον ἔμβασιν ποδός, 945
καὶ τοῖσδέ μ' ἐμβαίνονθ' ἁλουργέσιν θεῶν
μή τις πρόσωθεν ὄμματος βάλοι φθόνος.
πολλὴ γὰρ αἰδὼς δωματοφθορεῖν ποσὶν
φθείροντα πλοῦτον ἀργυρωνήτους θ' ὑφάς.
τούτων μὲν οὕτω, τὴν ξένην δὲ πρευμενῶς 950
τήνδ' ἐσκόμιζε· τὸν κρατοῦντα μαλθακῶς
θεὸς πρόσωθεν εὐμενῶς προσδέρκεται.
ἑκὼν γὰρ οὐδεὶς δουλίωι χρῆται ζυγῶι·
αὕτη δὲ πολλῶν χρημάτων ἐξαίρετον
ἄνθος, στρατοῦ δώρημ', ἐμοὶ ξυνέσπετο. 955
ἐπεὶ δ' ἀκούειν σοῦ κατέστραμμαι τάδε,
εἶμ' ἐς δόμων μέλαθρα πορφύρας πατῶν.

Κλ. ἔστιν θάλασσα, τίς δέ νιν κατασβέσει;
τρέφουσα πολλῆς πορφύρας ἰσάργυρον
κηκῖδα παγκαίνιστον, εἱμάτων βαφάς· 960
οἶκος δ' ὑπάρχει τῶνδε σὺν θεοῖς, ἄναξ,
ἔχειν, πένεσθαι δ' οὐκ ἐπίσταται δόμος.

934 lectio et interpretatio dubia   ἐξεῖπεν Auratus: -πον codd.
935 δοκεῖ Stanley: -κῆ codd.   936 δοκῆ F^{pc}Tr^{sscr}   937 αἰδεσθεὶς
F   942 τῆσδε Auratus: τήνδε codd.   943 fort. κρατεῖς (Weil)
μέντοι παρεὶς (Bothe; γ' del. Wecklein) ἑκὼν ἐμοί   946 καὶ F: σὺν Tr
948 δωματο- Schütz: σωματο- codd.   954 αὐτὴ codd.   956 κατ-
έσταμαι Tr (schol. εὕρηται καὶ κατέστραμμαι)   959 ἰσάργ- Salmasius: εἰς ἀργ- codd.   961 οἴκοις Porson

πολλῶν πατησμὸν δ' εἱμάτων ἂν ηὐξάμην,
δόμοισι προυνεχθέντος ἐν χρηστηρίοις
ψυχῆς κόμιστρα τῆςδε μηχανωμένηι·   965
ῥίζης γὰρ οὔςης φυλλὰς ἵκετ' ἐς δόμους
ςκιὰν ὑπερτείναςα ςειρίου κυνός·
καὶ ςοῦ μολόντος δωματῖτιν ἑςτίαν,
θάλπος μὲν ἐν χειμῶνι ςημαίνει μολόν·
ὅταν δὲ τεύχηι Ζεὺς ἀπ' ὄμφακος πικρᾶς   970
οἶνον, τότ' ἤδη ψῦχος ἐν δόμοις πέλει,
ἀνδρὸς τελείου δῶμ' ἐπιστρωφωμένου.
Ζεῦ Ζεῦ τέλειε, τὰς ἐμὰς εὐχὰς τέλει·
μέλοι δέ τοί ςοι τῶνπερ ἂν μέλληις τελεῖν.

Χο.   τίπτε μοι τόδ' ἐμπέδως   [ςτρ. α
          δεῖμα προστατήριον   976
          καρδίας τεραςκόπου ποτᾶται;
          μαντιπολεῖ δ' ἀκέλευςτος ἄμιςθος ἀοιδά,
          οὐδ' ἀποπτύςαι δίκαν   980
          δυςκρίτων ὀνειράτων
          θάρςος εὐπειθὲς ἵ-
          ζει φρενὸς φίλον θρόνον.
          †χρόνος δ' ἐπεὶ πρυμνηςίων ξυνεμβόλοις
          ψαμμίας ἀκάτα† παρή-   985
          βηςεν εὖθ' ὑπ' Ἴλιον
          ὦρτο ναυβάτας ςτρατός.

          πεύθομαι δ' ἀπ' ὀμμάτων   [ἀντ. α
          νόςτον αὐτόμαρτυς ὤν·

---

963 πατηςμὸν δειμάτων codd.   εὐξ- codd.   965 μηχανωμένηι
Abresch: -νης codd.   969 ςημαίνει Karsten: -εις codd.   μολόν
H. Voss: -ὼν codd.   970 ἀπ' Auratus: τ' ἀπ' codd.   972 -ςτρω-
φωμένου Victorius: -ςτρεφωμένου F, -ςτροφωμένου Tr   974 μέλοι
F^{sscr}Tr: -ληι F   τοί ςοι Tr: ςοι F   976 δεῖγμα F   978 ποτᾶτ'
Tr, idem 979 ἄμιςθος ἀοιδά. μαντιπολεῖ δ' ἀκέλ.   980 -πτύςας F
982-3 εὐπιθὲς codd.   ἵζει Scaliger: ἵξει F, ἵξει Tr   984-5 δ' ἐπὶ
Tr   ἀκάτας Tr; si χρόνος = χρόνος πολύς (quod valde dubium est),
fort. δ' ἐπεὶ πρυμνηςίων ξὺν ἐμβολαῖς (Casaubon) ψαμμίαις (Bothe) ἄτα
(Page) παρήβ.   παρήβης' Tr

τὸν δ' ἄνευ λύρας ὅμως ὑμνῳδεῖ   990
θρῆνον Ἐρινύος αὐτοδίδακτος ἔσωθεν
θυμός, οὐ τὸ πᾶν ἔχων
ἐλπίδος φίλον θράσος.
σπλάγχνα δ' οὔτοι ματάι-   995
ζει πρὸς ἐνδίκοις φρεσίν,
τελεσφόροις δίναις κυκλούμενον κέαρ·
εὔχομαι δ' ἐξ ἐμᾶς
ἐλπίδος ψύθη πεσεῖν
ἐς τὸ μὴ τελεσφόρον.   1000

μάλα †γάρ τοι τᾶς πολλᾶς ὑγιείας†   [στρ. β
ἀκόρεστον τέρμα· νόσος γὰρ
γείτων ὁμότοιχος ἐρείδει.
καὶ πότμος εὐθυπορῶν   1005
⟨   ⟩
ἀνδρὸς ἔπαισεν ἄφαντον ἕρμα.
καὶ τὸ μὲν πρὸ χρημάτων
κτησίων ὄκνος βαλὼν
σφενδόνας ἀπ' εὐμέτρου,   1010
οὐκ ἔδυ πρόπας δόμος
πλησμονᾶς γέμων ἄγαν,
οὐδ' ἐπόντισε σκάφος.
πολλά τοι δόσις ἐκ Διὸς ἀμφιλα-   1015
φής τε καὶ ἐξ ἀλόκων ἐπετειᾶν
νῆστιν ὤλεσεν νόσον.

τὸ δ' ἐπὶ γᾶν πεσὸν ἅπαξ θανάσιμον   [ἀντ. β
πρόπαρ ἀνδρὸς μέλαν αἷμα τίς ἂν   1020

---

990 ὅμως Auratus: ὅπως codd.   991 Ἐρινύος Porson: Ἐρινὺς
codd.   998 ἐξ ἐμᾶς F: ἀπ' ἐμᾶς τοι Tr   999 ψύθη H. Stephanus:
ψύδη codd.   1001 γάρ τοι FTrˢˢᶜʳ: γέ τοι Tr; μάλα γέ τοι τὸ
μεγάλας ὑγ. Paley   1005 post h.v. lacunam statuit Heath, post
1004 Klausen   1012 πλησμονᾶς Schütz: πημονᾶς codd.; παμονᾶς
Housman   1015 ἐκ om. Tr   1016 τε κἀξ F   1019 πεσὸν
Auratus: πεσόνθ' codd.   1020 προπάροιθ' ἀνδρὸς Tr   1020 seq.
τίς τ' ἀγκαλ- Tr

πάλιν ἀγκαλέςαιτ' ἐπαείδων;
οὐδὲ τὸν ὀρθοδαῆ
τῶν φθιμένων ἀνάγειν
Ζεὺς ἀπέπαυςεν ἐπ' ἀβλαβείαι.
εἰ δὲ μὴ τεταγμένα   1025
μοῖρα μοῖραν ἐκ θεῶν
εἶργε μὴ πλέον φέρειν,
προφθάσαςα καρδία
γλῶςςαν ἂν τάδ' ἐξέχει·
νῦν δ' ὑπὸ ςκότωι βρέμει   1030
θυμαλγής τε καὶ οὐδὲν ἐπελπομέ-
να ποτὲ καίριον ἐκτολυπεύςειν
ζωπυρουμένας φρενός.

Κλ.   εἴςω κομίζου καὶ ςύ, Καςςάνδραν λέγω·   1035
ἐπεί ς' ἔθηκε Ζεὺς ἀμηνίτως δόμοις
κοινωνὸν εἶναι χερνίβων, πολλῶν μετὰ
δούλων ςταθεῖςαν κτηςίου βωμοῦ πέλας,
ἔκβαιν' ἀπήνης τῆςδε, μηδ' ὑπερφρόνει·
καὶ παῖδα γάρ τοί φαςιν Ἀλκμήνης ποτὲ   1040
πραθέντα τλῆναι †δουλίας μάζης βία†.
εἰ δ' οὖν ἀνάγκη τῆςδ' ἐπιρρέποι τύχης,
ἀρχαιοπλούτων δεςποτῶν πολλὴ χάρις.
οἳ δ' οὔποτ' ἐλπίςαντες ἤμηςαν καλῶς,
ὠμοί τε δούλοις πάντα καὶ παρὰ ςτάθμην   1045
⟨   ⟩
ἔχεις παρ' ἡμῶν οἷάπερ νομίζεται.
Χο.   ςοί τοι λέγουςα παύεται ςαφῆ λόγον·
ἐντὸς δ' ἁλοῦςα μορςίμων ἀγρευμάτων
πείθοι' ἄν, εἰ πείθοι'· ἀπειθοίης δ' ἴςως.

1024 ἀπέπαυςεν Hartung: αὖτ' ἔπαυς' codd.   αὐλαβεία F, ἀβλαβείαι
γε Tr   1030 βλέπει Fᵃᶜ   1031 θυμαλγής τε καὶ οὐδὲν ἐπ om. Tr
1035 Καςάν- codd.   1041 δουλείας μάζης βία F, καὶ ζυγῶν θίγειν
(sic) βίαι Tr; δουλίας μάζης βίον Blomfield   1042 ἐπιρρέπει Tr
1045 παραςτάθμων F   post h.v. lacunam statuit Hartung   1046 ἔξεις
Auratus   1048 ἁλοῦςα C. G. Haupt: ἂν οὖςα codd.

Κλ.　ἀλλ' εἴπερ ἐςτὶ μὴ χελιδόνος δίκην　　　　1050
　　　ἀγνῶτα φωνὴν βάρβαρον κεκτημένη,
　　　ἔςω φρενῶν λέγουςα πείθω νιν λόγωι.
Χο.　ἕπου. τὰ λῶιςτα τῶν παρεςτώτων λέγει.
　　　πείθου λιποῦςα τόνδ' ἀμαξήρη θρόνον.
Κλ.　οὔτοι θυραίαι τῆιδ' ἐμοὶ ϲχολὴ πάρα　　　1055
　　　τρίβειν. τὰ μὲν γὰρ ἑςτίας μεςομφάλου
　　　ἕςτηκεν ἤδη μῆλα †πρὸς ϲφαγὰς† πυρός,
　　　ὡς οὔποτ' ἐλπίςαςι τήνδ' ἕξειν χάριν.
　　　ϲὺ δ' εἴ τι δράςεις τῶνδε, μὴ ϲχολὴν τίθει,
　　　εἰ δ' ἀξυνήμων οὖςα μὴ δέχηι λόγον,　　　1060
　　　ϲὺ δ' ἀντὶ φωνῆς φράζε καρβάνωι χερί.
Χο.　ἑρμηνέως ἔοικεν ἡ ξένη τοροῦ
　　　δεῖςθαι· τρόπος δὲ θηρὸς ὡς νεαιρέτου.
Κλ.　ἦ μαίνεταί γε καὶ κακῶν κλύει φρενῶν,
　　　ἥτις λιποῦςα μὲν πόλιν νεαίρετον　　　　1065
　　　ἥκει, χαλινὸν δ' οὐκ ἐπίςταται φέρειν
　　　πρὶν αἱματηρὸν ἐξαφρίζεςθαι μένος.
　　　οὐ μὴν πλέω ῥίψας' ἀτιμαςθήςομαι.
Χο.　ἐγὼ δ', ἐποικτίρω γάρ, οὐ θυμώςομαι·
　　　ἴθ', ὦ τάλαινα, τόνδ' ἐρημώςας' ὄχον·　　　1070
　　　εἴκους' ἀνάγκηι τῆιδε καίνιςον ζυγόν.

ΚΑΣΣΑΝΔΡΑ

　　　ὀτοτοτοτοῖ πόποι δᾶ·　　　　　　　　　[ϲτρ. α
　　　ὤπολλον ὤπολλον.
Χο.　τί ταῦτ' ἀνωτότυξας ἀμφὶ Λοξίου;
　　　οὐ γὰρ τοιοῦτος ὥςτε θρηνητοῦ τυχεῖν.　　1075

1052 λέγουϲα suspectum　　1054 πιθοῦ Blomfield　　1055 θυραίαι
Casaubon: -αίαν codd.　　τῆιδ' Musgrave: τήνδ' codd.　　1056 seq.
fort. πρὸ μὲν γὰρ ἑϲτίας (Bamberger) ... μῆλα, προϲφαγαὶ πυρός; ἑϲτίαι
μεϲομφάλωι C. G. Haupt　　1058 ante h.v. lacunam statuit Maas
1064 φρενῶν κλύει F, ordinem corr. ipse　　1067 denuo incipit M
1068 μὴ M (corr. Mˢ)　　1071 εἴκουϲ' Robortello: ἐκοῦϲ' codd.;
ἐκοῦϲ' ἀνάγκηϲ τῆϲδε Casaubon　　1072 et 1076 ὀτοτοτοὶ πομποῖ δᾶ
FTr　　1073 et 1077 ἄπολλον ἄπολλον FTr　　1074 ἀνωλόλυξας
schol. E. *Phoen.* 1028

Κα. ὀτοτοτοτοῖ πόποι δᾶ·   [ἀντ. α
    ὤπολλον ὤπολλον.
Χο. ἥδ' αὖτε δυcφημοῦcα τὸν θεὸν καλεῖ
    οὐδὲν προcήκοντ' ἐν γόοιc παραcτατεῖν.

Κα. ὤπολλον ὤπολλον,   [cτρ. β
    ἀγυιᾶτ', ἀπόλλων ἐμόc·   1081
    ἀπώλεcαc γὰρ οὐ μόλιc τὸ δεύτερον.
Χο. χρήcειν ἔοικεν ἀμφὶ τῶν αὑτῆc κακῶν·
    μένει τὸ θεῖον δουλίαι περ ἐν φρενί.

Κα. ὤπολλον ὤπολλον,   [ἀντ. β
    ἀγυιᾶτ', ἀπόλλων ἐμόc·   1086
    ἆ, ποῖ ποτ' ἤγαγέc με; πρὸc ποίαν cτέγην;
Χο. πρὸc τὴν Ἀτρειδῶν· εἰ cὺ μὴ τόδ' ἐννοεῖc,
    ἐγὼ λέγω cοι· καὶ τάδ' οὐκ ἐρεῖc ψύθη.

Κα. ἆ ἆ
    μιcόθεον μὲν οὖν, πολλὰ cυνίcτορα   [cτρ. γ
    αὐτοφόνα κακὰ †καρτάναι†   1091
    ἀνδροcφαγεῖον καὶ πέδον ῥαντήριον.
Χο. ἔοικεν εὔριc ἡ ξένη κυνὸc δίκην
    εἶναι, ματεύει δ' ὧν ἀνευρήcει φόνον.

Κα. μαρτυρίοιcι γὰρ τοῖcδ' ἐπιπείθομαι   [ἀντ. γ
    κλαιόμενα τάδε βρέφη cφαγὰc   1096
    ὀπτάc τε cάρκαc πρὸc πατρὸc βεβρωμέναc.

1078 ἥδ' FTr: ἡ δ' M   1080 et 1085 ἄπολλον ἄπολλον codd.
1084 περ ἐν Schütz: παρ' ἐν M, παρὲν F, παρὸν Tr   1088 εἰ cὺ· τὸ,
μὴ δ' ἐννοεῖc F, εἰ. τό περ μὴ δ' ἐννοεῖc Tr   1089 κᾶτα δ' οὐκ FTr
ψύθη Tr   1090 ἆ ἆ om. FTr   ξυνίcτ- M   1091 καρτάναι M,
κάρτάναι F, κάρτάναc Tr; κρεατόμα Weil   1092 ἀνδροcφαγεῖον
Casaubon (-γιον): ἀνδρὸc cφάγιον codd.   πέδον ῥαντ- MˢFTr: πεδορ-
ραντ- M   1093 εὔριc FTr, εὖριc Mᵖᶜ, εὖροc✶ Mᵃᶜ   1094 μαντεύει
M   ἀνευρήcει Porson: ἂν εὕρήcῃ M, ἐφευρήcει FTr   1095 denuo
incipit cod. G   μαρτυρίοιc codd.   μὲν γὰρ FGTr   τοῖcδ' ἐπιπείθ-
Abresch: τοῖcδε πεπείθ- codd.   1096 τάδε M: τὰ FGTr

Χο. ἦ μὴν κλέος σου μαντικὸν πεπυςμένοι
    ἦμεν, προφήτας δ' οὔτινας ματεύομεν.

Κα. ἰὼ πόποι, τί ποτε μήδεται;   [cτρ. δ
    τί τόδε νέον ἄχος; μέγα,   1101
    μέγ' ἐν δόμοιϲι τοῖϲδε μήδεται κακόν,
    ἄφερτον φίλοιϲιν, δυϲίατον· ἀλκὰ δ'
        ἑκὰϲ ἀποϲτατεῖ.
Χο. τούτων ἄιδρίϲ εἰμι τῶν μαντευμάτων,   1105
    ἐκεῖνα δ' ἔγνων· πᾶϲα γὰρ πόλιϲ βοᾶι.

Κα. ἰὼ τάλαινα, τόδε γὰρ τελεῖϲ;   [ἀντ. δ
    τὸν ὁμοδέμνιον πόϲιν
    λουτροῖϲι φαιδρύναϲα, πῶϲ φράϲω τέλοϲ;
    τάχοϲ γὰρ τόδ' ἔϲται· προτείνει δὲ χεῖρ' ἐκ   1110
    χερὸϲ ὀρεγομένα.
Χο. οὔπω ξυνῆκα· νῦν γὰρ ἐξ αἰνιγμάτων
    ἐπαργέμοιϲι θεϲφάτοιϲ ἀμηχανῶ.

Κα. ἒ ἒ παπαῖ παπαῖ, τί τόδε φαίνεται;   [cτρ. ε
    ἦ δίκτυόν τί γ' Ἅιδου·   1115
    ἀλλ' ἄρκυϲ ἡ ξύνευνοϲ, ἡ ξυναιτία
    φόνου· ϲτάϲιϲ δ' ἀκόρετοϲ γένει
    κατολολυξάτω θύματοϲ λευϲίμου.
Χο. ποίαν Ἐρινὺν τήνδε δώμαϲιν κέληι
    ἐπορθιάζειν; οὔ με φαιδρύνει λόγοϲ.   1120
    ἐπὶ δὲ καρδίαν ἔδραμε κροκοβαφὴϲ
    ϲταγών, ἅτε καὶ δορὶ πτωϲίμοιϲ
    ξυνανύτει βίου δύντοϲ αὐγαῖϲ.
    ταχεῖα δ' ἄτα πέλει.

1098 ἦ μὴν: ἦμην M, ἦμεν M^sscr FGTr; τὸ μὲν Headlam   1099 μα-
τεύομεν Schütz: μαϲτεύομεν codd.   1101˙ἄχος M^sFGTr: ἄχθοϲ M
1103 ἀλκὰν FG   1106 βοᾶι πόλιϲ FGTr   1110 seq. δὲ: γὰρ G
χεῖρ' M^pc: χεὶρ M^acFGTr   ὀρεγμένα FGTr; χεὶρ ἐκ χερὸϲ ὀρέγματα
Hermann   1113 ἐπ' ἀργ- FGTr   ἀμνημονῶ G   1115 ἦ M: ἢ
FGTr   γ' suspectum   Ἅιδου codd.   1117 ἀκόρετοϲ Bothe: -εϲτοϲ
codd.   1122 δορὶ πτωϲίμοιϲ Casaubon: δορία πτώϲιμοϲ M, δωρία
πτώϲιμοϲ FGTr (hic καὶ ὂμ.)

Κα.   ἆ ἆ ἰδοὺ ἰδού, ἄπεχε τῆς βοὸς   [ἀντ. ε
      τὸν ταῦρον· ἐν πέπλοισιν   1126
      μελαγκέρωι λαβοῦσα μηχανήματι
      τύπτει· πίτνει δ᾽ ⟨ἐν⟩ ἐνύδρωι τεύχει.
      δολοφόνου λέβητος τύχαν σοι λέγω.
Χο.   οὐ κομπάσαιμ᾽ ἂν θεσφάτων γνώμων ἄκρος   1130
      εἶναι, κακῶι δέ τωι προσεικάζω τάδε.
      ἀπὸ δὲ θεσφάτων τίς ἀγαθὰ φάτις
      βροτοῖς στέλλεται; κακῶν γὰρ διαὶ
      πολυεπεῖς τέχναι θεσπιωιδῶν
      φόβον φέρουσιν μαθεῖν.   1135

Κα.   ἰὼ ἰὼ ταλαίνας κακόποτμοι τύχαι·   [στρ. ζ
      τὸ γὰρ ἐμὸν θροῶ πάθος ἐπεγχέαι.
      ποῖ δή με δεῦρο τὴν τάλαιναν ἤγαγες
      οὐδέν ποτ᾽ εἰ μὴ ξυνθανουμένην; τί γάρ;
Χο.   φρενομανής τις εἶ θεοφόρητος, ἀμ-   1140
         φὶ δ᾽ αὑτᾶς θροεῖς
      νόμον ἄνομον οἷά τις ξουθὰ
      ἀκόρετος βοᾶς, φεῦ, ταλαίναις φρεσὶν
      Ἴτυν Ἴτυν στένους᾽ ἀμφιθαλῆ κακοῖς
      ἀηδὼν μόρον.   1145

Κα.   ἰὼ ἰὼ λιγείας βίος ἀηδόνος·   [ἀντ. ζ
      περέβαλον γάρ οἱ πτεροφόρον δέμας
      θεοὶ γλυκύν τ᾽ αἰῶνα κλαυμάτων ἄτερ·

1125 τῆς βοῆς Tr   127 -κέρωι M^{pc}: -κερων M^{ac}M^{sscr}FGTr λαθοῦσα M^Σ   1128 ἐν suppl. Schütz   1133 τέλλεται Emperius διαὶ Hermann: διὰ M, δὴ αἱ FGTr   1134 θεσπιωιδῶν Casaubon: -δὸν codd.   1137 ἐπεγχέαι anon.: ἐπεγχέασα M, ἐπαγχέασα FGTr; ἐπεγχύδαν Headlam   1139 οὐδέν ποτ᾽ M: οὐδέποτ᾽ FG, οὐ δή ποτ᾽ Tr   1142 ἄνομόν γ᾽ Tr   1143 ἀκόρετος Aldina: -εστος codd. βοᾶς FG: βοαῖς M, βορᾶς Tr   φεῦ om. FGTr   ταλαίναις ut vid. M (-νᾶς M^s): φιλοίκτοις ταλαίναις FG, φιλοίκτοισι Tr   φιλοίκτοις, deleto ταλ., Dobree   1145 μόρον Page: βίον codd.   1146 βίος ἀηδόνος Page: ἀηδόνος μόρον codd.   1147 περέβαλον Hermann (περιβ-): περεβάλοντο M, περιβαλόντες FGTr   1148 αἰῶνα M^{syp}: ἀγῶνα codd.

ἐμοὶ δὲ μίμνει σχισμὸς ἀμφήκει δορί.

Χο. πόθεν ἐπιccύτουc θεοφόρουc τ' ἔχειc   1150
    ματαίουc δύαc,
    τὰ δ' ἐπίφοβα δυcφάτωι κλαγγᾶι
    μελοτυπεῖc ὁμοῦ τ' ὀρθίοιc ἐν νόμοιc;
    πόθεν ὅρουc ἔχειc θεcπεcίαc ὁδοῦ
    κακορρήμοναc;   1155

Κα. ἰὼ γάμοι γάμοι Πάριδος ὀλέθριοι φίλων·   [cτρ. η
    ἰὼ Cκαμάνδρου πάτριον ποτόν·
    τότε μὲν ἀμφὶ càc ἀιόναc τάλαιν'
      ἠνυτόμαν τροφαῖc·
    νῦν δ' ἀμφὶ Κωκυτόν τε κἈχερουcίουc   1160
    ὄχθουc ἔοικα θεcπιωιδήcειν τάχα.
Χο. τί τόδε τορὸν ἄγαν ἔποc ἐφημίcω;
    νεογνὸc ἂν ἀίων μάθοι·
      πέπληγμαι δ' ὑπαὶ δήγματι φοινίωι
    δυcαλγεῖ τύχαι μινυρὰ θρεομέναc,   1165
    θραύματ' ἐμοὶ κλύειν.

Κα. ἰὼ πόνοι πόνοι πόλεοc ὀλομέναc τὸ πᾶν,   [ἀντ. η
    ἰὼ πρόπυργοι θυcίαι πατρὸc
    πολυκανεῖc βοτῶν ποιονόμων· ἄκοc δ'
      οὐδὲν ἐπήρκεcαν   1170
    τὸ μὴ πόλιν μὲν ὥcπερ οὖν ἐχρῆν παθεῖν,
    ἐγὼ δὲ †θερμόνουc τάχ' ἐμπέδωι βαλῶ†.
Χο. ἑπόμενα προτέροιcι τάδ' ἐφημίcω,

1150 τ' del. Hermann   1152 ἐπίφοβα: ἐπὶ φόβωι Mˢ et sscr. rell.   1153 μολοτυπεῖc FˢˢᶜʳTrᵃᶜ et ut vid. Gᵖᶜ   1154 ἔχη FᵖᶜG   1157 τόπον G   1159 post h.v. iterum deficit M   1163 ἂν ἀίων Karsten: ἀνθρώπων codd.   1164 πέπλημαι Tr   ὑπαὶ Tr: ὑπὸ FG   1165 δυcαλγεῖ Canter: δυcαγγεῖ codd.   μινυρὰ Schütz: μινυρὰ κακὰ codd.   1166 θαύμ[α]τ' Tr   1167 πόλεωc FG   ὀλομέναc Casaubon: ὀλωμ- FG, ὀλουμ- Tr   1171 τὸ μὴ οὐ Hermann   ἐχρῆν Maas: ἔχειν FG, ἔχει Tr   1172 desperatus   1173 προτέροιc codd.; -ροιc τάδ' ἐπεφημίcω Paley

καί τίς σε κακοφρονῶν τίθη-
σι δαίμων ὑπερβαρὴς ἐμπίτνων   1175
μελίζειν πάθη γοερὰ θανατοφόρα·
τέρμα δ' ἀμηχανῶ.

Κα. καὶ μὴν ὁ χρησμὸς οὐκέτ' ἐκ καλυμμάτων
ἔσται δεδορκὼς νεογάμου νύμφης δίκην,
λαμπρὸς δ' ἔοικεν ἡλίου πρὸς ἀντολὰς   1180
πνέων ἐφήξειν, ὥστε κύματος δίκην
κλύζειν πρὸς αὐγὰς τοῦδε πήματος πολὺ
μεῖζον. φρενώσω δ' οὐκέτ' ἐξ αἰνιγμάτων·
καὶ μαρτυρεῖτε συνδρόμως ἴχνος κακῶν
ῥινηλατούσῃ τῶν πάλαι πεπραγμένων.   1185
τὴν γὰρ στέγην τήνδ' οὔποτ' ἐκλείπει χορὸς
ξύμφθογγος οὐκ εὔφωνος· οὐ γὰρ εὖ λέγει.
καὶ μὴν πεπωκώς γ', ὡς θρασύνεσθαι πλέον,
βρότειον αἷμα κῶμος ἐν δόμοις μένει,
δύσπεμπτος ἔξω, συγγόνων Ἐρινύων·   1190
ὑμνοῦσι δ' ὕμνον δώμασιν προσήμεναι
πρώταρχον ἄτην, ἐν μέρει δ' ἀπέπτυσαν
εὐνὰς ἀδελφοῦ τῶι πατοῦντι δυσμενεῖς.
ἥμαρτον, ἢ θηρῶ τι τοξότης τις ὥς;
ἢ ψευδόμαντίς εἰμι θυροκόπος φλέδων;   1195
ἐκμαρτύρησον προυμόσας τό μ' εἰδέναι
λόγωι παλαιὰς τῶνδ' ἁμαρτίας δόμων.

Χο. καὶ πῶς ἂν ὅρκου πῆγμα γενναίως παγὲν
παιώνιον γένοιτο; θαυμάζω δέ σου,
πόντου πέραν τραφεῖσαν ἀλλόθρουν πόλιν   1200
κυρεῖν λέγουσαν ὥσπερ εἰ παρεστάτεις.

Κα. μάντις μ' Ἀπόλλων τῶιδ' ἐπέστησεν τέλει.

1174 καί τίς σε FG: τίς σε καὶ Tr   -φρονῶν Schütz: -φρονεῖν codd.
1175 δαίμων ποιεῖ ὑπερβαρὺς Tr (om. τίθησι)   1176 θανατη-
φόρα Tr   1179 νύμφας F   1181 ἐφήξειν Page: ἐς ἥξειν codd.
1182 κλύζειν Auratus: κλύειν codd.   1187 ξύμφογγος G, σύμφογγος F
1192 πρώταρχος FG   1194 θηρῶ Canter: τηρῶ codd.; κυρῶ Ahrens
1196 καὶ μαρτ- Tr   1198 ὅρκου πῆγμα Auratus: ὅρκος πῆμα codd.

Χο. μῶν καὶ θεός περ ἱμέρωι πεπληγμένος; [1204]
Κα. πρὸ τοῦ μὲν αἰδὼς ἦν ἐμοὶ λέγειν τάδε. [1203]
Χο. ἁβρύνεται γὰρ πᾶς τις εὖ πράccων πλέον. 1205
Κα. ἀλλ' ἦν παλαιστὴς κάρτ' ἐμοὶ πνέων χάριν.
Χο. ἦ καὶ τέκνων εἰς ἔργον ἠλθέτην ὁμοῦ;
Κα. ξυναινέcαcα Λοξίαν ἐψευcάμην.
Χο. ἤδη τέχναιcιν ἐνθέοιc ἡιρημένη;
Κα. ἤδη πολίταιc πάντ' ἐθέcπιζον πάθη. 1210
Χο. πῶc δῆτ' ἄνατοc ἦcθα Λοξίου κότωι;
Κα. ἔπειθον οὐδέν' οὐδέν, ὡc τάδ' ἤμπλακον.
Χο. ἡμῖν γε μὲν δὴ πιcτὰ θεcπίζειν δοκεῖc.
Κα. ἰοὺ ἰού, ὢ ὢ κακά·
       ὑπ' αὖ με δεινὸc ὀρθομαντείαc πόνοc 1215
       cτροβεῖ ταράccων φροιμίοιc ⟨δυcφροιμίοιc⟩.
       ὁρᾶτε τούcδε τοὺc δόμοιc ἐφημένουc
       νέουc ὀνείρων προcφερεῖc μορφώμαcιν·
       παῖδεc θανόντεc ὡcπερεὶ πρὸc τῶν φίλων,
       χεῖραc κρεῶν πλήθοντεc, οἰκείαc βορᾶc, 1220
       cὺν ἐντέροιc τε cπλάγχν', ἐποίκτιcτον γέμοc,
       πρέπουc' ἔχοντεc, ὧν πατὴρ ἐγεύcατο.
       ἐκ τῶνδε ποινάc φημι βουλεύειν τινὰ
       λέοντ' ἄναλκιν ἐν λέχει cτρωφώμενον
       οἰκουρόν, οἴμοι, τῶι μολόντι δεcπότηι 1225
       ἐμῶι· φέρειν γὰρ χρὴ τὸ δούλιον ζυγόν.
       νεῶν δ' ἄπαρχοc Ἰλίου τ' ἀναcτάτηc
       οὐκ οἶδεν οἷα γλῶccα μιcητῆc κυνόc,
       λέξαcα κἀκτείναcα φαιδρόνουc δίκην,
       ἄτηc λαθραίου τεύξεται κακῆι τύχηι. 1230
       τοιαῦτα τολμᾶι· θῆλυc ἄρcενοc φονεὺc

1203–4 ordinem versuum restituit Hermann   1205 βαρύνεται
Tr   1207 ἠλθέτην Elmsley: -τον codd.   ὁμοῦ Butler: νόμωι codd.
1211 ἄνατοc Canter: ἄνακτοc codd.   1212 οὐδὲν οὐδὲν codd.
1216 δυcφροιμίοιc suppl. Hermann: ἐφημένουc codd. (-νοιc Tr^sscr) ex 1217
1219 πρὸc: πρὸ G   1225 οἴμοι: ὠμὸν Blaydes   1226 eiecit A.
Ludwig   δούλειον Tr   ζυγω F^ac   1227 νεῶν δ' G. Voss: νεῶν τ'
codd.   1228–30 lectio et interpretatio incerta   εὖ οἶδεν Tr   κἀκ-
τείναcα Canter: καὶ κτείναcα codd.   1231 τοιαῦτα Tr: τοιάδε FG

ἔστιν· τί νιν καλοῦσα δυσφιλὲς δάκος
τύχοιμ' ἄν; ἀμφίσβαιναν ἢ Σκύλλαν τινὰ
οἰκοῦσαν ἐν πέτραισι, ναυτίλων βλάβην,
θύουσαν Ἅιδου μητέρ' ἄσπονδόν τ' Ἄρη   1235
φίλοις πνέουσαν; ὡς δ' ἐπωλολύξατο
ἡ παντότολμος, ὥσπερ ἐν μάχης τροπῆι·
δοκεῖ δὲ χαίρειν νοστίμωι σωτηρίαι.
καὶ τῶνδ' ὅμοιον εἴ τι μὴ πείθω· τί γάρ;
τὸ μέλλον ἥξει, καὶ σύ μ' ἐν τάχει παρὼν   1240
ἄγαν γ' ἀληθόμαντιν οἰκτίρας ἐρεῖς.
Χο.   τὴν μὲν Θυέστου δαῖτα παιδείων κρεῶν
ξυνῆκα καὶ πέφρικα, καὶ φόβος μ' ἔχει
κλύοντ' ἀληθῶς οὐδὲν ἐξηικασμένα·
τὰ δ' ἄλλ' ἀκούσας ἐκ δρόμου πεσὼν τρέχω.   1245
Κα.   Ἀγαμέμνονός σέ φημ' ἐπόψεσθαι μόρον.
Χο.   εὔφημον, ὦ τάλαινα, κοίμησον στόμα.
Κα.   ἀλλ' οὔτι παιὼν τῶιδ' ἐπιστατεῖ λόγωι.
Χο.   οὔκ, εἴπερ ἔσται γ'· ἀλλὰ μὴ γένοιτό πως.
Κα.   σὺ μὲν κατεύχηι, τοῖς δ' ἀποκτείνειν μέλει.   1250
Χο.   τίνος πρὸς ἀνδρὸς τοῦτ' ἄχος πορσύνεται;
Κα.   ἦ κάρτα ⟨μακ⟩ρὰν παρεκόπης χρησμῶν ἐμῶν.
Χο.   τοῦ γὰρ τελοῦντος οὐ ξυνῆκα μηχανήν.
Κα.   καὶ μὴν ἄγαν γ' Ἕλλην' ἐπίσταμαι φάτιν.
Χο.   καὶ γὰρ τὰ πυθόκραντα, δυσμαθῆ δ' ὅμως.   1255
Κα.   παπαῖ· οἷον τὸ πῦρ· ἐπέρχεται δέ μοι.
ὀτοτοῖ Λύκει' Ἄπολλον, οἲ ἐγὼ ἐγώ.
αὕτη δίπους λέαινα συγκοιμωμένη
λύκωι, λέοντος εὐγενοῦς ἀπουσίαι,
κτενεῖ με τὴν τάλαιναν· ὡς δὲ φάρμακον   1260
τεύχουσα κἀμοῦ μισθὸν ἐνθήσει κότωι·

1232 -φιλεὺς F   1235 Ἄρη Franz: ἀρὰν codd.   1240 μ' ἐν
Auratus: μὴν codd.   1242 παιδίων codd.   1244 ἐξεικ-
Tr   1247 κοίμισον Tr   1249 εἴπερ ἔσται Schütz: εἰ παρέσται
codd.   1252 κάρτα μακρὰν Fraenkel (μακρὰν post παρεκ. iam Eitrem):
κάρτ' ἄρ' ἂν codd.   παρεκόπης Hartung: παρεσκόπεις FG, παρεσκόπης
F^sscr G^sscr Tr   1255 δυσπαθῆ FG   1258 δίπους Victorius: διπλοῦς
codd.   1261 μισθὸν, sscr. μνείαν, F   ἐνθήσειν Tr   ποτῶι Auratus

ἐπεύχεται, θήγουσα φωτὶ φάςγανον,
ἐμῆς ἀγωγῆς ἀντιτείςεςθαι φόνον.
τί δῆτ᾽ ἐμαυτῆς καταγέλωτ᾽ ἔχω τάδε
καὶ ςκῆπτρα καὶ μαντεῖα περὶ δέρηι ςτέφη; 1265
ςὲ μὲν πρὸ μοίρας τῆς ἐμῆς διαφθερῶ·
ἴτ᾽ ἐς φθόρον· πεςόντα γ᾽ ὧδ᾽ ἀμείψομαι·
ἄλλην τιν᾽ ἄτης ἀντ᾽ ἐμοῦ πλουτίζετε.
ἰδοὺ δ᾽, Ἀπόλλων αὐτὸς ἐκδύων ἐμὲ
χρηςτηρίαν ἐςθῆτ᾽, ἐποπτεύςας δέ με 1270
κἀν τοῖςδε κόςμοις καταγελωμένην †μέτα†
φίλων ὑπ᾽ ἐχθρῶν οὐ διχορρόπως †μάτην†·
καλουμένη δὲ φοιτὰς ὡς ἀγύρτρια
πτωχὸς τάλαινα λιμοθνὴς ἠνεςχόμην·
καὶ νῦν ὁ μάντις μάντιν ἐκπράξας ἐμὲ 1275
ἀπήγαγ᾽ ἐς τοιάςδε θαναςίμους τύχας.
βωμοῦ πατρώιου δ᾽ ἀντ᾽ ἐπίξηνον μένει,
θερμῶι κοπείςης φοίνιον προςφάγματι.
οὐ μὴν ἄτιμοί γ᾽ ἐκ θεῶν τεθνήξομεν·
ἥξει γὰρ ἡμῶν ἄλλος αὖ τιμάορος, 1280
μητροκτόνον φίτυμα, ποινάτωρ πατρός·
φυγὰς δ᾽ ἀλήτης τῆςδε γῆς ἀπόξενος
κάτειςιν ἄτας τάςδε θριγκώςων φίλοις.
ὀμώμοται γὰρ ὅρκος ἐκ θεῶν μέγας, [1291]
ἄξειν νιν ὑπτίαςμα κειμένου πατρός. 1285
τί δῆτ᾽ ἐγὼ κάτοικτος ὧδ᾽ ἀναςτένω;
ἐπεὶ τὸ πρῶτον εἶδον Ἰλίου πόλιν
πράξαςαν ὡς ἔπραξεν, οἳ δ᾽ εἷλον πόλιν
οὕτως ἀπαλλάςςουςιν ἐν θεῶν κρίςει,

1263 -τείςεςθαι Blomfield : -τίςαςθαι codd.   1267 πεςόντα γ᾽ ὧδ᾽
Iacob : πεςόντ᾽ ἀγαθῶ δ᾽ codd.   ἀμείβομαι F^{ac}   1268 ἄτης Stanley : ἄτην codd.; ἄταις Schütz   1270 ἐπώπτ- Tr   1271 μέτα :
fort. ἐᾶι (μ᾽ ἐᾶι Heusde) ; μέγα Hermann   1272 ἐχθρῶν τ᾽ Rauchenstein   μάτην graviter corruptum   1277 ἀντεπίξ- codd.
1278 φοίνιον C. G. Haupt : -ίωι codd.   1279 ἄτιμόν F^{ac}G
1284 huc traiecit Hermann; post 1290 habent codd.   1285 ἄξειν
F : ἄξει GTr   1286 κάτοικτος Scaliger : -οικος codd.   1288 εἷλον
Musgrave : εἶχον codd.   1289 ἐν GTr : ἐκ F

	ἰοῦς' ἀπάρξω, τλήσομαι τὸ **κατθανεῖν**.	[1289] 1290
	Ἅιδου πύλας δὲ τάςδ' ἐγὼ προςεννέπω·	[1291]
	ἐπεύχομαι δὲ καιρίας πληγῆς τυχεῖν,	
	ὡς ἀςφάδαιςτος αἱμάτων εὐθνηςίμων	
	ἀπορρυέντων ὄμμα ςυμβάλω τόδε.	
Χο.	ὦ πολλὰ μὲν τάλαινα, πολλὰ δ' αὖ ςοφὴ	1295
	γύναι, μακρὰν ἔτεινας. εἰ δ' ἐτητύμως	
	μόρον τὸν αὑτῆς οἶςθα, πῶς θεηλάτου	
	βοὸς δίκην πρὸς βωμὸν εὐτόλμως πατεῖς;	
Κα.	οὐκ ἔςτ' ἄλυξις, οὔ, ξένοι, χρόνον πλέω.	
Χο.	ὁ δ' ὕςτατός γε τοῦ χρόνου πρεςβεύεται.	1300
Κα.	ἥκει τόδ' ἦμαρ. ςμικρὰ κερδανῶ φυγῆι.	
Χο.	ἀλλ' ἴςθι τλήμων οὖς' ἀπ' εὐτόλμου φρενός.	
Κα.	οὐδεὶς ἀκούει ταῦτα τῶν εὐδαιμόνων.	
Χο.	ἀλλ' εὐκλεῶς τοι κατθανεῖν χάρις βροτῶι.	
Κα.	ἰὼ πάτερ ςοῦ ςῶν τε γενναίων τέκνων.	1305
Χο.	τί δ' ἐςτὶ χρῆμα; τίς ς' ἀποςτρέφει φόβος;	
Κα.	φεῦ φεῦ.	
Χο.	τί τοῦτ' ἔφευξας, εἴ τι μὴ φρενῶν ςτύγος;	
Κα.	φόνον δόμοι πνέουςιν αἱματοςταγῆ.	
Χο.	καὶ πῶς; τόδ' ὄζει θυμάτων ἐφεςτίων.	1310
Κα.	ὅμοιος ἀτμὸς ὥςπερ ἐκ τάφου πρέπει.	
Χο.	οὐ Ϲύριον ἀγλάιςμα δώμαςιν λέγεις.	
Κα.	ἀλλ' εἶμι κἀν δόμοιςι κωκύςους' ἐμὴν	
	Ἀγαμέμνονός τε μοῖραν· ἀρκείτω βίος.	
	ἰὼ ξένοι·	1315
	οὔτοι δυςοίζω θάμνον ὡς ὄρνις φόβωι,	
	ἀλλ' ὡς θανούςηι μαρτυρῆτέ μοι τόδε,	
	ὅταν γυνὴ γυναικὸς ἀντ' ἐμοῦ θάνηι	
	ἀνήρ τε δυςδάμαρτος ἀντ' ἀνδρὸς πέςηι·	
	ἐπιξενοῦμαι ταῦτα δ' ὡς θανουμένη.	1320

1290 ἰοῦς' ἀπάρξω Page: ἰοῦςα πράξω codd.   1291 τάςδ' ἐγὼ
Auratus: τὰς λέγω codd.   1295 δὲ ςοφὴ FG   1296 ἔκτεινας
G   1299 χρόνον πλέω Hermann: χρόνωι πλέω codd. (πλέωι Tr)
1305 ςῶν Auratus: τῶν codd.   1309 φόνον Tr^sscr: φόβον FGTr
1317 μαρτυρῆτέ Orelli: -εῖτέ codd.

Χο. ὦ τλῆμον, οἰκτίρω σε θεσφάτου μόρου.
Κα. ἅπαξ ἔτ' εἰπεῖν ῥῆσιν ἢ θρῆνον θέλω
ἐμὸν τὸν αὐτῆς, ἡλίου δ' ἐπεύχομαι
πρὸς ὕστατον φῶς †τοῖς ἐμοῖς τιμαόροις
ἐχθροῖς φονεῦσι τοῖς ἐμοῖς τίνειν ὁμοῦ†   1325
δούλης θανούσης, εὐμαροῦς χειρώματος.
ἰὼ βρότεια πράγματ'· εὐτυχοῦντα μὲν
σκιᾶι τις ἂν πρέψειεν, εἰ δὲ δυστυχῆι,
βολαῖς ὑγρώσσων σπόγγος ὤλεσεν γραφήν.
καὶ ταῦτ' ἐκείνων μᾶλλον οἰκτίρω πολύ.   1330

Χο. τὸ μὲν εὖ πράσσειν ἀκόρεστον ἔφυ
πᾶσι βροτοῖσιν· δακτυλοδείκτων δ'
οὔτις ἀπειπὼν εἴργει μελάθρων,
"μηκέτ' ἐσέλθηις τάδε" φωνῶν.
καὶ τῶιδε πόλιν μὲν ἑλεῖν ἔδοσαν   1335
μάκαρες Πριάμου,
θεοτίμητος δ' οἴκαδ' ἱκάνει·
νῦν δ' εἰ προτέρων αἷμ' ἀποτείσηι
καὶ τοῖσι θανοῦσι θανὼν ἄλλων
ποινὰς θανάτων ἐπικράνηι,   1340
τίς ἂν ἐξεύξαιτο βροτῶν ἀσινεῖ
δαίμονι φῦναι τάδ' ἀκούων;

Αγ. ὤμοι πέπληγμαι καιρίαν πληγὴν ἔσω.
Χο. σῖγα· τίς πληγὴν ἀυτεῖ καιρίως οὐτασμένος;
Αγ. ὤμοι μάλ' αὖθις δευτέραν πεπληγμένος.   1345
Χο. τοὔργον εἰργάσθαι δοκεῖ μοι βασιλέως οἰμώγμασιν·

1323 ἡλίου Iacob: -ίωι codd.   1324 seq. e.g. δεσπότου (M. Schmidt) τιμαόροις / ἐχθροὺς (I. Pearson) φόνευσιν (Bothe) τὴν ἐμὴν (Heller) τίνειν ὁμοῦ   1328 σκιᾶι Wieseler: σκιά codd.   ἂν πρέψειεν Boissonade: ἀντρέψειεν codd.   δυστυχῆ codd.   1331 πράττειν codd. 1332 -δεικτῶν codd.   1334 μηκέτ' ἐσέλθηις Hermann: μηκέτι δ' εἰσέλθης codd.   1338 ἀποτείσηι Sidgwick: -τίσει codd.   1340 ἐπικράνηι Sidgwick: ἐπικρανεῖ FG, ἄγαν ἐπικρανεῖ Tr   1341 ἐξεύξ- Schneidewin: εὐξ- codd.

ἀλλὰ κοινωσώμεθ' ἤν πως ἀσφαλῆ βουλεύματ' ἦι.

— ἐγὼ μὲν ὑμῖν τὴν ἐμὴν γνώμην λέγω,
προς δῶμα δεῦρ' ἀστοῖσι κηρύσσειν βοήν.

— ἐμοὶ δ' ὅπως τάχιστά γ' ἐμπεσεῖν δοκεῖ   1350
καὶ πρᾶγμ' ἐλέγχειν σὺν νεορρύτωι ξίφει.

— κἀγὼ τοιούτου γνώματος κοινωνὸς ὢν
ψηφίζομαι τὸ δρᾶν τι· μὴ μέλλειν δ' ἀκμή.

— ὁρᾶν πάρεστι· φροιμιάζονται γὰρ ὡς
τυραννίδος σημεῖα πράσσοντες πόλει.   1355

— χρονίζομεν γάρ, οἱ δὲ τῆς μελλοῦς κλέος
πέδοι πατοῦντες οὐ καθεύδουσιν χερί.

— οὐκ οἶδα βουλῆς ἧστινος τυχὼν λέγω·
τοῦ δρῶντός ἐστι καὶ τὸ βουλεῦσαι †πέρι†.

— κἀγὼ τοιοῦτός εἰμ', ἐπεὶ δυσμηχανῶ   1360
λόγοισι τὸν θανόντ' ἀνιστάναι πάλιν.

— ἦ καὶ βίον τείνοντες ὧδ' ὑπείξομεν
δόμων καταισχυντῆρσι τοῖσδ' ἡγουμένοις;

— ἀλλ' οὐκ ἀνεκτόν, ἀλλὰ κατθανεῖν κρατεῖ·
πεπαιτέρα γὰρ μοῖρα τῆς τυραννίδος.   1365

— ἦ γὰρ τεκμηρίοισιν ἐξ οἰμωγμάτων
μαντευσόμεσθα τἀνδρὸς ὡς ὀλωλότος;

— σάφ' εἰδότας χρὴ τῶνδε μυθεῖσθαι πέρι,
τὸ γὰρ τοπάζειν τοῦ σάφ' εἰδέναι δίχα.

— ταύτην ἐπαινεῖν πάντοθεν πληθύνομαι,   1370
τρανῶς Ἀτρείδην εἰδέναι κυροῦνθ' ὅπως.

Κλ.   πολλῶν πάροιθεν καιρίως εἰρημένων
τἀναντί' εἰπεῖν οὐκ ἐπαισχυνθήσομαι·
πῶς γάρ τις ἐχθροῖς ἐχθρὰ πορσύνων, φίλοις
δοκοῦσιν εἶναι, πημονῆς ἀρκύστατ' ἂν   1375

1347 ἤν Paley : ἂν codd.   βουλεύματ' ἦι Enger: -ματα codd.   1348 ἡμῖν
Fᵃᶜ   1353 τὸ δρᾶν τι Musgrave : τι δρᾶν· τὸ codd.   1356 (ὧδε)
τῆς μελλοῦς Trypho π. τρόπ. Rhet. Gr. 8. 741. 9 Walz: τῆς μελλούσης FG,
μελλούσης Tr   κλέος codd. : χάριν Trypho   1357 πέδοι Hermann :
πέδον codd.   1359 πέρι : πάρος Auratus   1362 τείνοντες
Canter : κτείν- codd.   1364 κράτει codd.   1367 -μεθα F
1368 μυθεῖσθαι I. G. Schneider : μυθοῦσθαι codd.   1375 πημονῆς
Auratus : -νὴν codd.   ἀρκύστατ' ἂν Elmsley : ἀρκύστατον codd.

φάρξειεν ὕψος κρεῖccον ἐκπηδήματος;
ἐμοὶ δ' ἀγὼν ὅδ' οὐκ ἀφρόντιστος πάλαι
νείκης παλαιᾶς ἦλθε, cὺν χρόνωι γε μήν·
ἕστηκα δ' ἔνθ' ἔπαιc' ἐπ' ἐξειργασμένοιc.
οὕτω δ' ἔπραξα, καὶ τάδ' οὐκ ἀρνήcομαι,   1380
ὡc μήτε φεύγειν μήτ' ἀμύνεcθαι μόρον·
ἄπειρον ἀμφίβληcτρον, ὥcπερ ἰχθύων,
περιcτιχίζω, πλοῦτον εἵματος κακόν·
παίω δέ νιν δίc, κἀν δυοῖν οἰμώγμαcιν
μεθῆκεν αὐτοῦ κῶλα, καὶ πεπτωκότι   1385
τρίτην ἐπενδίδωμι, τοῦ κατὰ χθονὸς
Διὸς νεκρῶν cωτῆρος εὐκταίαν χάριν.
οὕτω τὸν αὑτοῦ θυμὸν ὁρμαίνει πεcὼν
κἀκφυcιῶν ὀξεῖαν αἵματος cφαγὴν
βάλλει μ' ἐρεμνῆι ψακάδι φοινίαc δρόcου,   1390
χαίρουcαν οὐδὲν ἧccον ἢ διοcδότωι
γάνει cπορητὸς κάλυκος ἐν λοχεύμαcιν.
ὡc ὧδ' ἐχόντων, πρέcβος Ἀργείων τόδε,
χαίροιτ' ἄν, εἰ χαίροιτ', ἐγὼ δ' ἐπεύχομαι·
εἰ δ' ἦν πρεπόντωc ὥcτ' ἐπιcπένδειν νεκρῶι,   1395
τάδ' ἂν δικαίωc ἦν, ὑπερδίκωc μὲν οὖν·
τοcῶνδε κρατῆρ' ἐν δόμοιc κακῶν ὅδε
πλήcας ἀραίων αὐτὸc ἐκπίνει μολών.

Χο. θαυμάζομέν cου γλῶccαν, ὡc θραcύcτομος,
ἥτιc τοιόνδ' ἐπ' ἀνδρὶ κομπάζειc λόγον.   1400

Κλ. πειρᾶcθέ μου γυναικὸc ὡc ἀφράcμονος,
ἐγὼ δ' ἀτρέcτωι καρδίαι πρὸc εἰδότας
λέγω· cὺ δ' αἰνεῖν εἴτε με ψέγειν θέλειc,
ὅμοιον· οὗτός ἐcτιν Ἀγαμέμνων, ἐμὸc

1376 φράξ- codd.   1378 νείκηc Heath : νίκηc codd.   1379 ἔπεc'
F   1381 ἀμύνεcθαι Victorius : -ναcθαι codd.   1383 -cτιχίζων
G, -cτοιχίζων F   1384 οἰμωγμάτοιν Elmsley   1387 Διὸc Enger :
Ἅιδου codd.   1388 ὀρυγάνει Hermann   1391 seq. διοcδότωι
γάνει Porson : διὸc νότωι γᾶν εἰ codd.; Διὸc νότωι γαθεῖ Lloyd-Jones
1395–8 locus difficilis; vid. Lucas, Proc. Camb. Phil. Soc. 1969. 60 seqq.
1395 πρεπόντωc I. Voss : -των codd.   1396 τῶιδ' Tyrwhitt
1397 τοcόνδε Blomfield   1401 μου om. G

πόcιc, νεκρὸc δέ, τῆcδε δεξιᾶc χερὸc   1405
ἔργον, δικαίαc τέκτονοc. τάδ' ὧδ' ἔχει.

Χο.   τί κακόν, ὦ γύναι,   [cτρ. α
χθονοτρεφὲc ἐδανὸν ἢ ποτὸν
παcαμένα ῥυτᾶc ἐξ ἁλὸc ὀρόμενον
τόδ' ἐπέθου θύοc, δημοθρόουc τ' ἀρὰc
ἀπέδικεc ἀπέταμεc; ἀπόπολιc δ' ἔcηι,   1410
μῖcοc ὄβριμον ἀcτοῖc.

Κλ.   νῦν μὲν δικάζειc ἐκ πόλεωc φυγὴν ἐμοὶ
καὶ μῖcοc ἀcτῶν δημόθρουc τ' ἔχειν ἀράc,
οὐδὲν τότ' ἀνδρὶ τῶιδ' ἐναντίον φέρων,
ὃc οὐ προτιμῶν, ὡcπερεὶ βοτοῦ μόρον,   1415
μήλων φλεόντων εὐπόκοιc νομεύμαcιν,
ἔθυcεν αὐτοῦ παῖδα, φιλτάτην ἐμοὶ
ὠδῖν', ἐπωιδὸν Θρηικίων ἀημάτων.
οὐ τοῦτον ἐκ γῆc τῆcδε χρῆν c' ἀνδρηλατεῖν
μιαcμάτων ἄποιν'; ἐπήκοοc δ' ἐμῶν   1420
ἔργων δικαcτὴc τραχὺc εἶ. λέγω δέ cοι
τοιαῦτ' ἀπειλεῖν ὡc παρεcκευαcμένηc
ἐκ τῶν ὁμοίων, χειρὶ νικήcαντ' ἐμοῦ
ἄρχειν· ἐὰν δὲ τοὔμπαλιν κραίνηι θεόc,
γνώcηι διδαχθεὶc ὀψὲ γοῦν τὸ cωφρονεῖν.   1425

Χο.   μεγαλόμητιc εἶ,   [ἀντ. α
περίφρονα δ' ἔλακεc· ὥcπερ οὖν
φονολιβεῖ τύχαι φρὴν ἐπιμαίνεται,
λίβοc ἐπ' ὀμμάτων αἵματοc ἐμπρέπει.

1406 δικαίωc Tr   1408 ῥυτᾶc Stanley: ῥύcαc vel ῥυcᾶc
codd.   ὀρόμενον Canter: ὁρώμ- vel ὁρώμ- codd.   1409 ἐπεύθου
Tr   1410 ἀπέτεμεc F^{pc}Tr^{ac}   ἀπόπολιc Casaubon: ἄπολιc codd.
1411 ὄμβρ- codd.   1414 οὐδὲν: οὐ cὺν F^{ac}   τότ' I. Voss: τόδ' codd.
1418 ἐπωδὴν G   ἀημάτων Canter: τε λημμάτων codd.   1419 χρῆν
Porson: χρή codd.   1420 βιαcμάτων G   1424 ἄρχειν c'
Dindorf   1428 λίβοc Casaubon: λῖποc codd.   ἐμπρέπει Auratus:
εὖ πρέπει codd.

AΓΑΜΕΜΝΩΝ

53

ἄντιτον ἔτι cε χρὴ cτερομέναν φίλων
τύμμα τύμματι τεῖcαι.   1430

ΚΛ. καὶ τήνδ' ἀκούεις ὁρκίων ἐμῶν θέμιν·
μὰ τὴν τέλειον τῆc ἐμῆc παιδὸc Δίκην,
Ἄτην Ἐρινύν θ', αἷcι τόνδ' ἔcφαξ' ἐγώ,
οὔ μοι φόβου μέλαθρον ἐλπὶc ἐμπατεῖ
ἕωc ἂν αἴθηι πῦρ ἐφ' ἑcτίαc ἐμῆc   1435
Αἴγιcθοc, ὡc τὸ πρόcθεν εὖ φρονῶν ἐμοί·
οὗτοc γὰρ ἡμῖν ἀcπὶc οὐ cμικρὰ θράcουc.
κεῖται γυναικὸc τῆcδ' ὁ λυμαντήριοc,
Χρυcηίδων μείλιγμα τῶν ὑπ' Ἰλίωι,
ἥ τ' αἰχμάλωτοc ἥδε καὶ τεραcκόποc   1440
καὶ κοινόλεκτροc τοῦδε, θεcφατηλόγοc,
πιcτὴ ξύνευνοc, ναυτίλων δὲ cελμάτων
ἰcοτριβήc· ἄτιμα δ' οὐκ ἐπραξάτην,
ὁ μὲν γὰρ οὕτωc, ἡ δέ τοι κύκνου δίκην
τὸν ὕcτατον μέλψαcα θανάcιμον γόον   1445
κεῖται φιλήτωρ τοῦδ'· ἐμοὶ δ' ἐπήγαγεν
εὐνῆc παροψώνημα τῆc ἐμῆc χλιδῆι.

Χο. φεῦ, τίc ἂν ἐν τάχει μὴ περιώδυνοc   [cτρ. β
μηδὲ δεμνιοτήρηc
μόλοι τὸν αἰεὶ φέρουc' ἐν ἡμῖν   1450
μοῖρ' ἀτέλευτον ὕπνον, δαμέντοc
φύλακοc εὐμενεcτάτου
πολλὰ τλάντοc γυναικὸc διαί;
πρὸc γυναικὸc δ' ἀπέφθιcεν βίον.

ἰώ
παράνουc Ἑλένα,   1455

1429 ἄντιτον Weil: ἀντίετον FG, ἀτίετον Tr   1430 τύμμα τύμματι
Casaubon: τύμμα τύμμα codd.   1433 Ἄτην τ' Butler   1435 ἐμῆc
Porson: ἐμὰc codd.   1437 μικρὰ codd.   1438 τῆcδ' ὁ Kayser:
τῆcδε codd.   1443 ἰcοτριβὴc Pauw: ἰcτο- codd.   1446 φιλήτωc
F   1447 παροψόνημα codd.   χλιδῆι Musgrave: -ῆc codd.
1452 seq. πολλὰ Franz: καὶ πολλὰ codd.   διὰ Tr   1455 παράνουc
Hermann: παρανόμουc codd.

μία τὰς πολλάς, τὰς πάνυ πολλὰς
ψυχὰς ὀλέϲαϲ᾽ ὑπὸ Τροίαι·
νῦν †δὲ τελείαν πολύμναϲτον ἐπηνθίϲω†
δι᾽ αἷμ᾽ ἄνιπτον. ἦ τις ἦν τότ᾽ ἐν δόμοις   1460
Ἔρις ἐρίδματος ἀνδρὸς οἰζύς.

Κλ.   μηδὲν θανάτου μοῖραν ἐπεύχου
τοῖσδε βαρυνθείς,
μηδ᾽ εἰς Ἑλένην κότον ἐκτρέψηις
ὡς ἀνδρολέτειρ᾽, ὡς μία πολλῶν   1465
ἀνδρῶν ψυχὰς Δαναῶν ὀλέϲαϲ᾽
ἀξύϲτατον ἄλγος ἔπραξεν.

Χο.   δαῖμον, ὃϲ ἐμπίτνεις δώμαϲι καὶ διφυί-   [ἀντ. β
οιϲι Τανταλίδαιϲιν,
κράτος ⟨τ᾽⟩ ἰϲόψυχον ἐκ γυναικῶν   1470
καρδιόδηκτον ἐμοὶ κρατύνεις·
ἐπὶ δὲ ϲώματος δίκαν
κόρακος ἐχθροῦ ϲταθεὶϲ᾽ ἐκνόμωϲ
ὕμνον ὑμνεῖν ἐπεύχεται ⟨   ⟩.

Κλ.   νῦν δ᾽ ὤρθωϲαϲ ϲτόματος γνώμην,   1475
τὸν τριπάχυντον
δαίμονα γέννης τῆϲδε κικλήϲκων·
ἐκ τοῦ γὰρ ἔρως αἱματολοιχὸς
νείραι τρέφεται· πρὶν καταλῆξαι
τὸ παλαιὸν ἄχος, νέος ἰχώρ.   1480

1459 desperatus; fort. νῦν τέλεον . . . ἐπηνθίϲω / τόδ᾽ αἷμ᾽   1460 ἦ
τις Schütz: ἥτις codd.   1461 vix intellegitur   1464 ἐκτρέχηϲ
F   1466 ὀλέϲαν FG   1468 ἐμπίτνεις Canter: -πίπτεις codd.
1468 seq. διφυίοιϲι Hermann: διφνεῖϲι codd. -λιδέϲιν FG   1470 τ᾽
suppl. Hermann   1471 καρδιόδηκτον Abresch: καρδία δηκτὸν codd.
1472 δίκαν Dindorf: δίκαν μοι codd.   1473 ϲταθεὶς codd.   ἐκνόμωϲ Tr^pc et schol. vet. Tr: ἐννόμωϲ FGTr^ac   1474 ὕμνον ὑμνοῦϲ᾽
Herwerden   ὕμνον epitheton desiderat, e.g. ⟨πικρόν⟩   1475 δ᾽
del. Wecklein   1476 τριπάχυντον Bamberger: τριπάχυιον codd.
1477 γέννης FG: γέννας Tr et sscr. FG   1479 νείραι Casaubon
(-ρηι): νείρει codd.

Χο.   ἦ μέγαν †οἴκοις τοῖσδε†   [στρ. γ
   δαίμονα καὶ βαρύμηνιν αἰνεῖς,
   φεῦ φεῦ, κακὸν αἶνον ἀτη-
    ρᾶς τύχας ἀκορέστου,
   ἰὼ ἰή, διαὶ Διὸς   1485
   παναιτίου πανεργέτα·
   τί γὰρ βροτοῖς ἄνευ Διὸς τελεῖται;
   τί τῶνδ' οὐ θεόκραντόν ἐστιν;

   ἰὼ ἰὼ βασιλεῦ βασιλεῦ,
   πῶς σε δακρύσω;   1490
   φρενὸς ἐκ φιλίας τί ποτ' εἴπω;
   κεῖσαι δ' ἀράχνης ἐν ὑφάσματι τῶιδ'
   ἀσεβεῖ θανάτωι βίον ἐκπνέων,
   ὤμοι μοι, κοίταν τάνδ' ἀνελεύθερον,
   δολίωι μόρωι δαμεὶς   1495
   ἐκ χερὸς ἀμφιτόμωι βελέμνωι.

Κλ.   αὐχεῖς εἶναι τόδε τοὔργον ἐμόν,
   τῆιδ' ἐπιλεχθείς,
   Ἀγαμεμνονίαν εἶναί μ' ἄλοχον·
   φανταζόμενος δὲ γυναικὶ νεκροῦ   1500
   τοῦδ' ὁ παλαιὸς δριμὺς ἀλάστωρ
   Ἀτρέως χαλεποῦ θοινατῆρος
   τόνδ' ἀπέτεισεν
   τέλεον νεαροῖς ἐπιθύσας.

Χο.   ὡς μὲν ἀναίτιος εἶ   [ἀντ. γ
   τοῦδε φόνου τίς ὁ μαρτυρήσων;   1506
   πῶ πῶ; πατρόθεν δὲ συλλή-

1481 ἦ μέγαν ἦ μέγαν οἴκοις Weil (cf. 1505 n.), ἦ μέγαν οἰκοσινῆ Wilamowitz   1484 ἀκόρεστον Todt   1486 πανεργέταν F^{pc}G, -εργάταν
F^{ac} 1489 ἰὼ semel F   1491 ποτ' ἄρ' εἴπω Tr   1493 ἐκπνέων
disyll. suspectum; ἐκπονέων Diggle, ἐκπνείων Tr   1494 ἀνελεύ-
θερα Tr   1495 δουλίωι Blomfield   1497 εἶναι τοὔργον
ἐμὸν τόδε Tr   1498 τῆιδ' Page: μὴ δ' codd.   ἐπιλεχθείς Scaliger:
-λεχθῆις codd.   1504 νεκροῖς Tr   1505 εἰ σὺ Schütz; cf. 1481
1507 δὲ om. Tr; fort. πῶ πῶ πατρόθεν γε (Burges) ... ἀλάστωρ;

πτωρ γένοιτ' ἂν ἀλάστωρ·
βιάζεται δ' ὁμοσπόροις
ἐπιρροαῖσιν αἱμάτων   1510
μέλας Ἄρης, ὅποι δίκαν προβαίνων
πάχναι κουροβόρωι παρέξει.

ἰὼ ἰὼ βασιλεῦ βασιλεῦ,
πῶς σε δακρύсω;
φρενὸς ἐκ φιλίας τί ποτ' εἴπω;   1515
κεῖσαι δ' ἀράχνης ἐν ὑφάσματι τῶιδ'
ἀсεβεῖ θανάτωι βίον ἐκπνέων,
ὤμοι μοι, κοίταν τάνδ' ἀνελεύθερον,
δολίωι μόρωι δαμεὶς
ἐκ χερὸς ἀμφιτόμωι βελέμνωι.   1520

Κλ.   οὔτ' ἀνελεύθερον οἶμαι θάνατον
         τῶιδε γενέсθαι ⟨   ⟩
         ⟨   ⟩
         οὐδὲ γὰρ οὗτος δολίαν ἄτην
         οἴκοισιν ἔθηκ';
         ἀλλ' ἐμὸν ἐκ τοῦδ' ἔρνος ἀερθὲν   1525
         τὴν πολυκλαύτην
         Ἰφιγένειαν ἀνάξια δράсας
         ἄξια πάсχων μηδὲν ἐν Ἅιδου
         μεγαλαυχείτω, ξιφοδηλήτωι
         θανάτωι τείсας ἅπερ ἦρξεν.

Χο.   ἀμηχανῶ φροντίδος στερηθεὶς   [στρ. δ
         εὐπάλαμον μέριμναν   1531
         ὅπαι τράπωμαι πίτνοντος οἴκου.

1511 δίκαν Butler: δὲ καὶ codd.   προβ- Canter: προсβ- codd.
1513–20 eadem ac 1489–96 excepto 1517 εὐсεβεῖ F   1522 post
γενέсθαι lacunam statuit Wilamowitz; suppleas e.g. ⟨δολίαις τε τέχναις |
ἐμὲ χρηсαμένην οὐκ εὖ μέμφεсθ'·⟩   1525 ἀερθὲν suspectum; fort.
θρεφθὲν   1526 seq. lectio incerta; πολυκλαύτην Porson: -κλαυτόν
τ' codd.   1529 ἔρξεν Spanheim   1530 φροντίδων Tr
1531 εὐπάλαμον Porson: -λαμον codd.; εὐπαλάμων μεριμνᾶν Enger
1532 ὅπη Tr^sscr

δέδοικα δ' ὄμβρου κτύπον δομοσφαλῆ
τὸν αἱματηρόν· ψακὰς δὲ λήγει.
Δίκα δ' ἐπ' ἄλλο πρᾶγμα θήγεται βλάβας   1535
πρὸς ἄλλαις θηγάναισι Μοίρας.

ἰὼ γᾶ γᾶ, εἴθε μ' ἐδέξω
πρὶν τόνδ' ἐπιδεῖν ἀργυροτοίχου
δροίτας κατέχοντα χάμευναν.   1540
τίς ὁ θάψων νιν; τίς ὁ θρηνήσων;
ἦ σὺ τόδ' ἔρξαι τλήσῃ, κτείνας'
ἄνδρα τὸν αὑτῆς ἀποκωκῦσαι
ψυχῇ τ' ἄχαριν χάριν ἀντ' ἔργων   1545
μεγάλων ἀδίκως ἐπικρᾶναι;
τίς δ' ἐπιτύμβιον αἶνον ἐπ' ἀνδρὶ θείῳ
σὺν δακρύοις ἰάπτων
ἀληθείᾳ φρενῶν πονήσει;   1550

Κλ.   οὐ σὲ προσήκει τὸ μέλημ' ἀλέγειν
        τοῦτο· πρὸς ἡμῶν
        κάππεσε κάτθανε, καὶ καταθάψομεν,
        οὐχ ὑπὸ κλαυθμῶν τῶν ἐξ οἴκων,
        ἀλλ' Ἰφιγένειά νιν ἀσπασίως   1555
        θυγάτηρ, ὡς χρή,
        πατέρ' ἀντιάσασα πρὸς ὠκύπορον
        πόρθμευμ' ἀχέων
        περὶ χεῖρα βαλοῦσα φιλήσει.

Χο.   ὄνειδος ἥκει τόδ' ἀντ' ὀνείδους,   [ἀντ. δ

1533 δημοσφ- G   1534 ψεκὰς codd.   1535 seq. fort. potius
δίκαν (Auratus) . . . θηγάνει (Hermann) . . . Μοῖρα   Δίκα G: δίκαι Tr,
δίκη FG^{sscr}Tr^{sscr}   θήγεται Pauw: θήγει codd.   βλάβης codd.   θηγάναις
codd.   Μοίρας Emperius: μοῖρα codd.   1537 εἴθ' ἔμ' FG
1539 ἐςιδεῖν Pauw   1540 δροίτης edd. plurimi   νῦν κατέχ- Tr
1541 νιν θάψων Diggle   1545 ψυχῇ τ' E. A. I. Ahrens: ψυχὴν codd.
1547 ἐπιτύμβιον αἶνον Casaubon: -ιος αἶνος codd.   1551 οὔ σε FG:
οὔτε Tr   μέλημα λέγειν codd.   1555 Ἰφιγένειά νιν Auratus: -ειαν
ἵν' codd.   1559 χεῖρε Porson   φιλήσει Stanley: -ση codd.

δύϲμαχα δ' ἐϲτὶ κρῖναι.　　　　　　　　　1561
φέρει φέροντ', ἐκτίνει δ' ὁ καίνων·
μίμνει δὲ μίμνοντοϲ ἐν θρόνωι Διὸϲ
παθεῖν τὸν ἔρξαντα· θέϲμιον γάρ.
τίϲ ἂν γονὰν ἀραῖον ἐκβάλοι δόμων;　　1565
κεκόλληται γένοϲ πρὸϲ ἄται.

Κλ.　　　ἐϲ τόνδ' ἐνέβηϲ ξὺν ἀληθείαι
　　　　χρηϲμόν· ἐγὼ δ' οὖν
　　　　ἐθέλω δαίμονι τῶι Πλειϲθενιδᾶν
　　　　ὅρκουϲ θεμένη τάδε μὲν ϲτέργειν　　1570
　　　　δύϲτλητά περ ὄνθ', ὃ δὲ λοιπόν, ἰόντ'
　　　　ἐκ τῶνδε δόμων ἄλλην γενεὰν
　　　　τρίβειν θανάτοιϲ αὐθένταιϲιν·
　　　　κτεάνων δὲ μέροϲ βαιὸν ἐχούϲηι
　　　　πᾶν ἀπόχρη μοι, μανίαϲ μελάθρων　　1575
　　　　ἀλληλοφόνουϲ ἀφελούϲηι.

ΑΙΓΙϹΘΟϹ
　　　　ὦ φέγγοϲ εὖφρον ἡμέραϲ δικηφόρου·
　　　　φαίην ἂν ἤδη νῦν βροτῶν τιμαόρουϲ
　　　　θεοὺϲ ἄνωθεν γῆϲ ἐποπτεύειν ἄχη,
　　　　ἰδὼν ὑφαντοῖϲ ἐν πέπλοιϲ Ἐρινύων　　1580
　　　　τὸν ἄνδρα τόνδε κείμενον φίλωϲ ἐμοί,
　　　　χερὸϲ πατρώιαϲ ἐκτίνοντα μηχανάϲ.
　　　　Ἀτρεὺϲ γὰρ ἄρχων τῆϲδε γῆϲ, τούτου πατήρ,
　　　　πατέρα Θυέϲτην τὸν ἐμόν, ὡϲ τορῶϲ φράϲαι,
　　　　αὐτοῦ δ' ἀδελφόν, ἀμφίλεκτοϲ ὢν κράτει,　　1585
　　　　ἠνδρηλάτηϲεν ἐκ πόλεώϲ τε καὶ δόμων·

1563 θρόνωι Schütz: χρόνωι codd.　　　1565 ἀραῖον Hermann:
ῥᾶον (ῥᾷ- Tr) codd.　　　　　1566 πρὸϲ ἄται Blomfield: προϲάψαι codd.
1567 ἐνέβηϲ Canter: -βη codd.　　　ϲὺν G　　　1568 χρηϲμόϲ, retento
ἐνέβη, Casaubon　　　1569 -θενιδῶν Tr^sscr　　　1570 θεμένα Tr (sscr. η)
1571 δύϲπλητά F　　　1573 om. Tr　　　1574 δὲ Auratus: τε codd.
1575 seq. μοι δ' ἀλληλοφόνουϲ μαν. μελ. ἀφελ. codd.; δ' del. Canter,
ἀλληλ. post μελ. traiecit Erfurdt　　　1582 χειρὸϲ Tr　　　1585 δ'
Elmsley: τ' codd.

καὶ προστρόπαιος ἑστίας μολὼν πάλιν
τλήμων Θυέστης μοῖραν ηὗρετ' ἀσφαλῆ,
τὸ μὴ θανὼν πατρῷον αἱμάξαι πέδον
αὐτοῦ· ξένια δὲ τοῦδε δύσθεος πατὴρ   1590
Ἀτρεύς, προθύμως μᾶλλον ἢ φίλως, πατρὶ
τὠμῷι, κρεουργὸν ἦμαρ εὐθύμως ἄγειν
δοκῶν, παρέσχε δαῖτα παιδείων κρεῶν.
τὰ μὲν ποδήρη καὶ χερῶν ἄκρους κτένας
†ἔθρυπτ' ἄνωθεν ἀνδρακὰς καθήμενος   1595
ἄσημα δ'† αὐτῶν αὐτίκ' ἀγνοίαι λαβὼν
ἔσθει, βορὰν ἄσωτον, ὡς ὁρᾷς, γένει.
κἄπειτ' ἐπιγνοὺς ἔργον οὐ καταίσιον
ᾤμωξεν, ἀμπίπτει δ' ἀπὸ σφαγὴν ἐρῶν,
μόρον δ' ἄφερτον Πελοπίδαις ἐπεύχεται   1600
λάκτισμα δείπνου ξυνδίκως τιθεὶς ἀρᾶι,
οὕτως ὀλέσθαι πᾶν τὸ Πλεισθένους γένος.
ἐκ τῶνδέ σοι πεσόντα τόνδ' ἰδεῖν πάρα·
κἀγὼ δίκαιος τοῦδε τοῦ φόνου ῥαφεύς·
τρίτον γὰρ ὄντα μ' †ἐπὶ δέκ'† ἀθλίωι πατρὶ   1605
συνεξελαύνει τυτθὸν ὄντ' ἐν σπαργάνοις,
τραφέντα δ' αὖθις ἡ Δίκη κατήγαγεν,
καὶ τοῦδε τἀνδρὸς ἡψάμην θυραῖος ὤν,
πᾶσαν ξυνάψας μηχανὴν δυσβουλίας.
οὕτω καλὸν δὴ καὶ τὸ κατθανεῖν ἐμοί,   1610
ἰδόντα τοῦτον τῆς Δίκης ἐν ἕρκεσιν.

Χο.   Αἴγισθ', ὑβρίζοντ' ἐν κακοῖσιν οὐ σέβω·
σὺ δ' ἄνδρα τόνδε φὴις ἑκὼν κατακτανεῖν,
μόνος δ' ἔποικτον τόνδε βουλεῦσαι φόνον·
οὔ φημ' ἀλύξειν ἐν δίκηι τὸ σὸν κάρα   1615

1590 αὐτός· Blomfield   ξενίαι Tr   1594 χρεῶν F   1595 seq.
fort. ἔκρυπτ' (Casaubon) ἄπωθεν (Fuhr) ἀνδρακὰς καθημένους
(Lawson) / ἄσημ'· ὁ δ' αὐτῶν (Dindorf); lacunas alii alias indicant
1599 ἀμπίπτει Canter: ἄν· πίπτει codd.   σφαγὴν Auratus: -ῆς
codd.   1602 ὀλέσθαι Tzetz. ap. An. Ox. Cramer 3. 378. 10: -θη
codd.   1605 ὄντα παῖδά μ' ἀθλίωι Herwerden   1609 συνάψας FG
1611 ἰδόντι Tr   1612 ὑβρίζοντ' Heyse: -ζειν codd.   1613 τόνδ
ἔφης codd.   1614 μόνος τ' Blaydes

δημορριφεῖc, cάφ' ἴcθι, λευcίμουc ἀράc.

Αι.   cὺ ταῦτα φωνεῖc, νερτέραι προcήμενοc
κώπηι, κρατούντων τῶν ἐπὶ ζυγῶι δορόc;
γνώcηι γέρων ὢν ὡc διδάcκεcθαι βαρὺ
τῶι τηλικούτωι, cωφρονεῖν εἰρημένον·   1620
δεcμὸν δὲ καὶ τὸ γῆραc αἵ τε νήcτιδεc
δύαι διδάcκειν ἐξοχώταται φρενῶν
ἰατρομάντειc. οὐχ ὁρᾶιc ὁρῶν τάδε;
πρὸc κέντρα μὴ λάκτιζε, μὴ παίcαc μογῆιc.

Χο.   γύναι, cὺ τοὺc ἥκονταc ἐκ μάχηc μένων   1625
οἰκουρὸc εὐνὴν ἀνδρὸc αἰcχύνων ἅμα
ἀνδρὶ cτρατηγῶι τόνδ' ἐβούλευcαc μόρον;

Αι.   καὶ ταῦτα τἄπη κλαυμάτων ἀρχηγενῆ·
Ὀρφεῖ δὲ γλῶccαν τὴν ἐναντίαν ἔχειc·
ὁ μὲν γὰρ ἦγε πάντ' ἀπὸ φθογγῆc χαρᾶι,   1630
cὺ δ' ἐξορίναc νηπίοιc ὑλάγμαcιν
ἄξηι· κρατηθεὶc δ' ἡμερώτεροc φανῆι.

Χο.   ὡc δὴ cύ μοι τύραννοc Ἀργείων ἔcηι,
ὃc οὐκ, ἐπειδὴ τῶιδ' ἐβούλευcαc μόρον,
δρᾶcαι τόδ' ἔργον οὐκ ἔτληc αὐτοκτόνωc.   1635

Αι.   τὸ γὰρ δολῶcαι πρὸc γυναικὸc ἦν cαφῶc,
ἐγὼ δ' ὕποπτοc ἐχθρὸc ἦ παλαιγενήc.
ἐκ τῶν δὲ τοῦδε χρημάτων πειράcομαι
ἄρχειν πολιτῶν· τὸν δὲ μὴ πειθάνορα
ζεύξω βαρείαιc, οὔ τι μὴ cειραφόρον   1640
κριθῶντα πῶλον, ἀλλ' ὁ δυcφιλὴc cκότωι
λιμὸc ξύνοικοc μαλθακόν cφ' ἐπόψεται.

Χο.   τί δὴ τὸν ἄνδρα τόνδ' ἀπὸ ψυχῆc κακῆc
οὐκ αὐτὸc ἠνάριζεc, ἀλλὰ cὺν γυνή,
χώραc μίαcμα καὶ θεῶν ἐγχωρίων,   1645

1621 δεcμὸν FG: -μὸc Tr; -μοὶ Karsten   1624 παίcαc schol.
Pind. *Pyth*. 2. 173^c: πήcαc codd.   1625 μένων Wieseler: νέον codd.
1626 αἰcχύνων Keck: -νουc' codd.; αἰcχύναc Butler   1630 ἀπὸ: ὑπὸ
Margoliouth   1631 νηπίοιc Iacob: ἠπ- codd.   1634 τῶιδε
βουλεύcαc FG   1635 τό γ' Lobel   1640 οὔ τι μὴν Wieseler
1641 cκότωι Auratus: κότωι codd.   1642 cύν- G   1644 ἀλλά
νιν Spanheim

ΑΓΑΜΕΜΝΩΝ 61

ἔκτειν'· Ὀρέστης ἀρά που βλέπει φάος,
ὅπως κατελθὼν δεῦρο πρευμενεῖ τύχηι
ἀμφοῖν γένηται τοῖνδε παγκρατὴς φονεύς.

Αι. ἀλλ' ἐπεὶ δοκεῖς τάδ' ἔρδειν καὶ λέγειν, γνώσηι τάχα.
Χο. εἶα δή, φίλοι λοχῖται, τοὖργον οὐχ ἑκὰς τόδε. 1650
Αι. εἶα δή, ξίφος πρόκωπον πᾶς τις εὐτρεπιζέτω.
Χο. ἀλλὰ κἀγὼ μὴν †πρόκωπος† οὐκ ἀναίνομαι θανεῖν.
Αι. δεχομένοις λέγεις θανεῖν γε, τὴν τύχην δ' αἱρούμεθα.
Κλ. μηδαμῶς, ὦ φίλτατ' ἀνδρῶν, ἄλλα δράσωμεν κακά·
     ἀλλὰ καὶ τάδ' ἐξαμῆσαι πολλά, δύστηνον θέρος. 1655
     πημονῆς δ' ἅλις γ' ὑπάρχει· μηδὲν αἱματώμεθα.
     †στείχετε δ' οἱ γέροντες πρὸς δόμους πεπρωμένους τούσδε†
     πρὶν παθεῖν ἔρξαντα †καιρὸν χρὴν† τάδ' ὡς ἐπράξαμεν.
     εἰ δέ τοι μόχθων γένοιτο τῶνδ' †ἅλις γ' ἐχοίμεθ' ἄν†
     δαίμονος χηλῆι βαρείαι δυστυχῶς πεπληγμένοι. 1660
     ὧδ' ἔχει λόγος γυναικός, εἴ τις ἀξιοῖ μαθεῖν.
Αι. ἀλλὰ τούσδ' ἐμοὶ ματαίαν γλῶσσαν ὧδ' †ἀπανθίσαι†
     κἀκβαλεῖν ἔπη τοιαῦτα δαίμονος πειρωμένους,
     σώφρονος γνώμης δ' ἀμαρτεῖν τὸν κρατοῦντα ⟨   ⟩.
Χο. οὐκ ἂν Ἀργείων τόδ' εἴη, φῶτα προσσαίνειν κακόν. 1665
Αι. ἀλλ' ἐγώ σ' ἐν ὑστέραισιν ἡμέραις μέτειμ' ἔτι.
Χο. οὔκ, ἐὰν δαίμων Ὀρέστην δεῦρ' ἀπευθύνηι μολεῖν.

1650 Aegistho tribuit Stanley 1651 Aegistho tribuit Fᵃᶜ, choro
FᵖᶜG, nota nulla in Tr 1652 Aegistho tribuunt codd. μὴν
κἀγὼ Porson πρόκωπος Gᵖᶜ: πρόκοπος FGᵃᶜ, πρόκοπτος Tr; πρόχειρος
Thomson οὐδ' Lobel, κοὐκ Fraenkel 1653 choro tribuunt
codd. γε Lobel: σε codd. αἱρούμεθα Auratus: ἐρούμ- codd.
1654 δράσωμεν Victorius: -σομεν codd. 1655 θέρος Schütz: ὁ ἔρως
codd. 1656 ὑπάρχει Scaliger: ὕπαρχε codd. αἱματ- Iacob: ἡματ-
codd. 1657 seq. desperati; e.g. στείχετ' ὦ (Heath) γέροντες ἤδη
(Porson) πρὸς δόμους· κρεῖσσον φρονεῖν (Fraenkel) / πρὶν παθεῖν ἔρ-
ξαντα· κυροῦν (Page) χρὴ (Hartung) κτλ. ἔρξαντες F ἐπράξαμεν Victorius: -μην codd. 1659 τῶνδε λύσις, ἐλοίμεθ' ἄν Blaydes, τῶνδ'
ἄκος Donaldson, δεχοίμεθ' ἄν Hermann 1660 πεπληγμένοις G
1662 τούσδε μοι codd. ἀκοντίσαι Wakefield 1663 δαίμονος
Casaubon: -νας codd. πειρωμένη G 1664 γνώμης θ' Stanley
ἁμαρτεῖν τὸν Casaubon: ἁμαρτῆτον codd. ⟨θ' ὑβρίσαι⟩ suppl. Blomfield
1666 Clyt. tribuit F 1667 δαίμων γ' Headlam

Αι.   οἶδ' ἐγὼ φεύγοντας ἄνδρας ἐλπίδας cιτουμένουc.
Χο.   πρᾶccε, πιαίνου, μιαίνων τὴν δίκην, ἐπεὶ πάρα.
Αι.   ἴcθι μοι δώcων ἄποινα τῆcδε μωρίας χάριν.   1670
Χο.   κόμπαcον θαρcῶν, ἀλέκτωρ ὥcτε θηλείαc πέλαc.
Κλ.   μὴ προτιμήcηιc ματαίων τῶνδ' ὑλαγμάτων· ⟨ἐγὼ⟩
      καὶ cὺ θήcομεν κρατοῦντε τῶνδε δωμάτων ⟨καλῶc⟩.

1671 θαρρῶν codd.   ὥcτε Canter: ὥcπερ codd.   1672 seq.
suppl. Canter et Auratus e schol. vet. Tr (ἐγώ, φηcί, καὶ cὺ κρατοῦντεc
τῶνδε τῶν δωμάτων διαθηcόμεθα τὸ καθ' αὑτοὺc καλῶc)

Commentary

Commentary

Prologue (1–39): The Watchman sights the beacon which brings Clytemnestra news of Troy's capture and so of Agamemnon's imminent homecoming. For the symbolic significance of the beacon-signal, see 1 n. The character corresponds to the spy posted by Aegisthus in *Od.* 4. 524–7 to warn him of Agamemnon's arrival. However, in Aeschylus he is under Clytemnestra's control (10–11) but loyal to Agamemnon (19, 34–5; see Intro. § 3). Although the news is joyful, the Watchman's speech establishes the atmosphere of deep foreboding which dominates the whole long build-up to Agamemnon's entrance, and also the conflict between words of good and bad omen (Intro. § 6). The sequences of thought and utterance in 16–21 and 31–9 are paradigmatic. The Watchman tries to dispel his fear by singing or humming, but in spite of himself he is drawn to lamenting the house's troubles; he can only pray, against the odds, for a positive outcome. When the signal does arrive, his initial joy soon cedes to anxieties which he dare not express openly. We will repeatedly see characters being led from encouraging words to pessimistic thoughts which they are wary of expressing, and which they often replace by a bland wish for the good.

The actor playing the Watchman probably (*pace* Metzger 2005) delivered his speech from atop the recently or newly introduced stage-building (Taplin 1977, 452–9). This may well have been an innovative and striking piece of staging. The Watchman has spent his watch lying prone, punctuated with moments of pacing about. In our view he stands to speak; Sommerstein (2010, 155) and others have suggested that he is still lying down, nearly invisible to the front rows, until verse 22.

1. The trilogy begins (as do *Cho.* and *Eum.*) in the language of prayer. This at once establishes the importance of the gods and—since the Watchman's prayer is soon answered—of the supernatural background that enables human language to affect the future.

μέν: the particle has no corresponding δέ, as often in the opening line of a speech. *τῶνδ' ἀπαλλαγὴν πόνων*: 'release from these toils', i.e. his wearisome vigil. The phrase may also have had a much broader connotation for Aeschylus' audience. Bowie (1993), 24 points out that it was used for the Eleusinian Mysteries' promise of a happy afterlife, and indeed the symbolism of torchlight blazing out from darkness featured at the climax of the Mysteries. The words gain prominence when they are repeated in ring-composition at 20, just before the beacon appears. However, in that line the reference has broadened to include the toils of the house of Atreus; see also *Eum.* 83 (Apollo to Orestes) ὥστ' ἐς τὸ πᾶν σε τῶνδ' ἀπαλλάξαι πόνων. The phrase in its three occurrences may therefore suggest a further type of 'release'—one from the cycles of retribution which the house and humanity as a whole will attain over the course of the trilogy (Intro. § 4.4).

2. φρουρᾶς ἐτείας μῆκος: φρουρᾶς is in apposition to πόνων. μῆκος is accusative of respect with ἐτείας: literally 'lasting a year in length'. **ἣν κοιμώμενος**: '[the watch], lying down through which'. ἥν is an internal accusative: the state of lying down constitutes the watch. κοιμάομαι evidently does not have its most common meaning 'lie down to sleep'.

3. στέγαις Ἀτρειδῶν: 'at the palace of the Atridae' (local dative). Plural στέγαι means 'dwelling', not 'roof'. The words set the scene for the audience. **ἄγκαθεν, κυνὸς δίκην**: 'on my elbows, like a dog'. δίκην plus genitive, 'like', occurs with unusual frequency in *Agamemnon*, perhaps as a subliminal reinforcement of the central theme of δίκη (Wilson 2006). ἄγκαθεν only recurs elsewhere at *Eum.* 80, where Orestes is instructed to embrace the image of Athena 'in his bent arms'; cf. ἀγκών, 'bend, esp. elbow', ἀγκάς 'in one's arms'. Here 'like a dog' amplifies that word and the Watchman's general situation: he has been lying on the roof (where the house-dog might well lie), probably belly-down and propped up on his elbows so that he can look for the beacon on the horizon. For dogs in the play, see Introduction § 9.2.

4–6. The Watchman has become familiar with the stars, which themselves indicate the passage of time which he feels so heavily. The ἄστρα (ordinary stars) are metaphorically viewed in a sweeping glance as a ὁμήγυρις, 'public assembly'. This opposes the 'bright potentates, conspicuous in the sky, which bring mortals winter and summer', i.e. constellations such as the Pleiades whose movements mark the seasons. The societal metaphor may suggest not only the Watchman's isolation from real human society, but also the play's audience, a ὁμήγυρις with officials conspicuous in the front row.

7. The text is uncertain. The OCT means literally 'I know the dynasts ... the major stars [ἀστέρας], whenever they set [φθίνωσιν] and at their risings.' τῶν is demonstrative, 'of them': compare e.g. 158 τοῖς, *Eum.* 137 τῶι. However, there is a metrical problem: Aeschylus and Sophocles seem only to allow a dactylic word at the beginning of a trimeter if it is a proper name. West assumes that ἀστέρας was a gloss on 6 δυνάστας which intruded, and suggests replacing it with a participle (e.g. Campbell's τηρῶν, 'as I watch') which can govern both a temporal clause and the manuscripts' accusative ἀντολάς. Thus perhaps: 'as I watch whenever they set, and their risings'. If the stars are an image of human society (4–6 n.), its dynasts such as Agamemnon likewise rise and set as regularly and ineluctably as stars (cf. 27–9 n.).

8–10. As the Watchman has been looking at the stars, so too now (καὶ νῦν) he is looking out for the beacon. The parallelism is pointed by φέρουσαν echoing 5 φέροντας. However, where nature's lights bring seasons, the man-made 'signal of a torch' brings a kind of speech (φάτιν) from Troy, subsequently redefined (by way of τε: Denniston 502) as a ἁλώσιμον βάξιν, 'report relating to capture', cf. 21 εὐαγγέλου ... πυρός, 23 φάος πιφαύσκων, 475–82, 589 φράζων, and see Goldhill (1984a), 8–12.

10–11. ὧδε γὰρ ... κέαρ: γυναικός is possessive, and κρατεῖ is absolute, 'exercises power'. The words establish a crucial aspect of Clytemnestra's characterization and Aeschylus lends v. 11 emphasis by composing it in just four weighty words. The idea of a woman with κράτος and the juxtaposition γυναικὸς ἀνδρο- emphasize that Clytemnestra's position in Argos conflicts with normal Greek gender-roles. Though a woman, she has a 'male-counselling heart', i.e. the kind of initiative which Greeks normally associated with men (see Intro. § 4.5). ἐλπίζον 'expectant' is reticently ambiguous: superficially, Clytemnestra sounds loyally optimistic, but the audience knows her real hopes for Agamemnon's return.

12–13. εὖτ᾽ ἂν δὲ ... εὐνήν: the Watchman's 'bed' (i.e. the floor where he is lying) is dew-sodden and paradoxically 'involves wandering in the night'. Because of the damp, he restlessly paces to and fro and shifts the spot where he lies.

13–15. ἐπισκοπουμένην and παραστατεῖ carry the medical connotations of visiting and attending the bed of a patient. The Watchman complains that *his* bed is not visited by comforting dreams: ἐμήν is emphatically positioned, with hyperbaton (i.e. it is markedly removed from the word with which it goes syntactically). Rather, he is kept awake by fear. He does not explain this, but the possibility that it is fear for Agamemnon's future sounds a first note of foreboding. For the recurring metaphor of sickness, see e.g. Fowler (1967), 40–4, 61–2, 72–3.

In 15, τὸ μή + infinitive expresses 'so that . . . not' after verbs such as 'prevent', 'avoid': Smyth § 2744.

16. ὅταν δ': 'Well, whenever . . .'. After the parenthesis in 14–15, the Watchman starts afresh with a new 'whenever' clause. This is a common form of anacoluthon. **δοκῶ:** 'I think to', which is usually δοκεῖ μοι.

17. The medical imagery from 13–14 continues. ἐντέμνων is 'tapping into a root to extract medicinal sap' (cf. LSJ supplement s.v.). His singing or humming flows slowly and smoothly as a 'remedy in the form of song', like a healing incantation.

ὕπνου, however, is difficult. It implies that the Watchman is singing to stave off sleep. This would be reasonable except that he has just said that he cannot sleep anyway, from fear (14). In fact, in the papyrus this line seems to have begun with τόδ' ἀντίμολπον. ὕπνου could then have intruded from a marginal comment (perhaps already based on misinterpretation), and displaced a word which followed ἀντίμολπον. (For example, τόδ' ἀντίμολπον <αὐτὸς> ἐντέμνων ἄκος, 'myself tapping into this song-remedy' might be appropriate: the Watchman becomes his own metaphorical doctor, and not just the patient.) The remedy would be for the fear he has just mentioned; as an apotropaic song, it can be characterized using the markedly ritual stem of μολπή. He sings to cheer himself up, but (18–19) is constantly driven back to pessimism. Lines 16–19 would then establish the pattern, repeated in the parodos, first stasimon, and second episode, of encouraging utterances which lead on to a discouraging conclusion (Intro. § 6).

19–21. Line 19 is a sinister one of deliberate understatement, which shows the Watchman's compunction in defining the situation explicitly. The household is 'not tended very well as in the past'. For the grammar of τὰ πρόσθε, compare τὸ πρίν (LSJ πρίν A II 2). The audience knows that the Watchman is referring darkly to Clytemnestra's adultery with Aegisthus, but it would be ill-omened to articulate the fact. The use of δια-πονέω perhaps suggests a link with v. 1: Agamemnon used to expend πόνοι on the household, whereas Clytemnestra is causing them πόνοι. In any case, when the

Watchman returns in v. 20 to a prayer about ἀπαλλαγὴ πόνων (see 1 n.), he expresses the hope that Agamemnon will return to sort out the house's troubles, as well as bringing an end to his personal chore. This prayer tries to counteract his allusion to the house's troubles with words of good omen (predicative εὐτυχής and εὐαγγέλου).

Line 21 is a genitive absolute: 'when the fire of the darkness appears with good news'. The sequence φανέντος ὀρφναίου πυρός elegantly emphasizes the symbolic contrast between light and darkness.

These lines are followed by a substantial pause, until the Watchman sights the beacon.

22–4. In 22 we prefer the punctuation ὦ χαῖρε λαμπτήρ, νυκτὸς ἡμερήσιον | φάος . . . , and thus the juxtaposition 'day-like light in the night'. φάος, as well as 'light', often metaphorically means 'relief' (cf. 20 ἀπαλλαγή). For this meaning, and the juxtaposition, cf. 522 φῶς ἐν εὐφρόνηι φέρων. πιφαύσκω is strictly 'bring to light', and cognate with φάος, but it generally means 'speak'; it is therefore the perfect verb to continue the metaphor from 9–10 of the light 'speaking', i.e. bringing an articulate message. In particular the fire-signal foretells 'the organization of many choral performances', which were a typical way to thank the gods for success. ἐν Ἄργει: Aeschylus locates Agamemnon in Argos, rather than in Mycenae (as in Homer) or Sparta: see Introduction § 2. τῆσδε συμφορᾶς χάριν: 'as thanks for this stroke of fortune'. But συμφορά has been used in 18 in its more common negative sense, and the audience may well think of how the beacon's arrival will eventually lead to Agamemnon's 'calamity'.

25. ἰοὺ ἰού: cries of joy (or sorrow or pain) often stand outside the metre in tragedy.

26. Ἀγαμέμνονος γυναικί: the Watchman no longer refers to Clytemnestra as a ruler herself (as in 10), but more traditionally via her husband. Aegisthus is not mentioned, although the bed which he shares with Clytemnestra is (27). The Watchman displays his hopes for a restoration of the old order. σημαίνω τορῶς: the emphasis impresses on the audience the recurrent questions in *Agamemnon* about the clarity of signs (see Intro. § 6).

27–9. εὐνῆς ἐπαντείλασαν . . . ἐπορθιάζειν: 'to rise from bed and as soon as possible to raise for [or possibly 'in'] the house an *ololygmos* of good omen at the occasion of this torch'. εὐνῆς is a genitive expressing separation. The participle ἐπαντείλασαν is accusative even though its referent has appeared in the dative (γυναικί), as quite often happens: see 342 n., Smyth § 1062. The verb links Clytemnestra's motion with the ἀντολαί of the potentate-stars in 6–7: her star is in the ascendant, but will not be so forever. τῆιδε λαμπάδι is governed by the ἐπ- in ἐπορθιάζειν.

The ὀλολυγμός is a ritual cry of thanksgiving performed by women, whose appearances in *Agamemnon* and *Choephoroe* are problematic responses to internecine murder or plans thereof (cf. 587 and 595, 1118, *Cho.* 387, 942; it is important that a positive *ololygmos* occurs in the last line of *Eumenides*). Already here the phrase ὀλολυγμὸν εὐφημοῦντα prompts us to consider why Clytemnestra is giving thanks, and whom her *euphēmia* will benefit. (This is the first explicit occurrence of the important idea of *euphēmia* in the trilogy.)

29. εἴπερ: 'since', rather than the more sceptical 'if in fact'.

30. ἀγγέλλων πρέπει: 'conspicuously announces'; compare φαίνομαι + participle.

31. The capture of Troy is to be celebrated by choruses (23) and the Watchman personally will dance a φροίμιον, a hymnic prelude addressed to the gods. He is not thinking that he will be involved in a formal ritual, nor is it likely that he performs a little jig now onstage. Rather, he will privately dance for joy before the ensuing public dances of thanksgiving.

32–3. The Watchman's motivation is explained in a metaphor from πεσσοί, a game in which counters were moved round a board in accordance with the throws of three dice. Line 32 means 'For I shall make my move in accordance with the happy fall of my master's affairs'. δεσποτῶν is plural for singular; τίθημι is used in a technical gaming sense. The metaphor by which Agamemnon's affairs have 'fallen well', like dice, is apt since they were beyond the Watchman's control and determine his future behaviour. In 33 he shifts his metaphor slightly. It is his present activity (φρυκτωρία, 'beacon-watching') which 'threw' the dice, in that it has enjoyed good fortune, and is the immediate cause of his ἀπαλλαγὴ πόνων.

34–35. δ' οὖν is 'Well, at any rate' (Denniston 461–2), and marks an ellipse of a thought which the Watchman is reluctant to utter (cf. 19–21 n.): dangers await Agamemnon at his return. All that his servant can do is pray: 'may it come about (for me) to grasp the dear hand of the palace's master when he arrives'. δ' οὖν recurs in several passages of *Ag.* where a disastrous alternative is euphemistically left unexpressed: see 255, 676, 1568.

36–9. The Watchman clams up, with a sudden change of style to short clauses which cross line-breaks. 'A great ox is standing on my tongue' was a proverbial expression for 'keeping mum'; the image of a key on the tongue is also found, associated with the secrecy of the Eleusinian Mysteries (e.g. Sophocles *OC* 1050–3 'rites whose golden key is standing on the tongue of the Eumolpid attendants'). Compare 1 n. for the implication that the story of the Atreid house is a kind of 'initiation' for the audience.

Lines 37–8 then refer guardedly to the brooding presence of the οἶκος with its sinister secrets (cf. 18) which, of course, it cannot express. Finally the Watchman explains his own euphemistic guardedness, with a further resonance to the Mysteries: 'For *I* choose to speak to those who know [(τοῖς) μαθοῦσιν] and to forget to those who do not know'. ἑκών qualifies both verbs. The initiated will understand his hints about the house's secrets; he is careful that the uninitiated will not. Aeschylus' audience, who would have been familiar with the outline of Agamemnon's story, are among the initiated. Aeschylus' character does not exactly address them, which would contravene tragic convention, but his words indirectly draw the spectators more closely into the ritualized enactment of Agamemnon's return and murder.

Parodos (40–257): This is the longest choral movement in extant Greek tragedy. The main divisions can be summarized as follows; for the metrical scheme, see Appendix § 5.

40–82: The Chorus of twelve old men with staves (75) enters slowly along an *eisodos* supposed to lead to the rest of Argos, and processes round the *orchēstra*. It declaims anapaests which first describe the mission of the Atridae to Troy as a just cause backed by Zeus, engendering casualties but moving to a fated conclusion; the men then introduce themselves as too old to have joined the expedition.

83–103: Still in anapaests, they address Clytemnestra *in absentia* (see further ad loc.), and explain that they have come to find out why there are sacrifices of all kinds throughout Argos, and whether their wavering optimism is justified.

104–59: After Clytemnestra fails to appear, the Chorus moves into song and returns to its narrative. It recounts an omen of two eagles devouring a pregnant hare, which appeared—probably at Aulis

(116 n.)—as the expedition set out. It quotes Calchas' interpretation: the Atridae will defeat Troy and its inhabitants; however, Artemis may be angry at the young animals' deaths, block the ships, and require a horrendous sacrifice in compensation; Calchas ends by envisaging a child-avenging Wrath waiting in a house.

160–257: The Chorus, seeking to make sense of its narrative, invokes Zeus since he laid down the rule πάθει μάθος, that from suffering comes learning. In the middle of the second pair of strophes, this invocation dovetails back into the story of Agamemnon, the winds which delayed the expedition at Aulis, and the decision to sacrifice Iphigenia. The Chorus ends by wishing for a positive future outcome.

This sequence is not a static narrative of part of the essential background to Agamemnon's return (the cause and course of the Trojan War; Iphigenia's sacrifice). Rather, by repeatedly shifting from confidence to foreboding—as the prologue did (1–39 n.)—the song helps to define the prevailing atmosphere; it also situates the events in the broader perspectives which are so important to Aeschylus' presentation (e.g. the functioning of Zeus and infatuation: Intro. § 4). Finally, its utterances can be seen as a form of dramatic action in their own right, in that they are ill-omened for Agamemnon (see Intro. § 6).

40. δέκατον μὲν ἔτος: another initial μέν without a correlated δέ (see 1 n.); as often, ἐστί must be understood. The opening words suggest that the elders know the prophecy that Troy would fall in the tenth year (as in *Il.* 2. 329), and that this conditions their concern about what the news might be. They articulate their mental state more clearly in their questions to Clytemnestra, at 98–103.

41. ἀντίδικος: legal imagery, as often in this trilogy which has different forms of δίκη as its central theme (Intro. § 4.1). Menelaus, with Agamemnon, is a 'plaintiff' against Priam.

42. ἠδ' Ἀγαμέμνων: the Chorus's first utterance of the king's name is emphasized in the first rhythmical swing from ∪∪ — to — ∪∪ (see Appendix § 3).

43–4. Literally 'the strong yoke-pair formed of the Atridae, consisting of double-throned and double-sceptred honour from Zeus'. Both τιμῆς and Ἀτρειδᾶν (where -ᾶν is the Doric ending of the first declension genitive plural) are genitives defining ζεῦγος. Διόθεν is the first mention of Zeus, the dominant god in the play; here, as often, the king of the gods is the source of royal authority among men. His name is so worked in as to create a striking alliteration of δι-. Menelaus is not, as normal, the king of Sparta, but apparently a joint ruler in Argos: for Aeschylus' focus on Argos see Introduction § 2.

47. ἦραν: 'got under sail' (LSJ ἀείρω I 5) rather than 'levied'. ἀρωγήν: the word has a special legal sense, 'support in a lawsuit': see e.g. *Supp.* 726 ἀρωγοὺς ξυνδίκους θ'. This therefore continues the imagery of 41 ἀντίδικος.

48. 'screaming "Ares!" loudly and from the spirit', i.e. as an angry war-cry. μεγάλ' is adverbial neuter plural, and is Page's emendation based on *Il.* 16. 428–9 where in a simile two vultures fight each other μεγάλα κλάζοντε. The manuscripts' μέγαν is bolder but possible (Fraenkel): the war-cry would not be quoted verbatim but paraphrased by 'great Ares'.

49–59. The metaphor κλάζοντες, which is used particularly of birds, develops into a simile comparing the Atridae to a pair of vultures, which gives our first view of justice as retribution. Aeschylus appears to remodel *Od.* 16. 216–18, where Telemachus has just recognized Odysseus: 'They cried shrilly, and more rapidly than birds—bearded vultures or bent-clawed αἰγυπιοί, whose children hunters have snatched before they were able to fly.' Aeschylus only implies, by the similarity to Paris' abduction of Helen, that his transgressors have stolen the chicks. Whereas the vultures have lost their helpless children, the Atridae have lost Helen, whose willingness to 'fly the nest' they do not doubt. And whereas the birds' cries are laments, which a god appeases by sending a separate Fury, the Atridae are themselves the agents of retribution, and their cries are no longer mournful but belligerent. This bird-image will soon receive a complement in the omen of the eagles (see 104–59 n.).

49–50. τρόπον αἰγυπιῶν: accusative τρόπον + genitive means 'in the manner of'; cf. τίνα τρόπον, 'In what manner?', 3 κυνὸς δίκην. Greek descriptions of αἰγυπιοί cannot be consistently identified with a modern species; they are mostly vultures, but occasionally attack live prey (Thompson 1936, 25–6). οἵτ': ὅσ-τε is rare in tragedy; here it strengthens the link to extended epic similes, where it is common ('generalizing' τε: LSJ s.v. B). ἐκπατίοις ἄλγεσι παίδων: παίδων is an objective genitive, i.e. 'distress for their children'. ἐκπάτιος is literally 'off the beaten track'. Either the adjective is transferred from the vultures' habitat to their distress; or their distress may be metaphorically 'off the track' of sense (cf. 194 ἅλαι with n.). παῖς is normally used of human children. It was perhaps chosen to anticipate a separate strand of retributive justice in the play, namely Clytemnestra's ἄλγος for Iphigenia. ὕπατοι λεχέων: possibly 'very high above their nests', but this usage of ὕπατος + genitive is unparalleled; West obelizes.

51. στροφοδινοῦνται: 'wheel eddying around' (LSJ); for such compounds see Introduction § 9.1.

52. The vultures' wings resemble oars, and conversely *Od.* 11. 125 mentions 'oars that are wings for ships'; the vultures correspond to the Atridae, who command rowers.

53–4. Lit. 'having lost the bed-watching toil over their chicks'. ὀρταλίχων is an objective genitive, like 51 παίδων. ὄλλυμι here means 'lose' not 'destroy' (LSJ s.v. A 2).

55–9. 'Some god on high—either Apollo or Pan or Zeus—hears the lament, shouted shrilly and in bird-cries, of these metics, and sends a late-avenging Erinys for the transgressors', i.e. those who took the chicks. The position of 55 τις is unusual, but the sense must be as above (cf. Soph. *OC* 95). For the idea, compare *Cho.* 382–3 Ζεῦ . . . ἀμπέμπων | ὑστερόποινον ἄταν.

The vultures are 'metics' or 'resident aliens' in the Olympians' domain of the sky. As Athenian metics could bring certain private suits directly before the Athenian polemarch (MacDowell 1978, 76, 221–3), so the birds' complaints are heard directly by the gods who govern their location, and punishment is delivered. Three particular Olympians are specified. Zeus is the supreme guardian of justice, and the supporter of the Atridae in the following sentence. Pan is the god of the vultures' habitat in the wilderness, and of hunting. Apollo's relevance is less obvious. One might think first of his ornithomancy, which involves observing the cries of large birds. Later in the trilogy, however, he becomes more prominent, in Cassandra's scene, then as Orestes' sponsor offstage in *Choephoroe* and onstage in *Eumenides*. In *Eum.*, a case between him and the Erinyes is judged by an Athenian court, and one eventual result is that the Erinyes become metics in Athens (*Eum.* 1011). Thus the differences between the first and last δίκαι of the *Oresteia* are marked by Apollo's appearance here, and the references to metics. Throughout *Ag.*, the chthonian Erinyes are not antagonistic towards the Olympians (as for most of *Eum.*), but are their agents: see Introduction § 4.2.

60–2. As a god sends the Erinys against the chick-hunters, so Zeus sent the Atridae to punish Paris (Alexandros) concerning Helen. Zeus is specifically 'the mightier one, Zeus of guest-friendship', since Paris had abused Menelaus' hospitality. πέμπει is a historic present. For the sense in which Zeus 'sends' them, see Introduction § 4.3.1 on divine determination.

Helen is described in uncomplimentary terms as a 'woman of many men'. The Chorus present Helen as a destructive force also at 403–8, 680–749, 1455–60.

63–7. In a few vivid phrases the hardships of war are summarized. Zeus' purpose in sending the Atridae, expressed with the future participle, is 'to lay down many and limb-wearying wrestling-bouts for the Greeks and Trojans equally'; the retribution harms both sides. From γόνατος to κάμακος come two genitive absolutes, neatly balanced with chiasmus; the first continues the image of wrestling from 63.

προτέλεια 'preliminary ritual' seems to have referred particularly to the sacrifice before a marriage-rite, which is not directly pertinent here since the war *follows* Paris' marriage to Helen (699–708). The word is probably chosen to suggest that both the τέλος of the war—the sack of Troy—and its preceding phase are sacrificial rituals. Perhaps too, on a different level, it is relevant that Aeschylus presents the whole Trojan War as an essential preliminary to the actions which are being ritually enacted for the Athenian audience.

67–71. The OCT means 'Those things are where they now are, and are moving to their fated end. Neither by lighting a fire underneath [i.e. by a burnt offering] nor by pouring libations from unburnt sacrifices [e.g. wine, milk] will someone charm cases of stubborn anger [i.e. in the gods].' ἱερῶν is a partitive genitive. The subject of παραθέλξει is probably τις (understood) rather than Paris, who has not been mentioned since 61. Although the Chorus is thinking primarily of the Trojans trying to win back Zeus, it expresses itself generally, and thereby sounds a more foreboding note about the ability of human beings to control their future, which will be pertinent to Agamemnon and Clytemnestra too.

The above text, however, rests on questionable emendations (see app. crit.). The manuscripts' ὑποκλαίων must be changed to ὑποκαίων, and δακρύων immediately below was probably a gloss on ὑποκλαίων, and therefore wrong. But whereas Page simply omits οὔτε δακρύων, it may have intruded on some other words. One might read οὔθ᾽ ὑποκαίων οὔθ᾽ ὑπολείβων | οὔτε <τραπέζαις> ἀπύρων ἱερῶν. This allows ἄπυρα ἱερά to have its normal sense of solid offerings such as fruit and cakes which were placed on offering-tables rather than being burnt on the altar (LSJ ἄπυρος I 5). The manuscripts' ὑπολείβων may be retained. At least in fifth-century Sicily, it meant 'pour a libation underground', for ancestor-spirits, and probably through a pipe (Jameson, Jordan, and Kotansky 1993, 30–1). Here such libation might aim to assuage an Erinys' anger. We suggest therefore that the overall meaning is that the spirits of retribution are not to be assuaged by any of the standard forms of offering: burnt sacrifice, libations, or unburnt sacrifice.

72–82. The Chorus introduces its own infirmity in contrast to the young soldiers. This infirmity becomes important for the plot when it motivates the Chorus's powerlessness at Agamemnon's murder and against Aegisthus' guards in the exodos.

72. ἀτίται: the meaning may be 'dishonoured' (from τίω) or 'not involved in vengeance' (from τίνω). We favour the latter. τίτᾱς means 'avenging' at *Cho.* 67; ἀτίτᾱς is 'unavenged' or 'not paying' at *Eum.* 256. **σαρκὶ παλαιᾶι:** dative expressing cause (Smyth § 1517).

73. τῆς τότ᾽ ἀρωγῆς ὑπολειφθέντες: genitive expressing separation.

75. νέμοντες ἐπὶ σκήπτροις: 'guiding on staves'. The Chorus's staves will doubtless have featured in its choreography; see also 1652 n.

76–82. The Chorus explains why its strength is ἰσόπαις, by two clauses linked with τε ... τε; the basic point is that old men, like children, cannot fight. The OCT prints ἀνάισσων, which is Hermann's conjecture. Although 'the young marrow leaping up within the breast' seems suitable to early and non-technical medical conceptions, it leaves ἰσόπρεσβυς unexplained. We therefore prefer the manuscripts' ἀνάσσων: 'the young marrow ruling within the breast is equal to an elder' because it has authority but not military power: 'there is no Ares [i.e. warlike spirit] in its χώραι'. Here, ἐνί = ἔνεστι, and χώραι might be military ('post'), or mean the 'territory' over which the marrow 'rules'. See M. West (1990*a*), 174–5 for further discussion.

From 79 there is further poignant description of 'the exceedingly old thing' (neuter rather than masculine) whose 'foliage is now withering away', i.e. the man in the late autumn of his life. With his staff, he 'goes along on his three-footed ways'; ὁδούς is a cognate accusative. (Similarly in the Sphinx's famous riddle: 'What has four legs in the morning, two in the afternoon, and three in the evening?

Man.') Finally, 'no better than a child, he wanders, a dream seen in the daytime': as we would say, he is in his 'second childhood', and purposeless, insubstantial, out of place.

83–103. The Chorus is by now established in the *orchēstra*. It turns towards the palace to ask Clytemnestra why she is now burning sacrifices on the altars of Argos, and to request that she relieve its profound anxiety.

Is Clytemnestra onstage? If so, she must make her first entrance unannounced (at 82 or earlier), occupy herself with sacrificial business at altars in front of the palace, then either depart without answering, or remain as a brooding presence until 258 while the Chorus does not wait for her answer. Such elaborate background stage business would wreck the audience's attention which Aeschylus' songs presuppose. In that case 83–103 must be an apostrophe, comparable to those in parodoi at Soph. *Aj.* 134 and Eur. *Hipp.* 141, except that Clytemnestra's entrance is postponed for longer. See Taplin (1977), 280–5 for fuller discussion.

83–4. Τυνδάρεω θύγατερ: the reference to Tyndareus perhaps recalls the myth that he forgot Aphrodite in a sacrifice, so she made all his daughters infamous for their sexual behaviour (e.g. Stesichorus *PMG* 223). For example, Helen betrays Menelaus and Clytemnestra betrays Agamemnon. The patronymic therefore not only immediately links Clytemnestra to Helen, but points to her adultery at the same time.

86–7. Lit. 'by persuasion of what message do you judge sent-round sacrifices?', i.e. ' . . . have you sent round orders for sacrifices and are now judging them?'. The things which are περίπεμπτα are understood from θυοσκεῖς. A θυοσκόος is someone who judges sacrifices for omens, e.g. how high the flame burns.

88–90. The 'city-governing' gods are divided first into the Olympians (ὕπατοι) and chthonians such as local heroes, then by location into those of doorways and those of the market-place.

92–3. 'The torches in their various quarters reach up as tall as heaven'; this is a good omen from the burnt offerings. The metaphor λαμπάς impresses on the audience that these fires are a response to the beacon-signal, to which the word referred in 8 and 28. The three dactyls in quick succession within an anapaestic context help express the Chorus's excitement.

94–6. The fires are 'medicined by the gentle, guileless encourage-ments of pure unguent, by a πέλανος owned by royalty, from the store'. A πέλανος is a thick or clotted liquid, in this case oil. φαρμασσομένη plays on the medical use of ointments to render something strong; then the slightly incongruous μαλακαῖς ἀδόλοισι παρηγορίαις sets up a contrast with Clytemnestra's later behaviour.

97–103. The first clause means 'consent in saying [i.e. 'please say'] whatever of these things is both possible and right'. The aorist participle λέξασα is aspectual, rather than marking a prior action. Clytemnestra is to *heal* the Chorus's concern with comforting *words*: λέξασα and παιών correspond to the preceding images of παρηγορίαις and φαρμασσομένη respectively. The Chorus's concern is for the fate of the Trojan expedition (cf. 40 n.), and 'currently at one moment grows malignant [i.e. deeply troubling], while at other moments hope, inspired by the sacrifices you show forth, wards off insatiable worry'.

In 103 read καὶ θυμοβόρον φρενὶ λύπην (so West, Sommerstein, based on the scholion). The final emphasis on 'insatiable worry and heart-devouring pain in the mind' casts a pall over the elders' optimism.

104–59. Clytemnestra does not come out to answer. So the Chorus returns to the narrative of the expedition, but switches into song with a lyric triad (strophe, antistrophe, epode) in rolling dactyls punctuated by occasional iambic or choriambic phrases. The dactyls give the passage an epic quality, and hexameters were also the metre of prophecy, which features powerfully. As normal in choral lyric, Doric vowels appear frequently from now on: ā for η, and -ᾶν for -ῶν in the first declension.

The omen which is recounted can be linked with the simile in 49–59. Here the Atridae are represented by two eagles rather than vultures, no longer complainants about their own young, but aggressors against a hare's young. However, there is still retributive justive from a god: Artemis will exact a penalty (the sacrifice of Iphigenia), which will in turn lead to a 'child-avenging wrath' embodied in Clytemnestra (155).

104–5. κύριός εἰμι θροεῖν: 'I have authority to utter'. θροεῖν is more powerful than λέγειν. Despite the elders' physical weakness (72–82), they can still relate and affirm the significance of past events in their lyric performance. The thought expresses fresh confidence. **ὅδιον κράτος αἴσιον:** 'the auspicious command on the road' is a compressed way of saying 'the commanders who met with auspicious omens on the road' (D–P). Aristophanes' Euripides quotes 104 and 108–11 in *Ran.* 1276–89, with ridiculous additions. ἀνδρῶν ἐκτελέων: the genitive depends on κράτος and is probably objective like the genitives in 108–9: command 'over men just grown up', so in their prime; cf. Eur. *Ion* 780 ἐκτελῆ νεανίαν. The men's vitality is implicitly contrasted with the Chorus's age in what follows.

105–7. Read πειθώ [acc.], μολπᾶν ἀλκάν: 'For still by divine favour the life born with me breathes over me persuasion, the vigour of song.' The σύμφυτος αἰών is the life which continues in a person from infancy through to old age. The elders lack the physical ἀλκή ('power', esp. defensive) to fight in war, but their singing has the metaphorical ἀλκή to 'win over' listeners. This is a strong opening statement of one way in which words have power to influence events in the context of the drama; for this as a function of lyric choruses, see Introduction § 7.

108–12. The elements compressed into 104 now recur more clearly: a 'swooping' (θούριος: of aggressive darting movements) bird-omen sent the command over the Greek youth on their way to Troy. ταγάν: a recherché, perhaps Thessalian, word for 'leadership'. πράκτορι: 'avenging'. πράσσω/-ομαι often means 'exact atonement' in the trilogy.

113–15. The bird (cf. singular ὄρνις, βασιλεύς) becomes two; in fact, ὄρνις retrospectively acquires the sense of 'bird-omen'. The chiastic patterning of οἰωνῶν βασιλεὺς βασιλεῦσι νεῶν 'the king of birds to the kings of the ships' at once suggests the interpretation. (Distinguish νεῶν < ναῦς from νέων < νέος.)

The 'king of birds' is the eagle. The black eagle is the μελανάετος, described by Aristotle as the strongest, and also known as the 'hare-killer' (*HA* 8(9). 32 618b 26–31); the white-rumped one is the πύγαργος, which was also large and considered bold but not as powerful. In 123 the two eagles are identified by Calchas with the two kings who are λήμασι δισσούς 'twain in temper'. Since cowardly humans might be called λευκόπυγος, some have argued that the omen suggests cowardice in Menelaus; but both he (at 124) and the πύγαργος are warlike; nor is Menelaus cowardly in the *Iliad*, although he is shown to be more merciful than his brother at 6. 37–65. This difference may be the point of Aeschylus' λήμασι δισσούς.

116. ἴκταρ μελάθρων: ἴκταρ was probably an archaic and solemn preposition in Aeschylus' time: 'nigh on'.

Are the μέλαθρα the 'palace' at Argos (Sommerstein 1995–6), or the Atridae's 'huts' at Aulis (J. Heath 2001)? Although at *Il.* 9. 640 and repeatedly in Euripides *Iph. Aul.* μέλαθρον is used of military huts, the reference in those passages is unambiguous whereas here nothing excludes the more usual meaning. Furthermore, the Greeks often located prodigies right at the start of journeys. Perhaps most awkward for Sommerstein's interpretation is the emphasis of 114–15 βασιλεῦσι νεῶν, which naturally suggests kings currently command-ing the whole flotilla, rather than kings who have ordered a flotilla but not yet taken charge of it. The other arguments on either side seem less significant. For example, the fact that the corresponding Homeric omen occurred at Aulis (*Il.* 2. 299–322) does not imply that this one does.

χερὸς ἐκ δοριπάλτου: a suitably military way to describe the right hand. ἐκ here and in the expression ἐκ δεξιᾶς means 'on' the right, not 'coming from' it. The omen therefore appears to be propitious. (Cf. 145 δεξιὰ μέν.)

117. παμπρέπτοις ἐν ἕδραισι: 'in an extremely conspicuous place to settle'. The omen is a public event.

118–20. Here λαγίναν … γένναν probably means 'one born of a hare'. βλάψαντε λοισθίων δρόμων means 'hindering it from its final runnings'; λοισθίων is 'proleptic', i.e. the eagles' action makes this run the hare's last. (βλάψαντε is Page's emendation of βλαβέντα. The latter is masculine, unlike γένναν, but might conceivably stand as a *constructio ad sensum* since λαγώς is always masculine: Barrett 1964, 367.)

121. This line is used as a refrain at the end of all three stanzas in the triad. The repeated cry αἴλινον is particularly associated with dirges (cf. Soph. *Aj.* 627). Combined with 'but may the good win out' it exemplifies a repeated pattern, already established at 17–21, whereby a character is led to an ominous or negative utterance which he or she can only hope to rectify by forced optimism.

122–30. Calchas, here called a στρατό-μαντις to emphasize his public role (cf. 117 n.), interprets the omen: the eagles symbolize the Atridae; the pregnant hare, Troy; its unborn young, innocent Trojans.

122–5. The OCT is most easily construed as: 'The careful army-seer, when he saw, understood the warlike hare-eaters, escorts of the command, to be the two twin-tempered Atridae.' M. West (see 1999,

48) plausibly reads πομποὺς τ' ἀρχάς 'escorting rulers' (sc. of the birds; cf. 113–14 οἰωνῶν βασιλεύς). ἐδάη appears in LSJ s.v. δάω.

126–7. χρόνωι μὲν ἀγρεῖ: the μέν is opposed to the thought of 131, not to 128 δέ. The verb means 'captures', but resembles words for hunting (ἀγρά, ἀγρεύω, etc.), which would suit the eagles as well as the Greeks. It is present for future, as often in prophecy (Smyth § 1882). **κέλευθος:** as the subject of ἀγρεῖ, 'journey, expedition' constitutes a metonymy.

128–30. The OCT would mean: 'Moira will violently ravage all the livestock of the city walls, made over [as to a creditor], abundant for public use.' But reading πρόσθε τά is easier, despite the unusual order of πύργων ... πρόσθε: 'Moira will violently ravage all the abundant livestock of the public before the city walls.' Lines 1168–9 confirm that animals were sacrificed there in an attempt to gain divine support. However, the prophetic language hints at a further point: the κτήνη δημιοπληθῆ represent the mass of the Trojan populace who will be slaughtered like cattle before the walls. For the sacrificial imagery, see Zeitlin (1965).

For Moira, see Introduction § 4.2. This is her first appearance in a trilogy where she will stand for more than 'fate'. She embodies also the system of violent retributive δίκη, and it is to her that the Erinyes trace their authority at *Eum.* 335, 392.

131–4. Literally 'Only (I fear) lest some jealousy from the gods may darken, stricken beforehand, the great curb of Troy, encamped.' For μή + subjunctive in this sense cf. 341, Smyth §§ 1801–2. Calchas begins in a powerful mixture of metaphors to outline his fear of Artemis, on which he spends far more time than the joyous prediction of 126–7. The 'curb' of Troy is the Greek army, as clarified by the participle στρατωθέν; Troy is figured now as a horse rather than a hare. The curb may be darkened, i.e. harmed—the opposite symbolism to the light of liberation and victory which we saw in the prologue. And this darkness will arise from it being struck before its application at the subjugation of Troy. (There is no parallel for LSJ's interpretation of προτύπτω as 'forge beforehand'.)

134–8. οἴκτωι 'from pity' is a dative expressing cause; κυσί depends on ἐπίφθονος 'resentful of'. Artemis was a goddess of childbirth (λόχου here suggests her cult-title 'Lochia') and as the patron of hunting controlled how game animals were killed. Specifically, hunters would not kill young hares out of respect for her (Xenophon *Cyn.* 5. 14), and Attic women dedicated hares to her (symbolizing fertility?) at Brauron, where she had connections to none other than Iphigenia: see further 232, 239 nn. She therefore pities the pregnant hare and is resentful against the eagles. The latter are called 'her father's winged dogs', since eagles were particularly associated with Zeus (who is thought to have sent this omen) and dogs are nature's hare-hunters.

Lines 136–7 offer a fine example of Aeschylus' ambiguous wording. The surface meaning is 'sacrificing a suffering hare, together with its brood, before labour'. But the words hint at the connection to Iphigenia's sacrifice: πτάξ 'hare' is etymologically a 'cowering female', αὐτότοκος could mean 'one's own child' and πρὸ λόχου could be 'in front of the army'. θυομένοισιν also draws out the parallel to the image of the slaughtered 'cattle' in 128–30.

140–55. Calchas explains Artemis' pity and grudge (140–3), and says that she requires fulfilment of the omen (144), which has a bad side as well as a good (145–6). He then specifies his fears more precisely, though still cryptically: she may hold up the ships and demand an unholy sacrifice (147–51). Finally he sets the omen within a longer-term chain of sin and retribution (152–5).

140. τόσον περ: 'to *such* an extent'. περ here adds emphasis (Denniston 482), rather than being concessive. ἁ καλά: the 'fair goddess' Artemis, one of whose cult-epithets was καλλίστη; cf. Eur. *Hipp.* 66 καλλίστᾱ with Barrett (1964). However, ἁ here is a fourteenth-century conjecture, and causes a dubious metre. M. West (cf. 1999, 50–1) therefore suggests τόσον περ εὔφρων Ἑκάτα. Hecate was often assimilated to Artemis, despite being generally more chthonic (see *NP* s.v. Hecate); according to Hesiod fr. 23 Iphigenia was worshipped as Hecate or 'Artemis on the Road' after her sacrifice.

141. δρόσοις: literally 'dews', here meaning 'young'. In *Od.* 9. 222 some of Polyphemus' lambs are ἔρσαι, also literally 'dews'. ἀέπτοις: perhaps conceived to mean 'unfollowing' (as if from ἕπομαι), i.e. helpless. The real etymology is uncertain. μαλερῶν: 'ravening', used of fire in epic.

144. τούτων αἰτεῖ ξύμβολα κρᾶναι: '(she) demands to fulfil the counterparts of these things', i.e. a matching sacrifice of another young female—Iphigenia. κραίνω is often used in contexts of oracles, dreams, and omens coming true (e.g. 249).

145–6. The manuscripts have the unmetrical φάσματα στρούθων, where the latter word must have intruded from a marginal comment about the omen of the sparrows and the snake in *Il.* 2. 311. It is metrically likely that it replaced a spondaic word. D–P's <κρίνω>, with a full stop at the end of 144, is a possible replacement: 'I judge the visions to be partly propitious, partly displeasing.'

147. Calchas calls on his patron god Apollo to intercede, both as the Healer and as Artemis' brother. Apollo is *ἰήϊος* because the cry *ἰή* is closely associated with paeans.

West suggests δή for δέ, which produces a more regular metre. The lack of contraction in καλέω is typical of epic or Pindar, but rare in Aeschylus.

148–55. In these long clauses, each noun has multiple adjectives in asyndeton, and each applies a brushstroke to the sinister picture. First the contrary gales are presented: ' . . . that she not wreak non-sailings caused by contrary winds—long-lasting, ship-detaining'. Then σπευδομένα governs 'another sacrifice', to complement that of the eagles, but this time one which is *ἄνομος* (both 'without music' and 'lawless') and without the joyful feasting that would normally follow a sacrifice, 'an inborn architect of quarrels, not husband-fearing'. The sacrifice is gradually personified: first *σύμφυτον* suggests that it is a facet of the inherited family troubles, then *οὐ δεισήνορα* may already suggest Clytemnestra, who will later be seen as the embodiment of the family *δαίμων* (1468–74). The next clause explains these personifications (*pace* Furley 1986) and, with its feminine endings, brings sharper focus: 'For there awaits a frightening, resurgent, crafty housekeeper—a remembering, child-avenging Wrath.' The *Μῆνις* is 'resurgent' in that after its period of waiting still (cf. *μίμνει*) it will return in the form of Clytemnestra to be unleashed upon the sacrificer.

We are now in a position to discuss Aeschylus' unique treatment of Iphigenia's sacrifice and its aftermath; see Conacher (1987), 76–83 for a survey of scholarship. Aeschylus chose not to follow the tradition of the epic *Cypria*, according to which the Greeks gathered twice at Aulis, with an abortive attempt to sail to Troy between. At the first gathering, a snake ominously ate a brood of sparrow-chicks and their mother (see *Iliad* 2. 301–30); at the second, the ships were delayed by winds and Iphigenia sacrificed. Aeschylus combines the two: the omen of the eagles eating a hare and her foetuses reworks that of the snake eating the sparrows, but is now causally linked to Iphigenia's sacrifice. Aeschylus' purpose was partly to avoid reference to extraneous events, but the combination has striking implications. In the *Cypria* Agamemnon had killed a deer at Aulis and boasted that he was a better hunter than Artemis, and is punished for this hubris (see also, with different focalization, Sophocles *Electra* 563–76). In Aeschylus, Zeus sends the Atridae to punish Paris for abducting Helen, which entails widespread suffering including that of innocent people. Zeus also sends his birds (the eagles), as an omen which gives a preview of this suffering. Artemis then demands the young and innocent Iphigenia in compensation for the death of the hares in this 'preview': unusually, Agamemnon must pay in advance for a *future* action. The point is not that Artemis opposes Zeus' plan as expressed in the omen: rather, 'Her anger is simply the counterpart of Zeus' own plan, that wrong shall be avenged by violence, and that in consequence the avenger must pay' (Kitto 1956, 71). Aeschylus also relates the passage to the chain of retributive justice by making Calchas end with an allusion to Clytemnestra's vengeance.

156–9. The Chorus sinisterly identifies Calchas' words as 'fateful for the royal palace' (rather than for the army). In ξὺν μεγάλοις ἀγαθοῖς, it makes a last attempt to emphasize the positive, but is pulled back at once by the negative: 'In harmony with these things, cry *ailinos ailinos*—but may the good win out.' τοῖς is demonstrative, and refers to the predominantly bad omens that have preceded. The integration of the refrain, which has been free-standing, into the overall syntax brings a sense of closure, just as ἀπ' ὀρνίθων ὁδίων rounds the triad off in ring-composition with 104.

160–83. The rhythm changes to solemn trochees for the so-called Hymn to Zeus. These three strophes interrupt the narrative of events before the war, to which they must refer. The transition of thought is natural, given the depressing conclusion of Calchas' interpretation of the omen, with its implications of Iphigenia's sacrifice and the future problems for the palace (154–5), and to which it was apt to say *ailinos* (158–9). To avert the detrimental effect of their words, they turn to Zeus as the only god on whom to rely if they are to rid themselves of this anxiety (163–7 with n.), since he is the source of good sense, in particular the rule that 'from suffering comes learning' (176–8 with n.). They are thus seeking the comfort of an enlightened purpose behind their gloomy narrative. Lecythia (— ∪ — ∪ — ∪ —) recur with remarkable frequency throughout the trilogy, beginning here: in *Agamemnon* they seem to be correlated with the Chorus's attempts to find a meaning behind the events described or enacted onstage (see Appendix § 4.4).

The main elements of Greek hymns are: an opening invocation (second-person) or naming (third-person) of the god; epithets and other descriptions of the god's attributes, and/or a narrative of the god's past deeds; a prayer. In this example, the elders begin by naming Zeus, say that only he can help (163–5) with the desire which they imply at 165–7, and sketch his accomplishments in overthrowing Cronus and directing mortals towards sense. From 179, however, they gradually move away from Zeus and back to their narrative.

Interpretation of the passage has raised numerous disputes: important contributions with which we disagree include Pope (1974) and P. Smith (1980), criticized by Conacher (1976) and (1983) respectively; Schenker (1994) includes a useful survey of opinions.

160–2. Literally 'Zeus, whoever he is—if this (name) is dear to him who is called it, it is by this that I address him.' ποτε intensifies the interrogative ὅστις. The contemplation of what name to use if the god is to listen is a common and traditional element in Greek prayers. The qualification 'whoever he is' is much rarer, and acknowledges Zeus' mysterious nature: compare Euripides *Tro.* 884–7, where Hecuba's prayer includes 'whoever you are, difficult to know by conjecture' and four philosophical options for Zeus' nature.

163–7. 'I have no comparison to make, when I weigh everything in the balance, except Zeus, if I must truly cast off the futile burden of anxiety'. The thought is 'I have no comparison to make *to* Zeus', but after the metrical colon πάντ' ἐπισταθμώμενος there seems to be a slight shift to '. . . except Zeus'. μάταν is an adverb used adjectivally (Smyth § 1096). ἀπο-βαλεῖν is separated in tmesis; ἀπό does not govern φροντίδος.

The Elders do not define their anxiety precisely. Gagarin (1976), 139–50 argued that its object is the success of the expedition (as in 99), but something more closely connected to the surrounding narrative is desirable and at hand. Possibly their thoughts are already turning to the troubling sacrifice of Iphigenia, but more simply the final words of Calchas' prophecy fill them with foreboding, and concern that by repeating them they have added to the forces stacked against Agamemnon's prosperity. Their anxiety is a weight (ἄχθος), and they metaphorically use scales (ἐπισταθμώμενος) to weigh up the various possible remedies for it.

In both 165 and 173 the change to dactyls coincides with Zeus'
name. It lends the lines grandeur, and links the hymn with the
preceding (mainly dactylic) narrative.

168–75. The elders mention without names two deities whose
effectiveness is past, and with whom they contrast Zeus: these are
his predecessors—his grandfather Uranus and father Cronus. The
locus classicus for the succession-myth is Hesiod *Theogony* 154–210,
459–506. Cronus' mother Earth incited him to castrate his father
Uranus. Later, Cronus was afraid of a successor and began swallow-
ing his children, but his wife Rhea saved Zeus. Earth made Cronus
vomit up the other children, and under Zeus' leadership they over-
threw Cronus and the Titans. Besides the Chorus's immediate concerns, this myth offers a comparandum for the sequence of internecine conflicts in Atreus' family, and at first Zeus' superiority is
figured with athletic imagery of violent power (contrast 175 n.). But
importantly, the chain of conflict on the divine plane has been ended
for good by Zeus' stable rule.

169. παμμάχωι θράσει βρύων: 'teeming with all-fighting boldness'.
Given the imagery which follows in 171–2, πάμμαχος may evoke
the παγκράτιον, which was a particularly violent and free form of
wrestling.

170. οὐδὲ λέξεται πρὶν ὤν: 'will not even [οὐδέ] be mentioned, since
he is of the past'. λέξεται is a future middle form with passive sense,
as often in 5th-century Greek.

171–2. τριακτῆρος: the wrestler who throws his opponent three
times (here referring to Zeus). The genitive is governed by
τυχών.

173–4. 'Anyone who gladly sings a celebration of Zeus as a victor'.
For Ζῆνα κλάζων compare 48 κλάζοντες Ἄρη, but the construction
here is harder: a verb and internal object effectively meaning 'hymn,
celebrate' (ἐπινίκια κλάζων ~ ὑμνῶν) are given a second object
which describes the topic of the song (Ζῆνα). See Renehan (1976),
51–2 for parallels.

175. τεύξεται φρενῶν τὸ πᾶν: 'shall hit the target of sense completely' (τυγχάνω + genitive). The emphasis here shifts from Zeus'
power to his civilizing qualities. His connection to human intelligence is underscored by the close sequence φρενῶν ... φρονεῖν
(which is supported by προφρόνως just before), and he is metaphorically a path-builder and lawgiver (176–8).

176–8. ' ... he who set mortals on the path of good sense—he who laid down "From suffering, learning" to be valid'. The Chorus explains the theology underpinning its turn to Zeus, which was done in search of comfort (165–7). φρονεῖν is opposed to τὸ μάταν φροντίδος ἄχθος there. Their initial purpose and vv. 179–81 show that πάθος is 'suffering' rather than just 'experience' (so LSJ), and that πάθει μάθος is 'From suffering comes *learning*' rather than the dispiriting 'From *suffering* (alone) comes learning'. So Croesus uses the proverb in Herodotus 1. 207. 1 'My παθήματα, though they were unpleasant, have become μαθήματα': compare the consolatory tone of 'We live and learn.' Aeschylus, however, elevates the saying to a natural law attributable to Zeus, who embodies the unity in inherited moral and religious ideas.

The elders cite the principle of πάθει μάθος with a particular application in mind. They are perhaps seeking some lesson from Iphigenia's πάθος, and in general cite the principle as an example of the positive aspects of Zeus' rule which give them hope of a positive meaning behind the story they are telling. (Schenker 1994, 6 argues that they have in mind that the Trojans will learn from the war not to abduct other people's wives: but this is rather far from the immediate context of the words.) However, the principle may have other applications in the context of the trilogy. Agamemnon himself does not learn from his suffering, but the principle is laid down for βροτοί in general (176), and the audience of a tragic performance were thought both to suffer with the characters, and to learn from it. The view that poets including tragedians could teach you something is pervasive in Greek sources (see most bluntly Ar. *Ran.* 955, 1009, 1025–6, 1055, though Aristophanes treats the idea jocularly). At the end of *Eumenides* the placated Furies greet the Athenian people 'sitting close to Zeus, dear to the dear virgin [Athena], σωφρονοῦντες ἐν χρόνωι' (*Eum.* 998–1000, again in lecythia). Under the guidance of Zeus and Athena (and Aeschylus), the Athenians and βροτοί generally have eventually learnt a system to escape the endless cycle of retributive homicides. See also Introduction § 4.4.

(In 177 the manuscripts have τῶι instead of τόν. This has two minor effects. It makes θέντα subordinate to ὁδώσαντα, so that the law-giving is *part* of the guiding-to-sense; but this is clear anyway from 179–81. Secondly, adding an article to πάθει brings a slight nuance of 'from the given suffering': see Fraenkel. But the proverb is likely not to have had this article.)

179–81. 'And before the heart there drips, in sleep at least, the suffering of remembered pain: wisdom comes even to those who are unwilling.' ἦλθε is a gnomic aorist. The first stage of learning from suffering is that memory of a πάθος percolates drop by drop into our inner consciousness. For anxiety being by the heart, cf. 976–7 and *Sept.* 289–90 γείτονες δὲ καρδίας μέριμναι. The manuscripts have ἔν θ' ὕπνωι, where θ' is wrong. Page's ἔν γ' ὕπνωι is acceptable (though he wanted γε to mean 'even', which it does not). The point would be that though one may suppress past pains during the day, such preoccupations still haunt one's dreams. Other editors including West prefer to emend to ἀνθ' ὕπνου: in this case, the point is that remembering pain keeps one awake at night.[1]

182–3. The OCT means 'The favour from the deities who sit on the awesome bench is characterized, I suppose, by force.' χάρις βίαιος is an oxymoron, drawn from what precedes: the χάρις of good sense may be bestowed against the recipient's will, i.e. is βίαιος. σέλμα denotes the raised seat of a helmsman, i.e. a position of authority (cf. 1617–18 n.).

The lines tentatively (που) suggest a belief that deities (probably Olympians and chthonians in concert: see Intro. § 4.2) can operate benignly. When in *Eumenides* the divine χάρις of Athena (and behind her Zeus) presents the institution of civic justice as a solution to the problem of violent retribution, this still admits an element of force. Nobody rejects the Erinyes' statements that 'it is beneficial to σωφρονεῖν under the pressure of sorrow' (*Eum.* 520) and that the audacious sinner must eventually 'lower his sail under compulsion [βιαίως]' (553–7). With this in mind, σεμνόν in *Ag.* 183 might anticipate the reference to the cult of the Σεμναὶ θεαί at *Eum.* 1041.

There are two textual issues: firstly ποῦ 'Where . . . ?' versus που; secondly βίαιος (which is incompatible with ποῦ) versus the manuscripts' βιαίως. With ποῦ, the rhetorical question would effectively express 'The gods show force and not favour', which contradicts the Chorus's general purpose (165–7) and comments about μάθος and τὸ σωφρονεῖν. One might defend βιαίως, though the omission of ἔστι 'there exists' would be very rare: 'There is, I think, some favour from the deities, though they sit on their awesome bench by force', i.e. though they exercise authority through force.

---

[1] These lines were memorably quoted by Robert Kennedy in his speech on the assassination of Martin Luther King (Indianapolis, 4 April 1968: Guthman and Allen 1993, 355–8). He referred to Aeschylus as his 'favourite poet'.

184–91. In 184, καὶ τότε 'So then' introduces an example of the preceding general claims. Moreover, we return to the past narrative in the middle of a strophic pair, which emphasizes how Agamemnon's dilemma and Iphigenia's sacrifice are a πάθος from which some μάθος may ultimately be expected. Indeed, the Chorus also relates the end of this narrative to the doctrine of πάθει μάθος (250–1).

186. μάντιν οὔτινα ψέγων: contrast Agamemnon's treatment of Calchas at *Il.* 1. 106.

187. ἐμπαίοις τύχαισι συμπνέων: 'breathing along with the events that struck against him'. i.e. Agamemnon's own impetus went along with them; they are explained in 188–98 as the contrary winds, so that the 'blowing' metaphor (cf. 219 πνέων) has added point.

188. ἀπλοίαι κεναγγεῖ: literally 'by a lack of sailing characterized by empty innards': the delay made their provisions run out (cf. 193 νήστιδες). κεν(ε)αγγέω is a technical medical term. The syncopated rhythm drags, to reflect the sense (as at 196).

189. βαρύνοντ': plural with the collective subject λεώς; in tragedy, the augment is sometimes omitted (as in Homer and lyric).

190–1. 'occupying the land opposite Chalcis in the backward-roaring region of Aulis'. πέραν is sometimes an adverb, but here a noun. Aulis and Chalcis face each other across the Euripus strait (see Map, p. 101), which was famous for its violent currents which frequently changed direction. With Page's punctuation, the sentence breaks off here without a main verb, as the description of the winds is fleshed out.

192–257. The metre for the rest of the parodos is dominated by taut syncopated iambics (Appendix § 4.3.1). The form ∪ — ∪ — | · — ∪ — | ∪ — · —, as in 192, recurs particularly often through the trilogy; for the view that it is correlated with contexts of sin and its retribution, see Appendix § 4.4. At this point, its employment to describe the contrary winds expresses Artemis' anger at the eagles' destruction of the pregnant hare.

192. πνοαὶ δ' ἀπὸ Στρύμονος: the Strymon is a large Thracian river; the northerly from there (Boreas) was known as particularly violent.

193. 'bringing bad leisure, famished, making the moorings terrible'. The outer adjectives are extremely rare, and have similar prefixes; νήστιδες is transferred from the troops to the winds. For such use of adjectives see Introduction § 9.1.

194. ἆλαι: usually related to ἀλάομαι—either 'wanderings' in search of food or '(mental) distractions' (as in Eur. *Med.* 1285). But the word might be related to ἀλεῖν 'grind down' (Housman 1888, 290).

195. ναῶν: Doric for νεῶν 'of the ships'. **ἀφειδεῖς:** 'unsparing'; governs a genitive, like φείδομαι. The winds cause the ships and tackle to decay.

196. παλιμμήκη: 'as long again'—twice the time it should have taken. For the dragged rhythm see 188 n.

197–8. 'were thinning out the flower of the Argives by wearing it down'. The Greek elite was both physically and mentally weakened. καταξαίνω is a metaphor from carding wool for spinning, and so gains extra point from the fact that ἄνθος could be used of the fluffy nap of a fabric (Borthwick 1976).

198–204. The Chorus returns us to the situation before the digression of 192–8, and adds a further temporal specification (ἐπεὶ δὲ καί, 'and when also'). Calchas 'cried aloud another cure for the bitter storm . . . citing [προφέρων] Artemis', i.e. as his authority. This picks up the glancing reference to Calchas in 186. ἄλλο suggests that various remedies—probably conventional sacrifices—have already been tried; but the new suggestion is βριθύτερον πρόμοισιν, 'heavier for the chiefs'.

For the metrical change at 199 and the colometry of 202–4, see Appendix § 5. The rhythmic pulse presumably contributed to the description of the Atridae beating the earth with their βάκτρα; this is an unusual word for 'sceptre', and more appropriate to the elders' walking-sticks, which they may well have used to mime the action here.

205–21. The story is skilfully arranged here. The Chorus was careful not to spell out the 'new plan', and compressed the earlier events to their essentials. But by contrast Agamemnon is made to voice his dilemma in extended direct speech and blunter terms: the tearing apart (δαΐξω is brutal) of his child and her blood running on his hands will be a hideous pollution, but he cannot abandon the expedition or the allies to whom he is committed. For Agamemnon's decision-making, see Nussbaum (2001), ch. 2.

205. ἄναξ δ᾽ ὁ πρέσβυς: a return to the subject of 184. δέ is apodotic (Denniston 179) to the long temporal clause of 198–204—translate 'then'.

206–11. βαρεῖα μὲν κήρ . . . βαρεῖα δ᾽ clearly points the dilemma, which is intensified by the candour of 207–11. Distinguish κήρ 'ruin' (fem.) from κῆρ 'heart' (neut.).

212–13. 'Ship-deserter' was an Athenian legal term (preserved once in oratory and in ancient dictionaries). For crimes of desertion in general see MacDowell (1978), 159–61. Agamemnon cannot afford to 'lose his alliance'. Alliances were sealed with sacred oaths of cooperation which he would have to break, and he could thereby expect to lose all his aristocratic prestige.

214–17. The OCT means 'It is right that they [the allies] should desire a wind-preventing sacrifice and a maiden's blood with an extremely passionate passion.' However, West points out that it is strange for a desire to be θέμις, rather than an action; and the moral issue centres not on the allies' desires but on the prescribed sacrifice. There is a palaeographical argument for including αὐδᾶι, which is a marginal variant. He proposes . . . ὀργᾶι περιόργως· ἀπὸ δ᾽ αὐδᾶι Θέμις, which we tentatively prefer: '(the alliance) passionately desires . . . but Right forbids it' (M. West 1990*a*, 178–81). This time, ὀργᾶι is a verb not a noun, and Agamemnon's speech does not itself include signs of the very misguided thinking which will be attributed to him in 219–21.

The juxtaposition of παυσανέμου θυσίας and παρθενίου αἵματος neatly oppose the public and familial sides of Iphigenia's death (Goldhill 1984*a*, 30). The sacrifice of a young person to ensure military success is a widespread motif in Greek myth. Plutarch *Themistocles* 13. 3–4 offers one parallel, probably without historical accuracy. Before the battle of Salamis a seer asserts that Themistocles should slaughter some young prisoners-of-war to ensure success in the battle. Themistocles is horrified at the thought, but the army pressures him into killing them.

217. εὖ γὰρ εἴη: the usual euphemistic rider when the situation looks bleak (cf. 121 τὸ δ᾽ εὖ νικάτω). The connection of thought with γάρ seems to entail an ellipse: '(I say that) because I (just) hope that things will be well.'

218. ἀνάγκας ἔδυ λέπαδνον: Agamemnon 'put on the halter of necessity'. ἀνάγκη is an overriding external constraint, in this case Agamemnon's obligations to his allies; but ἔδυ implies voluntary submission to it. See Introduction § 4.3.2 and, for the halter image, 235–8 n.

219–21. 'breathing an impious veering (wind) of the mind, an impure, unholy one—from that moment he changed his mind to thoughts of utmost daring'. For 'breathing' a decision, see 187 n. One could understand πνοήν with τροπαίαν, but a feminine adjective sometimes occurs when an idea cognate with the verb is understood, whatever the gender of the normal word for that idea; cf. 1459, and Wilamowitz (1933), 365–6. The idea of veering from piety anticipates μετέγνω which, like ἔδυ, suggests Agamemnon's active volition.

222–3. 'For shameful-counselling brazen derangement, first cause of woe, *emboldens* mortals.' The delay of γάρ throws emphasis onto θρασύνει. This sentence adds a further level of motivation (though not an exoneration), since the Greeks considered such 'derangement' to be sent by the gods. The obvious comparandum is Agamemnon's own famous excuse in *Iliad* 19. 86–144, where he claims that he was afflicted by Atē in his treatment of Achilles. The Chorus makes no suggestion as to why the gods might have afflicted Agamemnon: Aeschylus keeps the focus on understanding what state of mind enabled Agamemnon to kill his daughter. For psychological determination, see Introduction § 4.3.3.

224–5. The important particle combination δ' οὖν (see 34–5 n.) means 'However that may be . . .', i.e. 'Whatever the complexities of Agamemnon's motivation'. θυτὴρ . . . θυγατρός is now a brutally explicit counterpart (reinforced by alliteration) to the emphatic δυσσεβῆ τροπαίαν ἄναγνον ἀνίερον of 219–20.

225–6. **γυναικοποίνων πολέμων ἀρωγάν**: cf. 62 πολυάνορος ἀμφὶ γυναικός (with n. for its nuance). ἀρωγάν is an accusative in apposition to the idea of sacrifice in the preceding clause (Smyth § 991b).

227. **προτέλεια ναῶν**: for προτέλεια see 63–7 n. The 'preliminary ritual of the ships' probably refers to the normal sacrifice before embarkation, which is here perverted into a human sacrifice. The prenuptial association of προτέλεια may also allude to the normal pretext for summoning Iphigenia to Aulis, which was to marry her to Achilles. This version is reflected in 1523, and was present before Aeschylus in the epic *Cypria*, Stesichorus' *Oresteia* (Campbell 1991, 128), and on a *lekythos* by Douris from *c*.470 (*LIMC* Iphigenia 3).

228–47. The sacrifice is now described in poetry of great pathos and compelling economy of detail. Iphigenia struggles against her destiny, unlike the resolute figure on Douris' *lekythos* (227 n.) or in Euripides *Iph. Aul.* Similarly, there is no hint of the version where

Artemis saves Iphigenia at the last moment by substituting a clone (Hesiod fr. 23a, Stesichorus *PMG* 215) or by leaving a deer to be sacrificed in her stead (e.g. *Cypria*; *LIMC* Iphigenia 1 (Attic; *c*.425 BC)).

Sounds and their absence are a special focus: Iphigenia's prayers and addresses are ignored; by contrast, Agamemnon offers a prayer before his instructions, which include gagging Iphigenia in order to avoid a curse; nevertheless, the Chorus mentions her desire to address the men, and her past utterance of paeans at Agamemnon's symposia.

228. κληδόνας πατρώιους: bold Greek for 'her calls of "Father!"'. That κληδόνες are also 'omens' (Intro. § 6) may give the expression a sinister force.

229–30. παρ' οὐδὲν ... ἔθεντο is 'valued at nought' (LSJ τίθημι B II 3). For the unusual position of τε, following both noun and adjective, cf. *Supp.* 282. βραβῆς are usually 'umpires', but here decision-making 'chieftains'.

232. δίκαν χιμαίρας: 'like a young goat', a common sacrificial victim. This is a poignant context in which to find a form of δίκη. The passage probably evoked two related Attic cults of Artemis, at Brauron and Mounychia. The latter's foundation-myth involves a goat being substituted for a daughter who is about to be sacrificed; for the relevance of Brauron see 239 n., and in general Bowie (1993), 19–22.

233–4. Agamemnon instructs them 'to seize (her) with lifting, so as to be face-down'. προνωπῆ is predicative; the position ensures that her blood falls on the altar, as in the Timiadas Painter's famous vase depicting Polyxena's sacrifice—*LIMC* Polyxena 26 (*c*.565 BC).

The object of λαβεῖν is πέπλοισι περιπετῆ, with which understand νιν. The two main paths of interpretation are: (1) 'falling about her father's robes' in supplication (Lloyd-Jones 1952; D–P); (2) 'so that her robes fell round her' (Lebeck 1971, 83; Sommerstein). (1) suits other uses of περιπετής, such as Sophocles *Ant.* 1223, but some find it inelegant that Iphigenia's current state would intervene within the description of how she will be when lifted.

The choice is also relevant to interpreting παντὶ θυμῶι: with (2) the attendants are to lift 'with all their heart', i.e. without faltering; with (1), it is more likely that Iphigenia is supplicating 'with all her heart'. Either way the pathos is enhanced by alliteration.

235–8. In an effect which is very unusual for tragedy, the sentence crosses the formal boundary between antistrophe and the following strophe, as though to emphasize the violence of Iphigenia's gagging. The datives βίαι and μένει (which is from μένος not μένω) are in apposition to φυλακᾶι: literally 'a muzzle . . . , the might and voiceless [i.e. 'silencing'] force of bridles'. Compare the imagery of animal control in 133 στόμιον and 218 λέπαδνον. The Greek army will be a 'bit' applied to Troy. But as a counterpart to this, first Agamemnon 'yokes' himself into applying a 'muzzle' or 'bridle' to Iphigenia. **καλλιπρώιρου**: literally 'fair-prowed'. Adjectives in -πρωιρος are regularly used metaphorically of human faces, but this is particularly apt now that Iphigenia is horizontal. The genitive is objective with φυλακᾶι. **ἀραῖον οἴκοις**: It is typical of the emphasis of the trilogy that Agamemnon envisages Iphigenia's voice as 'a source of a curse on the palace' rather than on the expedition as a whole (cf. 156–9 n.). Distinguish ἀραῖος from ἀραιός/ἀραιός 'slender'.

239–47. The poetry softens as it concentrates on Iphigenia and, in the absence of speech, on vision. From her position on the attendants' shoulders, she can only beg for pity with her eyes; in her bright yellow dress she is 'conspicuous' (πρέπουσα) like the central figure in a painting. Effective details include the repetition of πατρός (244–5), the rich use of adjectives (εὔποτμον, ἀγνᾶι, ἀταύρωτος), and the polyptoton φίλον . . . φίλως (246–7). The description of φιλία, purity, and well-omened paeans contrasts poignantly with the perverted sacrifice of daughter by father.

239. 'Letting her saffron-dyed clothes hang to the ground'. χέουσα cannot be 'Letting . . . fall': Iphigenia does not have the freedom to expose her body as Polyxena does before she is sacrificed in Euripides *Hecuba* 557–61.

The periphrasis κρόκου βαφάς is naturally taken as a κροκωτός, a yellow *chitōn* worn at special events. Lynn-George (1993), 5–6 usefully observes that it introduces a motif of dyeing which will recur at important moments in the trilogy (see 612, 960). There seems to be an allusion to the practice at Brauron, where girls participating in the cult wore κροκωτοί. The cult's foundation-myth recalls Iphigenia's story in that it involves appeasing Artemis by the sacrifice of virgins, and at Euripides *IT* 1446–68 we hear of Iphigenia receiving hero-cult at nearby Halae: cf. 232 n.

240–1. **ἔβαλλ᾽ . . . βέλει**: Iphigenia's unveiled glance is like an arrow.

The most common theory of vision among the Greeks was that eyes emitted rays of light which illuminated the object seen.

242–3. πρέπουσά θ' ὡς ἐν γραφαῖς: for the sense see 239–47 n. If the text is sound, the words start a new sentence which never achieves a main verb. This is defensible (see 248–9 n.), but Maas's emendation τώς 'as' (cf. *Sept.* 637) is attractive. προσεννέπειν θέλουσ', ἐπεί: ἐπεί introduces the reason why she would be able to 'address them by name'.

244. κατ' ἀνδρῶνας: Attic girls would not have appeared at dinners in their father's ἀνδρών, but this detail of heroic society is touching.

245. ἀταύρωτος: 'unbulled' i.e. virgin, carefully positioned close to ἀγναί. The striking adjective suggests that Iphigenia is now like a sacrificial cow as well as a goat (232). πατρός: an emphatic repetition of the word from 244.

246–7. 'she lovingly used to perform the honour of the paean for good fortune at the third libation'. It was customary to sing a paean and pour three libations between dinner and the symposium: other references include Xenophon *Symp.* 2.1 and Plutarch *Mor.* 615b. For the third libation see further on 1387.

248–9. The narrative breaks off in appropriate reticence (cf. 36 with n.), and perhaps in mid-sentence (see 242–3 n.). The elders dare not actually say 'Then Agamemnon took a knife and slit his daughter's throat'. Rather, they sum up the event in a euphemistic litotes: 'The crafts of Calchas were *not without fulfilment.*' These τέχναι are his acts of presaging at 144–51. This raises foreboding that his prediction of Μῆνις waiting at home was also correct: Moritz (1979), 198.

250–2. The Chorus reverts importantly to the doctrine of πάθει μάθος (177–8), and now associates it with the central theme of Δίκη rather than only with Zeus. We tentatively interpret: 'Where Justice is concerned, she *does* [μέν] weigh out learning to those who have suffered; but what is to come— you may hear whenever it should happen.'

The position of μέν indicates that Δίκη is also the notional subject of the δέ-clause (τὸ μέλλον δ' ... κλύοις); a comma after ἐπιρρέπει might be preferable to a colon. One might be tempted to paraphrase '... but Justice does not weigh out learning with respect to future events'. However, it is more pertinent to the presentation of justice in the rest of the play if the Chorus begins with the thought 'As for what Justice will weigh out for Agamemnon in the near future ...', and then resorts to euphemistic remote optatives. At 177–8 they

introduced πάθει μάθος as a source of optimism in the face of
Iphigenia's plight; after confronting that plight more directly, they
seem reduced from genuine hope to despair that any good will
accrue to Agamemnon, and an empty and vague expression of hope
(255). This summing-up therefore clarifies the relationship of the
Hymn to Zeus to the story of Iphigenia, and contributes to the play's
repeated shifts from hope to euphemistic hope-against-hope.

The image in ἐπιρρέπει is of Justice having a pair of scales (cf.
Cho. 61 ῥοπὰ Δίκας) in which possible outcomes are weighed up;
the scale containing the fair outcome descends. The transitive use
'make the scale containing X descend for Y' is also found at *Eum.*
888. The image of the scales links Justice with Zeus (who laid down
πάθει μάθος), since he famously holds the scales of life and death
in the *Iliad* (8. 69–72, 22. 209–13). Zeus, Justice, and scales-imagery
are also linked by Aeschylus at *Supp.* 402–5, and at e.g. *Hom. Hymn
Herm.* 322–4.

252–3. Read the manuscripts' προχαιρέτω: 'Let it [= the future] be
greeted in advance: (that is) equal to [i.e. as good as] groaning in
advance.' Neither welcoming nor deploring the future will change it,
but the former is preferable. (The OCT's πρὸ χαιρέτω would mean
'Before then, dismiss it from your thoughts', but this balances
προ-στένειν less neatly.)

254. 'For it will arrive, clear and dawning along with the sunbeams';
probably a proverb (cf. 264). The rays of dawn are an image of
'illumination', but also suggest the passage of dramatic time during
the song, from the night when the beacon was seen to the new day.

255–7. 'However that may be, may the outcome following these
events be well—in accordance with the wishes of this closest sole-
guardian bulwark of the Apian land.' The revealing particles δ' οὖν
are again employed (cf. 34–5 n., 224), here in the recurrent formula
of hope against hope (see Intro. at n. 76). During 255 the central
doors in the *skēnē* open to reveal Clytemnestra emerging from the
palace. Her grandeur is matched by an elaborate description. ἄγχισ-
τον refers to her closeness to Agamemnon in terms of heredity, as
a justification of her sovereignty in his absence. (In historical Greek
societies, of course, the queen would not have taken over, but that is
how Aeschylus has set up his mythical Argos.) Indeed, μονόφρουρος
implies Clytemnestra's sole control: Aegisthus is elided here as in
most of the play. ἕρκος ('bulwark') gives her a touch of the male
Iliadic hero: compare e.g. *Iliad* 3. 229 'Ajax . . . the ἕρκος of the

Achaeans'. The 'Apian land' is the Argolid, named after Apis who had once purified it (see *Supp.* 260–70).

ὡς θέλει suggests a polite deference from the Chorus (cf. 258–60). However, we know that Clytemnestra's wishes are not aligned with theirs. Furthermore, πρᾶξις 'outcome' is used at Euripides *Iph. Aul.* 272 in the sense 'enactment of revenge' (cf. 111 χερὶ πράκτορι, 'with avenging hand'). If the audience feels that secondary meaning here, the queen's entrance instantly undermines the Chorus's wish. (We prefer the interpretation above to the alternative, that τόδ' ... ἕρκος refers to the Chorus itself.)

First Episode (258–354): The movement consists largely of a short passage of stichomythia between Clytemnestra and the Coryphaeus, followed by two long speeches for Clytemnestra. The first describes the chain of beacons, starting from Mt. Ida in the Troad, which has brought her the news of Troy's capture on the previous night. In the second speech the queen presents a picture of Troy after the sack and leads on to a warning of the various dangers that could befall the Greek host before its return to Argos. The sequence may not appear to advance the play's 'action', but it does have clear dramatic purpose. It characterizes Clytemnestra as an authoritative speaker and agent. Furthermore, her words have ambivalent connotations, and if these are understood as having an ominous power to damage Agamemnon's safety (Intro. § 6), the logic and dynamics of the episode within the broader plot become more evident.

258–63. In his opening speech the Coryphaeus addresses Clytemnestra in respectful terms, though honouring her essentially as the temporary substitute for her absent husband; the subsequent stichomythia will be more combative. Three points which were given importance in the play's first mention of Clytemnestra (10–11) have that importance reinforced here: Clytemnestra's κράτος and ἐλπίς, and the male–female antithesis.

259–60. 'It is justice [i.e. proper] to honour the wife of a ruling man, when the throne is left empty of the male'. θρόνου and ἐρημωθέντος form a genitive absolute; ἄρσενος is a genitive of separation governed by ἐρημόω.

261–3. Literally 'As for you, I should gladly hear whether you are sacrificing after learning something good, or (are doing so) not after learning, from (mere) *hopes* of good news.' θυηπολεῖς is construed with both limbs of 261, but εὐαγγέλοισιν ἐλπίσιν only with the second. The lines expand on the Chorus's initial request at 97–8.

264–7. Clytemnestra's impressive opening characterizes her with great verbal dexterity in picking up several of the Coryphaeus' words (εὐάγγελος, πυνθάνομαι, ἐλπίς, κλύω; also εὔφρων in εὐφρόνη). She splits the idea of 'hopes of good news' into a prayer for good news in the morning, followed by an announcement of some specific good news which is *beyond* hope.

Night is euphemistically εὐφρόνη, 'kindly time', i.e. when human beings forget their worries. The idea of night giving birth to day is common (e.g. Soph. *Trach.* 94–6), but sinister in Clytemnestra's mouth. She is herself a mother, kindly to Iphigenia, whose death she is set to avenge (see esp. 152–5): the Μῆνις τεκνόποινος is now before us in person. Moritz (1979), 207–9 discusses the sinister contexts in which εὐφρόνη and εὔφρων are used in the early part of the trilogy.

The precise proverb behind 264–5 is unknown.

268. τοὖπος = τὸ ἔπος ('crasis'). Clytemnestra's word has 'escaped' the Coryphaeus in that he cannot believe it. The alliteration of π/φ is expressive, of excitement and/or incredulity.

269. *Τροίαν Ἀχαιῶν οὖσαν*: probably sc. φημί from 268; however, a participle after a verb of speaking other than ἀγγέλλω is very unusual.

271. 'Yes [γάρ], for your (weeping) eye asserts your loyalty.' For this sense of γάρ in answers, see Denniston 73. κατηγορέω governs a genitive (σοῦ). εὖ φρονοῦντος continues the word-play of εὔφρων (262) and εὐφρόνης (265). See also Goldhill (1984a), 36.

272. τί γὰρ τὸ πιστόν; : 'What is it that makes you sure?' This time, γάρ signals a request for an explanation of 269 (Denniston 63). The Coryphaeus' tone seems to be sceptical, given Clytemnestra's response and his subsequent questions.

273. τί δ' οὐχί: 'Of course!'—a strong riposte. μὴ δολώσαντος θεοῦ: genitive absolute, 'unless the god has deceived me'. Line 281 identifies the θεός.

274. πότερα: here introducing a single question. ὀνείρων φάσματ': Clytemnestra's implication in 273 that a god is involved prompts the suggestion that she is influenced by a dream.

275. 'I would not accept the fancy of a dozing mind.' βριζούσης scornfully answers ὀνείρων. Clytemnestra's contempt of dreams here is belied in *Choephoroe*, where a nightmare prompts her to send libations to Agamemnon's shade.

(δόξαν λαβεῖν may also mean 'acquire a reputation for', but that concept is less directly pertinent to the question in 274.)

276. 'Well, has some unfledged rumour puffed you up?' The particles introduce a further sceptical suggestion (Denniston 27). πιαίνω is literally 'fatten', and contemptuous (also in 1669). We interpret ἄπτερος as above, suggesting a rumour which is not fully grown or detailed; others take ἄπτερος less picturesquely as 'swift'—see Russo in *CHO* iii 22–4.

277. παιδὸς νέας ὥς: 'as of a young girl'. The genitive depends on φρένας; ὥς (accented) goes with what precedes. The reference to childishness would fit ἄπτερος if it means 'unfledged'.

278. The genitive ποίου χρόνου is used slightly unusually with the perfect πεπόρθηται to mean 'Since what time?', though it is answered in 279 by a normal genitive of 'time within which'. ποίου (rather than τίνος) may suggest a note of scepticism, as does the emphatic καί, 'actually'.

279. 'I declare it was during the night which just now bore this daylight.' The ambiguous resonances of 265 (see n. there) are emphasized.

280. 'Exactly who [καὶ τίς] of messengers could arrive at such speed?' τόδε τάχος is an 'adverbial' accusative (Smyth § 1606–8). The Coryphaeus' sceptical questioning reaches its climax.

281–316. Clytemnestra's so-called 'Beacons Speech' introduces us to her eloquence and tremendously vivid imagination.[2] As a description of beacons being lit repeatedly, the passage is impressively varied, though certain key ideas (φάος, πέμπω) recur. For example, mountains are mentioned by proper name alone, or with λέπας, αἶπος, σκοπή; this cycle repeats from 298, with the insertion of ὄρος. The beacons are referred to with even greater variety and, for most, adjectives describe the brightness, strength, or motion of their light. The subject is now the flame, now the groups of watchmen; but the flame is itself often given the animate qualities of a messenger, and metaphorical verbs to suit. Complementary similes (288, 297–8) compare the light to the sun and moon moving through the sky. All

---

[2] It may recently have inspired Peter Jackson, who replaced Tolkein's brief reference to a beacon-chain with a stirring sequence in his film *The Return of the King* (Jackson 2003, 0: 44: 55–0: 46: 48). We thank Alex Hadcock for this suggestion.

this turns what was probably a familiar military procedure to the Athenians (see Hdt 9. 3. 1; Hershbell 1978), into a marvel of cosmic dimensions (cf. 318 ἀποθαυμάσαι).

The speech has some puzzling features: some of the geography is obscure, and it can seem to be a set-piece of catalogue poetry with no relevance to Agamemnon's murder. The main geographical difficulties are the huge distances between some pairs of beacons, and our inability to locate three of the toponyms (289 Macistus, 302 Lake Gorgopis, 303 Mt. Aegiplanctus). The former issue may be insignificant: *pace* most articles on the beacons, we do not think that Aeschylus felt bound to cartographic precision. The obsure toponyms we would connect to the question of the speech's relevance. The chain of fires symbolically links the events at Troy with what is to come in Argos. Owen attractively saw Clytemnestra 'beckoning on' the destructive vengeance of Zeus 'as it comes . . . in the tiger-leaps of her sentences to strike the palace of Agamemnon' (1952, 71). Furthermore, many of the toponyms (and possibly all) have ominous associations with female treachery, ambushes, and the death of kings: D.A.R. has suggested an allusion for each location ad locc. Thus Clytemnestra's description gains an aggressive dimension. The suggestive connections with these types of destruction not only create foreboding, but are malevolently ill-omened and contribute practically to the dramatic momentum towards Agamemnon's murder (see Intro. § 6).

In terms of staging, Clytemnestra may well advance at 281 from her position in front of the central door towards the centre of the *orchēstra*, where she will be closer to the audience and also in among the Chorus (see Intro. § 5.1).

281. Ἥφαιστος: a magnificent one-word answer to the Coryphaeus. Even the lame god Hephaestus can easily travel at this superhuman pace. Ἴδης: the genitive is governed by ἐκ-. Ida and the next two locations (Lemnos and Athos) occur in reverse order in Hera's journey to the summit of Ida where she famously deceives her husband in *Iliad* 14. This undermines the positive appearance of Hephaestus, Hermes, and Zeus fostering the message's first stages.

282. ἀγγάρου πυρός: 'the courier flame'. ἄγγαρος is a Persian word used by Herodotus (8. 98) to describe their system for carrying despatches by horse in day-long relays.

283–4. Ἑρμαῖον λέπας Λήμνου: the 'crag of Hermes on Lemnos', also mentioned at Sophocles *Philoctetes* 1459; it may be the north-east or north-west promontory of the island (see Jebb 1898, who

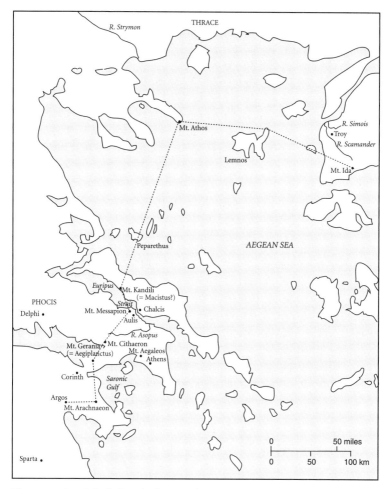

Places mentioned, including the beacon-chain. Adapted with permission; base map of the Aegean Sea available from http://d-maps.com (accessed 17 December 2010). © Daniel Dalet.

prefers the former). Hermes is relevant as a god of communication, but also as a god of trickery, who made woman deceitful (Hesiod *Op.* 67–8). One of Lemnos's principal associations was the myth of the Lemnian women who killed all but one of their menfolk (mentioned at *Cho.* 631–4).

285. Ἀθῷον αἶπος Ζηνός: 'the steep of Athos belonging to Zeus', i.e. sacred to him. The adjective–noun–genitive sequence recalls

Ἑρμαῖον λέπας Λήμνου, but with variation, so that the god now appears in the genitive rather than the adjective.

286. 'Rising aloft, so as to clear the back of the sea'; if correct, a unique use of νωτίζω (see LSJ).

287–8. The OCT (like Fraenkel, West, and Sommerstein) posits a lacuna to account for the impossible syntax, and to insert an intermediate station in the 100 miles between Athos and Macistus. See e.g. M. West (1990*a*), 181–3, who argues for Peparethus. The second issue is less significant, since travellers have reported seeing Athos from Euboea (Thomson 1938, 36; Beattie 1954, 78), and anyway the audience scarcely required geographical realism.

Emendation is a possible alternative. If πεύκη τό were replaced by a verb, such as Kock's ἐπέσυτο (from ἐπισεύω), the sense could be 'The power of the travelling torch <sped on> joyfully, relaying its golden radiance like a kind of sun to the watch-towers of Macistus'. However, it is hard to see how πεύκη would have entered the manuscript tradition.

289. παραγγείλασα: probably (lacuna or not) an aorist participle used aspectually, to describe coincident rather than prior action: see Barrett (1964), 213–14 for a good discussion. **Μακίστου**: lit. 'Tallest'; even in spoken passages, tragedy always uses the form with Doric ā, rather than μήκιστος. That the next stage is from Macistus to the modest hills by the Euripus (292) strongly suggests that Macistus is in Euboea, but the name is not otherwise recorded. Scholars have generally identified it with Mt. Kandili. A sinister poetic association is harder to find here, but it is curious that the adjective's only occurrence in the *Iliad* is at 7. 155, where it applies to a man being killed: τὸν δὴ μήκιστον καὶ κάρτιστον κτάνον ἄνδρα (Nestor about Ereuthalion; κτανεῖν ἄνδρα could also mean 'to kill a husband').

290–1. 'It did not neglect its messenger's share [i.e. turn in the relay] by delaying or by being insensibly overcome by sleep.' ὁ δ᾽ refers to Macistus, and so by metonymy to its watchmen. The negatives οὔτι and οὐδ᾽ apply to the main verb as well as to the participles.

293. 'signals to the watchmen of Messapion its coming over the streams of Euripus'. μολόν is a participle after a verb of showing (Smyth § 2106–7). Messapion is a chain of coastal hills on the Boeotian side of the Euripus strait. The mention of this strait reminds us of Iphigenia's sacrifice (cf. 190–1).

297–8. Ἀσωποῦ: a river in Boeotia. A possible ominous association is that Tydeus was ambushed there by fifty Thebans, according to

Iliad 4. 392–6. δίκην: the recurrent usage (see 3 n.) is here markedly planted between a comma and the end of the verse. Κιθαιρῶνος: Mt. Cithaeron is notorious among other things for the death of King Pentheus at the hands of his mother Agave and the other bacchants (as told in Euripides *Bacchae*). Another possible resonance is the Great Daidala festival held there which involved a huge bonfire, and commemorated King Cithaeron's advice to Zeus on how to deal with his wife's anger (Pausanias 9. 3. 5–8).

301. φρουρά: 'the watch' is another metonym for the watchmen (cf. 290–1 n.). Here, they burn 'more than what had been ordered'— an exuberant touch.

302–3. Given the specific toponyms in the rest of the speech Γοργῶπις ('Gorgon-eyed') and Αἰγίπλαγκτος ('Roamed by goats') are generally taken as proper names, though not by Fraenkel. Cratinus fr. 189 seems to have referred to a Lake Gorgopis near Corinth, whose exact location may well have been unclear to Aeschylus' audience. Aegiplanctus is not otherwise recorded; it is generally equated with Mt. Gerania, north of Corinth, since this gives the simplest route. (Quincey 1963, 129–31 thought the name would have suggested Aegaleos, a modest hill near Athens. But in this local instance the Athenians would have noticed that the route Cithaeron–Aegaleos–Arachnaeum is too contorted.)

Whether the audience took them as real or fictitious, the names may be symbolically suggestive. 'Gorgon-eyed' may recall Agamemnon's shield 'on which was embossed Γοργὼ βλοσυρῶπις, with a fearsome glance' (*Il.* 11. 36–7), while Αἰγί-πλαγκτος suggests Αἴγι-σθος. Then by an ingenious metonymy, the φάος (a common metaphor for 'victory', here in vengeance) swoops over Gorgopis (the warrior Agamemnon) to Aegiplanctus (~ Aegisthus).

ἔσκηψεν: intransitive 'shot downwards'; an aggressive word, repeated in 308, 310.

304. θεσμόν: i.e. Clytemnestra's instructions (cf. 312 νόμοι). †μὴ χαρίζεσθαι†: a different middle infinitive is needed (a passive one would be unusual in an indirect command), meaning something like 'disregard'. Musgrave's παρίεσθαι fits the sense (cf. 291 παρῆκεν), but is less convincing palaeographically than Casaubon's χρονίζεσθαι 'delay'.

305. ἀνδαίοντες: i.e. ἀναδαίοντες (poetic 'apocope' of the final vowel of a preposition; compare e.g. 7 ἀντολ- for ἀνατολ-). μένει: dative of μένος (as in 238).

306–8. †καὶ Σαρωνικοῦ ... φλέγουσαν†: neither West nor Sommerstein obelizes, and the OCT is reasonably smooth: 'they send a great beard of flame to leap over the conspicuous [κάτοπτον] headland of the Saronic strait as well [καί]'. ὑπερβάλλειν is an infinitive expressing the aim of a verb of sending (Smyth § 2009); καί might be translated 'even' or 'actually', but this seems to give a false emphasis. The main difficulty is that φλέγουσαν has no noun to agree with. Possibly, φλόγα is to be understood from the imaginative metaphor φλογὸς πώγωνα. West alternatively suggests φλογὸς μέγαν πώγων', ὅσην Σαρωνικοῦ . . . . , where φλογὸς ὅσην + infinitive is straightforward. (West and Sommerstein both prefer κατόπτην: 'the headland overlooking the Saronic strait'.)

    Whichever 'strait' in the Saronic Gulf is referred to, it is named after Saron, a mythical king of Trozen. He supposedly built a coastal sanctuary to Artemis, but drowned while chasing a stag into the sea; his body washed ashore in Artemis' grove. The myth therefore again involves the death of a king, but overlaps more precisely with Iphigenia's story (death at Artemis' coastal sanctuary).

308. εἶτ' ... εἶτ': distinguish εἶτ' < εἶτα and εἶτ' < εἶτε. The unusual repetition 'Then ... then' has a forceful and effective succinctness.

309. Ἀραχναῖον αἶπος: Spider Mountain in the Argolid, within sight of the palace. The name anticipates the image of 1492 (and 1516) where the robe which Clytemnestra has woven to entrap Agamemnon is a spider's web.

310. σκήπτει: the verb is used for a third time, as the light finally descends on the house of Atreus—a deeply uneasy moment to which all the preceding detail of the language has contributed.

311. οὐκ ἄπαππον: 'not without descent from'. Many α-privative adjectives govern a genitive, as here (Smyth § 1428).

312–13. 'Such, I tell you, (were) my dispensations for torch-bearers, fulfilled in succession one from another.' The five οι sounds in 312 are powerfully assertive; τοι carries a boasting nuance (Denniston 540). Whereas 282 alluded to the Persian ἀγγαρήϊον, here λαμπαδη-φόρος would suggest the torch-races documented at eight festivals in Attica, where fresh fire was conveyed from one altar to another. For example, at the festival of Hephaestus relay teams from each tribe competed in different age-categories. Clytemnestra is like an official prescribing the rules of the festival. Unlike the torch-races, of course, there is only one 'team' and the fire is not physically transported from station to station, but the fast relay of firelight grounds the comparison.

314. Interpretation is difficult since the 'runners' could be (1) the watchmen who sent the message on at each stage, or (2) the firelight itself.

(1) 'The runner of the first leg and that of the last leg are victorious', i.e. all the signallers share in the success of the operation. For the omission of a second article with τελευταῖος, cf. 324; for the singular verb with a compound subject, see Smyth § 966. (*Pace* Sommerstein n. 71, we would not take Clytemnestra herself as the 'last runner'.)

(2) 'He who ran both first and last legs [i.e. Hephaestus] is victorious.' On this interpretation, Clytemnestra alludes to a further difference from normal torch-races, namely that a single 'runner' has performed every stage.

In either case, given the absence of a proper relay contest, the emphatic νικᾶι stands out and implies Clytemnestra's desire for a victory of her own, to follow on Agamemnon's victory at Troy (see esp. 940–3).

315–16. σύμβολον παραγγέλλειν is a technical term for 'pass on the watchword': Struck (2004), 80 n. 12. τέκμαρ is in ring-composition with 272, implying that Clytemnestra has now completed her proof of Troy's capture. Also, σύμβολον and ἐκ Τροίας echo the Watchman's words at 8–9 and confirm the fulfilment of his duty.

The first syllable of τοιοῦτος often scans short, as if the iota were a single consonant 'y'. This anomaly is largely confined to τοιοῦτος.

317–19. The Coryphaeus will invoke the gods later on (αὖθις), as the elders do after 354. But first, 'I would like to hear and marvel greatly [ἀπο-] at these words from start to finish, as you would tell it again'. It may seem puzzling that the Coryphaeus does not immediately express more enthusiasm for the conviction of Clytemnestra's account and the news of Agamemnon's victory. Aeschylus seems to be suggesting that a second hearing of her words might allow one to detect their underlying resonances. **λέγοις**: optative by assimilation to θέλοιμ᾽ ἄν (Smyth § 2186).

320–50. Instead of responding to the Coryphaeus' 'remarkable request' (D–P), Clytemnestra imagines the scene at Troy, again with great vividness and authority. Her utterances continue to be ominous for Agamemnon's cause. She begins by contrasting the cries of the vanquished and the victors: the Trojans are lamenting their loved ones, while the Greeks . . . We expect them to be joyfully celebrating their victory, but Clytemnestra paints a bleak picture for them too. The ambivalent description continues down to 347: for the moment, the Greeks are safe and warm, but their fortunes are still subject to luck and divine vengeance.

321. πρέπειν: 'to be conspicuous' rather than 'to be appropriate', as at 241.

322–3. 'If you were to pour both vinegar and oil into the same vessel, you would call the two of them enemies [literally 'non-friends'] as they take separate positions.' ταὐτῶι = τῶι αὐτῶι. οὐ is stronger if taken with φίλω (which is dual) rather than with the verb.

324–5. ἔστι = πάρεστι (LSJ εἰμί A VI). συμφορᾶς διπλῆς could be genitive absolute (sc. οὔσης: 'the turn of fortune being twofold'), but more likely defines φθογγάς, 'cries (expressive) of the twofold turn of fortune'.

These lines express the opposition of two groups in several ways: first ἄμεικτον, then δι-χοστατοῦντε, the dual φίλω, δί-χα, and δι-πλῆς.

326–9. There is no need to obelize. 'Those on one side [the Trojans], prostrate around the bodies of husbands and brothers, and children (prostrate around the bodies) of the elders who begot them, from a throat no longer free lament aloud [ἀπ-] the death of their dearest.' For the affecting juxtaposition of young and old, cf. 75–8, 721–2, Lebeck (1971), 18–19.

330–3. Literally 'Night-roaming toil after battle posts the other side starving to breakfasts consisting of what [ὧν = ἐκείνων ἅ] the city affords, according to no token in turn, but as each has drawn fortune's lot.' νυκτίπλαγκτος and πόνος recall the Watchman's speech (1, 12, 20) as does 336 δρόσων τ' ἀπαλλαχθέντες and (by opposition) 337 ἀφύλακτον εὐδήσουσι. The Greeks are in a happier position now than the Watchman was, but the echoes of the prologue also link them with the mood of foreboding established then. Lines 332–3 use military terminology to contrast the Greeks having to fend for themselves with the normal procedure for rationing; but the details are not wholly clear. Perhaps the soldiers normally received a token based on a ballot (cf. πάλον), which determined the order in which they received provisions.

334–7. At least the Greeks have a roof over their heads and can enjoy a decent night's sleep without guards being posted. But ὡς εὐδαίμονες is overstated: call no one happy until they are dead (see e.g. 928–9 and Hdt. 1. 32 for this commonplace). Clytemnestra is deliberately 'tempting fate', to counteract the superficially good news (cf. 895–905). The sinister implication is reinforced by the assonance of εὐδαίμονες with εὐδήσουσι, εὐφρόνην, and 338 εὐσεβοῦσι.

338–47. The sense of danger comes to the fore in these lines. In the excitement of victory the Greeks must beware of desecrating the temples of the gods, if they want a safe return home. Aeschylus' audience could not have missed the sinister significance of this warning: Priam's murder at the altar of Zeus and Cassandra's abduction from the temple of Athena were among the most famous episodes of the tradition. Then from 345 Clytemnestra goes on to list all the possible risks: 'If the army should return without error in the eyes of the *gods*, the suffering of the dead [e.g. Iphigenia, the innocent Trojans] might be awakened, unless suddenly-striking [πρόσπαια] disasters should occur.' The last clause includes any remaining contingency, and suggests the blows of Agamemnon's murder (cf. 1384 παίω). By mentioning each possibility, Clytemnestra offers a κληδών which makes it more likely to occur.

338. πολισσούχους: the most common gods 'who hold the citadel' are Athena and Zeus (as in Athens: Athena Polias and Zeus Polieus). These are precisely the gods whose sanctuaries are most famously desecrated (338–47 n.).

340. τἄν = τοι ἄν (crasis). ἄν is thus repeated. This often lends extra emphasis to the preceding word(s), here ἀνθαλοῖεν (Smyth § 1765).

341. μή + subjunctive expresses 'I rather fear that' (see 131–4 n.), whereas a plain wish would have an optative. This distinction is very apt given Clytemnestra's real hopes.

342. νικωμένους: this refers to the soldiers implied in στρατῶι, attracted into the accusative under the normal construction of χρή (see Smyth § 1062).

343–4. δεῖ is construed first with the genitive σωτηρίας ('There is need of'), then with the infinitive κάμψαι ('There is need to'). The Greeks' return journey is described as the second 'leg' (κῶλον) of a hairpin-shaped running track (δίαυλος); κάμψαι includes both rounding the turn at half-way (καμπή), and completing the home straight.

345–7. See 338–47 n. for a gloss. ἐγρηγορός 'awakened' is the perfect active participle from ἐγείρω, but with intransitive sense. It suggests the common idea that the dead are in some sense 'asleep'. Sommerstein has παρήγορον and West a lacuna, but we see no reason to alter the text.

348. τοιαῦτά τοι γυναικός: once again an assertive τοι (cf. 312–13 n.). Here for the first time Clytemnestra proudly asserts her womanhood (cf. 592, 1661 nn.).

349. 'But may the good prevail, not ambivalently in appearance.' In τὸ δ᾽ εὖ κρατοίη, Clytemnestra chooses a formula which else-where in the play fights against despair (see 121 n.), and thus again focuses attention on the danger in the Greeks' situation; and the mention of ambivalence (διχορρόπως), even when negated, emphasizes its importance in all that Clytemnestra has said. The emphasis on the visual over other qualities (ἰδεῖν, explanatory infinitive) looks forward to what the theatregoers will themselves witness.

350. 'For many are the blessings of which I have chosen the enjoy-ment for myself.' Prayers not only for goods but for the continued ὄνησις of them were common (see Fraenkel, though he interprets differently). Clytemnestra expands on her inclusion of 'unambigu-ously' in her preceding prayer: she wants both *many* goods and the ability to enjoy them. For the public, πολλὰ ἐσθλά refers to the sack of Troy and ὄνησις to the safe return of Agamemon. But privately, πολλὰ ἐσθλά may refer to her current life of adultery and power, and ὄνησις to the ability to enjoy these after killing Agamemnon on his safe return, to avenge Iphigenia. The middle verb perhaps hints that *her* good might not be the same as Agamemnon's. The line is thus a beautifully sinister parting shot.

There is an alternative interpretation: 'For I prefer enjoyment (of my current fortune) to many blessings (in the future)'; ἐσθλῶν is now a genitive of comparison. Clytemnestra would be explaining why she did not instead pray for further future goods in 349: we consider this far-fetched.

351–3. The Coryphaeus, picking up 348, credits Clytemnestra with a man's good sense; κατά means 'in the fashion of' (LSJ s.v. B IV 3). εὐφρόνως differs from σῶφρον᾽ and means 'with kindly intent' (cf. 271): the Coryphaeus has not perceived Clytemnestra's malevolent ambiguity. For the moment the elders' mood has changed from ἀπιστία (268) to trusting the beacon-signals as πιστὰ τεκμήρια. They return to their intention (317) of addressing the gods in well-omened fashion (εὖ, qualifying προσειπεῖν).

354. Literally 'A not unvalued recompense for toils has been achieved.' For this sense of χάρις, see LSJ s.v. III 1a; the word is the main term used to describe the mutual favours of human worship and divine benefaction. LSJ seem wrong to translate ἄτιμος here as 'unworthy'.

Clytemnestra probably withdraws into the palace during 353–4.

First Stasimon (355–487): After twelve lines of introductory anapaests the Chorus embarks on another long ode of three strophic pairs, followed by an epode in a different vein. The whole is remarkable for its gradual shifts of thought. What begins as a hymn of praise to Zeus and Night for the capture of Troy ends up mentioning popular resentment at the Atridae's campaign and the dangers of conquest. This conclusion leads the elders to wonder whether the beacon-signal was trustworthy after all.

Troy's capture is ascribed to Zeus finally punishing Paris, and the first strophic pair (367–402) consists largely of reflections on the path from wealth to sin to divine punishment as exemplified by his fate. At the transition into the second pair (403–36), the trail leads via Helen's departure to Menelaus' sense of loss in the palace, and from there to the distress of women in houses throughout Greece at the loss of their husbands in the Trojan war. As in the three preceding stanzas, the final four lines of the antistrophe introduce an idea which is then expanded: this time it is of war as a gold-trader exchanging warriors for ashes. The third pair (437–74) builds up to the general Argive resentment at the war, and the Chorus's foreboding of punishment from above for those who are mass killers (461), overly successful (468), and city-sackers (472). Lines 461–70 recall 367–84 in mentioning the unjust rich man and the blow from Zeus (Lebeck 1971, 43–4). From a positive and hopeful starting-point, the Chorus must again confront a negative and troubling conclusion about Agamemnon's fortunes.

The ode's metrical form (Appendix § 5) contributes to its significance. The syncopated iambic rhythm associated in the parodos with sin and retribution (192–257 n.) prevails throughout from 367; moreover, each strophe has a short, metrically identical tailpiece ('ephymnion'). The metre therefore emphasizes the unity of idea which pervades the shifting sequence of subject-matter and imagery. This idea is the course of retribution. Paris was rich, sinned, and has been punished. Agamemnon is rich, has blood on his hands, and . . . The Chorus can draw the conclusion, but dare not voice it. Instead, they seek to avoid it by a remarkable volte-face in the epode, where they (or some of them: see 475–87 n.) revert to mistrusting the beacon-signal, in marked contrast to their attitude at the beginning of the song (352). Troy's sack will bring trouble—but perhaps it has not come to that yet.

355–66. In the introductory anapaests, victory over Troy and over Paris is attributed to Zeus Xenios (cf. 61–2) and Night, under whose cover the city was traditionally captured. These lines have a typical hymnic form: an invocation to Zeus and Night, epithets, then a relative pronoun forming a transition into a description of past events.

356. μεγάλων κόσμων κτέατειρα: κτέατειρα only occurs here, and two interpretations are canvassed: (1) 'possessor of mighty ornaments', i.e. the moon and the stars: compare the cosmic perspective of 6–9; (2) 'obtainer of great glories'. For κόσμος verging on 'victory' see e.g. Pindar *Olympian* 8. 83. (2) is more relevant to the context, whereas (1) is purely decorative.

357. ἥτ': the relative has a causal force, 'in that you . . .' (Denniston 523–4); with interpretation (1) above it explains φιλία, and with (2) also κόσμων κτέατειρα.

358. στεγανὸν δίκτυον: 'a covering net'. Troy has been captured under *cover* of darkness, cast over the city from the sky. The image here and in 361 γάγγαμον ('dragnet') will recur later in the 'net' of the robe which Clytemnestra uses to entrap Agamemnon (1115, 1382). See Introduction § 9.2. **ὡς:** consecutive (normally ὥστε in prose), as the following infinitive suggests. **μέγαν:** here 'grown up'.

359. μήτ' οὖν νεαρῶν τιν': 'nor yet any of the young'. οὖν throws a slight emphasis (Denniston 419; it does not mean 'therefore' here). The unsettling focus on the innocent Trojan children perhaps recalls how the hare's young were a symbol of innocent victims at 118–20.

360–1. 'the great slavery-net of all-taking ruin'. δουλείας is a defining genitive with γάγγαμον; ἄτης is possessive. The net belongs to ἄτη in that Troy's capture and enslavement are retribution for Paris' folly in abducting Helen. The thought is developed at length in 367–402.

362. Δία . . . ξένιον: recalling 61–2, as does ἐπ' Ἀλεξάνδρωι.

363–6. 'who has long been drawing his bow against Paris, to ensure that he might not shoot his arrow in vain, either short of the target or beyond the stars'. Zeus is metaphorically an archer (as Paris was), whereas normally he hurls his missiles. ὑπὲρ ἄστρων suggests both that πρὸ καιροῦ is spatial (not temporal 'prematurely') and that σκήπτω is transitive 'shoot' (with βέλος as object) rather than intransitive 'fall' (with βέλος as subject).

367–8. 'From Zeus is the blow that they [= the Trojans] can tell of. This at least [i.e. whatever else remains unclear] it is possible to track down.' The Trojans can trace their city's fall to Zeus; but the impersonal πάρεστιν suggests that the Chorus too, in its present song, is pursuing a trail in its attempt to make sense of events.

369. ἔπραξεν ὡς ἔκρανεν: 'He [= Zeus] acted as he ordained.' ἔπραξεν picks up 363 πράξαντ'. The assonance (repeated ἔ-ρᾱ-εν) has a portentous ring.

369–73. 'People have denied that the gods deign to be concerned with any mortals by whom the grace of inviolate things is trampled on.' The Greek idiom is literally 'Someone has denied ...' in the singular. For the personal construction of μέλω governing a genitive, see LSJ s.v. B. ὅσοις πατοῖθ' is an indefinite clause, in the optative because ἔφᾱ is historic. The dative ὅσοις expresses the agent, as often in verse (ὑφ' ὅσων would be normal in prose). Paris tramples on Menelaus' hospitality; but the whole phrase looks forwards to Agamemnon trampling on the precious garments in the third episode, and χάρις ἀθίκτων may also recall Iphigenia at her sacrifice. See also Lebeck (1971), 74–8.

ὁ δ' οὐκ εὐσεβής: 'But such a man (is) impious'. Demonstrative ὁ δέ refers to the τις; as often, ἐστίν is omitted.

374–8. A passage with no certain solution. (1) With ἀρή for ἄρη, the OCT might mean 'The ruin attendant on what may not be dared stands revealed for the descendants of those whose pride is greater than right, when their house abounds with wealth in excess, beyond what is best' (Lloyd-Jones 1979, amended). Here, ἀτολμήτων is neuter (cf. 408 ἄτλητα). πνεόντων depends on ἐγγόνοις; for μέγα πνεῖν 'be proud' see e.g. Eur. *Andr.* 189, *Bacch.* 640. φλεόντων δωμάτων is a genitive absolute, and πνεόντων ... φλεόντων is a marked assonance. The argument would be: 'The gods *do* have regard for sin: (even if it does not come immediately) their punishment is visited on the sinner's descendants', combined with 'Extreme

wealth leads to pride and thence to daring and sin.' For the first
point, cf. *Sept.* 742–5, Introduction § 4.3.4. However, the Chorus
before and after speaks of the *direct* punishment of Paris, without
reference to any ancestral crime for which he is paying.

(2) Emendation produces quite different readings, such as
Hartung's πέφανται δ' ἐκτίνουσα τόλμᾱ τῶν Ἄρη πνεόντων
μεῖζον ἢ δικαίως, 'The audacity of those who breathe Ares more
fiercely than is just has been shown paying a penalty.' However,
the Chorus would not attribute excessive militarism to Paris and the
Trojans, and Ἄρη πνεῖν μεῖζον is dubious Greek (see Fraenkel).

378–80. 'Let there be a non-harmful amount, so as to be enough for
one who has a good allotment of wisdom.' ἔστω/ἔστι first in the
sentence most often means 'Let there be/There is'.

381–4. We take πλούτου πρὸς κόρον (uncapitalized) together: 'For
there is no defence for a man who in excess of wealth has kicked
the great altar of Justice into obscurity.' κόρος is also the attitude
engendered by extreme wealth. πρός effectively means 'in a manner
involving' (cf. 130 πρὸς τὸ βίαιον). The image of 'kicking Justice's
altar' signifies spurning the hallowed canons of proper behaviour,
and is echoed at *Eum.* 539–42 'Show respect for Justice's altar, and do
not, with an eye to profit, dishonour it with a godless kick' (Podlecki
1989).

One could alternatively construe πλούτου with ἔπαλξις, 'defence
afforded by wealth against Excess'; but this fits the conventional
wisdom less well. The doctrine enounced here and the following idea
in 385–6 already appear in Solon fr. 4. 5–18. Wealth in excess (cf.
πλούτου κόρος) leads to insolent thoughts and acts above one's
station (i.e. ὕβρις). The insolent man is further assailed by
infatuation (ἄτη), which makes him susceptible to persuasion
(πειθώ) into impious crimes (cf. the effect of παρακοπή in 222–3).
Ruinous retribution then follows for himself, or his descendants
(374–8 n.) or his fellow-citizens (397–8).

385–6. 'Relentless Persuasion forces (him) on—the irresistible child
of πρόβουλος Infatuation.' Atē is the spirit who sends the folly
associated with ὕβρις, and uses her daughter Πειθώ as her instrument to effect come-uppance: the sinner, through folly, can be
persuaded to horrendous actions. For similar genealogical relationships among personifications, see Fraenkel; in general, see Introduction § 4.3.3. βία and πειθώ are normally contrasted, but the
language here paradoxically unites the two ideas.

πρόβουλος admits two interpretations: either Infatuation 'sets up the agenda' which Persuasion carries through, as the Athenian Council prepared προβουλεύματα for discussion in the Assembly (see Rhodes 1972, 52–87); or Infatuation 'exercises forethought' by marking out her victim in advance and planning how to undo them.

For Aeschylus' use of ἄφερτος, and the elegant translation 'more than our nature will bear', see Dodds (1973), 56 with n. 2.

387. ἐκρύφθη: gnomic aorist.

388–95. The sinner's exposure and the inevitability of his demise are described in a magnificent blend of images. 'Rather, the contamination is conspicuous, a grim-shining light. Like bad bronze, by rubbing and knocks he turns out indelibly black [literally 'fixed with black', related to πήγνυμι] when brought to justice, for he is a boy chasing a fluttering bird, once he has brought an intolerable smear on his city.' For τρόπον + genitive see 49 n. The sinner's wickedness is brightly manifest (πρέπει, φῶς), yet shows up dark (μελαμ-παγής) like low-quality bronze whose admixture of lead is gradually revealed by wear and tear. πρόστριμμα is that which rubs off the sinner on to his city. The process of rubbing (see the two occurrences of τριβ-) therefore simultaneously infects his society and reveals his unclean heart. That is why, in hoping to escape conviction, he seeks the unattainable, like a boy pursuing a bird (a proverbial expression—compare our 'wild goose chase').

396–8. (1) Usually construed: 'As to his prayers, none of the gods listens to them, but (one) destroys the unjust man who is conversant with those things.' θεῶν τις is understood as the subject of καθαιρεῖ from the preceding οὔτις θεῶν; the sense of the rare ἐπίστροφος is suggested by *Od.* 1. 177 ἐπίστροφος ἀνθρώπων; τῶν is demonstrative.

(2) However, the position of μέν suggests that λιτᾶν should be common to both clauses, picked up in the second by the slightly vaguer neuter τῶν. Then ἐπίστροφος could mean 'paying attention to' (cf. LSJ ἐπιστρέφω II 3). The δέ-clause is then ' . . . while the unjust man who respects them he [= the sinner] destroys', i.e. brings down with him. This gives a good contrast between the μέν- and δέ-clauses; the latter picks up the idea of 395 πόλει πρόστριμμα θείς.

Blomfield's emendation φῶτα Δίκα for φῶτ' ἄδικον is attractive with either (1) or (2).

399–402. The Chorus returns to specify the intended relevance of the preceding general statements to Paris (not named since 363) and his disgraceful treatment of Menelaus' hospitable board.

403–5. The subject switches to Helen after 402 γυναικός. Literally 'Leaving for her fellow-citizens shield-bearers' turmoils, settings of ambushes, and instances of sailors' arming-up.' ἀσπίστορας and ναυβάτας are normally nouns ('shield-bearer', 'sailor'), here used adjectivally instead of in the genitive. λοχισμούς might mean 'instances of forming into companies'. The lines are carefully discussed by Gannon (1997), though his interpretation of ὁπλισμούς (via ὅπλα, 'ships' tackle') does not square with extant usage of ὁπλίζω.

406. ἀντίφερνον ... φθοράν: instead of a dowry (φερνή), Helen brings to her new home destruction; this is no better than what she left to the Argives in 403–5.

407–8. βεβάκει: pluperfect of βαίνω without augment—'she was gone'. διά: a long syllable is 'resolved' into two shorts for the first time in the stasimon, to reflect the sense of a sudden, uncatchable departure. The rhythmic effect is duplicated in the responding line (424, also with διά and βεβακ-), where the dreams of Helen slip away.

The Chorus at 60–7 suggested that Helen was not a worthy object of war, and here it presents her willingly leaving with Paris (see esp. ῥίμφα, 'lightly', conveying both speed and ease, and ἄτλητα τλᾶσα). This probably seemed tendentious, since Aphrodite's role was emphasized in the *Cypria*, and mentioned alongside Helen's guilt in Alcaeus fr. 283, Sappho fr. 16, and frequently in the *Iliad* (3. 64, 164, 399–412, 6. 349; but the self-loathing Helen also blames herself, particularly at 3. 174). Makron painted the abduction on two cups, *c*.485 BC (*LIMC* Alexandros 63–4): on one Paris is armed, Helen looks modestly at the ground, and Aphrodite and Persuasion are present; on the other, Helen's family urge the other Trojans to stop the abduction (contrast Aeschylus' ῥίμφα).

409. δόμων προφῆται: 'the palace spokesmen', perhaps certain elders in the Atridae's retinue, who speak here while Menelaus is silent. προφήτης can mean 'seer', but their prediction for the future (415) is hardly difficult, so this meaning seems less apt.

The editor must decide where their speech ends—not before 415 δόξει, whose tense does not make sense from the Chorus's perspective, nor after 426 since the δέ-clause (and thus the preceding μέν-clause) is located in the Chorus's present. As alternatives to the OCT, it is worth considering whether the speech ends after 415 or 419.

410. πρόμοι: Agamemnon as well as Menelaus.

411. στίβοι φιλάνορες: literally 'man-loving footprints'—but are they from when Helen was loyal to Menelaus, or are they the 'philandering' steps by which she followed Paris? φιλάνορες may well recall 62 πολυάνορος (also of Helen), which suggests the latter interpretation here; the adjective will be carefully ambiguous in 856. Furthermore, the idea of 'stepping' has just been evoked (βέβακει: the precise core of βαίνω is 'take a step') in connection with Helen's departure. (Sommerstein takes στίβοι as the impress of Helen's body on Menelaus' bed, but στείβω and related words normally refer to footsteps.)

412–13. A heavily emended but readable text is Hermann's: πάρεστι σιγὰς ἀτίμους ἀλοιδόρους ἀλίστους ἀφειμένων ἰδεῖν, 'One can observe the rejected party's silences, which are without honour, without revilement, without entreaty.' The plural participle from ἀφίημι alludes to a single person, namely Menelaus (see Smyth § 1007). The three accusative a-privative adjectives are transferred from him to his silence; for their cumulative emotional intensity cf. 769–70, *Cho.* 55 σέβας δ' ἄμαχον ἀδάματον ἀπόλεμον.

414–15. 'Through (Menelaus') longing for the woman across the sea, a ghost will seem to rule the palace.' The ghost is almost certainly that of Helen, whose spirit seems to Menelaus to continue her reign; cf. the subsequent idea of her appearances to him (420–1 ὀνειρό-φαντοι δόξαι). (Schütz and others have taken the ghost as Menelaus, now 'a phantom of his former self', but this strains the single word φάσμα.)

416–19. Menelaus' situation paradoxically leads him to 'hate the grace' of statues in his house. κολοσσοί probably suggest a rather archaic figure with the legs not carved separately; Steiner (1995), 178 suggests that this static quality contrasts with Helen's mobility. Menelaus' hatred is explained by 418–19 ('apodotic' δέ: Denniston 169), of which the first words are tricky. They might mean 'In his situation of lacking (Helen's) eyes, all Aphrodite [≈ 'loveliness'] goes to ruin', including the beauty of statues. Alternatively, 'Because they lack (real) eyes, all their loveliness goes for nothing': the statues' painted or inset eyes just remind Menelaus of the real ones he is missing. We do not find the idea that the κολοσσοί represent Helen herself at all attractive.

420–1. πενθήμονες ... δόξαι: while waking, Menelaus sees statues as a pale substitute for Helen. This is continued by 'a mourner's fantasies' of her while he is asleep. Housman's πειθήμονες, 'persuasive', is an attractive possibility given ὀνείρων φάσματ' εὐπιθῆ (274).

423–5. 'For vainly, whenever someone sees what appears good, is the vision gone, having slipped aside through his hands.' δοκοῦνθ' ὁρᾶι is Salzmann's emendation of δοκῶν ὁρᾶν which produces a hanging participle (but is accepted by West). For παραλλάσσω in this sense, see LSJ s.v. II 5–6; the *locus classicus* for dreams slipping through one's fingers is *Iliad* 23. 99–101 (Achilles and Patroclus' ghost).

425–6. 'not thereafter attending on wings the paths of sleep'. When the vision has roused the dreamer once, it does not return. The 'paths of sleep' are probably the routes which take dreams from the underworld to dreamers.

428. τάδ' ἐστί: here—as perhaps in 417, 419, and 421 if one ends the speech of the προφῆται earlier (409 n.)—the Chorus speaks of Menelaus' sorrows in the present tense, as though he were still in the palace. τῶνδ' ὑπερβατώτερα: 'ones surpassing them' (genitive of comparison), i.e. Menelaus' distress during the day. But the vague phrase and present tense might suggest to the audience Clytemnestra's ἄχη for Iphigenia.

429–31. The picture broadens to include the grief in the other families of the Greek men who went to war. The corrupt text demands caution, but the OCT means: 'And, in general [τὸ πᾶν, which more often means 'utterly'], for those who set out together from the land of Greece, a mourning woman with an enduring heart is conspicuous in the house of each.' συνορμένοισι is aorist participle from συνόρνυμαι. δόμωι 'ν would be an example of 'prodelision' of ἐν.

πένθεια, which is not found elsewhere, causes more difficulty. Murray's interpretation (above) is more vivid than Stinton's 'grief'. Fraenkel and West considered ἀπένθεια ('non-lamentation'), an attested word which could follow συνορμένοις. However, in 445–7 it is clear that the bereaved do express their sorrow (to complement Menelaus' πενθήμονες δόξαι, if that text is right). For further discussion on either side see D–P, M. West (1990a), 187.

432. γοῦν: the particle introduces a piece of evidence for the claims of the preceding statement (Denniston 451). There is certainly much cause for distress: an urn containing ashes is all that comes home from the war. θιγγάνει πρὸς ἧπαρ: 'touch right to the liver', i.e. cause bitter grief.

433–4. οὓς μὲν γὰρ <τις> ἔπεμψεν οἶδεν: 'For people *know* those whom they sent out', but cannot recognize them when they return as ashes; (ἐκείνους) οὓς ἔπεμψεν is a relative clause, not an indirect question.

434–6. τεύχη 'urn' (LSJ s.v. II) is plural for singular. The practice of returning the ashes of Athenian soldiers killed in battle after their bodies had been cremated seems to have been introduced within the decade before the *Oresteia*; by contrast, in the *Iliad* (except for 7. 332–8 and 16. 678–83, the latter being quite exceptional) the warriors' bones are generally burnt in a common pyre, and the ashes buried at Troy. Besides this specific contemporary reference, the whole following passage would have resonated powerfully with Athenians who had suffered heavy casualties on multiple fronts in 460–59 BC (see Intro. § 2).

437–44. In a striking image, War is presented as a 'gold-trader of bodies, who carries his weighing-scales amid a spear-battle'. The idea modifies the scales of the *Iliad* in which the heroes' fates are weighed in order to indicate who will die (e.g. 22. 209–13). Here Ares takes a corpse and offers in exchange a weight of πυρωθὲν ψῆγμα, 'refined gold-dust' in the terms of the metaphor and 'cremated ash' in actuality. This dust is βαρύ—simultaneously 'weighty' on Ares' scales and a 'heavy' burden to the dead man's relatives. The ash is ἀντήνωρ—a fair exchange for a man according to Ares' scales, yet quite the opposite in the eyes of the bereaved. In 444, read εὐθέτους to provide a more even distribution of adjectives among the nouns: 'loading easily-stowed urns with ash' (genitive after the idea 'fill').

445–51. Private eulogies (cf. εὖ λέγοντες) lead into suppressed resentment at the purpose of the expedition, in which most Argives have no investment, and at the Atridae generally; with ἀλλοτρίας διαὶ γυναικός cf. 62, 225–6. The attitude contrasts markedly with the civic ideology of e.g. Pericles' funeral oration (Thucydides 2. 35–46), where private grief is subordinated to the glorious goals of the *polis* as a whole. The stanza ends emphatically with the Atridae: the ode's original focus on Paris seems distant.

For the switch in rhythm at 448–51 (=467–70), see Appendix § 5.

449. βαΰζει: 'snarls', like a dog—connoting criticism and probably also bitter sorrow: see Garvie (2009), 53–4.

450. ὑπ' . . . ἕρπει: = ὑφέρπει in tmesis.

451. προδίκοις: 'principals in the lawsuit'. cf. 41 n.

452–5. 'Others, of beautiful form, occupy graves in Trojan soil on the spot [αὐτοῦ], around the wall.' εὔμορφοι was recently used of Menelaus' statues at 416; the adjective is poignantly re-applied to the slain youths, whose beauty is also mentioned in the *Iliad* to increase pathos at their death (Vernant 1991, ch. 2). ἐχθρὰ δ' ἔχοντας ἔκρυψεν: Understand γῆ with ἐχθρᾷ: 'The hostile earth has hidden its occupiers.' The Greeks now 'hold' Troy, but the soil holds some graves. MacNeice attempted to capture the assonance (ἐχ-/ἐκ-) and paradox with 'holding and hidden in enemy soil'.

456–8. The atmosphere is growing very dark. The citizens' angry muttering will be 'heavy' for the Atridae, as the bereavements they have caused were βαρύ to their populace (441). It 'is paying the debt of a publicly ordained curse'. The denunciations of the leaders have imposed a debt whereby harm is to be visited upon them. This will soon be exacted by the anger expressed and fostered by the populace's talk.

The nature of these Argive 'public curses'—which are also mentioned in 1409, 1413, 1616—is unclear. The Athenians had curses against traitors read out by heralds at the beginning of assemblies and council-meetings: see Aristophanes *Thesmo.* 331–67, with Austin and Olson (2004), 160. But the rest of the play does not suggest a regular meeting of the assembly in Argos, so less formal denunciations may be meant (see Intro. at n. 34).

459–60. μέριμνα is used again (cf. 99) of the elders' foreboding, no longer for the fate of the expedition but for Agamemnon's safety. 'My anxiety waits to hear something roofed in night.' νυκτηρεφές is particularly atmospheric. We are a long way from the beginning of the ode, where night was praised for roofing over Troy with a στεγανὸν δίκτυον (358).

461–7. The Olympian gods and chthonian Erinyes are again working to the same end (Intro. § 4.2). 'For the gods do not fail to watch mass killers, and the dark Erinyes in time make dim [i.e. kill] the man who is fortunate without justice, by wearing-away his life in a reversal of fortune, and once he is among the invisible there is no defence.' πολυκτόνων and βίου are objective genitives, after ἄσκοποι and τρίβαι respectively. τιθεῖσ' is an epic form for Attic τιθέασιν. τελέθοντος (sc. αὐτοῦ) is a genitive absolute. The 'mass killer' prospers through bloodshed, and so incurs the Erinyes' attentions;

their relentless pursual of their victims even beyond death is mentioned at *Eum.* 175, 334–40.

468–9. 'To be spoken of excessively well [i.e. to be too famous] is a heavy burden.' βαρύ returns again. For this sense of κλύω see LSJ s.v. III and ἀκούω III.

469–70. οἴκοις: 'to his house'. But the manuscripts' ὄσσοις is preferable: 'For a lightning bolt from Zeus is hurled by his eyes.' Zeus' eyes are the seat of his φθόνος (see 947). His angry, flashing glance here causes lightning, which in other sources he hurls. Compare Iphigenia's eyes as the source of a 'missile' of light at 240–1.

471–4. The final ephymnion is devastating. The Chorus prefer (LSJ κρίνω 7) prosperity which does not inspire φθόνος, and do not wish to be sackers of cities; ' . . . *nor* may I be captured myself, and see my life subject to another'. For μήτ᾽ οὖν, see 359 n. Superficially, the Chorus pray not to have their own city sacked. However, since Agamemnon is already a πτολιπόρθης (cf. 783), we may notice that αὐτὸς ἁλούς and ὑπ᾽ ἄλληι are shortly to apply to him. (The manuscripts have ὑπ᾽ ἄλλων: ' . . . *nor* may I look on my life after myself being captured by others'. This is possible, but leaves βίον κατίδοιμι weaker.)

475–87. The Chorus's track of lyric utterance and movement has led it to another ominous conclusion. This is not just mood-setting; its words considered as speech-acts have moved the drama on towards Agamemnon's destruction (Intro. § 6). In the epode the tone changes completely, and the question is raised whether the message conveyed by the beacon-signal (which prompted its song, 351–3) may perhaps be false after all. Clytemnestra's τεκμήρια, which the Coryphaeus had accepted as πιστά (352), are now challenged—a reversal which any reader must interpret. It is not enough to say that their doubts raise our anticipation of the Herald's entrance at 489. Rather, Clytemnestra's declaration of Troy's capture, which has seemed to be grounds for optimism, has turned out to bode ill, and the Chorus—as if in denial—grasps at the possibility that the whole business has not yet come to pass. The volte-face makes still better sense if the passage is split between different speakers (475–8, 479–82, 483–7: as in Murray's older OCT). Although the lyrics of extant tragedy never demand this kind of division, a slight dissolution of the Chorus's corporate body is appropriate to its confusion and the change of tone. It would anticipate the total disintegration at 1346 after Agamemnon's death-cries. See also 496–7 n.

476. διήκει θοά: the words perhaps suggest that the talk *caused by* the fire has also spread through the city *like* fire.

477–8. 'Who knows if (it is) true, or whether it is somehow a divine falsehood?', i.e. a deception inspired by the gods. The idea recalls 273, as the subsequent lines revert to the patronizing attitude towards women seen in 274–6.

479. τίς ὧδε παιδνός: sc. ἐστίν. **φρενῶν κεκομμένος:** 'knocked from his mind' (κόπτω + genitive of separation); compare the etymology of παρα-κοπή 'infatuation'.

480–2. 'that he is fired in his heart [acc. of respect] by newfangled fire-messages, then is distressed at a change of story?' Or νέοις may simply be 'recent'. No sensible adult would allow him- or herself to get excited by beacon-signals, only to be confounded when contradictory news arrives. The accusative participle πυρωθέντα is very unusual, since there is no change of subject before the infinitive καμεῖν (which has a consecutive sense after ὧδε). Interested readers may consult Fraenkel's lengthy discussion.

483–4. 'It fits the command of a *woman* to approve thanksgiving before the manifestation.' αἰχμή (literally 'spear-point') is probably used as a metonym for 'rule', with a military colour which is particularly paradoxical besides γυναικός (contrast Theseus' more natural use of δορύ for his rule at Euripides *Hipp.* 975). The speaker makes the sexist suggestion that a woman in charge, as Clytemnestra is, *would* intemperately sanction the offering of sacrifices on the strength of wishful thinking, before things have become clear.

485–7. The most likely interpretation is: 'Overly persuasive, a woman's decree ranges far at a swift rate. However, it is with a swift fate that a rumour [κλέος] uttered by a woman perishes.' In other words, Clytemnestra's news and instructions have had the suspect persuasiveness which Greeks often attributed to women, but the widespread excitement will fade as fast as it arose. Whether ὅρος can mean 'decree' is debated, but it is attested in the lexicographer Hesychius, and ὁρίζω often means 'I decree' (LSJ s.v. III). ἐπινέμομαι (middle) is used of a fire or disease spreading, and thus fits the spread of altar-fires through the city after Clytemnestra's orders (88–93; cf. 476 n.). There is a marked word-play, and several long syllables are resolved into shorts (an unusual effect in Aeschylean lyrics) to suggest the swiftness.

The alternative interpretation is: 'Overly persuadable, the female boundary offers a swift crossing and is grazed on by others.' The metaphor from shepherding means 'It is easy for extraneous ideas to enter and prey on a female mind.' However, the passive senses of πιθανός, ἐπινέμομαι (LSJ s.v. II A), and ταχύπορος are hard to parallel.

Second Episode (489–680): The Coryphaeus now announces the approach of a Herald, who will establish whether the beacon-signal was to be trusted. Time has tacitly passed during the preceding stasimon: in 476 the beacon has very recently been sighted; by 489 Agamemnon's fleet has endured a storm and the few survivors have returned. As Aristotle observed (*Poet.* 5 1449b 12–16), earlier tragedy was less concerned than later to focus on a unified sequence of events lasting under a day. *Eumenides* similarly abbreviates the time taken for Orestes and the Furies to travel from Delphi to Athens.

The new arrival, a soldier back from the war, in a first *rhēsis* greets his native land before reporting that Agamemnon is on his way, and proclaiming exultantly that Troy has been sacked. After a brief passage of stichomythia, during which the Coryphaeus hints at the elders' anxieties at home during the army's absence, the Herald goes on in a second long speech to describe the hardships that the Greeks had to endure at Troy—though all that is over now. Clytemnnestra enters and, in a sinister *rhēsis* of her own, sends a message of simulated loyalty for the Herald to take to Agamemnon. After her exit, the Coryphaeus asks about Menelaus, and the Herald delivers a third speech revealing the dreadful storm which has almost entirely destroyed those who sailed with Agamemnon. As with the first episode, these 190 lines do not seem at first to contribute to the plot. But again, there is a forceful shift from optimism to gloom, and ominous words prevail over and undermine the apparent good news of Agamemnon's safe return. The pattern underlying the four speeches is explored further in the comments below.

489–502. The speech must be delivered by the Coryphaeus rather than Clytemnestra. The latter would not dismiss the beacon as an inferior messenger (491–2), and 498–500 are much better suited to the Coryphaeus than to her. Furthermore, there are numerous dramatic benefits of having her enter just before 587, for which see

585–6 n. It is unusual for the Coryphaeus to have such a long speech: see 1577–1673 n., and Griffith (1977), 130–4 for other examples.

489–90. All three genitive nouns may depend on παραλλαγάς: 'the exchanges of torches, of beacon-watches and of fire' (for the structure 'A, B τε, καὶ C', cf. 403–4). However, Wilamowitz's emendation φρυκτωρίας (acc. pl.) would produce more natural syntax and phrasing: 'the beacon-watches and fire-relays of the light-bearing torches'.

491–2. οὖν here means 'in fact' rather than 'therefore' (Denniston 418; cf. 359 n.). The idea of dreams being pleasing but deceptive has already arisen at 274 and 420–1.

493. τόνδ': the deictic ὅδε in tragedy often accompanies a pointing gesture when a new character is introduced; compare e.g. 256.

493–4. κατάσκιον κλάδοις ἐλαίας: the Herald is 'shaded by twigs of olive', i.e. wearing a wreath which normally signifies good news (e.g. Sophocles OT 82–3, Trach. 179). However, the Coryphaeus wishes to hear the news from his mouth rather than to make this inference (498–9).

494–5. The arrival kicks up a cloud of dust, which is evidence that he has urgent news to announce. 'Thirsty dust' is first described as 'mud's neighbouring sibling'; διψία suggests their precise relationship. This kind of riddling description is not uncommon in Greek, and is termed a γρῖφος or 'kenning'. Compare Septem 493–4 where the monster Typhon within Mount Etna breathes forth 'black smoke, fire's variegated sibling'. The use of the γρῖφος-device here fits a context which is concerned with the puzzle of interpreting various kinds of sign, such as beacons, dreams, olive-wreaths, dust-clouds, and smoke-signals.

τάδε refers forwards to the ὡς-clause: 'this, namely that . . .'—a more common turn of phrase in Greek than in English.

496–7. 'that he will neither give a signal dumbly, nor with fire's smoke by kindling you a flame from mountain wood'. It is difficult to see to which individual σοι is addressed unless a particular chorus-member spoke 479–82 (see 475–87 n.). Otherwise Butler's οὔτε μοι is one simple conjecture.

498–500. Literally 'No, either in words he will proclaim greater rejoicing— but I abominate the speech opposing that. For may an addition [i.e. confirmation] arise happily on top of what has appeared happily [i.e. the beacon].' The Coryphaeus characteristically refuses to articulate the 'or' to follow 'either', because it would be too ominous; instead, he ends in 500 with a prayer for good, with εὖ repeated. Cf. 251–5 with notes.

501–2. A typical rider introduced by ὅστις to end the speech. Sophocles *Aj.* 1038–9 is particularly similar: ὅτωι δὲ μὴ τάδ' ἐστὶν ἐν γνώμηι φίλα, | κεῖνός τ' ἐκεῖνα στεργέτω κἀγὼ τάδε.

503–37. The Herald begins his opening speech with a moving address to his native soil, perhaps kneeling to touch and kiss it like Agamemnon at *Od.* 4. 521–2 or Odysseus at 13. 354. He calls on Argos and its gods to receive the Argive army, then on the palace and its gods to receive Agamemnon, before announcing the conqueror's arrival. All this bodes excellently, but some details in his subsequent report of what has happened to Troy unwittingly prompt unease (see 527, 530 nn.).

503. ἰώ: Aeschylus uses this exclamation more in lyrics than in trimeters, which suggests its emotional intensity here and in 518; we would favour a quiet delivery to an outburst.

504. φέγγει: the shift from 'light' to 'daylight' to 'day' is fairly common: see LSJ s.v. 1d.

505. πολλῶν ῥαγεισῶν ἐλπίδων is genitive absolute, whereas μίας is genitive after τυγχάνω. ῥήγνυμι is rarely used metaphorically, so 'broken hopes', even if these are unspecified, is a more striking phrase in Greek than in English. The rhetorical antithesis πολλῶν . . . μιᾶς is explained in 506–7: his hope of dying in his native soil *has* been realized, though the failure of many other hopes had inclined him to despair.

506. ηὔχουν: from αὐχέω, 'I feel confident' (elsewhere 'I boast'); it governs a future infinitive μεθέξειν (from μετέχω). Ἀργείαι χθονί: the repetition from 503 communicates his deep emotion.

509. Zeus, 'supreme in the land', and Apollo are given special prominence. This can be explained from within the trilogy, though naturally both had important cults in historical Argos. Zeus is the most important god throughout *Ag.*, and Apollo will protect Orestes in the other plays. See Introduction § 4.2, 55–9 n.

510. ἰάπτων μηκέτ': μηκέτι (rather than οὐκέτι) shows that the participial phrase is effectively a prohibition: 'and no longer shoot'. The Herald alludes to the famous instance of Apollo shooting plague-bearing arrows against the Greeks in *Iliad* 1. 43–52.

511. Σκάμανδρον: one of the rivers in the Troad (see Map, p. 101).

512. σωτήρ ... παιώνιος: common titles for Apollo at his most supportive.

513. ἀγωνίους θεούς: perhaps 'the gods in assembly', as at *Supp.* 189, which might suggest one of the cults where twelve gods were worshipped as a group (see Long 1987). However, the alternative interpretations 'gods of assemblies' (already in Schol.ₐ bT *Il.* 24. 1) or 'gods of contests' could suit the build-up to Hermes, who is often associated with both areas.

514–15. Hermes, as the herald of the gods, is the Herald's special 'protector' (τιμάορον).

516–17. In πέμψαντας (sc. 'us'), εὐμενεῖς, and δέχεσθαι the Herald is using the formulaic language of prayers by armies setting forth on an expedition. Compare Xenophon *Cyr.* 2. 1. 1 'After praying to the Persian deities to πέμπειν them favourably [ἵλεως καὶ εὐμενεῖς], they crossed the border; after crossing, they in turn prayed to the Median gods to δέχεσθαι them favourably.' See Burkert (1985), 203–8 for an introduction to the distinctive local hero cults of Greek religion. λελειμμένον δορός: 'which remains from the spear', i.e. which survived the war. δορός is a genitive expressing separation.

519. θᾶκοι: stone seats before the palace, where the kings would give judgment. δαίμονές τ' ἀντήλιοι: 'deities facing the sun'. Like the ἀγώνιοι θεοί of 513, this group (though attested in passing elsewhere) is obscure to us. One can only speculate on the purpose of south-facing cult statues close to a palace. The deictic τοισίδ' in 520 suggests that these statues were present onstage, but along with the θᾶκοι they seem to have very little dramatic function and could be simply imagined, if one accepts Triclinius' conjecture τοῖσιν. See Introduction § 5.1.

520. εἴ που πάλαι: 'if ever in the past'. Another formula of prayers, calling for a continuation of past favours (the so-called *da quia dedisti* structure). φαιδροῖσι ... ὄμμασιν: the adjective is predicative: 'with eyes which are beaming' for the occasion. This expresses gladness: cf. 725 φαιδρωπός, 1120 φαιδρύνει.

521. κόσμωι: 'with pomp'. πολλῶι χρόνωι: 'after a long time', like σὺν χρόνωι.

522–3. The central 'message' ἥκει ... Ἀγαμέμνων ἄναξ is emphasized by the powerful placement of the words at beginning and end of the sentence. The emphasis is underlined in 530–1, which also contain ἄναξ and ἥκει in strong positions. φῶς ἐν εὐφρόνηι: Agamemnon has brought the literal light of beacons through the darkness (24–5), but also the metaphorical light of relief to a dark place (see 1 n. for the symbolism).

524. ἀλλ' εὖ νιν ἀσπάσασθε: the Herald started by expressing his personal feeling without regard for the Chorus; in 523 he mentioned them in the third person (τοῖσδ' ἅπασι), and now he turns to address them. **καὶ γὰρ οὖν:** 'for in fact'—both καί and οὖν contribute to the assertive tone.

525–6. 'who has dug Troy into the ground with the fork of justice-bearing Zeus, with which [τῆι: relative] the soil has been worked over'. A δίκελλα is a two-pronged agricultural fork, which brings out the metaphor in κατασκάπτω—generally 'destroy' but literally 'dig downwards'. But whereas normally agriculture has a productive purpose, it is here twisted to the purely destructive. The metaphor is continued in 528 σπέρμα χθονός (i.e. the people) and 529 ζευκτήριον, 'plough-yoke'.

527. This line is suspect, as it interrupts the agricultural imagery and closely resembles *Pers.* 811 βωμοὶ δ' ἄϊστοι δαιμόνων θ' ἱδρύματα. However, it would certainly be effective. The overenthusiastic Herald would inspire a shudder in the Chorus and the audience, as he unwittingly confirms Clytemnestra's ominous warning at 338–47 (see n.) from which θεῶν ἱδρύματα is repeated. This is the kind of bad news which 'pollutes' a moment where εὐφημία is required (as he puts it below: 636–7). Furthermore, ἄϊστοι might remind us of the train of thought at two points in the preceding stasimon— 381–4 'no defence for one who kicks the altar of Justice into obscurity' and 461–7 'the Erinyes send killers among the ἄϊστοι, at which point there is no defence'. By annihilating the altars, Agamemnon and the Greeks were prompting a divine response which would annihilate them in turn—such as we learn of in the last speech of the episode.

530. Ἀτρείδης πρεσβύς: this way of specifying Agamemnon may already prompt us to wonder about Menelaus' fate, which will become the crushing climax of the episode. **εὐδαίμων:** tempting fate, as in 336 (see 334–7 n.). This is therefore (if 527 is genuine) a second link between Clytemnestra's malicious words in the first episode and the Herald's incautious exuberance.

531. Understand ἐστίν. τίεσθαι depends on ἀξιώτατος, 'most worthy to be honoured'.

532–3. 'For (neither) Paris nor his city, which jointly paid the due, boasts that his action (was) greater than the suffering.' Understand οὔτε before *Πάρις* and *εἶναι* in 533. Paris' action (abducting Helen) has brought Troy down with him, and met a suitably serious retribution. The juxtaposition of *δρᾶμα* and *πάθος* gives the first clear expression of the theme that *παθεῖν τὸν ἔρξαντα* (1564), which summarizes the law of retribution (see Intro. § 4.1).

534–5. 'For, convicted in a lawsuit of robbery and theft, he both lost his forfeiture and . . .'. *ὀφλών* is from *ὀφλισκάνω*. *ἁρπαγή* and *κλοπή* are normally distinguished in that the former entails violence and the latter stealth, but here the two are grandly combined to describe the (consensual) abduction of Helen and the theft of Menelaus' possessions; the latter are also mentioned as a cause for complaint in the *Iliad* (e.g. 3. 70). *ῥύσιον* is property which may be seized on the basis of a legal claim: Paris' conviction gave Menelaus the right to confiscate his possessions, including the stolen goods. For the important series of legal metaphors applied to the sack of Troy, see again Introduction § 4.1.

535–6. 'and mowed down his ancestral home, soil and all, in complete destruction'. *αὐτόχθονον* = *αὐτῆι τῆι χθονί*, for which see Smyth § 1525. *πανώλεθρον* is 'proleptic', i.e. describes the condition of Troy effected by Paris' action. The whole clause expands on 532 *συντελής*, and returns to the image of destructive agriculture from 525–9. However, this time Paris is the agent.

537. 'Double is the penalty the sons of Priam have paid.' Distinguish *τὰ ἁμάρτια* ('payments for a wrong') from *ἡ ἁμαρτία*. According to the Solonian law, the basic sentence for unaggravated theft in Athens was to 'pay double', by returning the stolen goods and paying a fine of equal value (Demosthenes 24. 114). In this case, Helen has been recovered and (more importantly) their country destroyed.

539. *τὸ τεθνάναι*: the article + infinitive would be attached loosely to what follows (see D–P): 'As to death, I shall no longer refuse the gods', i.e. from now on he can die happy. But *τὸ τεθνάναι* is itself an emendation for *τεθνᾶναι*, which is regarded as an impossible form and difficult to construe with *ἀντερῶ*; West obelizes.

540. *ἔρως*: throughout the next few lines, the power of nostalgia is conveyed with the language of sexual desire (cf. *ἀντεράω, ἵμερος, ποθέω*). *ἐγύμνασεν*: a paradoxically physical verb (more so than English 'exercise') to describe emotional stress, in troops who have significant bodily discomforts too.

541. ὥστ' ἐνδακρύειν γ': '(Yes,) so much so that I have *tears* in my eyes for joy.' The consecutive clause implies the answer 'yes'; γε throws emphasis.

542–4. From 540–1, the Coryphaeus enigmatically concludes (ἄρα + imperfect) that the soldiers' nostalgia, which he calls a 'disease', was 'pleasant' (τερπνῆς: predicative position). The oxymoron confuses the Herald, so the Coryphaeus explains: the desire was reciprocal, and reciprocated desire is pleasant. For metaphors of sickness, see 13–15 n.

ἐπήβολοι 'having a share of' governs a partitive genitive νόσου (cf. μετέχω + gen.). δεσπόσω governs a genitive like other verbs meaning 'rule'; the metaphor 'master the meaning' is bolder in Greek than in English. ἀντερώντων is objective genitive after ἱμέρωι, 'desire *for*'. Line 544 continues the construction of 542—a common effect in stichomythia.

545. A very elegant way of expressing the reciprocal feeling. τῆνδε γῆν is both subject of ποθεῖν and object of ποθοῦντα.

546. ὡς: consecutive, as in 550 and perhaps 575 (prose would have ὥστε). As in 541, the consecutive clause implies the answer 'yes'. ἀμαυρᾶς: literally 'faint', i.e. troubled (the opposite of 'bright' implying cheerfulness). This line, followed by 548 and 550, gives a rare glimpse of the Chorus's anxiety over what has been going on in Agamemnon's absence.

547. στύγος: 'sullenness', bringing to an end the language of desire. †στρατῶι†: gives the wrong sense. Read Heimsoeth's λεῶι, 'the (Argive) people'; στρατῶι would be an inept gloss based on the commoner sense of λεώς.

548. 'For a long time I have had silence as my medicine against harm.' Compare the imagery of 542 νόσου.

549. ἀπόντων κοιράνων: genitive absolute.

550–1. 'So much so that now—in your words—even death (would be) a great favour.' The Coryphaeus refers to 539, but means something different: not 'I am so happy that I no longer crave life' but 'I am so anxious that I crave death'. The Herald gives the wrong interpretation, and responds '(Yes), for the deed turned out well'.

551–82. The Herald's second *rhēsis* starts on a note of good omen. The introduction speaks of both good and bad aspects to the Greeks' life at Troy, but the detailed account, starting with μόχθους (555) is all about the bad. The fine description of war's discomforts would have stirred memories in the Athenian audience: see Introduction § 2. At 570 the Herald reverts to more cheerful language and a triumphant mood prevails till the end of the speech.

551–2. 'As for these things, someone might well say that in that long duration some of them fell favourably.' For ταυτά read the manuscripts' ταῦτα, which suits τὰ μέν and τὰ δ' better; 'these things' are the tasks of the Trojan expedition, corresponding to the unexpressed subject of πέπρακται. εὐπετῶς ἔχειν represents the direct speech εὐπετῶς εἶχεν, effectively = εὐπετῆ ἦν (as often with ἔχω + adverb). For the metaphor, cf. 32 εὖ πεσόντα.

553. κἀπίμομφα: perhaps reminiscent of 145–6 δεξιὰ μὲν κατάμομφα δέ, of the eagle-omen which showed the same ambivalence as the fortunes of the expedition as a whole.

554. Understand ἐστίν. The accusatives express duration, and ἅπαντα is emphatically placed: 'for the *whole* time'.

555–66. These rich lines treat of the soldiers' troubles. The Herald first focuses on their difficulty in sleeping: this consists of a general headline (555), then subsections about conditions on the voyage (556–7) and on land (557–62). From 563 he describes the weather they suffered. Both parts are expressed by conditionals (εἰ λέγοιμι, εἰ λέγοι τις) which—if the text is to be trusted—tail off without an apodosis to indicate the Herald's unease.

556. During the voyage, the soldiers had to set up uncomfortable makeshift beds by spreading rugs over the narrow gangways (σπαρνὰς παρήξεις) along the sides of the ship.

556–7. D–P take τί with both στένοντες and λαχόντες: 'what not lamenting, (what) not having got as the *day*'s portion?' The soldiers lamented everything—not only the bad beds they were in (556), but also the whole gamut of troubles they had had during the day. Others take οὐ λαχόντες ἤματος μέρος as subordinate to στένοντες: 'and what lament did we not utter when we did not get our daily rations?' But this sense of μέρος is doubtful.

558. Literally 'Then again, as for the situation on dry land, there was even more to disgust (us) in addition [προσ-].' τά is accusative of respect; καί belongs with πλέον.

560. λειμώνιαι: belongs closely with κἀπὸ γῆς, 'and the droplets in meadows coming from the earth', as opposed to the drops ἐξ οὐρανοῦ in the form of rain which 'drizzled over' the soldiers.

561–2. With the comma after σίνος, the δρόσοι are 'a continual ruin, rendering the hair of our clothes [wool] infested with lice'. Others have placed the comma after ἐσθημάτων: 'a continual ruin of our clothes, and rendering our hair infested with lice'. Either way δρόσοι (fem.) is awkwardly followed by τιθέντες (masc.), which may indicate corruption; the *apparatus* suggests the makeshift τιθεῖσι δ'. Aristotle bears witness to the belief that lice were born directly from flesh, particularly if damp (*HA* 5. 31 556b 24–557a 1).

563–4. The snow on Mount Ida caused icy winds around the Greek camp.

565–6. 'or the heat, when the sea fell and slept waveless in a windless midday rest'. The sultriness is finely expressed in the liquid consonants (μ,ν), long vowels, and diphthongs of the drawn-out phrase.

567. τί ταῦτα πενθεῖν δεῖ: the Herald breaks off, to avoid further clouding his news. παροίχεται πόνος: the idea of ἀπαλλαγὴ πόνων (1) returns.

568–9. '(The toil) is past, so that not even getting up (each morning) will ever be a concern again for the *dead*, and as for us . . .'. The articular infinitive τὸ μὴ μέλειν is consecutive after the main idea of 'escape, avoid': cf. 13–15 n.

570–4: The lines as ordered in the manuscripts are impossibly contorted, and best rearranged as in the OCT. The general sense is 'Why should the living tot up our losses?' Their profit is compared with their suffering, first on a balance (ἀντιρρέπει) and then on an accountant's abacus: the dead are τοὺς ἀναλωθέντας, 'the expended'; ἐν ψήφωι. λέγειν ('to reckon by the pebble') implies a precise tally.

571 [574]. νικᾶι τὸ κέρδος: recalling κέρδεσιν νικωμένους (340–2) in Clytemnestra's warning (cf. 527 n.).

573 [571]. τύχης: the genitive after ἀλγεῖν expresses the cause of pain.

574 [572]–5. Either (1) 'I think it right actually [καί] to rejoice greatly at what has happened, since [causal ὡς] it is right . . .' (so D–P); or (2) 'And [καί] I think it right to say a long farewell to disasters, so that [consecutive ὡς] it is right . . .'. The latter requires taking χαίρειν as if it were χαίρειν εἰπεῖν; for the colloquial πολλὰ χαίρειν εἰπεῖν see e.g. Eur. *Hipp.* 113. We prefer the basic sense of this: 'Goodbye to all that!' West inserts a lacuna, where εἰπεῖν might have stood.

575–6. εἰκός (sc. ἐστί, as in 586) governs the dative ποτωμένοις (sc. ἡμῖν) and the infinitive; τῶιδ' . . . φάει is either temporal ('on this day') or the indirect object (boast 'to this sunlight'). The Argives are 'borne on wings over land and sea' in that their fame spreads far and wide. Pindar uses the same metaphor at *Nem.* 6. 48–9.

577–9. ποτ᾽, ταῦτα, the tense of ἐπασσάλευσαν, and ἀρχαῖον give the sentence the character of an accompanying epigram to be read by future generations for whom the spoils are an antiquity and tourist attraction; such epigrams do typically contain an aorist verb such as ἀνέθηκεν 'dedicated', i.e. are oriented to future visitors. M. West (1990*a*), 193–4 suggests a lacuna 577 in which the 'future onlooker' was brought in explicitly. But possibly κομπάσαι + quotation can refer to a boast made in a public piece of writing, or the original dedicator is thought of as reading out his epigram after making the dedication. At any rate, the words both praise Argos (see 580 εὐλογεῖν πόλιν) and show a sense of pan-Hellenic unity against barbarians.

Dedicating spoils in temples (with a commemorative inscription) was a common Greek practice; one might compare the flags in some British cathedrals which preserve past military glories. The temple of Athena at Lindos in Rhodes actually contained alleged spoils from the Trojan War (see Fraenkel).

τοῖς καθ᾽ Ἑλλάδα δόμοις: locative dative, 'in their temples across Greece'. γάνος: literally 'brightness, gleam'; here approximately 'treasure'.

581. τιμήσεται: future middle form with passive sense (cf. 170 n.). The Herald allows credit to Zeus as to the generals. Cf. 810–12, and Introduction § 4.3.1 on divine and human levels of causation.

582. πάντ᾽ ἔχεις λόγον: a common formula of conclusion. But it is *not* the end of the Herald's story.

583–4. Literally 'I do not reject [i.e. deny] being defeated by your words. Being a good learner is always in its prime for old men.' For ἀναίνομαι + participle compare Euripides *Heracles* 1235 εὖ δράσας δέ σ᾽ οὐκ ἀναίνομαι. The Chorus must accept that its scepticism at the beacons (477–82, 496–7) was misplaced. The metaphor of words 'defeating' somebody will turn into reality at 940–3.

Line 584 contrasts the decline of their physique, with which ἡβάω is usually connected, with their continuing mental capacity.

585–6. '(It is) reasonable that these things are of most interest to the palace and to Clytemnestra, but that they enrich me into the bargain.' σύν is adverbial.

We now expect the Herald to enter the palace, and he should be envisaged moving up to the door. However ('Speak of the devil', as we might say), Clytemnestra enters—the watchdog (607) who guards and controls the interior and the threshold across which Agamemnon is soon to be lured to his destruction (see Taplin 1977, 229–30). By having her enter on cue to frustrate the Herald's journey, Aeschylus gives us a powerful and unsettling symbol of her control. Although the preceding lines have ended on a sunny note, the atmosphere suddenly becomes heavily overcast, and Clytemnestra's presence now will act as a catalyst for the more depressing mood which continues after her exit to the end of the episode. Her entrance and exit thus play a significant part in the dramatic structure; for a definitive discussion of their timing, see ibid. 299–302.

587–614. There is a magnificent defiance and menace in Clytemnestra's speech. She tells the Herald that his news is superfluous as far as she is concerned, and speaks scornfully of those who treated her responses to the beacon-signal as the demented fantasies of a woman. Her sinister authority is strengthened by Aeschylus' making her speak as if she knew all that has been said about her. The message she sends Agamemnon via the Herald is loaded with deception and reaches a grim climax in the ambiguity of 611–12.

587. ἀνωλόλυξα μὲν πάλαι: the delivery of πάλαι can catch Clytemnestra's tone immediately: she raised the women's cry of triumph '*long* ago'. Uncorrelated μέν at the start of a speech, as at 1.

588. ὁ πρῶτος ... ἄγγελος: rather belittling the Herald's job.

589. φράζων ἅλωσιν: cf. 10 ἁλώσιμόν τε βάξιν.

590–2. Clytemnestra might almost be quoting the Chorus's sentiments in 477–87.

590. φρυκτωρῶν: with this accentuation, 'beacon-watchers'; but φρυκτώρων may have meant 'beacons'.

591. δοκεῖς: 'you consider' not 'you seem'.

592. 'Truly, (it is) just in the nature of a *woman* to be elated in one's heart.' For αἴρω see LSJ ἀείρω II; κέαρ is accusative of respect (cf. 481 καρδίαν). Clytemnestra presents her womanhood as an issue for others; she asserts it again in 594 and 614, also exploiting her role as a γυνή in the sense of 'wife' in 602 and 606.

593. πλαγκτὸς οὖσ' ἐφαινόμην: φαίνομαι with participle: 'I was clearly crazed', spoken with heavy sarcasm.

594–6. ὀλολυγμὸν ... εὐφημοῦντες: cf. 28 ὀλολυγμὸν εὐφημοῦντα, and for Clytemnestra's appropriation of other words from the

Watchman's speech cf. 589, 330–3 nn. The masculine participle and ἄλλος indicate that she has been involving men in the 'female custom' of ὀλολυγή.

597. 'putting the incense-consuming flame to rest and rendering it fragrant'. εὐώδη is 'proleptic' (cf. 535–6 n.). Adding incense makes a fire stop flaming and produces a fragrant smoke.

598–9. 'And as for now, what need is there to tell a longer story to *me*? I shall learn the whole tale from the king himself.' μάσσω is the neuter plural of μάσσων, a comparative of μακρός. The emphatic ἐμοί in 598 both looks back to her initial point that the Herald has nothing new to tell *her* (587–8) whatever he might have to tell others; and it also looks forward to 599, where she introduces Agamemnon and (hypocritically) their 'special relationship' into her train of utterance.

600. ὅπως δ' ἄριστα: 'as well as possible', like the more common ὡς + superlative (similarly 605 ὅπως τάχιστ'). Construe with δέξασθαι not σπεύσω. αἰδοῖον: 'venerable'. Clytemnestra's open insincerity begins here, with the pretence that she feels a wife's proper αἰδώς towards her husband.

601. δέξασθαι: the word of three long syllables at the end of the sentence, followed by an unusual sense-break before the final two syllables, makes the word ring out, and makes us consider the 'reception' which awaits. For whom will it be 'as good as possible'?

602. τούτου: 'than this sc. φέγγους' (not 'of this man', taken with γυναικί). φέγγος: 'day(light)'; cf. 504 n.

603. ἄνδρα is the object of σώσαντος, which is part of a genitive absolute.

604. πύλας ἀνοῖξαι: Clytemnestra does not foresee Agamemnon opening the gates himself. In fact, she will rejoice to watch him submitting to a final entrance over which she has total control.

605. ἐράσμιον πόλει: 'the country's darling' (Headlam 1904). The sensuous expression is practically indecent in public, and invites damaging disapproval of Agamemnon.

606. εὕροι: it is interesting that she expresses herself with a wish, as if there was some uncertainty, rather than with e.g. εὑρήσει.

607. οἷάνπερ οὖν ἔλειπε: '*exactly* as he left her'; -περ and οὖν both strengthen the pronoun (Denniston 421), and underline Clytemnestra's dissimulation. δωμάτων κύνα: superficially refers to an obedient guard-dog, but female dogs were also a symbol of shamelessness: see Introduction § 9.2.

609–10. σημαντήριον οὐδὲν διαφθείρασαν: 'having destroyed no seal'. During his absence, Agamemnon's valuables are presented as having been locked up, and the locks stamped with his seal (see Austin and Olson 2004, 184 for parallels). Clytemnestra declares she has not broken in to any of these.

611–12. 'I know no pleasure, nor scandalous rumour, derived from another man, any more than I know the dipping of metal.' The smith tempers iron by rapidly cooling it in water after heating. χαλκός is used rather loosely here, just as χαλκεύς is a 'smith' generally rather than a 'bronzesmith'. Agamemnon is to assume that Clytemnestra, like a normal wife, is equally *ignorant* of adultery and metallurgy. But we and the Chorus know about Aegisthus, and thus receive a hint to confirm our suspicion that she has plans for a weapon to be dipped in Agamemnon's blood. The double meaning is both extremely malevolent and ominous.

613. κόμπος: the Herald's preceding speech also ended with a κόμπος (575), but one which was favourable to Agamemnon. τῆς ἀληθείας γέμων: Clytemnestra's boast is 'laden with the truth' (English 'loaded' can be used similarly); even the Herald might sense that she 'doth protest too much'.

614. 'not base to shout, at least for a noble wife'. For ὡς + noun limiting a more general assertion, see LSJ ὡς Ab II 2. λακεῖν is an explanatory infinitive after αἰσχρός (cf. 621 καρποῦσθαι after καλά). Loud boasting might be shameful, but not if it is true (613) and uttered by a γενναία woman who is both morally and socially the opposite of τὸ αἰσχρόν. This exit-line is composed for a powerful delivery, with the juxtaposition αἰσχρός/γενναίαι, the alliteration γενναίαι γυναικί, and the choice of λακεῖν over a verb describing less powerful utterance. All this sharpens Clytemnestra's defiant final assertion of her womanhood against her sexist detractors.

As the self-proclaimed 'guard-dog' withdraws into her kennel, the forecast is decidedly ominous.

615–17. The details of the text are complicated, but the basic structure is the antithesis αὕτη μὲν οὕτως εἶπε . . . σὺ δ' εἰπέ, κῆρυξ. We would read εὐπρεπῆ for εὐπρεπῶς and delete the comma after μανθάνοντί σοι: 'Well, *she* has spoken like that—a fair-seeming speech, if you learn (its sense) by clear interpreters. Now *you* speak, herald.' The Coryphaeus implies that Clytemnestra's words, when clearly understood, only *seem* good; εὐπρεπὴς λόγος is used similarly at Euripides *Tro.* 951. The tone of uneasiness matches that of 548 and 550.

617. Μενελέων ... πεύθομαι: the sense 'inquire about' + accusative is comparatively rare: see LSJ πυνθάνομαι I 4.

620–35. The ensuing dialogue is composed in 'distichomythia', which offers scope for longer units of thought than in the single-line exchanges. The form recurs at 1348–71 (when the individual chorus-members deliberate), *Cho.* 1051–64, *Eum.* 711–30.

620–1. Literally 'There is no way that I might speak falsehoods which are good, for friends to reap the fruits of for the long term.' The Herald's laboured language shows his reluctance to answer, but he sees that lying is not a durable solution.

622–3. The Coryphaeus' reply mimics the Herald's sentence-structure: 'Oh, how might you manage to speak truths which are welcome? When these things [the true and the welcome] are split, they are not easily hidden', i.e. a cover-up is soon detected. πῶς ἄν with optative effectively expresses a wish.

624. ἀνὴρ ἄφαντος: the dreadful truth tumbles out quickly. ἀνήρ = ὁ ἀνήρ; ἐστίν is omitted.

626–7. 'Did Menelaus vanish after putting out to sea †visibly†, or did a storm, a shared affliction, snatch him from the army?' στρατοῦ is a genitive expressing separation. ἐμφανῶς is obelized, since one would need an adverb meaning 'separately' to provide the contrast. But it can be retained with the smaller change of πότερον (which is not required: Smyth § 2657) into πρότερον or Heyse's πρότερος.

This question is motivated in part by the epic version of the story, where Menelaus set out separately: see Introduction § 3.1. Many scholars have conjectured that the *Oresteia*'s satyr-play staged Menelaus' adventures, which would add a further reason for his introduction here (Intro. n. 1).

628. ὥστε here is 'like' (a predominantly epic usage), and ἄκρος is 'excellent' not 'topmost'. For the common metaphor of 'well-aimed' words, see also 1194; compare 'hitting the nail on the head' in English.

630–1. 'And was the rumour spoken by the other sailors of him as living or as dead?' For γάρ here and in 634, see 272 n.

633. The Greeks often thought of the Sun as all-seeing. χθονὸς φύσιν: 'what grows on the Earth', an unusual sense of φύσις.

634–5. Of the two datives, ναυτικῶι στρατῶι expresses an interested party, while δαιμόνων κότωι expresses instrument: the storm came and ended *for* the fleet *by* divine wrath. In δαιμόνων κότωι, the Coryphaeus assumes that the storm was an act of divine retribution; if 527 is genuine, it gives a good reason for this assumption. δαίμονες, as often, is used for gods whose identity is mysterious: 'Daimon is the veiled countenance of divine activity' (Burkert 1985, 180). In 645 the Herald will identify them with the retributive Furies. (In *Od.* 3. 135 Athena causes the storm; possibly Aeschylus wished to limit her role to that of *Eumenides.*)

636–80. The Herald's third and final *rhēsis* starts with a long and syntactically disjointed preamble of profound distress at his having to combine news of victory with a report of disaster. There follows a grand poetic description of the storm which destroyed all except Agamemnon's ship, and left Menelaus' survival in doubt. The speech concludes with the usual euphemistic formulas which arise from deep foreboding.

636–7. The Herald is reluctant to '*pollute* a day of good omen with a tongue of ill tidings'. This emphasis on the tussle between detrimental speech and εὐφημία is a good encapsulation of how powerful words are important to the drama's dynamics (Intro. § 6). χωρὶς ἡ τιμὴ θεῶν: 'Honouring the gods (is) separate' [sc. from bad tidings]. The comment explains why the strong religious colour of μιαίνειν is apt.

638. ἀπευκτά: 'abominable' (related to εὔχομαι 'pray'); a further piece of the language of religious pollution.

639. στυγνῶι προσώπωι: Hesychius' dictionary has an entry for σμοιῶι προσώπωι which should probably be read here. στυγνῶι would be an intrusive gloss on the rarer adjective, which has approximately the same meaning. See M. West (1990*a*), 195. στρατοῦ: construe with πήματα.

640–2. Two πήματα are contrasted: 'one wound, the public one, for the *state* to meet' (τυχεῖν: explanatory infinitive), versus the many *individual* 'men who have been taken as sacrificial victims [ἐξα-γισθέντας, a *hapax*] from their many homes by the double whip which Ares loves'. The punctuation could be clearer with a comma after ἄνδρας and none after μάστιγι. The natural way to understand the 'double' whip is that it inflicts both types of πήματα. (The text does not, *pace* Fraenkel, entail that the whip inflicts only the individual wounds.) φιλεῖ is particularly poignant in this context.

643. The two πήματα are further described in apposition as 'a two-pronged ruin, a bloodied pair'. In the latter image, Ares whipping the pair of horses on his war-chariot becomes an allegory for the twin destruction of war.

644–5. 'Well, it is fitting that (someone) packed with troubles like *that* speak such a paean to the Furies.' The Herald makes a fresh start on the sentence after the chain of associations in 638–43. μέντοι does not here mean 'however', but adds emphasis to τοιῶνδε (Denniston 399–400). The metaphor of σεσαγμένον (sc. τινα) is from pack-animals; the present is σάττω.

'Paean to the Furies' is a 'blasphemous paradox' (Fraenkel) to express the idea that a description of the effective storm will implicitly praise the Furies who instigated it. The paean is normally a hymn to Apollo, who is not to be associated with troubles (cf. 1074–9) and who in *Eumenides* will openly oppose the Furies. The phrase encapsulates the discordance between εὔφημον and κακαγγέλωι from the speech's beginning, and belongs to a broader thematic strand of misdirected hymns (e.g. 709–16, 1186–92).

646–7. πραγμάτων is objective genitive dependent on εὐάγγελον, 'with good news of'. The lines seem to start a balancing accusative and infinitive with πρέπει, but we only get the accusative ἥκοντα (like σεσαγμένον, a participle used on its own as a noun): at 648, the Herald breaks off in another anacoluthon.

649. Read Ἀχαιοῖς ... θεῶν. The storm 'experienced by the Achaeans' was 'not without the anger of the gods'. The Herald implicitly acknowledges Greek impieties (one naturally thinks of the desecration of shrines: cf. 341, 527 n.), and confirms the Coryphaeus' δαιμόνων κότωι (635). For ἀμήνιτον + genitive, cf. 311 n.

650–2. The storm was a conspiracy between two inveterate enemies, the elemental forces of fire and water (i.e. lightning and the sea), who 'proved their good faith by destroying the hapless army of Argives'. ἐδειξάτην and φθείροντε are duals.

653. ὠρώρει: pluperfect from perfect ὄρωρα, 'I arise' (see LSJ ὄρνυμι).

δυσκύμαντα is a *hapax*, as are 655 κεροτυπουμέναι, 656 ὀμβρο-κτύπωι, and 657 στρόβωι: for such clusters see Introduction § 9.1.

654–7. 'The gusts from Thrace smashed the ships against each other and they, rammed violently by the storm consisting of a tornado [τυφῶ: genitive] together with the beating rain, disappeared and were gone by the whirling of a mischievous shepherd.' The Thracian winds previously afflicted the Greeks at Aulis: 192 n. The image in κεροτυπούμεναι and ποιμένος is of the fleet as a flock of goats whose herdsman panics them into butting each other. Metaphorically, the 'herdsman' stands for the god controlling the storm. κερο-τυπούμεναι is particularly apt, since Homeric ships with a raised prow and stern could be called ὀρθόκραιρος, literally 'with upright horns'.

For χειμῶνι τυφῶ West suggests πρηστῆρι τυφῶι 'with a burning tornado', as some mention of fire is expected (651).

659. ἀνθοῦν: 'flowering'; a poignant image for the corpses and timbers varying the colour of the sea's surface, where normal flowers do not grow; furthermore the corpses are of the ἄνθος Ἀργείων (197–8).

661. σκάφος: accusative of respect after ναῦν ἀκήρατον.

662–4. The ship was saved by stealth or begging by a god, who also steered. But Fortune the Saviour must also have been on board. θέλουσα reflects a common formula in prayers, such as 'Fortune, save us θέλουσα' ('willingly, graciously'). We know, however, that the gods are merely 'saving' Agamemnon for his fate at home.

665–6. Consecutive ὡς + infinitive. The sailors were preserved from a dilemma between anchoring and being swamped, or not anchoring and being wrecked on the rocky coast.

667–70. 'Then, having escaped from death at sea [πόντιον Ἅιδην], in the light of day [λευκὸν ἦμαρ] we brooded in our anxious thoughts, unable to believe our fortune, over the fresh affliction of the army, which had suffered and was (still) being badly pulverized [present σποδουμένου; i.e. by the waves].' The sailors contemplate the disaster with the attention a cowherd pays to his animals (ἐβουκολοῦμεν); the herding metaphor of 655–7 is reintroduced in a different configuration.

672. τί μήν: an idiom meaning approximately 'That's natural'.

673. ταῦτ' ἔχειν: 'be in the same condition'. ταῦτ' = τὰ αὐτά.

674. γένοιτο δ' ὡς ἄριστα: the usual prayer when the outlook looks really bleak (cf. Intro. at n. 76). This precise formulation marks a decisive shift at *Cho.* 782: the Nurse thinks Orestes is dead and utters the words from a position of despair, but we and the Chorus know then that for once things *are* turning to the speaker's favour.

674–9. 'For [γὰρ οὖν: Denniston 112], where Menelaus is concerned, expect first and foremost that he has got back [aorist μολεῖν]. Well, at any rate [δ' οὖν], if some sunbeam traces him to be alive and seeing,

thanks to the contrivances of Zeus, not yet willing to destroy the
family utterly [ἐξ-], there is some hope that he will come back to his
palace.' The Herald ends by addressing the Coryphaeus' question
from 617–19 about Menelaus' homecoming. He initially expresses
the best-case scenario (following γένοιτο ὡς ἄριστα), that Menelaus
has safely reached Greece. But δ' οὖν marks a change to a more
realistic view as the unexpressed alternative enters his mind (cf. 34
with n.). He is reduced to *some hope* that, *if* Zeus is not *yet totally*
against the family, Menelaus *will* get back.

680. κλύων would seem here to mean approximately 'knowing'
(see LSJ κλύω I 1, at end). Other editors prefer κλυών (aorist),
which repeats ἀκούσας with variation. Either way, the Herald
affirms to the Coryphaeus that *this* is the true story—in contrast to
his declaration at 582 (see n.). He then leaves despondently, the
enthusiasm of his arrival shattered, to take Clytemnestra's message to
Agamemnon.

Second Stasimon (681–781): This ode is the climax of ominous and
efficacious performance in the first half of the play, culminating in
Agamemnon's grand entrance (Intro. §§ 6, 7). The Chorus begins,
significantly, by exploring the meaning of Helen's name (the root
ἑλ-, as in ἑλεῖν, implies 'destruction') and of her κῆδος, the
'marriage-alliance' with Paris, which was also a source of κῆδος in
the sense 'grief'. The Greeks often saw names as omens of character,
but the principle has special point here. Owen phrased this well
(1952, 78): '[Helen's] career is the translation into fact of the significance of her name. Words are coming alive, incarnating themselves in acts.' This occurs just before the transition between the
build-up of words which are ominous for Agamemnon, and their
'incarnation' before the audience's eyes, as Persuasion (embodied in
Clytemnestra) forces him towards new hubris and destruction.

In the second strophic pair and str. γ, the situation of Helen at
Troy is illustrated by a fable of a lion-cub, first reared as a household
pet, and later growing up to create havoc. Then from ant. γ through
the fourth strophic pair the Chorus utters γνῶμαι which point the
moral (but which it never applies to a specific individual) about
prosperity conjoined with impiety: hubris breeds in such a house,
which is plunged into ruin; Justice rejects it—she who guides all
to its end. The winding of the dramatic spell is complete: Enter
Agamemnon.

For the ways in which rhythm enhances this magnificent ode, see Appendix § 5.

681–8. The trochaic rhythm of the Hymn to Zeus returns (160–83 n.), and again the Chorus is seeking to make sense of an aspect of the Trojan War (in this case, Helen's destructive allure) by appeal to a superhuman authority. Here it is a vague, unseen, and prescient being; but since children were normally named by their fathers one may suspect Zeus' work again, inspiring Helen's human father Tyndareus (Lloyd-Jones 1978, 53–4). In any case, Helen is perceived as having played a part in the divine plan for punishing the guilty.

683–5. This suggestion about the nature of the name-giver interrupts the basic question (and is better punctuated, as by West, as parenthetical), and delays the name 'Helen' as long as possible. Indeed, this is the first time that Helen's name is actually given (Goldhill 1984*a*, 14). On the importance of naming, see Introduction at n. 77.

For the overawed tone of μή introducing a question ('Was it someone . . . ?') see Barrett (1964), 314–15; the common rule of thumb that it 'expects the answer "no"' is inadequate. **γλῶσσαν ἐν τύχαι νέμων**: 'plying an accurate tongue' (MacNeice). τύχη here is not 'chance', but related to the sense of 'hitting the mark' in τυγχάνω. For νέμω meaning 'employ', see LSJ s.v. III 2.

686–7. τὰν δορίγαμβρον ἀμφινεικῆ θ' Ἑλέναν: the object and object-predicate of ὠνόμαζεν: 'Who named . . . that spear-relationed and quarrelled-over woman "Helen"?' γαμβροί are male in-laws (usually brothers-in-law), so δορίγαμβρον implies that war was the inevitable consequence of marrying Helen. Aeschylus seems to have coined the word, but with reference to *Iliad* 3. 49 νυὸν ἀνδρῶν αἰχμητάων, 'female in-law of spearsmen' (of Helen).

688. πρεπόντως: first her name was ἐτήτυμος to her. Now we have the converse: her actions, expressed in the following predicates, are suitable to her name.

688–90. ἑλένας ἕλανδρος ἑλέπτολις: the significance of Helen's name depends on the pun with ἑλ-εῖν, 'capture, overpower'. Browning caught the wordplay with 'Ship's-hell, man's-hell, city's-hell' (1877, l. 709). West and Fraenkel rightly prefer the spelling ἑλέναυς.

From ἐκ τῶν, the Chorus takes off into ionic rhythm as it resumes from the first stasimon the narrative of Helen's abduction and its consequences, this time from the Trojan viewpoint and in the light of Troy's known destruction.

690–1. 'she left her delicately precious chamber-curtains and sailed'. -τιμος would be related to τιμή in the sense 'cost' not 'honour'; but Salmasius' ἁβροπήνων ('delicately woven') is an attractive suggestion. προκαλυμμάτων probably refers to the 'chamber-curtains' of Helen's marriage-bed in Argos; for the alternative that Helen removes her veils, in a first reference to marriage ritual, see Seaford (1987), 123–7 at 124.

692. Ζεφύρου γίγαντος: the west wind is needed to blow Helen from Greece to Troy. Zephyrus is more commonly a gentle breeze, but here (in a kind of oxymoron) has the power of a 'giant' to sweep Helen swiftly across the sea. This contrasts starkly with the winds which delayed the Greek force (192).

By Aeschylus' time various accounts of Helen's journey with Paris had been put forward. The *Cypria* seems to have existed in two ancient versions: in one, they had a smooth two-day journey, as in Aeschylus; in the other Hera diverted them to Sidon (see Finkelberg 2000). Stesichorus' famous *Palinodes* seem to have suggested that Helen was whisked off to Egypt and that Paris, without realizing, sailed away with only a phantom of her: Campbell (1991), 92–7.

693–8. There is a textual difficulty at κέλσαν τάς.

(1) With the OCT, the picture of Helen in her voyage over the sea is linked almost simultaneously (τε rather than δέ) with the 'shield-bearing huntsmen, in their multitudes, on the vanishing trail of oars' who 'put in at banks of the Simois'.

(2) The manuscripts' κελσάντων is possible. One can understand ἔπλευσαν in 693–5, from ἔπλευσε and the connective τε. The genitive participle would refer to Paris and Helen putting in, and could be construed as a possessive genitive with either ἴχνος or πλατᾶν, or as a genitive absolute with the pronoun αὐτῶν understood. The last interpretation would leave 696–8 not only metrically but also syntactically separate.

With either reading, πολύανδροι may recall πολυάνορος ἀμφὶ γυναικός (62); the πολλοὶ ἄνδρες would no longer be Helen's lovers, but her pursuers. The Simois was one of the rivers in the Troad (see Map, p. 101).

698. δι' Ἔριν αἱματόεσσαν: Eris, excluded from the wedding of Peleus and Thetis, sowed the discord among Hera, Athena, and Aphrodite which led to the Judgement of Paris. For the personification

of Eris cf. 1461 (again with Helen). However, with the OCT's κέλσαν
τάς there is the option of reading ἔριν and translating 'for the sake of
bloody war'.

αἱματόεσσαν contrasts grimly with the pastoral colour of
ἀεξιφύλλους. The stem αἱμ- recurs in the corresponding syllable at
the end of the antistrophe (716).

699–700. κῆδος ὀρθώνυμον: 'rightly-named' because κῆδος means
not only 'marriage alliance' but also 'cause of sorrow'. MacNeice
essays this wordplay with a 'marring marriage'.

701. Μῆνις ἤλασεν: Μῆνις is the personified wrath of the gods
(especially here of Zeus Xenios). ἤλασεν is 'impelled, set in
motion'.

701–6. The construction centres on πρασσομένα (fem. nom. sing.),
which governs two accusatives, and means 'exacting requital for
X from Y'. The offence is τραπέζας ἀτίμωσιν καὶ ξυνεστίου Διός,
'dishonouring the table and Zeus of the shared hearth'—a slight
zeugma for 'dishonouring hospitality'. The offenders are (τοὺς) τὸ
νυμφότιμον μέλος τίοντας, 'those performing the observance of the
bride-honouring song'. **ὑστέρωι χρόνωι**: the sinner pays *in time*;
cf. 58 ὑστερόποινον, 766 τότ' ἢ τοθ'. **ἐκφάτως**: 'outspokenly, loudly'
(a *hapax*). Paris' family are, at this point, enthusiastic about his
match, in the Chorus's view.

706–8. ὑμέναιον is in apposition to νυμφότιμον μέλος. There
were various moments for song during the extended Greek marriage
ritual: this hymn is sung after Helen's arrival at her groom's house.
It 'fell to' (ἐπέρρεπε) Helen's in-laws to perform, since her family
were neither present nor supportive.

709–11. The Trojans now have to 'relearn the song as full of lamentation' (predicative πολύθρηνον)—not a ὑμέναιος but a θρῆνος. **που**:
'I suppose', as in 182.

714–16. παμπρόσθη is meaningless, and 715 unmetrical. The
apparatus gives a solution παμπορθῆ πολύθρηνον | αἰῶνα διαὶ
πολιτᾶν | μέλεον αἷμ' ἀνατλᾶσα, 'having endured a life of utter
destruction and much lamentation because of the pitiful bloodshed
of her citizens'. This yields reasonable sense, though the corruption
of διαί to ἀμφί is difficult to explain. For discussion and a different
reconstruction see M. West (1990*a*), 198–9.

717–49. The next strophic pair is occupied by a fable: a man once
tried to keep a lion as a pet, but when it grew up its nature asserted

itself and it caused havoc, by the will of the gods. This fable is also
put in Aeschylus' mouth in Ar. *Ran.* 1431–3, and alluded to in
Pl. *Gorg.* 483e. One expects an animal fable to have a central point of
applicability to its context, but also to develop a picture whose details
are not all bound by that context. In Aristophanes and Plato the
moral is 'However you nurture something, expect it to obey its
natural dispositions', but the Trojan War is not caused by Paris' or
Helen's natural dispositions being revealed. The fable is linked by
οὕτως to what precedes, and implicitly to what follows: Troy at first
fostered and celebrated Paris and Helen, but came to lament them;
Helen arrived in an atmosphere of calm but after a 'swerving aside'
(744) it was an Erinys' arrival which came to prominence. The
lion, like Helen, is removed from where it belongs and welcomed,
rather naively; but in time the divine plan of retribution behind its
migration becomes clear, and the situation turns tragic. The lion's
domestication cannot forever overlay the innate dispositions which
oppose it; Helen's sensuous arrival on the level of human explanation
cannot forever overlay the arrival of an ugly Erinys as part of the
divine plan (see Intro. § 4.3.1). The relevance of the fable here, then,
seems to be about the natural development of a *situation* under
divine guidance from joyous to lamentable, rather than specifically
about Paris' and Helen's natural dispositions coming out in time.

Knox (1952) influentially suggested that the details of the fable
also allude, without the Chorus intending it, to various events in
Agamemnon's family. The 'house awash with blood' (732) may naturally suggest the Atreid house, and the lion's innate tendency to
cause σίνος may suggest the house's innate δαίμων. Then the lion
might stand for Orestes, nurtured by Clytemnestra but eventually to
kill her, or Clytemnestra, who will fawn on Agamemnon before
'sacrificing' him, and who is a 'lioness' at 1258. Knox also, more
tenuously, suggested that the lion might be an antitype of Iphigenia,
whom Agamemnon nurtured only to kill while still helpless, or
Atreus, who created a meal of Thyestes' children. We wonder how
important or prominent these associations are: Orestes, for example,
has not been in our thoughts so far.

717–19. ἔθρεψεν: Greek fables characteristically begin with a verb;
the effect may be rendered with 'Once upon a time a man reared . . .'.
ἀγάλακτον ... φιλόμαστον: probably 'deprived of (its mother's)
milk, when longing for the breast'. The lion-cub is not in its natural
element.

720. ἐν βιότου προτελείοις: the cub's harmless condition is called the 'preliminary ritual' to the carnage that is to be wreaked by the grown lion. For the word προτέλεια see 63–7 n., 227; its special sense 'sacrifice before marriage ritual' is relevant given the fable's application to Helen and Paris' arrival at Troy. Moreover, this stasimon as a whole might be seen as the completion of the dramatic προτέλεια preceding the 'sacrifice' of Agamemnon.

721. ἄμερον: Doric for ἥμερον, 'tame'.

721–2. εὐφιλόπαιδα, καὶ γεραροῖς ἐπίχαρτον: the context suggests that εὐφιλόπαιδα is 'beloved of children', though 'friendly to children' is also possible. γεραροῖς ἐπίχαρτον perhaps recalls *Iliad* 3. 146–60, where Priam's aged councillors are captivated by Helen's beauty. The association could be confirmed by the epicism πολέα immediately afterwards. For the phrasing which juxtaposes young and old, cf. 326–9 n.

723. πολέα δ' ἔσχ': 'It got many things'; the lion-cub is now the subject. πολέα is an epic form for πολλά. Casaubon suggested the further epicism ἔσκ' (frequentative imperfect of εἰμί), with which πολέα would be adverbial: 'It was often'.

725. φαιδρωπὸς ποτὶ χεῖρα: 'bright-eyed towards the hand' which fed it solid food (cf. 718 ἀγαλακτον). For φαιδρός used of eyes see 520 n.

727–8. 'But when matured by time, it revealed the character inherited from its parents', i.e. its savagery. The imagery of parents, breeding, and children pervades the ode from here to 771, and implies a unity of thought (see 750–81 n.). Knox (1952) and Perradotto (1969) applied it to the Atreid family: thus the latter suggests that Agamemnon, like the lion in the fable, acquired a 'predatory and teknophonous *ethos*' from Atreus (p. 256). But we disagree: Agamemnon may display a hint of bloodthirstiness in 810–56 (see n.), but his decision to sacrifice Iphigenia was not presented in 205–27 as predatory or derived from an inherited disposition.

728–9. The Greeks placed particular value on θρεπτήρια, i.e. repaying the debt of having been raised by looking after one's aged parents. Here the lion perverts the custom.

731. ἀκέλευστος: in the terms of a δαίς, the lion is 'uninvited'.

732–4. ἄλγος and σίνος are accusatives in apposition to the general idea of 732. The sense is probably that members of the household as well as sheep (730) are being slaughtered by the full-grown lion.

735–6. While the man nurtured the lion-cub as a pet, a god *in addition* (προσ-) nurtured it as 'a kind of priest of Atē'. There is a clear ring-composition with 717–19, which expresses the complementarity of the divine and human type of nurture (ἀνήρ/θεοῦ; δόμοις repeated; ἔθρεψεν/προσεθρέφθη). The god destroys the household through the lion's actions, presumably in punishment. So the Trojans fostered Helen, but in time realized that Zeus had sent an Erinys into their midst in punishment for Paris' breach of hospitality (this is amplified in the next strophe); a higher power was thus at work in Helen's journey, as well as in her name (681–90).

The lion is a 'priest' whose 'sacrificial victims' are the sheep and οἰκέται; for the Trojans as sacrificial victims see 128–30 n.

737. πάραυτα δ': the adverb here means 'at first', i.e. when Helen and Paris first eloped. The fable is simply linked to its application by δέ.

738–43. λέγοιμ' ἄν, 'I might say', acknowledges that the following descriptions are rather bold metaphors. The four neuter phrases adumbrate Helen with more power than any direct description of her. She is 'a spirit of windless calm', and 'a gentle adornment to wealth', i.e. to Priam's wealthy house (cf. Iphigenia at 208). We prefer <τ'> to <δ'> in 741. Lines 742–3 then beautifully suggest the transformation from the pangs of loveliness to those of war: the poignant 'soft dart of her eyes' (cf. Iphigenia's glance at 241) and the 'soul-biting' quality of this 'flower of love' will become the sharpened missiles and heartache of fighting.

744–9. The changed situation is reflected in the change to ionic rhythm (cf. 757 n.). The opening participle gives us a singular feminine subject, which we naturally assume at first to be Helen, continued from the previous sentence. The idea that she 'swerved aside and ordained a bitter conclusion to the marriage' is bold, but not so as to make us doubt our identification. (παρακλίνασ' could be transitive 'turning aside', with γάμον understood as the object; but that is less vivid.) δύσεδρος καὶ δυσόμιλος also fits Helen: she brought harm to those with whom she sat and associated. However, συμένα (middle: 'swooping down') is less applicable to her; we therefore advocate adding a comma before, and removing the comma after Πριαμίδαισιν. The subject is then literally 'swooping down on the sons of Priam through the sending of [i.e. 'sent by'] Zeus Xenios'. This clearly echoes the Chorus's words at 59–62 where the Atridae are agents of a god-sent Erinys. Here, the final words of the strophe indeed reveal the subject to be an Erinys. The shifting of the sentence's subject and the revelation in its final word brilliantly mirror its overall meaning. As the family in the fable welcomed a lion-cub, but in time the divine plan for it as a priest of Ruin became clear, so the Trojans welcomed Helen, but in time recognized Zeus' plan which sent an ugly Fury against them at the same time. For Helen as an instrument of destruction in Troy, see also 1455–67.

νυμφόκλαυτος: a *hapax*, probably with the bold sense 'involving the lamenting of a bride': see Winnington-Ingram (1983), 208. The word opposes 705 νυμφότιμον, which described the wedding-hymn in Helen's early days at Troy, which was replaced in time with a dirge when the Erinys was revealed.

750–81. As in the first stasimon the focus shifted from Paris and the Trojans to the Greeks and Agamemnon, so now the elders turn away from Helen and the Trojans, to γνῶμαι about Justice and the wealth–folly–hubris syndrome (Intro. § 4.3.3) whose implications are more obviously relevant to Agamemnon, and which end with his entrance. The transition (as at 184) occurs half-way through a strophic pair, which suggests a dovetailing in thought with what has preceded. The links are 'in time' (766–7 ~ 727) and 'breeding': as the lion-cub in due course showed the savagery inherited from its parents, so one impious (758) or hubristic (763) action in time generates another of the same character. There is also a verbal link in ἄμαχον (768, cf. 733).

750–62. The Chorus refers to an old doctrine that a man's prosperity, if it becomes too great, breeds sorrow for his family. On this view, the gods are jealous of extreme prosperity and visit misery on its owner or his descendants. Compare Polycrates' attempts to reduce his wealth in Herodotus 3. 40–3. In 757 this doctrine is rejected. Rather, it is *impious actions* breeding more of the same which involve a family in 'insatiable misery', as divine punishment. The Chorus advances this view as unique (δίχα δ' ἄλλων μονόφρων), whereas in fact similar ideas—though with more focus on greed than piety—had long since been articulated at Athens by Solon. See his fr. 13. 9–32: hubristic greed leads to unjust action and detrimental susceptibility to πειθώ, which leads to eventual punishment from Zeus in the form of ruin to himself or a family member. Fragment 4. 5–29 contains similar ideas, except that ruin affects the whole state. cf. Doyle (1970) for other earlier authors, and Introduction § 4.3.3.

751. γέρων λόγος: γέρων is adjectival; cf. *Cho.* 314 where 'the doer suffers' is a τριγέρων μῦθος. The idea 'There is a saying . . .' is followed by an accusative and infinitive (751–6).

754. μηδ': this use of μή in an indirect statement is exceptional, as is μηδέ in the sense 'and not' without a preceding negative.

757. As in the strophe at 744, the change of rhythm marks a switch to a different thought.

758–60. 'For it is the impious act which after a time [adverbial μετά] breeds *more* acts, but ones *resembling* their lineage', i.e. the next generation differs (μέν) in quantity, but not (δέ) in quality.

761–2. 'The just house's destiny always has fair children' in that deeds in the household continue fair down the generations.

763–81. The fourth strophic pair is composed almost entirely in syncopated iambics, a taut, relentless pulse which contrasts with the metrical variety of the stasimon up to here. Again, the iambics deal with retribution of the impious (see Appendix § 4.4): they thus combine musical vigour with ominous content.

763–6. 'Old hubris is wont to breed a hubris which flourishes anew in the evil deeds of mortals.' The Chorus speaks these words generally, but one should ask how they apply within the dramatic context to Agamemnon. The previous hubris may be interpreted as the sack of Troy's shrines (cf. 527 with n.), and the next will be shown in the third episode: both are certainly δυσσεβῆ ἔργα (758).

(ἐν κακοῖς βροτῶν could mean 'among evil mortals', but taking κακά as 'evil deeds' brings home the point; 'among the misfortunes of mortals' does not suit the argument so well. An alternative candidate for the old hubris influencing Agamemnon would be Atreus butchering Thyestes' children, but this has not been mentioned yet, and the generations of hubris are not said to coincide with those of a family.)

766–7. 'now or later, when the appointed day of birth comes'. The OCT both here and in 775–6 follows Ahrens' attempt to restore a corrupt text (see *apparatus*). Fraenkel and West have κότον νεώρη where the OCT prints τόκου. That stays closer to the manuscripts, but the hubris is not a κότος ('anger').

768–71. 'and also that spirit which cannot be fought or warred against, the unholy boldness of black ruin for [or 'in'] the palace, (children) like their parents'. δαίμονα is a further object of 763 τίκτειν; τάν—an emendation for the unmetrical τόν—shows that a female daemonic personification is meant. This is identified by the apposition of θράσος ἄτας (or better, Ἄτας), which is a periphrasis for θρασεῖαν Ἄτην, i.e. the reckless infatuation which leads to destruction. εἰδομένας τοκεῦσιν is better taken as accusative plural qualifying both ὕβριν (766) and τὰν δαίμονα, rather than as genitive singular qualifying ἄτας alone; the two words balance 760 in content.

Again, applying these phrases to Agamemnon's imminent situation, daemonic Atē resulting from his hubris, against which he cannot defend himself, will presently make him disregard the dangers of treading over the purple garments into his palace. But in using δαίμων Aeschylus may also have had in mind the 'evil genius' which haunts the house, as invoked by the Chorus and embodied in Clytemnestra (1468–74).

773–9. 'As for Justice, she shines in dwellings acrid with smoke and honours the righteous man, but leaves gold-spangled abodes which are conjoined with filthy hands, and goes to the pure . . .'. The contrast is between the hovel of the poor but righteous, and the palace of the rich but polluted. For Agamemnon's hands, see 209–10 μιαίνων παρθενοσφάγοισιν | ῥείθροις πατρῴους χέρας. For the juxtapositions of light and dark (λάμπει/δυσκάπνοις; χρυσόπαστα/πίνωι) cf. 21–2, 388–9. †προσέβα τοῦ†: unmetrical, and τοῦ is senseless. Read Thierach's προσέμολε, a gnomic aorist on which προσέβα would be a gloss. The article τοῦ would initially have been added just before and above πλούτου, then misplaced here (West).

779–80. 'not revering the power of wealth falsely stamped with praise'. παράσημος is an adjective applied to counterfeit coinage. Praise is often wrongly accorded to the power of the wealthy without regard to their true 'metal', i.e. their characters and actions. This lends them a spurious currency, which Justice ignores. Compare the imagery at 387–93.

781. πᾶν δ' ἐπὶ τέρμα νωμᾶι: 'And she guides everything to its end.' The spell of Justice, in the sense of the active power of words accumulated in the first half of the play to bring Agamemnon to his retribution and 'end', is now complete. The cue for Agamemnon's entrance is similar in effect to the conclusion of the Witches' spell-ritual before the first entrance of Macbeth, 'Peace!—the charm's wound up' (*Macbeth* I. iii. 38).

Third Episode (783–974): This is the central scene of the play, and the only one in which Agamemnon himself appears on stage. The whole drama so far—the prevalence of ill omen, the repeated plunges back from momentary optimism, all that the Chorus and Clytemnestra have said about the punishment of the sinner—has been gradually building towards Agamemnon's appearance and interaction with Clytemnestra.

After an initial greeting from the Chorus, Aeschylus gives the king a formal address in which he thanks the gods and outlines what he proposes to do. Clytemnestra enters to deliver the longest speech of the play, at whose culmination she invites her victorious husband to enter his palace across a path of rich purple garments—a temptation to hubris which Agamemnon at first resists but eventually, after a crucial passage of stichomythia, yields to. He then briefly introduces his foreign captive, Cassandra, before moving towards his house to the accompaniment of a concluding speech by Clytemnestra. When the king finally passes inside the palace, we know that his death is inevitable.

Agamemnon enters the *orchēstra* along one of the *eisodoi* in an ἀπήνη (906), which in Homer is a four-wheeled wagon with seats, drawn by mules (as opposed to a ἅρμα, a two-wheeled war-chariot drawn by horses, in which one stood). Probably, the wagon was drawn on by attendants: animals notoriously create problems onstage, though their use in Greek tragedy cannot be excluded; see Sommerstein (1996), 241. The appearance of a wagon rather than a war-chariot could make Agamemnon seem less heroic; certainly, nothing suggests a spectacular crowd of returning troops, body-guards, or welcoming Argive citizens. After all, the conqueror has lost all but one ship from his fleet, and Aeschylus has every reason to emphasize his vulnerability in this scene. For general consideration of vehicular entries in Aeschylus, see Taplin (1977), 76–8.

More controversial is how Cassandra entered. She is sitting (cf. 1054 θρόνον) in a wagon (1039 ἀπήνη, 1054 ἁμαξ-). But is it the same one as Agamemnon, or a separate one behind him? Most scholars currently prefer a single vehicle: Cassandra's closeness to Agamemnon would be emphasized, and indeed their entrance would reflect fifth-century wedding iconography, since an Athenian husband drove his bride home beside him in a cart; this would be part of what motivates Clytemnestra to kill Cassandra. So e.g. Taplin (1977), 304–6; Rehm (1992), 84; Ewans (1995); Mitchell-Boyask (2006). However, Cassandra is not actually a new bride—rather a captive whose status as a concubine is merely implied at this stage

(955). Clytemnestra is not motivated to kill her by simple jealousy, nor does she ever speak of Cassandra as a rival 'bride' (1431–47 n.). We therefore feel that the iconographic parallel would introduce a disruptive idea and argues rather for a separate vehicle. Secondly, given the focus on wealth in the Chorus's preceding words, it is plausible for Agamemnon to enter with rich spoils, whose vain pomp would perfectly illustrate the elders' point (perhaps cf. 954). Since Cassandra is classed among Agamemnon's booty, she would enter along with the spoils, which would probably require a second vehicle. Thirdly, the visual focus up to 950 must be on Agamemnon and Clytemnestra. Cassandra's august presence in full prophetic garb and bearing a staff (1264–5) cannot be totally occluded, but if she is central beside Agamemnon it distracts from the battle of wits between husband and wife. Fourthly, Agamemnon's wagon needs to be fairly close to the centre of the *orchēstra*, so that he can step directly onto the long path of purple garments which lead to the central door. The wagon would then be moved by attendants after Agamemnon's exit, to leave the *orchēstra* clear for the Chorus to perform their ode. The stagecraft is tidier if Cassandra is located in a second wagon close to the *eisodos* throughout both episode and stasimon. Fifthly, this episode is reworked at length in Euripides *Electra* 988–1146 (Intro. § 10), which almost certainly involves the entrance of two vehicles (Raeburn 2000, 163–4).

Therefore, although the writer of the ancient *hypothesis* of the play (early second century BC?) could not have known how Aeschylus directed it, the performance-tradition he knew may reflect the original situation on this point: 'Agamemnon enters on a wagon, followed by another wagon containing the spoils and Cassandra.'

783–809. The Chorus addresses the victorious king in a passage of anapaests. The opening greeting has a very sinister resonance (see 783–4 n.) and the overall tone of what follows is far from congratulatory. The emphasis in 788–98 on the theme of insincerity is an implicit warning to Agamemnon to beware of Clytemnestra and this is reinforced in the final lines.

In this speech, one might imagine 783–4 shouted in unison, with the Coryphaeus perhaps taking over on his own at 785.

783–4. The king is hailed in ironically ominous terms as the 'city-sacker of Troy, offspring of Atreus'. πτολίπορθε recalls 472, where it was a dangerous thing to be. After that, we may wonder if Ἀτρέως γένεθλον is also ominous, since it could suggest Atreus' crimes against Thyestes, which Aegisthus will avenge. Four words would then succinctly comprehend the guilt for which Agamemnon is responsible and that for which he is not. (For the treatment of inherited liability see Intro. § 4.3.4.)

784–7. The questions reflect the desire prominent in the play to use the right description of a person (cf. 896–91, 1232–6), and also the Coryphaeus' desire to utter the appropriate word which will not incur divine φθόνος—just after the Chorus has greeted Agamemnon inauspiciously. The phrase 'neither overshooting nor dipping under the target of gratitude' is comparable to 365 μήτε πρὸ καιροῦ μήθ' ὑπὲρ ἄστρων. Recollection of that passage might suggest the thought 'As Zeus aimed successfully at Paris, so now he is aiming at Agamemnon.'

ὑπεράρας, ὑποκάμψας, and 789 παραβάντες are 'coincident' aorist participles: cf. 289 n.

788. τὸ δοκεῖν εἶναι: 'the semblance of being', as opposed to actually being such-and-such.

792. ἐφ' ἧπαρ: see 432 n.

793–4. Editors posit a lacuna after 794, because of the interlinear hiatus βιαζόμενοι | ὅστις, which is not as a rule found in anapaests. ξυγχαίρουσιν is then taken as a dative plural participle with ὁμοιοπρεπεῖς, 'looking like people who share one's joy'. The missing line would have contained the main verb, perhaps something to the effect of <χαλεπῶς τὰ δέοντα λέγουσιν>.

If the hiatus, at a sense-pause, were defensible one might translate 'they rejoice with (a man), appearing like him [i.e. hypocritically assuming happiness], forcing their unsmiling faces', i.e. into a smile.

795–8. The structure is 'It is impossible [οὐκ ἔστι] that a man's eyes deceive [λαθεῖν] (one) who (is) a good flock-judge.' ὅστις stands for ἐκεῖνον ὅστις. προβατογνώμων is another fine coinage, which adds the notion of discernment to the epic formula of the king as 'shepherd of the people'. Lines 797–8 then describe ὄμματα further: literally 'which seem out of kindly purpose to be fawning with friendship that is watered-down'. This is a compressed way of saying 'which seem kindly, but are only fawning with . . .'. δοκοῦντα repeats the idea of 788 δοκεῖν. As the scene develops, Clytemnestra will prove to be testing Agamemnon's judgement with such false appearances. For the nuance of εὔφρων in contexts involving her, see 264–7 n.

799–801. σὺ δέ contrasts the general situation (788–98) with the Coryphaeus' candidness towards Agamemnon: 'To me, you made a very inartistic [i.e. ugly] picture—I will not hide it—when launching the fleet back then for Helen's sake'. For Ἑλένης ἕνεκα as an inadequate grounds for war, cf. 62, 448–9, and the same attitude in e.g. Euripides *Cyclops* 283–4.

802. 'and not wielding the tiller of your mind correctly': a further description of their 'image' of Agamemnon, using a metaphor which fits the leader of a naval expedition. Compare 380 where a person εὖ πραπίδων λαχών would abjure Agamemnon's extreme wealth.

803–4. (1) The OCT (based on Ahrens' emendation) means 'conveying confidence to dying men from sacrifices', i.e. bringing hope to the soldiers who were dying at Aulis (188, 193, 197) by sacrificing Iphigenia. But a reference to her is not at all 'in place' from the Chorus (as D–P claim), and θράσος is an unusually abstract object for κομίζων.

(2) The manuscripts have the unmetrical θράσος ἑκούσιον. Most promising is West's <αἰπὺ γυναικός> θάρσος ἑκούσιον: 'recovering the <sheer>, willing wantonness <of a woman>, by means of dying men'. The lacuna is probably necessary, since without a qualification like γυναικός, θάρσος would be an exceedingly bold metonymy.

805. The Coryphaeus' former doubts have been replaced (νῦν δ' balancing 799 τότε μέν), but his sincerity remains: οὐκ ἀπ' ἄκρας φρενός, 'not from the surface of my mind', i.e. felt deeply, picks up the contrast of surface appearance versus 'reaching the liver' in 788–98.

806. The OCT's emendation πόνον and supplement <ἐγώ> (sc. εἰμί) produces: 'I am well-disposed to those who have ended their toil successfully.' But the line may be more deeply corrupt. For example, West sought to make the proverbial nature of the sentiment explicit in a longer lacuna after εὔφρων, along the lines of

εὔφρων <αἰνῶ τόδ' ἔπος προτέρων·
εὕδει> πόνος εὖ τελέσασιν.

807–9. 'By careful [δια-] enquiry, you will learn in time the man among the citizens who minded [literally 'house-sat'] the city justly, and the man who did so inappropriately.' But Agamemnon will not be allowed any time. The Coryphaeus perhaps hints in τὸν δικαίως οἰκουροῦντα at himself and the rest of the Chorus, and in τὸν ἀκαίρως at Clytemnestra and Aegisthus. But he will not name names or give a clear warning. πόλιν οἰκουροῦντα: the metaphor interestingly melds the king's *polis* with his *oikos*, and indeed it is the two οἰκουροί of his palace (1225, 1626) who have political control. In the presence of δικαίως, the melding may suggest that at this stage of the *Oresteia*, there is still no independent *polis*-justice independent from the king's house—a situation which will change in *Eumenides*. See Introduction § 4.1.

810–54. Agamemnon's address begins with a long 'prelude' (829 φροίμιον, cf. 31 n.), in which he acknowledges his debt to the gods and celebrates his destruction of Troy. He places great emphasis on justice (811–13 δίκη ... δικαίων ... δίκας, then the language of law-courts in 813–17), which he associates with blood, smoke, and fire. The splendour of the metaphors and sonority of the verse help to create the impression of a magnificent warrior king who revels in the glory of the punishment he has exacted and the blood that has been shed. In 830–44 he goes on to respond to the Chorus's warning revealingly (see 830–7, 841–2 nn.). Then he announces his future programme of civic action (844–50), and finally his intention of entering the palace to greet the gods within. For the striking but economical portrait, see Introduction § 8.

811. τοὺς ἐμοὶ μεταιτίους: Agamemnon attributes to the gods a *share* in his return and in his treatment of Troy. This, with the emphatic form ἐμοί, may indicate arrogance. On the one hand, the Greeks commonly thought of human and divine action as proceeding in parallel (Intro. § 4.3.1), and Agamemnon does give the gods a large measure of acknowledgement (813–17, 821–2, 829, 844, 852–3). However, in an event such as escaping from a storm the gods deserve sole credit (cf. 661–6).

812. πράσσομαι is used with one accusative of the justice exacted and another of the offender (cf. 701–6 n.). Here, however, the former is a relative which has been attracted to agree with its antecedent (δικαίων ἅ → δικαίων ὧν: see Smyth § 2522).

813–16. The gods paradoxically listened to 'pleas coming not from a tongue', i.e. the Greek and Trojan cases, which were not asserted in a law-court speech but in action by arms. The image is then elaborated. The gods are like a jury unanimously casting their 'pebbles' (voting-counters) into the αἱματηρὸν τεῦχος, the urn for votes calling for the death-penalty.

With the OCT, the pebbles are ἀνδροθνῆτας and Ἰλιοφθόρους, and the gods cast their votes while listening (κλύοντες: present). But it is sharper to read κλυόντες (aorist), place a comma after ἀνδροθνῆτας (so that it qualifies δίκας), then read Ἰλίου φθορᾶς depending on ψήφους, as in Euripides *Orestes* 1013 ψήφωι θανάτου: see M. West (1990*a*), 204–8. Thus: 'The gods, after hearing unspoken pleas involving the deaths of men, cast their votes for the destruction of Troy unambiguously into the urn of blood.'

816–17. Two interpretations of χειρός are possible:

(1) It depends on πληρουμένωι: '(Only) Hope [but none of the gods] approached the opposite vessel, which was not filled with any hand.'

(2) It is objective genitive after ἐλπίς: '(Only) hope for a hand approached the opposite vessel, which was not filled.'

On either interpretation (though perhaps more vividly with the former) the passage suggests the gods as jurors approaching the urns and dropping in their voting-counters, as will be enacted on stage by the Athenian jurors during *Eum.* 711–33. In the present passage, however, a contrastingly different kind of court is described: no speeches are made by the parties to the case (813), and there is no ambivalence (οὐ διχορρόπως) in the voting which could imply two sides to the question. The slaughterous justice of the gods on Troy seems much more arbitrary than the deliberative justice of the Athenian court on Orestes.

818. Different deliveries could give slightly different possible meanings: either 'The city's capture is still now conspicuous by smoke' or possibly 'The city is still now conspicuous after its capture, (but only) by smoke.' In the former, εὔσημός εἰμι governs a participle, like other expressions for 'to be clearly such-and-such'.

819–20. 'The storm-winds of ruin are alive, and the ash as it dies a painful death sends forth fat gusts of wealth.' The metaphorical 'storm of ruin' fuses with the literal winds which fan the flames amid Troy's ruins, and cause the smoke to remain visible. The winds are still 'alive', whereas the powdered ruins are slowly 'dying'. (Enger's δυσθνήισκουσα is a convincing emendation for the less intelligible συνθνήισκουσα.) The image then shifts again: the emanations from the burning ruins of wealthy Troy are like the fatty savour rising to the gods from a rich sacrifice (cf. 128–30 n.). In 820 the alliteration of π magnificently reflects Agamemnon's triumphalist tone in evoking a typical fifth-century picture of eastern luxury.

822–4. Several features in these lines suggest that the treatment of Troy was disproportionate. Agamemnon doubtless means 'since we have exacted recompense for extravagant robbery', but his words could also suggest 'since we have exacted recompense *consisting in* extravagant robbery'. Then γυναικὸς οὕνεκα ironically communicates the nuance of 62, 448–9, and 800, that Helen was too slender a justification. Thirdly, διημάθυνεν ('ground to powder') and the following imagery of the Greeks as beasts of prey suggests the inhumanity of their behaviour.

824–8. The Greek army is first a δάκος, a beast defined by its bite. Then it shifts species to become 'the brood of the horse', i.e. of the Wooden Horse. Their jump from the Horse's belly *down* to the ground again suggests a predatory animal, 'launching its leap'. Finally, the λεώς becomes a λέων which eats raw flesh, and which leapt *up*, over Troy's walls, and 'licked its fill of tyrannical blood'. The heroes of the *Iliad* are often compared to predatory animals (e.g. Agamemnon to a lion at 11. 113–19), but Aeschylus has added an unsettling exuberance as various images merge.

ἀμφὶ Πλειάδων δύσιν: Fraenkel takes this as a poetic way of saying 'in the dead of night', as in Sappho (?) *PMG* 976 'The moon and Pleiades have set, and it is the middle of the night.' Alternatively, Sommerstein (n. 171) suggests that Aeschylus may have changed the normal date of Troy's sack (early summer) to early winter in order to suggest Agamemnon's short-sightedness in trying to sail in the stormy season. See Pfundstein (2003) for further discussion: he elegantly observes that when the Pleiades set the constellation Leo is at its zenith (cf. 827). τυραννικοῦ: continuing the picture of eastern luxury (see 819–20 n.). These hints are preparing the way for 919–20, 935–6.

830–7. Agamemnon now responds to the Coryphaeus' remarks. In 830, τὰ δ' ἐς τὸ σὸν φρόνημα introduces the new topic without being syntactically integrated: 'As for your thinking . . .' (cf. 558 n.). Agamemnon recalls the Coryphaeus' unease (799–804) and in 831 emphatically agrees with his general comments (788–98). However, he revealingly focuses only on 793–4, and limits his interpretation of the warning against insincere flattery to a single cause of it, namely the envy which the successful (e.g. he himself) can inspire in a less fortunate *philos*. But Clytemnestra's insincerity will have very different roots. Agamemnon then rather sententiously declares that envy of another's fortune is a 'poison', which 'doubles the burden for one who already has an ailment [i.e. his own problems]'. Here, πεπαμένωι is the perfect of πάομαι ('acquire').

838–40. Agamemnon seems now to come closer to the Coryphaeus' warnings, but the exact sense is disputed.

(1) The OCT's punctuation suggests: 'I can speak from knowledge, for I well understand that those who seemed to be thoroughly loyal to me (were just) a reflection of friendship, the ghost of a shadow [i.e. very illusory].' This, unlike (2) and (3), retains the attractive chiastic balance of the two phrases in 839. However, κάτοπτρον is 'mirror' not 'reflection', and ὁμιλία is normally not 'friendship' but 'social intercourse'. The omission of the article with δοκοῦντας here and in (2) is also unusual, though cf. 39 μαθοῦσιν, 706 τίοντας.

(2) Remove the comma after εἴδωλον σκιᾶς and take as a complement of (τοὺς) δοκοῦντας; take κάτοπτρον as the object of ἐξεπίσταμαι. 'I can say from knowledge—for I well understand the mirror of social intercourse [i.e. how it truly reflects men's characters]—that those who seemed to be thoroughly loyal to me (were just) a ghost of a shadow.' S. West.

(3) Punctuate as in (2) but add a lacuna after 839: so Kitto (1956), 23 n. 2, Sommerstein. The idea would be e.g. 'I can say from knowledge—for I well understand the mirror of social intercourse— that <the loyalty of friends> is a ghost of a shadow. <Achilles and Ajax, for example, let me down> though they seemed to be thoroughly loyal to me, and only Odysseus . . .'.

841–4. οὐχ ἑκών is an allusion to the story in the *Cypria*: Odysseus feigned madness to escape having to enlist, but Palamedes uncovered his deception by the trick of threatening the baby Telemachus. Odysseus was a 'trace-horse' (σειραφόρος), i.e. a right-hand man to the 'yoke-pair of Atridae' (44). The trace-horse was attached directly to the chariot rather than to the yoke (so ζευχθείς is used loosely): see further 1640–1 n.

Agamemnon's remark that Odysseus *alone* proved faithful is intriguing. What of Nestor or Diomedes, for example? The fact that Odysseus is more often presented in fifth-century tragedy as deceptive may suggest that Agamemnon, here and in his tender concern in 843–4, lacks the perspicacity of the ἀγαθὸς προβατογνώμων (795). But the mention of Odysseus, and the uncertainty about his fate, also recalls the contrast in the *Odyssey* between the returns of Odysseus and Agamemnon—the latter having no happy ending. Agamemnon, who takes his success as certain (833), perhaps appears blinkered to the audience in that he misreads the contrast.

844–50. Agamemnon now announces his plans for the *polis* in admirable and sympathetic terms, which we know will go unfulfilled. The change of topic is introduced much as in 830 (see n.): 'As for the rest, with reference to the state and gods'. He emphasizes that his assemblies (ἀγῶνας) will be open to all (κοινούς, ἐν παν-ηγύρει); he will take counsel to ensure the continuation of what is good and the cure of what is bad, rather than acting as an absolute monarch. In 848–50 he presents himself as the paternalist healer of the body politic; this builds on the medical imagery of 834–5 (particularly εὐφρόνως vs. 834 δύσφρων; cf. 13–15 n.). He refers in 848 to φαρμάκων, which must have the general meaning 'remedies' rather than 'medicines', since in 849 he describes his practice as surgical—using either cautery or incision.

θέντες and βουλευσόμεσθα are examples of 'the royal we'. The sense of 846–7 is 'And as for what is in a good state, one must plan how it will, continuing, remain well.' In 848, ὅτωι is also neuter; for impersonal δεῖ τινί τινος, see Smyth §§ 1400, 1467.

851–2. εἰς μέλαθρα καὶ δόμους ἐφέστιος ἐλθών: literally 'after going into my halls and palace, to the hearth'; ἐφέστιος is proleptic (see 535–6 n. for this term). The hearth is the appropriate place to give greeting to the gods of the house, who are distinguished from the θεοὶ ἐγχώριοι addressed in the first part of his speech.

853. πρόσω πέμψαντες: cf. 516–17 n.

854. Both Agamemnon's desire to enter the palace and his concluding prayer for continued victory are frustrated by the opening of the doors, the appearance of Clytemnestra (with maids), and her speech. The moment is discussed well in Taplin (1977), 306–8; cf. 585–6 n. Whereas Agamemnon has made no reference to greeting his wife indoors, she now dominates the threshold and Agamemnon can only enter on her terms; indeed, for now he does not even leave his cart. Clytemnestra's sudden appearance suggests that the prayer for a stable victory can be answered in her favour as well, so that Agamemnon's νίκη begins to pass to her (see also 941–2).

855–913. Clytemnestra's *rhēsis* occupies fifty-nine lines, many of them addressed to the Chorus, rather than to Agamemnon himself. The action seems to be suspended, but once again Clytemnestra is deploying ominous language malevolently, to intensify the 'spell' she has been casting on her husband. She dwells with morbid fascination on the 'malignant rumours' which reached her about Agamemnon's wounds and deaths at Troy, and on the horrible dreams which (she says) haunted her in his absence. She uses as a cover for powerful language the susceptibility to rumour which she scorned as 'girlish' in 274–7 (cf. George 2001, 80). From 895 she moves on to extravagant expressions of praise, whose aim is to provoke divine φθόνος against Agamemnon. This concludes with her instructing her maids to unfurl patterned cloaks over which she invites him to enter the house.

855. ἄνδρες πολῖται: Clytemnestra very strikingly begins by addressing the Chorus rather than her long-absent husband. Agamemnon does not receive his first vocative until 905. **πρέσβος Ἀργείων τόδε:** a πρέσβος is a person or corporate body which is honoured, especially (as here) for its age. In the vocative, ὅδε does not mean 'this', but marks proximity: 'you Argive elders who are gathered here'.

856–8. The insincerity and ambiguity of 'I shall feel no shame' and 'my man-loving ways' are inescapable to the audience—though not to Agamemnon. Then in ἀποφθίνει τὸ τάρβος, the surface meaning is that 'shyness fades' with respect to speaking; but any fear of acting that Clytemnestra may have had has also been replaced by boldness.

858–9. οὐκ ἄλλων πάρα μαθοῦσ': i.e. from first-hand experience.

861–2. 'First, that a woman should sit at her home deserted, apart from her man, (is) a terrible evil.' ἐρῆμος is normally a two-termination adjective, as here. The words might easily be used by a man expressing anxiety about being cuckolded in his absence, and indeed we know that Clytemnestra has not been entirely deserted in the palace.

863. κληδόνας παλιγκότους: 'malignant rumours', but κληδόνες can specifically be ominous words whose mere mention makes them more likely to come about. And this is Clytemnestra's purpose in repeating the details of these reports of Agamemnon's death here. Line 874 κληδόνων παλιγκότων underscores the point. See Introduction § 6.

864–5. καί takes the place of e.g. ἔπειτα δέ, to balance 861 τὸ μὲν πρῶτον; as before, accusative-and-infinitive phrases are the subject with ἔκπαγλον κακόν as the complement. The plural λάσκοντας indicates to amplify τὸν μέν with κακὸν πῆμα λάσκοντα.

866–8. Literally 'And if this man kept receiving so many *wounds* as the rumour was channelled into the house, he has more holes to speak of than a net.' It is striking that Clytemnestra presents the conditional as real rather than unfulfilled: Agamemnon's wounds are made as vivid as possible.

τραυμάτων is emphatically placed before εἰ. The number of wounds is correlated with the 'flow' of rumours directed towards the palace; for the image cf. *Supp.* 469 'a spate of troubles approaches like a river'. τέτρηται is from τετραίνω. The net image anticipates the δίκτυον Ἅιδου of Cassandra's vision that is Clytemnestra herself (1115–16), and also the robe which the murderess eventually casts round her husband in his bath like a fishing-net (1382–3).

869–73. The lines have a similar structure to 866–8, but we pass from wounds to deaths. 'If he had died (as many times) as the stories multiplied, then three-bodied—a second Geryon—he could be boasting of having got a threefold cloak of earth after dying once per form.' Or ἐπλήθυον may continue the metaphor of ὀχετεύω, since the verb means 'flood' in Herodotus 2. 19. 1 (of the Nile). Geryon was a triple-formed monster whose exact representation varies; here, he has three torsos probably imagined as joined at the waist. He lived in the far west and was killed by Heracles.

Line 871 is suspect because of πολλὰς ἄνωθεν in 875. If authentic, one should perhaps read πολλῆς (qualifying χθονός rather than χλαῖναν) and transpose after 872: '(of earth) ... a lot on top of him—I do not speak of that below'. The second part of the line perhaps adds a macabre touch not unworthy of Clytemnestra in this passage.

874. κληδόνων: see 863 n.

875–6. Hanging oneself is typical behaviour of faithful wives in Greek tragedy (e.g. Jocasta in Soph. *OT* 1263–4, Phaedra in Eur. *Hipp.* 777), and this is the role Clytemnestra is acting.

Two basic ideas may be expressed by πρὸς βίαν and λελημμένης. The point may be (1) 'Others loosed many halters from my neck, which was violently caught in them.' Three other possible construes draw attention to Clytemnestra's resistance to her supposed rescuers. (2) Take πρὸς βίαν λελημμένης sc. μου as a genitive absolute, 'when

(I) was grabbed [by them] violently', i.e. against her will. (3) πρὸς βίαν could govern λελημμένης sc. μου, 'in despite of (me), who was caught [in the halters]'; cf. *Eum.* 5 οὐδὲ πρὸς βίαν τινός for this construction. (4) λελημμένης modifies δέρης, and πρὸς βίαν modifies ἔλυσαν ἄλλοι: 'Others loosed by force the halters from my neck, which was caught in them.'

877–86. Only now does Clytemnestra turn to Agamemnon, to explain why Orestes is not present to greet him. She has sent him away to Agamemnon's associate, King Strophius of Phocis. Strophius is a standard element in the myth; it is from Phocis that Orestes receives instructions at Delphi, then returns home with his companion Pylades (already in the Cyclic *Nostoi*). Here, Clytemnestra alleges that she sent Orestes away for safety, after some friendly advice from Strophius. This is disingenuous, as we sense in her over-protesting denial that there is any deception in her excuse (886). Orestes will eventually allege that she cast him away into misfortune and shamefully sold him into slavery (*Cho.* 913–15). However, Aeschylus does not tell us whether Clytemnestra's real motives, as well as the fear that Orestes might warn Agamemnon, also included a more motherly desire to protect him from Aegisthus. Orestes has a narrower escape in several alternative accounts, where a slave has to smuggle him away as Agamemnon is murdered (P. *Pyth.* 11. 17–18, Soph. *El.* 11–14, Eur. *El.* 16–18), or at an earlier assassination attempt by Aegisthus (Pherecydes frr. 134, 180).

877. ἐκ τῶνδέ τοι: 'For these reasons, you see'. Clytemnestra first explains Orestes' absence with reference to the rumours of Agamemnon's death (863–74).

Orestes' name is effectively reserved for the end of the sentence. Possibly on hearing 877 one thinks of their other absent child, Iphigenia. But soon the masculine κύριος clarifies who is meant.

878. Orestes is 'sovereign' over his parents' pledges, i.e. their shared affection for him guarantees their loyalty to each other.

879. μήδε θαυμάσῃς τόδε: presumably responding to a reaction from Agamemnon.

880. δορύξενος: an aristocratic guest-friend with whom Agamemnon had a previous military alliance.

881. ἀμφίλεκτα πήματα: the adjective means 'spoken in two ways', i.e. doubtful, disputed (cf. 1585). Clytemnestra must mean that Strophius was warning her of serious possibilities rather than certainties. However, the word neatly draws attention to the

disputable character of her explanations of Orestes' absence. (The
rendering 'twofold', referring to the two πήματα described in 882–4,
would lack parallels.)

883–4. This εἰ-clause functions like a noun: 'and the danger arising if
...'. ἀναρχία can have two slightly different meanings: the sense
'civil disobedience' is otherwise first attested at Sophocles *Ant.* 672;
the sense 'state of being leaderless' is older, and used by Aeschylus
at *Supp.* 907. Either way, this situation is 'accompanied by the
people's clamour', and Clytemnestra is envisaging a noisy popular
rising against the βουλή and (by implication) the palace. That
this is a consequence of Agamemnon dying at Troy is explicit on
the second interpretation of ἀναρχία, but in any case becomes clear
from 885.

   This interpretation presupposes that βουλή means 'council', but
the rest of the play is silent on this institution and its relationship
to Clytemnestra's power (see Intro. n. 34). It is possible that
Clytemnestra has discontinued the council, but here pretends to be
concerned about it. Fraenkel took βουλή rather as 'deliberation',
but this strains the metaphor of καταρρίπτω. Others have followed
Scaliger's conjecture βουλὴν καταρράψειεν, 'were to stitch up a
plot'.

884–5. Literally 'since it is something innate in mankind to give a
further kick to the man who has fallen'. 'To kick the man who's
down' was a phrase, then as now; compare e.g. Sophocles *Ajax*
1348 'Should you not also trample on one who has died?' In the
context of discussing Agamemnon's hypothetical death, τὸν
πεσόντα applies best to the king, and the 'further kick' would be
the damage done thereafter to his family (including Orestes) by the
lawless *dēmos*.

886. See 877–86 n. For the sense of μέντοι cf. 644–5 n.

887–8. ἔμοιγε μὲν δή marks the start of a new point. 'Well, for *me*
the gushing fountains of lamentation are quenched, and not a drop
is in them', i.e. her eyes are dry of tears. Of course, they *are* dry, but
because she has no drop of compassion in her, rather than because
extreme compassion has used up all her tears (cf. 856–8 n.).

889–91. This contrasts with 887 μέν: her eyes do not cry, but they are
sore with watching late at night in bed. Then, literally, 'as I bemoaned
the holding of lamps [cf. 312] about you, which were always
untended', i.e. as she bemoaned the fact that for a long time the
beacons were not lit to report his success.

892–3. λεπταῖς ὑπαὶ ... ῥιπαῖσι: for the instrumental use of ὑπό + dative, see 1164, LSJ s.v. B II 1. ὑπαί does not go with κώνωπος.

893. θωύσσοντος: the gnat's soft (cf. λεπταῖς) buzzing comes to Clytemnestra in her supposed nightmares as a terrifyingly loud noise. But the verb is normally used of dogs barking, or huntsmen shouting to their hounds, and these more precise associations perhaps suggest that Clytemnestra is dreaming of dogs barking around Agamemnon's corpse. See *Iliad* 1. 4, where the heroes' bodies become 'prey for dogs and birds'; Aeschylus also alludes to that line at *Supp.* 800–1.

894. πλείω τοῦ ξυνεύδοντος χρόνου: literally 'more than the time that slept with me', i.e. more than could have occurred in the actual duration of the nightmare.

895. νῦν: signalling another transition of thought. At some point (see 920) Clytemnestra performs the type of προσκύνησις associated with obeisance to oriental monarchs: this involves kneeling, then full-length prostration, then rising again. The timing of these actions is not indicated in the text, but Clytemnestra probably at least kneels here, as she starts to lard Agamemnon with the luxuriant third-person praise of 896–901. See Hall (1989), 96–7, 206–7 for the gesture.

896–901. After ἄνδρα τόνδε there follows a long series of complements in the accusative. The central idea behind these laudatory images is that of the saviour or preserver.

896. σταθμῶν: a herdsman's farmstead, where the dog guards livestock against thieves and predators.

897. σωτῆρα ναὸς πρότονον: the 'forestay' secures the mast to the bow; as one of the two ropes keeping the mast upright, it can be 'the preserver of a ship' in a storm. Here and in 900–1 there is a certain malicious irony in the application of nautical metaphors to Agamemnon who has lost so many sailors at sea.

898. ποδήρη: literally 'foot-fixed', i.e. firmly based. **μονογενὲς τέκνον:** a sole (male) heir, uniquely able to carry on the line; similarly *Cho.* 505–7, though it is probably interpolated.

899 [901]. The manuscripts give this line after κάλλιστον ... χείματος, and we see no need for the transposition. The manuscript text gives a balanced sequence of three lines, then καί (900), then three lines.

(It is true that Asclepiades *Epigram* 1 (early third century BC) presents the idea of a thirsty man drinking, *followed* by that of sailors seeing something after bad weather: see Sens (2011) for text and translation, though we retain some doubts about whether the passage is a 'reworking' of Aeschylus, as he states.)

902. This free-standing *gnōmē* is otiose and splits 903 'these appellations' from the expressions to which it refers. It may have been inserted from a marginal parallel to the preceding line.

903. νιν ἀξιῶ: 'I honour him', a poetic sense of ἀξιόω (LSJ s.v. I 2).

904. φθόνος δ' ἀπέστω: a common pious formula in encomiastic writing, but blatantly hypocritical on Clytemnestra's lips. It acknowledges that her praises might inspire divine envy, and this was precisely their point, as it is the point of the spreading of tapestries which follows.

904–5. πολλὰ γὰρ τὰ πρὶν κακὰ ἠνειχόμεσθα: perhaps another everyday phrase (cf. Aristophanes *Pax* 347, πολλὰ γὰρ ἀνεσχόμην). But her implication that one who has suffered deserves to be exempt from *phthonos* is disingenuous. Given the context of ominous utterance, τὰ πρὶν κακά must refer not only to the upsetting rumours and nightmares she mentioned, but also secretly to the sacrifice of Iphigenia.

905–11. Clytemnestra now stage-manages Agamemnon's entrance into the house. She calls on her handmaidens to spread the ground between the threshold and Agamemnon's wagon with a path of purple fabrics. These are εἵματα, i.e. large rectangular pieces of cloth used principally for cloaks and robes or occasionally as blankets, but not as carpet-rugs (921, 960, 963; εἷμα is related to ἕννυμι). They have been woven at great expense with patterns or images (949 ἀργυρωνήτους ὑφάς, 923 ποικίλοις). They are like the ceremonial robes offered to some gods, to clothe their statues or simply as a valuable dedication (922).

For Agamemnon to walk into his palace over these, particularly after Clytemnestra's prostration, will amount to a barbaric act of extravagance and hubris, as he appreciates. In fact, though the Greeks may have thought that the Persian king always walked on rugs (cf. Athenaeus 12 514c), Agamemnon's action would be beyond barbaric since these εἵματα are not rugs. S. West (1992) notes some interesting parallels from the Near East and from later Greece for crowds spontaneously acclaiming someone with a path of cloaks; but even if this practice were familiar to Aeschylus' audience, the fact that Clytemnestra is stage-managing the scene on her own is a very significant difference. Clytemnestra is thus contriving a temptation which, if Agamemnon yields, will provoke the divine *phthonos* which will be, as it were, the final nail in his coffin, and also sanctify her vengeance. For the main discussion of Agamemnon's action, see 944–9 n.

The line of purple garments is also a striking and significant piece of spectacle. It suggests a long trail of blood (regularly characterized in Greek as πορφύρεος: cf. πορφυρόστρωτος), which links the blood that Agamemnon has spilt at Troy with the blood soon to be shed in the house.

905. φίλον κάρα: Clytemnestra finally turns to Agamemnon again in a form of affectionate address, here deeply sinister. This is followed in 907 by the more obsequious ὦναξ (something like 'Your Majesty').

907. πορθήτορα: a further ominous reference to Agamemnon as πτολίπορθος (see 783–4 n.). Fraenkel interestingly suggests a connection with Near Eastern depictions of a conqueror stepping triumphantly on his victims. The choice of word also suggests that Agamemnon's trampling of the garments is in some way symbolic of his 'trampling' of Troy, i.e. that it is not only hubristic in itself, but also symbolic of the more serious acts of hubris in the desecration of Troy's shrines and the slaughter of innocent victims (cf. 763–6 n.).

908. ἐπέσταλται τέλος: for ἐπέσταλται see LSJ ἐπιστέλλω 2. τέλος here is 'duty' or 'function', but the path of fabrics will lead Agamemnon to another kind of τέλος, his 'end'. The ambiguities in the noun and its cognates are further exploited in 972–4.

909. πέδον κελεύθου: 'the ground of his path'; κέλευθος is here not a pre-existing made-up pathway, but the route which Agamemnon needs to traverse. **πετάσμασιν:** the word does not imply that the textiles are intrinsically for spreading out (i.e. that they are something other than garments)—only that they are used as such here. Clytemnestra perhaps chooses this initial description to gloss over her inappropriate use of clothes for the purpose.

At the end of this line we may assume that pairs of δμωιαί bring on the πετάσματα from the central door of the house, and lay them down in a line leading back from the *orchēstra* to the threshold (see also 973–4 n.).

911. Splendid ambiguity again. Like the Herald (506–7), Agamemnon may never have expected to return home from Troy, so his palace is ἄελπτον. And to him, Justice will lead him indoors as she has, in his words, guided the whole Trojan expedition. But for Clytemnestra, 'Justice' refers to vengeance for Iphigenia, and the palace is ἄελπτον because Agamemnon has no inkling of the reception awaiting him.

912–13. In her closing lines, Clytemnestra systematically links her watchful φροντίς, 'undefeated by sleep', with justice, the gods, and destiny all at once. It will 'arrange everything else justly, with the gods' help [σὺν θεοῖς], as it is fated'.

914–30. In his reply Agamemnon firmly resists Clytemnestra's blandishments and makes it clear how the action she has proposed would be repugnant to a normal Greek. His tone is cold, but his sentiment correct. His assertiveness comes out in the use of the first-person pronoun or adjective five times at the ends of lines.

914. Λήδας γένεθλον: a rather formal opening, which may also suggest what Helen and Clytemnestra share (cf. 83–4 Τυνδάρεω θύγατερ with n.). δωμάτων ἐμῶν φύλαξ: the phrase inevitably reminds the audience *how* Clytemnestra has watched over Agamemnon's house in his absence, and with whom.

915–17. First, Agamemnon ostensibly compliments Clytemnestra on the propriety of her speech. But his explanation (the γάρ-clause) limits this in a backhanded way: it was appropriate because, like Agamemnon's absence, she 'stretched it out for a long time [μακράν]'—a common turn of phrase for which Fraenkel gives close parallels. (In tone, this remark could be meant seriously, or as a gentle pleasantry, rather than as derisive.) Then he mentions a failure of propriety (ἀλλ' contrasting with μέν). 'But as for praising properly, this prize [τόδε γέρας apposed to αἰνεῖν] should come from others.' His point seems to be that public eulogies should be delivered by people from outside one's own household, since they will not be biased. (See Schol. 89b to P. *Nem.* 7: 'It is not that I praise them because they are my fellow-citizens. In that case I would seem to be favouring them with an encomium just on account of our connection: "For praise from home is diluted with reproach."') Agamemnon does not mention Clytemnestra's far-fetched descriptions of his possible injuries.

918–19. καὶ τἄλλα: accusative of respect, 'And as to the rest . . .', which turns out to mean the business with the garments. Agamemnon saves his most serious criticism for last. μὴ γυναικὸς ἐν τρόποις ἐμὲ ἄβρυνε: 'don't pamper *me* in the ways of a woman', i.e. as if Agamemnon were a woman. ἁβρός and its cognates often occur when Greeks express their view that oriental luxury is effeminate (e.g. Eur. *Bacchae* 493).

919–20. 'And don't gape for *me* with that grovelling clamour, like a barbarian man,' i.e. as if Clytemnestra were a barbarian man. The gender-swap (cf. 'as if I were a woman' in 918) is apt, especially for this ἀνδρόβουλος woman. βόαμα is an internal accusative. Alliteration (β, μ, π, χ) enhances this caustic and compressed reproof. For the staging of the prostration see 895 n.

921–4. Agamemnon appreciates that to walk over the garments would excite the gods' envy, as they alone should be honoured with such dedications. τιμαλφεῖν is a verb associated with cult, closer to 'worship' than to 'honour' (cf. *Eum.* 15, 626). The reference is to dedicating garments as a form of wealth, and particularly to rituals where a new robe was made to clothe a cult statue. The best-known example of this is the Panathenaea: see Barber (1992), 112–17 for details.

Lines 923–4 mean 'But that a person who is *mortal* should step on patterned things of beauty [κάλλεσι] is, for *me* at least, (a matter) not free of trepidation.' The contrasting δέ-clause need not be expressed (see Denniston 381).

925. Understand κατά before θεόν. Though forceful in itself, the line has been suspected (e.g. by Fraenkel) because it interrupts the thought linking 924 with 926 and the rest of the speech.

926–7. Probably χωρίς is an adverb: literally 'The appellation of foot-towels and that of tapestries cry aloud quite separately.' The underlying thought is that the *uses* of foot-towels and tapestries should be kept distinct; the former are textiles in standard use for cleaning the feet; the latter must not be used for anything similar. By expressing himself with κληδών and αὐτεῖ, which normally apply to words, Agamemnon is probably implying that abuse of the tapestries would 'convey a clear message' to onlookers. However, a κληδών is often a specifically ominous message (Intro. § 6): it therefore enhances the audience's sense that, when he eventually treads on the clothes, it is a deeply ill-omened act which contributes to his ruin.

The alternative interpretation is to take χωρίς as a preposition governing the genitives: 'My fame cries aloud without foot-towels and tapestries,' i.e. 'I don't need these accessories to advertise my glory.' But this loses the opposition between ordinary use of foot-towels and abnormal use of tapestries, which is a natural continuation of the preceding lines.

927–30. In his employment of conventional maxims, Agamemnon ends sententiously but pertinently. Avoiding τὸ κακῶς φρονεῖν includes 'knowing oneself' and so not hubristically overstepping one's position, as Clytemnestra is advocating. Indeed, it is a gift which only the gods can bestow. Agamemnon next quotes the commonplace that 'One should (only) call a man prosperous when he has ended his life in congenial wellbeing' (cf. e.g. Hdt. 1. 32, Soph. *OT* 1528–30). In other words, one must not be carried away by ephemeral triumphs, and always take care not to arouse divine anger. 'If I should act thus [ὥς: a mainly epic usage] in all things, I (may be) confident,' as opposed to feeling trepidation after walking on the garments (924).

931–43. This is the play's only passage of stichomythia between two actors rather than between an actor and the Coryphaeus. This formal point marks it as a confrontation of central importance. In only thirteen economical and powerfully compelling lines, the conqueror Agamemnon is himself conquered by Clytemnestra's persuasion into doing what he has just refused as decadent, hubristic, and dangerous. Each pair or triad of lines can be regarded as a point in their match of wits. The result has been prepared: Clytemnestra's 'unwomanly' intelligence has been established from the outset (10–11), while Agamemnon's lack of discernment has been revealed in his opening address (830–7, 841–4 nn.). Furthermore the Chorus's general comments about the function of Atē (especially in the first stasimon; see also Intro. § 4.3.3) are now exemplified. Agamemnon, surrounded by wealthy spoils, is induced to 'trample on the grace of inviolate things' (372–3) by an infatuation which makes him susceptible to compulsive persuasion (cf. 385–6); ruin must follow. The fact that Paris was the main focus of the first stasimon has a clear point: Agamemnon is now reduced to Paris—the conqueror to the conquered, the despiser of eastern luxury to a paragon of it. For the question of why Agamemnon yields, see 944–9 n.

931–2. In an introductory cast, Clytemnestra asks Agamemnon to answer her μὴ παρὰ γνώμην, according to his true 'opinion'. Agamemnon replies that he will not corrupt his γνώμη, now more in the sense of 'judgement'. The wordplay seems to be programmatic for the shifting sands of the argument that develops. The clash of wills is well reflected in the line-ends of 930–2, ἐγώ ... ἐμοί ... ἐμέ.

933–4. 'Would you have vowed to the gods in a moment of fear to sacrifice [LSJ ἔρδειν 2] these objects [i.e. garments] like this?' The question supposes a hypothetical situation where Agamemnon, in terrifying danger, vows that if the gods rescue him he will sacrifice some precious garments by having them trampled in their honour. Clytemnestra in 963–5 suggests that she herself might have done such a thing to secure Agamemnon's life.

Agamemnon's response does show some caution: 'Yes, *if* some *expert* had pronounced this duty.' But he omits the more forceful point that an instruction to offer up garments in *this* way, which so resembles hubris, would have been quite extraordinary. For the word τέλος (a 'duty', but leading to Agamemnon's 'end'), see 908 n.

935–6. Clytemnestra moves swiftly on. 'And what do you think *Priam* would (have done), if he had achieved all this?' Agamemnon replies 'I am certain he would have stepped on tapestries', but does not add ' . . . like the barbarian he is—all the more reason for me *not* to do so.' This allows Clytemnestra her next move.

937–9. 'Then [νυν] have no qualms about human criticism.' Clytemnestra distracts Agamemnon away from the idea of divine φθόνος with this mention of human ψόγος. In ἀνθρώπειον she subtly assumes a coincidence of Greek and Trojan viewpoints. However, Agamemnon does not complain at this illogicality. Instead he responds solely to the conclusion: one *should* consider human ψόγος because the *vox populi* is indeed powerful. This thought, especially with δημόθρους, picks up Clytemnestra's account at 883–4; see also 1413 n.

Agamemnon's overly general point lets Clytemnestra counter with a respectable commonplace: 'But the *unenvied* man attracts no emulation,' i.e. must be an unsuccessful one. For the thought that it is better to be successful and envied than unimpressive, compare e.g. Pindar *Pythian* 1. 95, 'Envy is better than pity', and recall Agamemnon's own connection between success and envy at 832–3. The crucial issue that Agamemnon will presently inspire *phthonos* in the gods, not in humans, and by hubris, not success, has been left behind.

940–1. Agamemnon senses that he is losing ground and snaps back: 'It's not a *woman's* part to desire a fight.' The military victor introduces the language of battle, but Clytemnestra turns the tables on him: 'But for the successful it's proper even to be conquered,' i.e. a victor can afford to and should be able to 'yield gracefully' in certain circumstances.

942. 'Do *you really* value victory in this struggle?' δήριος is objective genitive after νίκην, rather than genitive of value with τίεις. The particles ἦ καί and the nominative pronoun suggest a tone of particular interest or even surprise (Denniston 285, 316), with a slight pause before the line. Agamemnon appears to be entertaining an uneasy suspicion about Clytemnestra's motives.

943. Normally emended to πιθοῦ· κρατεῖς μέντοι παρεὶς [or παρείς γ'] ἑκὼν ἐμοί: 'Give in! You win, assuredly [μέντοι: Denniston 399], if you willingly hand it [sc. νίκην] over to *me*.' Clytemnestra finally beguiles Agamemnon with a bogus paradox; the diphthong of πιθοῦ and its circumflex accent can be delivered with a seductive cooing effect. For the thought compare Sophocles *Ajax* 1053 παῦσαι· κρατεῖς τοι τῶν φίλων νικώμενος, where Odysseus is flattering Agamemnon into allowing Ajax's burial.

The emended line still lacks a main caesura, but its division into six disyllabic words could be a special effect to mark Clytemnestra's final insistence which causes Agamemnon to yield.

944–9. Agamemnon gives in and calls for his shoes to be removed. This sign of humility—a barefoot king—is unusual. However it is only an illogical token gesture, which can save him from neither the possibility of divine envy nor the charge of extravagantly wasting his house's wealth—two things about which he expresses fear even now, in grandiose terms which attempt to maintain his dignity. Nor can anything distract from the 'victory' of the wife over the husband.

Why does Agamemnon yield? Older discussions took the matter as one of character, and ranged from the view that Agamemnon's latent arrogance is seduced by oriental splendour, to Fraenkel's (pp. 441–2) that he is a 'great gentleman, reluctant to get the better of a woman' and too tired to resist any further. Scholars now generally appreciate that Greek tragic characters are hardly ever rounded personalities whose characteristics are to be glimpsed by reading between the lines (see Intro. § 8). However, this does not mean that Agamemnon's reasons are not an issue at all. Our view is that the psychology is best interpreted in the light of the abstract considerations which Aeschylus has given us so far (369–89, 750–81), which suggest that Agamemnon's action does not arise directly from his normal dispositions. Rather, he exemplifies the man whom excessive prosperity has pushed towards Atē (away from his basic character), the man whom overbearing persuasion compels to act even against his better judgement, and to commit the new hubris of 'trampling on the grace of inviolable objects' (372–3) as he 'trampled' (907) on the shrines of Troy. Although stylized, the stichomythia has presented us with a plausible human portrayal of this process of being persuaded into an action about which one feels the severest misgivings.

Easterling (1973) and Taplin (1978), 78–82 are good short discussions of the scene. Dover (1987), 156–60 adds the useful parallel of Pausanias, the Spartan king who in 479 BC had led the Greeks to victory over the Persians at Plataea, shortly before succumbing to the lifestyle of an oriental potentate himself. However, as mentioned, Agamemnon feels no enthusiasm for his un-Greek behaviour.

944. ἀλλ᾽ εἰ δοκεῖ σοι ταῦθ᾽: the phrase is used in contexts of resigned acceptance (cf. e.g. Soph. *Ant.* 98). The actor might pause both before and after it.

944–5. ὑπαί . . . λύοι: = ὑπολύοι in tmesis. **ἀρβύλας:** the word strictly seems to mean 'ankle-boots', but may well be used loosely for 'travelling-shoes', of any design (so Fraenkel). **τάχος:** adverbial, 'quickly' (cf. 280 n.). **πρόδουλον ἔμβασιν ποδός:** 'which serves my foot as something to step on', an elaborate description of shoes. With ἔμβασιν cf. 946 ἐμβαίνονθ᾽: the repetition underscores how the fabrics replace the function of his shoes.

946–7. The phrasing suggests that θεῶν depends on ἁλουργέσιν ('sea-worked', i.e. dyed with murex) rather than ὄμματος: the vestments, as objects of possible dedication, are regarded as belonging to the gods, whose φθόνος Agamemnon wants to avoid. For divine φθόνος coming from a god's eye, see 469–70 n.

948–9. 'For (it is) a matter of great compunction to despoil the house, destroying with my feet its wealth, and its weavings bought with silver.' The words show that Agamemnon removed his shoes primarily as an apotropaic gesture of humility rather than to spare the fabrics: even barefoot he is 'destroying' them. His grandiloquence continues in δωματοφθορεῖν . . . φθείροντα and ἀργυρωνήτους.

950–5. While his shoes are still being removed, Agamemnon introduces Cassandra and asks Clytemnestra to treat her kindly. (For Cassandra's position onstage see 783–974 n.). By ancient standards no less than by modern, Agamemnon's off-hand way of introducing his wife to a slave-woman who naturally appears to be his concubine (955 ἄνθος suggests her attractions) is insensitive. This is a touch of arrogance at a critical moment, though 953 shows that Agamemnon is not entirely lacking in empathy towards Cassandra.

950. τούτων μὲν οὕτω: 'So much for that.' For the unusual genitive see Smyth § 1381.

951–2. Agamemnon is still thinking about how the gods will be looking on (cf. 947).

956–7. Agamemnon acknowledges that he has been 'overturned, subdued' (κατέστραμμαι: a strong verb) into giving ear to Clytemnestra's persuasion (ἀκοῦσαι: explanatory infinitive). The powerful alliteration πορφύρας πατῶν would be a good cue for him to step on the purple garments.

958–74. Agamemnon's slow walk up the purple trail into the palace (he only crosses the threshold at 972) is accompanied by a gloriously exultant speech by Clytemnestra, remarkable both for its luxuriant and ominous imagery, and for its incantatory assonances, alliterations, and repetitions (on which see McClure 1999, 80–92).

Clytemnestra starts by rejecting Agamemnon's economic qualms; then through a series of metaphors about the seasons she articulates the pleasure which his return brings. The constant references to the house (961?, 962, 964, 968, 971, 972) emphasize her excitement at the thought that Agamemnon will never replace her as its master.

958–60. 'The sea exists (and who will quench it?), nurturing the all-renewable ooze of much purple, worth its weight in silver, the dye for clothes.' The sea has an infinite supply of the murex shellfish, from which Tyrian purple was derived at proverbial expense. It will therefore be possible to acquire replacement garments. The purple κηκίς may again hint at blood: at *Cho.* 1012–13 the κηκίς of gore contrasts with the dyed robe in which Agamemnon was trapped.

961–2. οἶκος δ' ὑπάρχει ... ἔχειν: with the OCT's text we must construe 'Lord, with the gods' favour the house [*qua* store of property] subsists for possessing (a quantity) of these.' Porson's οἴκοις makes ὑπάρχει easier: 'it is available for the house to possess ...'. (Although West's ἄκος also avoids the unusual partitive genitive τῶνδε, Clytemnestra's point seems stronger if a form of οἶκος is retained.)

963–4. Clytemnestra recalls her point at 933, though the situation of visiting an oracle is slightly different. The emphatic πολλῶν reinforces her claim that the garments presently being trampled onstage are a small price to pay, but this certainly does not imply that there are actually only a few of them. **προυνεχθέντος:** 'if it had been commanded', a genitive absolute with an impersonal expression, rather than the normal accusative. For προφέρω used of oracular instructions, see LSJ s.v. I 5.

965. Magnificent ambivalence: Clytemnestra is 'cunningly contriving' an expense to ensure τὸ κομίζειν of Agamemnon's soul: κομίζω can mean not only 'convey to safety' but also 'take as a victory-prize, acquire' and (of corpses) 'convey to burial'.

966–7. There now begins a series of seasonal imagery. Agamemnon is the root of a great tree, whose existence ensures that foliage will shade the house in summer. ἵκετο is gnomic aorist. The 'dog star' Sirius rose at the hottest time of the year. For σκιὰν . . . κυνός, 'shade *against* the dog star', compare e.g. *Il.* 15. 646 ἕρκος ἀκόντων.

968–72. The next images come in a pair (μέν . . . δέ), enclosed by genitive absolutes. 'And now that you have arrived at your palace hearth, warmth signals its arrival in winter, and conversely, at the time when Zeus is making wine from the sour [i.e. unripe] grape, there is already coldness in the house, when the ἀνὴρ τέλειος ranges within his hall.' For σημαίνει μολόν see 293 n.; μολών is pointedly repeated. Zeus is connected with growing vines in that he sends rain and is a general patron of agriculture (cf. 1015); it is natural that Clytemnestra mentions him rather than Dionysus in this connection, given 973. (The manuscripts, West, and Sommerstein have σημαίνεις μολών with θάλπος as object. It is awkward for 'you' to shift from genitive in 968 to subject in 969.)

Agamemnon's return is metaphorically warmth in winter and coolness in late summer; i.e. it ensures steadiness, and avoidance of unpleasant extremes. But the images build towards the ominous. Wine is like blood (cf. 1395–8). ψῦχος can be the chill of death (see e.g. Sophocles *OC* 621–2 ψυχρὸς νέκυς). ἀνδρὸς τελείου is prima facie the man ἐν τέλει, but τέλειος also has particular application to full-grown animals which are ripe for sacrifice. This build-up is timed to coincide with Agamemnon being swallowed up in the dark interior of the *skēnē*. The long ἐπιστρωφωμένου is an impressive word to cover his exit.

973–4. Here perhaps Clytemnestra moves upstage, and mounts the threshold herself, taking care not to tread on the purple garments, which can be arranged to allow this. She may then turn round in the centre of the doorway, raise her arms, and fling out a prayer which amounts to a final gloat behind her victim's back before she exits herself. Euripides alludes to the effect in his *Electra* (1142–6) after

Clytemnestra herself has been lured by her daughter into the house where she is going to be murdered (see Intro. §10).

Clytemnestra appeals to Zeus Teleios, a widespread cult-title which seems to have referred to various nuances of $\tau\acute{\epsilon}\lambda os$—in Athens particularly marriage, and the third and final libation at a symposium; also, Zeus was constantly turned to as the most effective fulfiller of prayers. Here, the last nuance is explicitly relevant; the second is intriguing given 1386–7 (see n.); the first must have struck the Athenian audience as they watched husband and wife being reunited—but only in perverted disharmony. Given 972 $\tau\epsilon\lambda\acute{\epsilon}iou$ and its sacrificial nuance, the wordplay might suggest the extra point that Agamemnon is a suitable victim for Zeus Teleios to lead to his end.

In 974, $\tau\hat{\omega}\nu\pi\epsilon\rho$ is an epicism for $\hat{\omega}\nu\pi\epsilon\rho$, i.e. $\dot{\epsilon}\kappa\epsilon\acute{\iota}\nu\omega\nu$ $\ddot{\alpha}\pi\epsilon\rho$. The assonance (-$oi$) and the wordplay $\mu\acute{\epsilon}\lambda oi$ ... $\mu\acute{\epsilon}\lambda\lambda\eta\iota s$ (translate e.g. 'May you at*tend* to the things you in*tend* to fulfil!') contribute to the power and spell-binding quality of this exit-line.

The following stage directions can be conjectured after Clytemnestra's exit, assuming that Agamemnon has occupied a separate wagon from Cassandra. The handmaidens gather up the trampled garments and carry them in; the doors close. Agamemnon's cart is wheeled off by his attendants, down the *eisodos* opposite the one by which he entered. Meanwhile the Chorus regroups for the ensuing stasimon.

Third Stasimon (975–1034): Agamemnon's entry into the palace now inspires a song of fear and deep foreboding. The ode is no longer structured by a narrative of *past* events as in the earlier choral movements. The metre, predominately trochaic with dactylic elements, recalls the hymn in the parodos (160–91), and again the Chorus is groping after an interpretation of their responses to what they have witnessed. But whereas in the parodos Zeus was invoked in a spirit of hope as the god who ordained that suffering leads to understanding, now Clytemnestra has just called upon Zeus to bring about suffering, and the Chorus's hope is banished in a 'dirge of the Fury' (991), the thrust of which is that Agamemnon's doom is sealed. The metre reminds the audience of the Chorus's earlier perspective and, for the moment, gives the lie to it.

It may be helpful to summarize what we take to be the train of thought in this difficult ode.

First strophic pair: 'Why do I feel fear and foreboding which I cannot shake off? The expedition sailed and has returned, but I cannot sing a victory song. My sense of justice provokes these forebodings of retribution, which are not vain. I can only pray that they will prove false.'

Second strophic pair: 'Like excessive health, excessive wealth often comes to an abrupt end, though a man can forestall this by sacrificing some of his property. Among illnesses, Zeus can remedy famine, but no songs can remedy bloodshed. And divine justice ensures that no one person can get away with more than their fair portion. That being so, it is hopeless to express my fears openly.'

975–83. In performance, the alliteration of dental consonants (δ, τ, θ) in these lines powerfully expresses the Chorus's foreboding.

975. τίπτε: an epic form of τί ποτε.

976–7. προστατήριον καρδίας τερασκόπου: 'presiding before my portent-seeing heart'. The phrase generally recalls 178 πρὸ καρδίας, though here it is fear rather than distressing memories which has penetrated the inner consciousness. However the fear has the role of a προστάτης, here in the sense 'governor' rather than 'patron': the fear governs their divinations. And τερασκόπου is specific: the Chorus's heart is an augur which has seen a portent, namely Agamemnon walking over the purple garments into the palace.

977. ποτᾶται: fear 'hovers' constantly (ἐμπέδως) like a bird; this image interacts with the preceding idea of augury.

978–9. The heart's augury is expressed in song, as Greek prophecies often were, but one which is prompted by no external commission or payment. The responding verses (991–2) contain a similar idea, of the 'self-taught' θυμός singing a dirge for the Erinys.

980–3. 'Nor does persuasive confidence, to spit it [i.e. my song] out like hard-to-interpret dreams, sit on its customary throne in my mind.' ἀποπτύσαι depends on θάρσος. φίλον is little more than a possessive, as occasionally in Homer (LSJ s.v. I 2c). θρόνον continues the imagery of προστατήριον: fear rather than confidence is in the position of sovereignty.

984–7. Restoration is uncertain. We suggest χρόνος δ' ἐπεὶ πρυμνησίων ξὺν ἐκβολαῖς | ψάμμος ἄμπτα παρήιβησεν, 'Time has grown old [lit. 'passed its prime'] since the sand flew up together with the casting-out of the stern-cables.' ἄμπτα = ἀνέπτη from ἀναπέτομαι. Ships were rowed stern-first onto a beach, and weighted stern-cables then used to anchor them to something on the shore.

The general sense up to 994 seems to be: 'The Greeks' journey is far in the past, and I have seen their return, so my old anxieties can be forgotten, yet I am still afraid.' Thus the structure χρόνος παρήβησεν ἐπεί ... is suitable. ψαμμίας ἀκάτα must be altered since the words neither make sense nor respond metrically with 998. Wilamowitz's ψάμμος ἄμπτᾱ seems a reasonable way to introduce the subordinate verb. Fraenkel suggested that the sand went flying πρυμνησίων ξὺν ἐμβολαῖς, i.e. when they hauled in the ropes and set sail from Aulis. But the extra change ἐκβολαῖς has two benefits. ὑπό + accusative Ἴλιον suggests *arrival* on the shore below Troy; and sand more obviously flies up when a weighted rope is hurled onto a beach than when it is hauled off one.

990–3. The Chorus has witnessed Agamemnon's return (988–9), but its forebodings will not admit the joyful victory-song, and it sings a dirge. Dirges were not accompanied on the lyre (rather on the *aulos* alone) whereas hymns and epinicians could be. The fact that the dirge belongs to an Erinys is an important indicator that their fear includes thoughts of retribution.

993–4. 'not having at all [adverbial τὸ πᾶν] the agreeable confidence of hope'.

995–7. 'And close by my mind where justice dwells, my guts are not acting emptily—my heart which is circling round in eddies that bring fulfilment.' κέαρ is in apposition to σπλάγχνα: though strictly they are different organs, both are sites of emotion, in contrast with the φρένες (here located around the diaphragm) which hold the mind or understanding. The close conjunction (πρός + dative) of the heart and the ἔνδικος mind implies that the Chorus's rational sense of justice is having a profound effect on its emotions, as it contemplates what lies ahead for Agamemnon. ματάιζειν is acting or speaking μάτην: their emotional response is not vain; rather it is τελεσφόρος. The crucial adjectives ἐνδίκοις and τελεσφόροις between them suggest how Justice and Zeus Teleios are moving in concert towards Agamemnon's death.

κυκλούμενον is probably middle not passive, and from κυκλέω not κυκλόω. Two principal interpretations of the heart's circling motion seem particularly important. (1) Internal whirling is connected with the throes of prophecy in 1214–15 ὑπ' αὖ με δεινὸς ὀρθομαντείας πόνος στροβεῖ. (2) The heart might be doing a round-dance (a performance which can be described by δινέω: cf. δίναις). That would be appropriate both to its fear (cf. *Cho.* 167, the heart ὀρχεῖται in fear) and to τελεσφόροις, since a round-dance could have a particular efficacy; for example, the Furies' binding-song (*Eum.* 307–96) is intended to bring delirium on Orestes.

998–1000. 'But I pray that they [i.e. the forebodings] fall out as falsehoods [ψύθη: complement], out of my expectation, into the realm of non-fulfilment.' ἐλπίδος can be contrasted with its more positive sense in 994. The final move in this train of thought is one we have seen repeatedly: after unpropitious and despairing utterance, pray that the good may win out anyway, and move on (Intro. at n. 76). It is specifically the statement that their forebodings are τελεσφόρος (997) which was unpropitious and which they wish to revoke.

1001–17. In strophe β, health and wealth are compared in respect of the danger which comes from excess. After that the possibility of remedying an excess of wealth is explored, to be contrasted in the antistrophe with the irremediability of blood once shed, which brings us to the primary issue. The text is particularly corrupt here.

1001–4. The underlying thought appears to be that even health, like other good states including wealth, is a mean between extremes. Physical fitness can be taken to excess; the heavy training of an Olympic athlete, for example, can affect his immune system. We tentatively suggest the following restoration:

$$\mu\acute{\alpha}\lambda\alpha \; \gamma\acute{\epsilon} \; \tau o\iota \; <\sigma\phi\alpha\lambda\epsilon\rho\acute{o}\nu \; \dot{\epsilon}\sigma\theta'> \; \dot{\upsilon}\gamma\iota\epsilon\acute{\iota}\alpha\varsigma$$
$$\dot{\alpha}\kappa o\rho\acute{\epsilon}\sigma\tau o\upsilon \; <\tau\iota\nu\grave{\iota}> \; \tau\acute{\epsilon}\rho\mu\alpha\cdot \; \nu\acute{o}\sigma o\varsigma$$
$$\gamma\epsilon\acute{\iota}\tau\omega\nu \; \acute{o}\mu\acute{o}\tau o\iota\chi o\varsigma \; \dot{\epsilon}\rho\epsilon\acute{\iota}\delta\epsilon\iota.$$

'Assuredly, the end-point of health of which a person cannot get enough [i.e. when pursued obsessively] is extremely <dangerous for him>: illness, its neighbour who shares a partition-wall, presses on it.' <σφαλερὸν> τέρμα suggests both 'dangerous limit' and 'fragile boundary'. Health and sickness are seen as next-door neighbours; only a thin 'wall' divides them, and the threat that disease will encroach on health is ever-present for the addict of physical exercise. For this idea compare Hippocrates *Aphorisms* 1. 3 'A peak condition in athletes is dangerous [σφαλεραί] if it reaches its limit', and similarly e.g. Aristotle *Nic. Eth.* 2. 2. 6 1104a 11–18.

The problem of restoring the transmitted text begins from the scansion of the responding verses (1018–21):

$$∪∪∪ - ∪∪∪ - ∪∪∪ -$$
$$∪∪ - - ∪∪ - ∪∪ -$$
$$∪∪ - ∪∪ - ∪∪ - -$$

τᾶς πολλᾶς is probably a gloss on a genitive ἀκορέστου, which intruded and disrupted the whole passage. γάρ (1003) is frequently added by scribes at an asyndeton. We accept that ὑγιείας could have the diphthong scanned short: cf. 147 Πᾰιᾶνα. The passage is usefully explored in M. West (1990*a*), 207–9.

1005–7. The antistrophe implies that there is a lacuna somewhere of seven syllables, whose likely cause is that a scribe's eye skipped a line between words with similar beginnings or endings. We suggest something like:

ἀνδρὸς ἔπαισεν <ἄφαρ
δυστυχίας πρὸς> ἄφαντον ἕρμα.

The whole is then: 'And a man's fate, when following a straight course, <suddenly> strikes <against> the invisible reef <of misfortune>'. ἔπαισεν is gnomic aorist, as are ἔδυ and ἐπόντισε below. Like health, prosperity (metaphorically here a ship) can come to an abrupt end. Compare *Eum.* 552–65, though there the 'ship' specifically belongs to an *unjust* plutocrat.

1008–13. 'And nervousness, after casting in advance one part of the objects in one's possession from a sling of proper measure— the entire house does not sink, overladen with excess, nor does it [i.e. excess] drown the keel.' There is an anacoluthon, as if 1008–10 had been a genitive absolute; hence τὸ μέν 'the one part' is not followed by τὸ δέ. Our gloss takes πρό as a temporal adverb ('in advance'); it could also be a preposition with χρημάτων, 'in defence of one's things'. Regarding σφενδόνη, there is little evidence for cranes on fifth-century ships, though that sense might support an elegant wordplay with ὄκνος, which means 'derrick' in a few late sources: Skeat (1975). More likely, σφενδόνη is an impromptu sling (see Sommerstein).

The metaphor of the prosperous house as a cargo ship continues. But the precise picture changes from a vessel which has struck a reef (where jettisoning cargo cannot help) to one caught in a storm. As a ship runs less risk of sinking in a heavy sea if an appropriate amount of cargo is jettisoned in time, so the house can be preserved by disposing of a part of its wealth. Both prosperity and ship recall the story of Polycrates of Samos, who tried to avert the jealousy of the gods after a run of success by casting a treasured ring into the sea (Herodotus 3. 40–3). The image also ties in with Clytemnestra's suggestion in the preceding episode that Agamemnon might have been told to destroy the house's rich garments for fear of the gods (933–4).

1014–17. Literally 'To be sure, plentiful bestowal from Zeus, abundant and proceeding from yearly furrows, destroys the illness of hunger.' The *gnōmē* (marked, as often, with τοι) takes the idea of averted disaster from the preceding words about jettisoning excess wealth, and illustrates it from the field of sickness: famine can in time be allayed by good harvests, thanks to Zeus' gifts of rain. νόσον at the end of the stanza balances νόσος at the beginning. Though the immediate contexts are different, the word's repetition helps to transmit the unity of thought and of imagery in the complex poetic texture.

1018–21. 'But as for black blood that has fallen in death in front of a man, who could call it back again by incantation?' πρόπαρ is a rare form of προπάροιθε. We take it as a preposition with ἀνδρός, since the thought of Iphigenia's blood falling before Agamemnon would appear to be near the front of the Chorus's mind. Alternatively πρόπαρ is adverbial ('beforehand') and ἀνδρός depends on αἷμα. Homicide (in contrast to hunger) is irremediable, even by the powers of song. Similarly *Cho.* 48 'What payment can release blood once it has fallen to the ground?', *Eum.* 261–3, and 647–8 'When the dust has absorbed the blood of a man once dead, there is no rising again.'

1022–4. 'Not even the man who knew rightly how to bring up (someone) from the dead [genitive of separation] did Zeus restrain without injury.' ἐπ' ἀβλαβείαι is literally 'in a circumstance of non-injury' (LSJ ἐπί B 1 i). The reference is to the healer Asclepius, who was credited with restoring various heroes to life, and was punished by Zeus with his thunderbolt: see Frazer (1921), ii. 16–19 for sources.

1025–9. This very difficult passage has attracted a variety of inter-pretations, of which Thalmann (1985) gives a useful survey, though we reach different conclusions. We will argue for the translation 'But were it not that one appointed allotment, by the gods' workings, constrains another allotment from getting more than its due, my

heart, outrunning my tongue, would be pouring out these matters',
with the general sense 'There is a divinely ordered pattern of justice
bringing people like Agamemnon down; this makes it useless for me
to give voice to my fears.' The basic structure is an unfulfilled conditional clause referring to the present (imperfect εἶργε in protasis;
imperfect ἐξέχει + ἄν in apodosis); μή ... φέρειν is a clause of
hindering after εἶργε (Smyth § 2739), and the aorist participle
προφθάσασα expresses coincident rather than prior action (cf.
289 n.).

The first points of interpretation are which two μοῖραι the Chorus
has in mind, and in what sense one constrains the other from
'winning too much'. The thought should be related to the dramatic
context (their fear of Agamemnon's death) and to the preceding
ideas, namely that sickness presses on the wall of extreme fitness, that
prosperity can come abruptly unstuck, that excessive prosperity is
remediable by timely humility whereas bloodshed is irremediable,
and that Asclepius was punished for acting beyond his situation. This
suggests that the constrained μοῖρα is the 'portion' of Agamemnon,
who is extremely prosperous, who has just demonstrated imperfect
humility and acted beyond his situation, and who has blood on his
hands.

The Chorus has revealed (990–3 n.) that it fears that Agamemnon's
prosperity is about to be limited by retributive justice. τεταγμένᾱ
μοῖρα can represent an element in the workings of this. Personified
Μοῖρα ('Destiny') is the source of the Erinyes' authority in matters
of retribution at e.g. *Eum.* 333–5; uncapitalized μοῖρα—an individual's portion as predefined by Moira—may retain her connection
to retribution. In this sense, the boundaries between individual
μοῖραι, where they limit each other from expanding, are policed
by δίκη such as Agamemnon is about to face. There are a number
of related ideas before Aeschylus: see Thalmann (1985), 103–4. For
example, in Anaximander fr. 1 the μοῖραι of *opposing qualities* are
constantly paying each other compensation for injustice, i.e. δίκη is
the principle of balance between them. The continuity between this
idea, which is particularly close to 1001–4 on health and sickness,
and δίκη policing the balance of *individuals'* μοῖραι, suggests the
unity of thought throughout this strophic pair. See also Intro. § 4.3.2
on conceptions of Moira.

Although there are close parallels for taking μοῖραν and ἐκ θεῶν
closely together, here it would produce a very artificial opposition

with τεταγμένᾱ μοῖρα (*pace* Scott 1969). We therefore prefer to take ἐκ θεῶν with εἶργε: the constraint proceeds from the gods, i.e. they govern it. The Olympians are thus authorities for retributive justice, as well as the Erinyes. Compare *Eum.* 391–3 where the Erinyes speak of their θεσμὸν Ι τὸν μοιρόκραντον ἐκ θεῶν Ι δοθέντα τέλεον, 'charter ordained by Moira and conceded as authoritative by the gods'.

In 'the heart outstripping the tongue', the Chorus revives the idea of the heart 'speaking' internally (977–8, 990–3) with a 'voice' that should not dictate what the tongue expresses publicly. The allusion to the proverb 'Don't let your tongue outstrip your mind' (see Fraenkel for examples) suggests that their point is that their feelings would run away with their words so as to blurt out their fear openly (for instance by going to warn Agamemnon or praying for his safety), were it not for the divine pattern they have just articulated. That pattern constrains them because it renders such speech futile.

(The most plausible alternative is to take the second μοῖρα as that of the Chorus members, constrained by their human condition from being cognitively capable of identifying and giving clear expression to their fears. But the hints in the first strophic pair suggest rather that they *can* identify their fears, even if they still do not know the exact mechanism of Agamemnon's death. Furthermore, the connection of thought with 1001–24 is lost.)

1030–3. As it is, the Chorus's heart can only murmur inarticulately in the dark, 'in grief of spirit' (MacNeice) 'and expecting never to accomplish anything καίριον'. ἐκτολυπεύσειν is literally to 'wind off' a ball of newly-spun wool, i.e. to complete. καίριον includes both 'timely' and 'well-targeted', which when applied to a speech-act would approach 'well-omened' (see e.g. *Sept.* 1). Whereas we have repeatedly—and as recently as 998–1000—met a prayer for good following desperately on a pessimistic conclusion, the Chorus no longer feels that such prayers can help Agamemnon.

1034. ζωπυρουμένας φρενός: genitive absolute, and probably with a temporal not a causal nuance: 'while my mind is being set on fire'. The proximity of mind and heart returns (cf. 995–6), but now where the heart is ὑπὸ σκότωι, the mind is paradoxically ablaze. For similar language relating reason and emotion to the fire of fear, cf. *Septem* 288–9 γείτονες δὲ καρδίας Ι μέριμναι ζωπυροῦσι τάρβος, 'anxieties neighbouring my heart are kindling fear'.

Fourth Episode (1035–1330), including *kommos* (1072–1177): There follows a scene of exceptional power and pathos, potentially the emotional peak of a performance. From now on the audience is expecting to hear news of Agamemnon's death, but the drama is held in suspense for about twenty minutes while attention is concentrated on Cassandra.

Lines 1035–71: First, Clytemnestra re-enters from the house and attempts to lure Cassandra inside. Those gifted with second sight cannot be left alone and the prophetess is to be murdered beside Agamemnon. But where the queen's persuasion succeeded with the king, with the captive it fails. She is greeted with stony silence, and soon leaves in frustration. The contrast between her domineering tone and the Coryphaeus' gentleness helps to establish sympathy for the prophetess.

What follows is in two parts, of carefully constructed form. (1) 1072–1177: Cassandra is not a mute role after all, and bursts into utterance. She and the Chorus have an extended *epirrhēma*, i.e. alternating turns which include song; since much of the tone, especially from Cassandra, is threnodic, the passage is sometimes also called a *kommos* following Aristotle's terminology (*Poet.* 12 1452b 24). The complex interplay of speech and song is unusual, and essential to this passage's power; as usual, we can only imagine how movement contributed to the effect. In the first four strophic pairs Cassandra expresses herself in a combination of sung lyrics, mainly in the jerky dochmiac rhythm, and a few spoken iambic trimeters, while the Coryphaeus speaks more measured responses in iambic couplets. In pair ϵ his couplets are followed by the whole Chorus singing dochmiacs, as it catches Cassandra's agitation. Then in the final two pairs the Coryphaeus has no speech, whereas Cassandra's shifts to trimeters become more regular.

In her various utterancs Cassandra mentions her horror of the house, has visions of Thyestes' children and of Clytemnestra killing Agamemnon in his bath, and predicts her own death. Her gift of inspired visions contrasts with that of Calchas, who makes inferences from omens: Cassandra's method seems to have been associated by Greeks with the Pythia and foreign sibyls. For her exclamatory style and irregular sentence-structures in this sequence, see with caution Mazzoldi (2002).

(2) 1178–1330: A spoken section in iambics, during which the topics mentioned above are recapitulated. Cassandra has three

extended *rhēseis*, each followed by a comment of four lines from the Coryphaeus and a passage of stichomythia. The episode concludes with two shorter speeches for Cassandra, and her exit into the palace.

The episode has a crucial function in the dramaturgical design of the trilogy, beyond the creation of prolonged suspense. As Knox observes in a stimulating analysis of Cassandra's dramatic position, Aeschylus uses the recently established third actor imaginatively, not to 'make the dialogue more flexible' but 'to make the drama transcend the limits of space and time' (1972, 104; see also Intro. § 5.2). Cassandra not only prophesies the murder of Agamemnon and herself, but is used as an ideal mouthpiece to look back to Thyestes' adultery with Atreus' wife Aerope and to the slaughter of his children as primal acts of folly in the house (cf. 1192 πρώταρχον ἄτην), and forward to the return of Orestes who will put the θριγκός—the 'coping stone'—on the structure of follies, by killing his mother and Aegisthus (1283). Aeschylus thus presents the death of Agamemnon not as an isolated personal tragedy, but as one of a series with antecedents and a sequel. The series typifies the tragic situation of the law παθεῖν τὸν ἔρξαντα, 'that the doer must suffer' (1564; cf. *Cho.* 313), the self-perpetuating chain of crime and punishment which is such a central issue of the *Agamemnon* and *Choephoroe*, and in *Eumenides* finds a resolution in civic justice (Intro. § 4.1). This broader perspective is combined with the first allusions to Aegisthus' role in Agamemnon's assassination (1223–5), and thus the latter's 'inherited guilt', i.e. the need for him to pay for his father's outstanding crimes (Intro. § 4.3.4). The perspective is also given vivid expression throughout by a pervasive concentration on the *oikos*, both as the looming onstage presence which Cassandra must enter, and as a subject for imaginative poetic treatment—it is a human slaughterhouse (1090–2), haunted by a revelling band of Furies (1186–93).

Given the Chorus's fears in the preceding stasimon, their inability to comprehend Cassandra may seem strange. Aeschylus exploits the story (made explicit at 1202–13) that Apollo had punished her with a curse that her prophecies would never be believed. This generates sustained dramatic irony, as the audience understands Cassandra's words better than the Chorus. Where there is no room for lack of comprehension, the Coryphaeus resorts characteristically to desperate protests (1246–7).

1035. Clytemnestra's sudden and surprising re-entry is marked with a peremptory instruction, which sets the tone for what follows. Aeschylus makes Clytemnestra know Cassandra's name and background, although Agamemnon did not name her at 950–5.

1036–8. 'Since Zeus has without wrath made you a sharer in the house's lustrations, standing among *many* slaves near Ktesios' altar'. Clytemnestra brazenly suggests in ἀμηνίτως that Zeus has kindly brought Cassandra to a 'good home'. The purificatory 'lustration' before a sacrifice involved the sacrificers washing their hands, and sprinkling the victim. Many houses contained an open-air altar of Zeus Ktesios, the protector of possessions, where the household slaves would attend domestic rituals. Of course, Clytemnestra has a malevolent 'sacrifice' in mind.

1039. The repetition of ἔκβαιν᾽ ἀπήνης τῆσδε from 906 suggests that Clytemnestra is preparing the same fate for Cassandra as for Agamemnon. We can infer from the text that Cassandra has already remained motionless longer than Clytemnestra expected; her first assumption is that the cause is pride.

1040. καὶ γάρ is used to introduce an *exemplum* and τοι gives it extra force: 'Even the son of *Alcmene*, they say, once . . . !' The reference is to Heracles' servitude to Omphale, queen of Lydia.

1041. πραθέντα: see under πέρνημι in LSJ. †δουλίας μάζης βία†: the manuscripts' major divergence may go back to ancient variants (see app. crit., D–P). Blomfield's emendation of βία to βίον gives a reasonable sense: 'put up with a life of servile barley-bread'. Barley-bread was coarse compared to wheat-bread (ἄρτος).

1042–4. Literally 'But anyway, if the necessity of this fortune [i.e. slavery] should fall to one's lot [intransitive, as in 707], there is a great blessing in (having) masters of *ancient* wealth: those who have reaped a good harvest [ἀμάω] without ever having expected it are both cruel to their slaves . . .'. Clytemnestra cites as a reason for Cassandra to feel some consolation the view, common in the sixth and fifth centuries (see Fraenkel), that nouveaux riches cannot be trusted to behave properly.

1045–6. παρὰ στάθμην is adverbial ('along the plumbline', i.e. 'exactly') and therefore does not balance ὠμοί τε δούλοις. In the absence of emendations, editors posit a lacuna of one or more lines. Since παρὰ στάθμην suggests propriety, it probably does not belong with the preceding description of cruelty but with the following words—'and you are getting [or ἕξεις, 'will get'] from us precisely the sort of treatment which is reckoned customary'. Thus the lacuna should come earlier than in the OCT, before or straight after πάντα. See M. West (1990*a*), 210.

1047–9. The Coryphaeus' comment is rich in dramatic irony. He thinks that Clytemnestra's speech is σαφής, whereas the audience and Cassandra see it as dissembling: Cassandra will not be welcomed into the house's rituals, but killed at one—the recurrent motif of perverted sacrifice. Furthermore, whereas by μορσίμων ἀγρευμάτων ('fatal traps') he is thinking only of the capture of Troy (cf. 121 n., 357–61), we understand Clytemnestra's imminent trap.

Pauses in which Cassandra fails to respond may be posited before 1047 and after the second πείθοι' in 1049. For Cassandra's silence, see Introduction § 5.2.

1049. 'please comply, if you will comply—but perhaps you might not comply'. The first optative expresses a polite command, as often; the second arises by attraction in this idiom; with the third, supply another ἄν. The Coryphaeus' tone with his three optatives is very polite and non-coercive, by contrast with Clytemnestra's imperatives (κομίζου, ἔκβαινε; cf. 1393–4 n.). The triple emphasis on the stem of πειθώ (and see πείθειν twice and λεγ- three times in 1052–4) is significant: we are waiting to learn whether Clytemnestra's persuasion, which was successful with Agamemnon, will also work with Cassandra.

1050–2. Literally 'Well, unless like a swallow she is possessed of an unknown barbarian language, I *am* prevailing on her by speaking within her mind,' i.e. transmitting words which Cassandra at least understands. The twittering swallow was a common simile in Greek for foreign speech (e.g. Ar. *Ran.* 678–82).

This is the first of a striking series of metaphors between Cassandra and animals: she becomes a game animal (1063), a horse (1066–7), probably an ox (1071), a bloodhound (1093), a nightingale (1145), a general bird (1316), and finally a swan (1444).

1053. 'Follow the advice: she is saying the best course of what is available.' For this sense of ἕπομαι, see LSJ ἕπω B I 7; there is no need to assume (with Sommerstein) that Clytemnestra starts to move off, with ἕπου meaning 'follow her'.

1055–6. 'I certainly do not have leisure to waste time here [τῆιδε], out of doors.' πάρα = πάρεστιν. For the sense of τρίβειν see LSJ s.v. II 2.

1056–7. The simplest solution is to emend πυρός to πάρος, which would govern ἑστίας (though the long separation is unusual): 'For the sheep are already standing in front of the hearth at the central navel (of the palace), for the slaughter.' The idea that a house's altar should be at its 'navel' derives from the religious space of Delphi, where a large stone was supposed to be the Navel of the Earth.

1058. 'as for ones [sc. ἡμῖν] who never expected to have this favour'. ὡς introduces a consideration which explains the urgency of the sacrifice. If the line is genuine, Aeschylus allows Clytemnestra one further gloating ambiguity regarding the nature of the χάρις. However, the repetition of words from 1043–4 is suspicious, and Fraenkel deletes the line.

1059. σὺ δ' is emphatically placed, and opposes τὰ μὲν ... μῆλα. We would place heavier punctuation after τίθει to mark another expectant pause.

1060–1. The point of ἀξυνήμων is 'unable to understand Greek'. Cassandra's hand is κάρβανος (a rare word for 'outlandish, barbarian') not just because she is a Trojan, but specifically because her foreignness causes her to have to use hand-gestures.

Clytemnestra is growing more and more exasperated. The nominative σύ, repeated from 1059, expresses her impatience. Her words are often taken as illogical.[3] But it is quite human for her in the context to ask Cassandra to communicate in gestures, especially if she herself is gesturing in exasperation.

1063. Why is Cassandra's manner 'like that of a newly-captured animal'? This phrase and 1067 (see below) have suggested to some commentators that her body is quivering, like an animal in 'spasms of terror' as she goes into a prophetic seizure: Ewans (1995) ad loc. However, we far prefer to think that she stays absolutely motionless until 1071. This gives a better motivation for Clytemnestra's angry exit, clarifies the crucial dramatic point that Cassandra is impervious to Clytemnestra's persuasion, and seems to fit the action at 1070–1 better (see n.). As Fraenkel put it, 'As long as Cassandra remains motionless, she is unassailable' (p. 485). Furthermore, after Clytemnestra's request that Cassandra use gesture, her supposed

---

[3] A. E. Housman parodied them in his *Fragment of a Greek Tragedy*: 'But if you happen to be deaf and dumb | And do not understand a word I say, | Then wave your hand, to signify as much.' The *Fragment* also alludes to *Ag.* 494–5, 975–9, and 1092. See Housman (1997), 244–7.

prophetic twitches seem unlikely to generate the response 'She seems
to need an interpreter.'

It may be that *νεαιρέτου* is wrong. Although the recurrence of
νεαίρετον in 1065 is not impossible, it does raise suspicion. A word
like *ἀφράσμονος* might suit the context of incomprehension (cf.
1401). There remains the discrepancy between the stillness which
we suppose and Clytemnestra's description of Cassandra as raving
(a typical behaviour for eastern seers, which she does display later).
But that inaccuracy would aptly signify the pitch of Clytemnestra's
frustration, and the irony that in assuming that Cassandra has
no understanding she herself fails to comprehend Cassandra's
behaviour.

1064. *κλύει*: here effectively 'obeys', governing the genitive.

1066–7. 'but does not know how to endure the bridle before foaming
out her spirit in blood'. *αἱματηρόν* is predicative. Cassandra's
attitude to slavery is like that of a recalcitrant horse to a sharp Greek
bit, which might produce both blood and foam at its mouth. (Dio
Chrysostom 63. 4–5 has an interesting description of Apelles finding
this hard to paint.) Clytemnestra is implying that Cassandra will
not do as she is told until she has been roughly treated. She replaces
the Coryphaeus' simile in 1063 with a less pitying metaphor also
drawn from animals, which unsympathetically merges the raving of
prophetic inspiration with the raving *pride* of a horse.

The words might suggest that Cassandra is starting to foam at the
mouth in a prophetic seizure. But this is not necessary, since at least
the word *αἱματηρόν* is simply metaphorical. See 1063 n.

1068. *πλέω ῥίψασ'*: 'throwing out more words', i.e. wasting them.
Clytemnestra leaves angrily after this line.

1070–1. *ὦ τάλαινα*: the Coryphaeus addresses Cassandra com-
passionately, and she responds by leaving her wagon. This seems
more appropriate to a figure that has remained silent and still than
one already in the throes of mantic possession. *καίνισον ζυγόν*:
'accept your new yoke'. The imagery now is probably of an ox or
mule.

1072–81. Cassandra leaves the cart, which is discreetly removed by
attendants. Her movements thereafter have been variously envisaged.
She may move slowly towards a central position in the *orchēstra*
while the Chorus regroups around her. A popular view is rather that
she turns towards the palace at 1081, then recoils and cries out to

Apollo Agyieus because she sees a conical pillar representing him by the door. Later in the fifth century, it was common practice to place an altar and/or pillar near the *skēnē* door to represent Apollo Agyieus (Poe 1989, 131–7). But here it is quite natural for Cassandra to cry out to her guardian deity and to use the epithet which refers to him directing journeys, so the inference from her cry is insecure. Indeed, Cassandra's recoil at 1307 is more forceful without a similar action here.

1072–3. Until now, the audience has been kept guessing as to whether Cassandra is a mute supporting role or a substantial, Greek-speaking character, employing the recently introduced third actor (see Intro. § 5.2). Now she bursts into utterance with three cries expressing respectively lamentation, pained surprise, and horror, then an invocation of Apollo. ὀτοτοτοῖ is mostly uttered by effeminate and/or oriental characters in tragedy (Heirman 1975, 258–9).

1074. Λοξίου: a common title of Apollo, especially in oracular contexts. The name was explained by reference to λοξός 'slanting', and the obliqueness of Apollo's oracles.

1075. 'For he (is) not one to come to meet a mourner.' For Apollo's avoidance of the miasma of death and consequently of lamentation, see e.g. *Septem* 854–60, Euripides *Alcestis* 22.

1078–9. The Coryphaeus repeats his point from 1074–5, adding that Cassandra's creepy and cryptic cries are ill-omened; he has also switched from addressing her to addressing his fellow elders. For the personal construction of προσήκω here, see LSJ s.v. III 3b.

1081. ἀγυιᾶτ', ἀπόλλων ἐμός: Aeschylus takes Cassandra into dochmiacs, the agitated metre which dominates her subsequent utterances. Cassandra makes a bitter pun on Apollo's name and ἀπόλλυμι (clarified in ἀπώλεσας). She calls on his epithet Agyieus, 'god of the ways' (cf. ἄγυια) because as her guardian he has led her to destruction in Argos (cf. 1087 ἤγαγες).

1082. οὐ μόλις τὸ δεύτερον: 'without difficulty, for the second time'. For the first, see 1202–13.

1083–4. The Coryphaeus already knows of Cassandra's divinely inspired prophetic power (τὸ θεῖον; cf. 1098–9). He expects Cassandra to talk about her own lot, but she will have unpleasant home truths to tell first.

1087–8. The Coryphaeus gives a simple answer and is made to express an exaggerated confidence in his correctness, to be refuted by Cassandra in 1090–2 with a very different kind of description.

1090 ἆ ἆ: the cry does not recur in the antistrophe and some scholars athetize. If it is right, it is tantamount to two horrible screams *extra metrum*.

1090–1. 'No! To a god-hating house, conscious of many evils of self-slaughter'. μὲν οὖν corrects a preceding statement. The noun συνίστωρ governs an object as σύνοιδα would. Adjectives compounded with αὐτο- are often used in tragedy of bloodshed within a family (see e.g. Soph. *Ant.* 52–6).

†**καρτάναιτ**: meaningless, and failing to correspond metrically with 1096. A possible emendation, though the word does not occur elsewhere, is Weil's κρεᾱτόμα, 'involving cutting of flesh', which could refer to the Thyestean banquet (see 1096–7).

1092. ἀνδροσφαγεῖον: 'slaughter-house of men', a *hapax*; though ἀνδρο- could suggest men in general, the audience naturally thinks of Clytemnestra's ἀνήρ in particular. **πέδον ῥαντήριον:** literally 'a floor besprinkled', i.e. with blood. M's reading πεδορραντήριον would be 'a place where the floor is sprinkled'. Either way, ῥαντήριον suggests the sprinkling of lustral water rather than blood (see Fraenkel), and thus the recurring motif of perverted sacrifice.

1093. εὔρις: 'with a keen nose'. Cassandra seems to be scenting out blood like a hound.

1094. 'and she is seeking the blood of those whose blood she will detect'. In other words, the 'bloodhound' Cassandra is on to a trail which does lead somewhere. It is best to take ὧν = ἐκείνων ὧν, and φόνον with both verbs.

1095–7. γάρ implies the response 'Yes, since . . .' (cf. 271 n., 552). With the deictic pronouns τοῖσδε and τάδε Cassandra is pointing to the horrible vision before her of Thyestes' children, who were cooked by Atreus and eaten by their father. The dative μαρτυρίοισι is followed in apposition by an accusative (βρέφη), as if 1095 had said something like 'I witness'; the loose syntax suits Cassandra's visionary fervour, though we would add a comma at the end of 1095. It is unclear whether ὀπτάς τε σάρκας is parallel to σφαγάς (i.e. a second object of κλαιόμενα) or to βρέφη, but either is suitably gruesome.

1098–9. The combination ἦ μήν ('I assure you') is defended by D–P, but it normally introduces an oath (Denniston 350), and the similarity to 1099 ἦμεν arouses suspicion. Headlam's τὸ μέν would sharpen the distinction between a μάντις who predicts the future, and προφῆται who announce and interpret a present sign by means of special insight. The Coryphaeus recognizes Atreus' infanticide in Cassandra's vision (cf. 1106), and politely acknowledges her reputation as a seer, but declares that the elders 'do not wish the horrors of the past to be dragged into the light' (Fraenkel).

1100–4. The exclamation ἰὼ πόποι alerts us that Cassandra's next vision has arrived. It is vague at first (someone planning a terrible pain in the house) but comes increasingly into focus down to 1129. The subject of the repeated μήδεται is unspecified, but may suggest the name Κλυται-μήστρα, as in *Od.* 3. 261 μέγα μήσατο ἔργον.

1106. Unlike the previous vision (ἐκεῖνα) which the Coryphaeus recognized and with which 'the whole city resounds', this one prompts no comprehension—Apollo's curse on Cassandra's prophecies seems already to be in operation.

1107–11. The plotter comes into sharper focus: she is a wife bathing her husband.

1107. 'Agh! Brazen woman—is it *this* you're going to carry through?' The horror-struck tone of the question explains (cf. γάρ) Cassandra's use of τάλαινα. τελεῖς here is probably future rather than present.

1109–10. φαιδρύνασα has no main verb, as the syntax effectively breaks off in the exclamation πῶς φράσω τέλος. As in 1107, γάρ explains her choice of words: she means 'end', 'since that will occur quickly'. τάχος is adverbial, as in 945.

1110–11. 'She stretches forth hand after [LSJ ἐκ I 3] hand as she reaches out.' This is left enigmatic; we will later understand that the wife is preparing to throw the fatal robe over her husband (1380–3).

1112–13. ἐξ αἰνιγμάτων: the emphasis of οὔπω and νῦν suggests that ἐξ αἰνιγμάτων expresses a previous state: 1100–4 were 'riddles'; 1107–11, which include future verbs, were 'prophecies', but still baffling. ἐξ would then be 'after' (LSJ ἐκ II 2). Alternatively, Fraenkel and Sommerstein interpret it to mean 'as a result of riddles'. ἐπαργέμοισι: 'obscure'; ἄργεμον is a medical term for a white film on the eye.

1115–17. Cassandra now sees not only Clytemnestra's hands, but the cloak which will entrap him in the bath ('net': cf. 1382–3). Punctuated as a statement, 1115 answers 1114: 'Indeed, it is some net of Hades,' i.e. a lethal net. Alternatively, 1115 could be a second question. Either way, 1116 ἀλλ' ('But more . . . !') adds a qualification: Clytemnestra—the female 'sharer in the bed and in responsibility for murder'—is herself a net or trap. ξυν-αιτία gives a fleeting suggestion of Aegisthus' involvement.

1117–18. 'Let Discord, of which the family cannot have enough, raise a cry of triumph over a sacrifice associated with stoning.' στάσις here is probably discord personified. The alternative is to translate 'company' (cf. *Cho.* 458, referring to the chorus as a whole), i.e. a chorus of Furies who haunt the house, as described at 1186–90. However, the Coryphaeus understands στάσις as an allusion to a single Fury (1119).

For the genitive θύματος expressing the cause of a verb implying emotion, see Smyth § 1405. Agamemnon's murder is again a perverted 'sacrifice', which will pollute the whole community and thus merit the collective punishment of public stoning; see 1616 where the Coryphaeus threatens Aegisthus with curses and stoning (λευσίμους ἀράς).

1119–20. The Coryphaeus can recognize a Fury in Cassandra's hints about a wife killing a husband, but not the precise application. His words produce an echo of 27–9 δόμοις ὀλολυγμὸν . . . ἐπορθιάζειν, where it was Clytemnestra who was to raise the shout; this may be a hint of her character's connections to the Furies and other destructive powers (Intro. § 8).

1120. φαιδρύνει: 'gladden' (cf. 520 n.).

1121–3. Here, probably, the whole Chorus makes its entry singing dochmiacs, as it catches Cassandra's mood. 'And to my heart there has run the saffron-dyed drop which [feminine ἅτε] also for men felled by a spear reaches its endpoint together with the rays of their setting life.' In other words, they feel as faint and grow as pale as a dying warrior.

Either of two physiological ideas may be understood in 'saffron-dyed': that fear makes blood drain towards the heart from the cheeks, turning them pale (cf. *Supp.* 566 χλωρῶι δείματι); or that faintness is caused by yellow bile or gall approaching the heart (cf. *Cho.* 183–4 'a wave of gall assailed my heart too' with Garvie 1986). Both this yellow colour and the suggestion of completion in ξυνανύτει befit the image of the dying soldier at life's sunset.

1124. ἄτη here is 'ruin'. The remark picks up 1110 τάχος γὰρ τόδ' ἔσται, underlining the Chorus's fear of imminent disaster.

1125–6. The sacrificial imagery continues in Cassandra's vision of the victim as a bull; this is, paradoxically, to be kept away from its dangerous cow (i.e. Clytemnestra).

1126–8. 'Taking (him) in robes, a black-horned contrivance, she strikes.' μελαγκέρωι μηχανήματι cannot be construed as instrumental with τύπτει, since the sword which Clytemnestra uses (1262, 1529) is not a 'contrivance'. Rather it is in apposition to πέπλοισιν; at *Cho.* 980 μηχάνημα is again used of the robe in which Clytemnestra entrapped Agamemnon (1081–3). The robe is 'black' because it is sinister, stained with mortal bloodshed, and envelops its victim in darkness (Collard 2002 ad loc.); it is 'horned' because it is the weapon of a metaphorical 'cow'. The confusing mismatch between robes and black horns suits the prophetess's language, and the anomalous situation which she is describing.

1129. 'I tell you a misfortune of [i.e. involving] a vessel of treacherous murder.' See LSJ τύχη III 2.

1130–5. No elder 'could claim to be a consummate discerner of prophecies' (distinguish γνώμων from γνωμῶν, the genitive plural of γνώμη), but they can conjecture that something terrible is behind these ones. They explain this with reference not to Cassandra's hints, but to the general comment that prophets rarely prophesy good, which may well be proverbial. **κακῶν γὰρ διαί**: the sense seems to be 'through terrible [i.e. ominous] words', as in Sophocles *Trach.* 1131 διὰ κακῶν ἐθέσπισας.

1136–77. Cassandra now has a vision of her own impending death, which prompts a lament for Troy's general misfortunes. Her dochmiac cola from now on are capped with two presumably spoken iambic trimeters—a move towards the clearer insights of her iambic *rhēsis* from 1178. Meanwhile the bewildered Chorus's responses from now are dochmiac throughout. For the shifting balance between speech and song see 1035–1330 n.

1136. **ταλαίνας**: referring to herself, as clarified in 1137–8 τὸ γὰρ ἐμὸν πάθος and με τὴν τάλαιναν.

1137. **ἐπεγχέαι**: explanatory infinitive, 'to pour on top', sc. of Agamemnon's suffering. The metaphor suggests both the flow of her speech and the flow of blood which will constitute the πάθος.

1138–9. The question must be addressed to Apollo given its echo of 1087. But as 1139 makes clear, ποῖ here is 'To what purpose?' rather than 'To where?' οὐδέν seems syntactically unattached in this idiom where it goes closely with εἰ μή: '(to do) nothing except share in death' (cf. οὐδὲν ἄλλο ἤ: LSJ ἄλλος III 2). **τί γάρ;** : also idiomatic, 'Because what (other purpose is there)?'

1140. Faced with Cassandra's more lucid prophecy of her own death, the Chorus becomes more forthright in its disbelief: she must be out of her wits (the tone is clear in 1151 ματαίους).

1141. αὐτᾶς: for σεαυτᾶς.

1142. νόμον ἄνομον: 'unmusical music' (LSJ νόμος II; cf. 151), a common type of oxymoron (see 1545). Cassandra's singing is disordered and disturbing.

1142–5. The Chorus now compares Cassandra to Procne, who punished her husband Tereus for raping her sister Philomela, by killing their son Itys and serving him to his father. To save Procne from Tereus' revenge, the gods turned her into a nightingale, which often features in Greek literature as a type of the mourning mother.

ξουθά: an adjective commonly applied to the nightingale (ἀηδών, delayed to 1145); it may refer to tawny colour or trilling sound, but Silk (1983), 317–19 has argued that even in the fifth century it may have had no stable core meaning. **ἀμφιθαλῆ κακοῖς ... μόρον:** of the two accusatives, Ἴτυν quotes Procne's cry (the nightingale was apparently thought to sing 'ee-toose'), and μόρον describes what it is a lament for. ἀμφιθαλής means basically 'blooming on both sides', and is used in e.g. *Iliad* 22. 496 of children who have both parents living. Aeschylus twists the word to the negative: both his parents, as chef and diner, took part in his κακά.

The manuscripts have βίον here, then μόρον in 1146 (where it would be a rare exclamatory accusative). Page swapped to μόρον ... βίος on the grounds that μόρος entails death, and so is unsuited to 1146 (see D–P); this claim about μόρος is disputed in e.g. Lloyd-Jones (1978), 57.

1146–9. Cassandra objects to the comparison with Procne because her own fate is worse: she presents the nightingale, preserved by metamorphosis, as living on without troubles, whereas a 'rending' awaits her. This—particularly κλαυμάτων ἄτερ, 'without any (new) cries of distress'—is a very unusual perspective, since the nightingale's famous song was normally seen precisely as a lament.

περέβαλον for περιέβαλον is an unusual form for metrical convenience. The verb governs οἱ, which is the dative of the enclitic pronoun (not an article), and two objects which produce a slight zeugma—the tangible 'body' and intangible 'lifetime'. **δορί:** a 'weapon' in general rather than a spear, since we assume that Cassandra is right, and she is killed with a sword. The meaning would be unique, but she has 'prophetic licence'. Cf. 1496 βελέμνωι.

1150–1. The adjectives recall those in 1140 (and θεοφόρ- responds exactly), but this protestation asks after the *source* of Cassandra's distress.

1152–3. 'and (why do you) mould the melody of these fearful things, simultaneously in ill-omened clamour and in high-pitched strains?' Or δυσφάτωι may mean 'unintelligible', as the scholiast thought.

1154–5. 'Whence are the boundary-stones of your prophetic path that involve evil utterance?' The ὅροι define the edges of the course of Cassandra's ill-omened song.

1156–61. Cassandra does not respond to the two πόθεν ἔχεις questions, but resumes her lament for herself and recalls Paris' fatal marriage and her childhood home in Troy, soon to be replaced by one in the underworld. The thought is expressed by contrasting the banks of the Trojan river Scamander with those of Cocytus and Acheron in Hades. ἠνυτόμαν τροφαῖς: literally 'I grew up by rearing', i.e. 'I was raised and grew up'; this is an unusual sense of ἀνύ(τ)ω.

1162–6. The Chorus can now comprehend Cassandra's 'excessively clear' words and its fear becomes more aggressive (beating, stinging, and shattering). Its understanding may arise in part from a calmer delivery of the iambics 1160–1, which it describes as μινυρά, 'whimperings'.

1164. ὑπαὶ δήγματι: for the sense of ὑπό, see 892–3 n. For the δῆγμα of pain see 791.

1165. We take μινυρὰ θρεομένας as a genitive absolute (sc. σου), whose circumstances are expressed by δυσαλγεῖ τύχᾱι: 'while you, in your grievous misfortune, utter whimpering sounds'.

1166. θραύματ' ἐμοὶ κλύειν: 'for me [emphatic], things shattering to hear'.

1167–72. Cassandra now makes Troy not just a background for her miserable fate, but something to lament in its own right. Priam's sacrifices before the walls (see 128–30 n.) did not prevent the city suffering 'just as, in fact, was fated' (ὥσπερ οὖν ἐχρῆν). Then in her final line she reverts to her own death, which balances the deaths of the sacrificial animals. ἄκος δ' οὐδὲν ἐπήρκεσαν τὸ μή . . . : 'They supplied no remedy to prevent'. In prose one would expect (τὸ) μὴ οὐ: Smyth § 2744. ἐγὼ δὲ †θερμόνους . . . βαλῶ†: Musgrave emended to ἐγὼ δὲ θερμὸν ῥοῦν τάχ' ἐν πέδωι βαλῶ, 'and I will soon cast a hot stream [of blood] upon the ground'. ἐν is in tmesis with βαλῶ. The infinitive result clause in 1171 is balanced by an indicative one.

1173. 'These utterances of yours follow your former ones.' Which former ones? The content from both Cassandra in 1172 and the Chorus resembles 1149–55 more than 1156–66, and the moment of clarity has elapsed. ἑπόμενα may well mean not only 'follow (in content)' but also 'follow (in tone)', i.e. refer to a more passionate delivery of Cassandra's preceding line.

1174–6. 'And some malevolent deity, falling on you with excessive weight, is making you sing of lamentable, death-bringing sufferings.' τις is indefinite rather than interrogative: its accent comes from the enclitic σε. The point is that Cassandra has reverted to divinely inspired talk of death which they cannot comprehend.

τέρμα δ' ἀμηχανῶ: the Chorus concludes the lyric exchange on a note of general perplexity: where will the πάθη end? τέρμα is accusative of respect.

1178–1330. The third part of the episode is to some extent a recapitulation of the second, but the switch from lyric to trimeters marks a significant change of tone. Not only does Cassandra describe her insights with more fluency, and at times more clarity, but she also relates them with greater logic to the central theme of a chain of crime and retribution (see 1035–1330 n.), and in her final lines complements her insight into her own tragic situation by compassion for the whole of humanity.

1178–97. Cassandra begins her first *rhēsis* by declaring that she will speak in a different way, and asserting her abilities as a bloodhound tracking the past events of the house (cf. 1093). She then articulates a knowledge of Thyestes' adultery with Atreus' wife Aerope, and the potent image of the palace haunted by a chorus of Furies. This introduces the motif of inherited liability which becomes more important from this point on (Intro. § 4.3.4).

1178–9. καὶ μήν marks a new departure (Denniston 352). Cassandra's prophecies 'will no longer have their fixed gaze from behind veils, like a newly-wedded bride'. ἔσται δεδορκώς is a periphrasis for the future of δέδορκα (itself a perfect with present meaning). The verb suggests a piercing, perceptive look, while the veils stand for the riddling language in which her insights have been couched. Greek brides wore a veil during the feast in their parents' house on their wedding day, and the unveiling (ἀνακαλυπτήρια) at the end of that meal and before the journey to the groom's house was an important moment in the marriage ritual. The comparison with a bride has extra poignancy in Cassandra's mouth, since she has been denied marriage, and since her closest brush with it was the moment that she frustrated Apollo's seduction and received the mixed blessing of her riddling χρησμός (cf. Collard 2002 ad loc.).

1180–3. Cassandra's χρησμός will be clear in its expression instead of veiled. It is therefore λαμπρός, 'bright'; then it is λαμπρός in the sense of a 'fresh' wind (LSJ λαμπρός I 5), blowing towards (or 'from': see below) the bright East; then it is like the more menacing wave that such a wind would cause. The chain of metaphors characterizes the prophetic mode of speech, even as Cassandra declares that it will be more straightforward.

The repetition πρὸς ἀντολάς ... πρὸς αὐγάς is weak, and reading πρὸς ἀντολῆς ... πρὸς ἀγάς ('from the East to the shore') produces a better sense. The Greeks knew that sunrise causes a dawn wind blowing off the sea *from* the East. See Lavery (2004*a*), 12–13.

Lines 1182–3 can be construed in two slightly different ways, since κλύζειν may be transitive 'make to break over' (χρησμός still the subject; μεῖζον sc. πῆμα the object) or intransitive 'break over' (μεῖζον πῆμα the subject). The metaphor of a wave or heavy sea of troubles is common. τοῦδε πήματος must refer to the sorrow which has just been described (her own death, and probably Agamemnon's). The identification of the πολὺ μεῖζον πῆμα is more difficult. Fraenkel interprets that the same topics will be recapitulated but will cause more anguish because they are more comprehensible. But we (like Sommerstein) prefer to think that it is the new topic of Clytemnestra's future murder by Orestes, which is to feature as the ultimate atrocity in 1280–5.

1184–5. Cassandra asks the Chorus to 'act as witnesses', i.e. testify to the truth of what she is saying, as she smells out the trail of past crimes συνδρόμως, like a sleuth-dog running closely on the scent. For the image, cf. 1093–4.

1186–90. The house is perpetually haunted by a chorus, singing about crimes in unison but in ugly and ill-omened strains (both nuances of οὐκ εὔφωνος are present). Furthermore (καὶ μὴν ... γ') it is a κῶμος, a band of drunken revellers who would normally go on from house to house. But instead of having drunk wine, this κῶμος is drunk (perfect participle) on human blood, which has emboldened it (consecutive ὡς + infinitive) to stay where it

is—it cannot be sent away to another house. Finally the choreuts
are revealed: 'kindred' Erinyes, which implies partly that they are
sisters, but chiefly that they avenge crimes committed among
kinsmen. Their perpetual presence implies the inexorable nature
of the chain of crime and retribution in which the Atreids are
involved. The picture is related to that of 1117–20 (see n.), but
more terrifyingly specific. For the Erinyes drinking blood, see also
Eum. 264–6.

1191–3. The Erinyes, now a hymnic χορός again, are 'besieging the
inner rooms' (δώμασιν προσήμεναι), and 'chanting as their hymn
the primal act of ruinous madness' (πρώταρχον ἄτην); in this, they
literally 'spit out a brother's bed which was inimical to its trampler',
i.e. they abominate Thestes' adultery with Atreus' wife, which
resulted in the horrific vengeance of the banquet. Thyestes' adultery
is a further act of 'trampling', which recalls Agamemnon trampling
on the garments and the general comment at 370–3. The Erinyes'
position in the house, and the fact that it is adultery which causes
and forms the subject of their singing, suggests a perversion of the
epithalamion, the hymn performed outside the bedroom door of
newly-weds.

ἐν μέρει δ' ἀπέπτυσαν: the verb seems to be a rather unusual
example of a 'dramatic' aorist which refers to the present: see Lloyd
(1999), esp. 26–8, though he explains our passage differently. ἐν
μέρει ('in turn') is normally referred to the Erinyes themselves.
Given 1187 ξύμφθογγος, the round of abominations would have to
follow the main unison song (so Fraenkel). But possibly one could
refer the phrase to the sequence of actions entailed in 1193—the
adultery, and the punishment implied in δυσμενεῖς.

1194. Cassandra is no longer a hunting dog, but a hunting archer
striking or missing the quarry. The emendation κυρῶ produces
a better contrast with ἥμαρτον than θηρῶ, and is accepted by
Fraenkel, West, and Sommerstein.

1195. 'Or am I a false seer, a knocker at doors, a babbler?' The three
predicates are probably a comprehensive picture of a mendicant
prophet who visits the houses of the rich, dispensing indulgences
which he or she falsely claims to be empowered to sell (cf. Plato *Resp.*
2 364b–c).

1196–7. With the OCT, Cassandra bids the Chorus testify on oath
(reworking her opening instruction: 1184 μαρτυρεῖτε) that she
knows the house's past history; λόγωι must modify παλαιάς and

mean 'ancient in story'. Her knowledge of the past is a sign of divine possession, which also validates her forecasts of the future; compare *Iliad* 1. 70 where Calchas' knowledge of past, present, and future are mentioned side by side as components of seercraft.

However, the positive articular infinitive with the subject expressed (τό μ' εἰδέναι) is hard to parallel from Aeschylus, as is λόγωι παλαιάς. West simply obelizes λόγωι. Fraenkel emends to τὸ μὴ εἰδέναι, which scans with synizesis, as often where μή precedes a vowel. Cassandra is then challenging the Chorus to *deny* on oath that *it* knows the house's murky history from hearsay (λόγωι this time modifying εἰδέναι). The Chorus has already indicated as much in 1106.

1198–1201. The Coryphaeus' response is somewhat evasive. 'How could the striking of an oath, genuinely struck, be curative?', i.e. curative for the past crimes—but he keeps them unmentioned. He is however surprised that a foreigner is as knowledgeable as a native Argive.

θαυμάζω governs both a genitive σου, expressing the cause of an emotion (cf. 1117–18 n.), and an accusative and infinitive expressing its content (τραφεῖσαν sc. σε . . . κυρεῖν). The syntax of ἀλλόθρουν πόλιν is harder. It might be the object of λέγουσαν, 'when speaking about a city of foreign speech'; compare transitive verbs of speaking such as *Od.* 1. 1 ἄνδρα μοι ἔννεπε. Alternatively one can emend, e.g. to ἀλλόθρωι 'ν πόλει (Enger).

1202–13. In this first stichomythic exchange, Cassandra responds to the Coryphaeus' surprise by revealing her relationship with Apollo. Aeschylus only sketches the story, but it seems basically compatible with the ancient handbook's statement that 'Apollo wished to sleep with Cassandra so promised to teach her prophecy; she learnt it but did not sleep with him, so Apollo removed the persuasiveness of her prophecies' (Ps.-Apollodorus *Bibl.* 3. 12. 5). That version includes Apollo's agreement to delayed gratification and eventual failure to get his way, which have undeservedly aroused suspicions about Aeschylus' text (1205–8 nn.).

1202. τῶιδ' ἐπέστησεν τέλει: 'set me to this function'; τέλος as in 908.

1203–4. μῶν—for whose nuances see Barrett (1964), 314–15—marks the Coryphaeus' tone as politely hesitant. In καὶ θεός περ the Coryphaeus seems to expect that the gods are free from sexual desire, which is far from the assumption in many Greek authors.

Cassandra's αἰδώς would be prompted by the code that any sexual liaison outside marriage was a possible source of dishonour.

1205. 'Indeed: during prosperity everyone is more delicate.' Conversely, Cassandra is no longer εὖ πράσσουσα, so she cannot afford the reticence of αἰδώς.

(Kovacs (1987) objects that ἁβρύνομαι is normally more pejorative. This leads him to reject the transposition of 1203–4, and to insert a lacuna on either side, so that there could be a reference to Cassandra's pride in refusing Apollo's advances. However, the verb's basic meaning is 'I make myself ἁβρός', and the adjective is often used positively of adolescent girls, such as Cassandra was.)

1206–8. 'The fact is, he was a wrestler, powerfully breathing his χάρις on me.' κάρτα better qualifies what follows, rather than the verbal idea in παλαιστής ('a real wrestler'). χάρις often entails ἔρως (LSJ χάρις IV), and sex is often described in terms of wrestling. In speaking of Apollo as a παλαιστής, Cassandra must be implying that he *tried* to take her by force. Thus the Coryphaeus assumes that the god got his way and, with his unerring divine potency, impregnated her. But Cassandra agreed to sleep with Apollo some time in the future, then reneged (1208; cf. 1202–13 n.).

(We do not think Kovacs (1987) is justified in supposing that Apollo could not possibly have accepted delayed gratification, and inferring that for Aeschylus—uniquely—Cassandra *did* sleep with Apollo, and was punished for some subsequent infidelity.)

ἠλθέτην ὁμοῦ: the manuscripts' ἤλθετον νόμωι ('in the customary way') is possible. The emendation ὁμοῦ requires the change to -την, which is a poetic form of the historic second person dual ending.

1210. Cassandra either received the gift of prophecy as part of Apollo's seduction (as in Ps.-Apollodorus) or at the moment of her bargain with him. This detail, like the details of how she escaped Apollo's advances, are left vague so as not to overshadow the central points.

1212–13. The conversation ends with an attractive irony. Cassandra's punishment for cheating Apollo was never to be believed. The Coryphaeus cannot even accept that: 'Well, to *us* at least your inspired utterances seem credible enough.' But in fact he will remain baffled by her predictions (1245).

1214–41. Cassandra suddenly undergoes a fresh paroxysm of possession but remains in spoken trimeters. This leads to a second *rhēsis*:

she has a further vision of Thyestes' children which she describes in greater detail than at 1096–7, then from 1223 she connects it to the vengeance being plotted, first hinting at Aegisthus, then dwelling on Clytemnestra's deception (though names are still withheld). Finally she adds, returning to the point reached in 1212–13, that whether or not she convinces the Chorus of anything it will witness the truth soon enough.

1215–16. ὑπ' ... στροβεῖ: in tmesis, 'whirls me underneath', i.e. from deep inside. φροιμίοις <δυσφροιμίοις>: the uncertain supplement is Hermann's, and produces an expression similar to 1142 νόμον ἄνομον; other adjectives such as <δυσχειμέροις> would also suit. The manuscripts have ἐφημένους, which is evidently imported from the line below.

Lines 1214–16 form a 'prelude' of pain to the *rhēsis* as a whole. Thereafter we envisage a quieter, horror-stricken tone, gradually building from 1223 towards a strong climax at 1236–7.

1217–22. Cassandra has a vision of Thyestes' children 'sitting close to the palace' (ἐφημένους is not necessarily 'sitting on top of'). At first they are not defined, and 'resemble the forms of dreams'. Then more details are added—some visual (they are holding their flesh and innards), others not (they are sons whose father ate of them).

1219. ὡσπερεὶ πρὸς τῶν φίλων: 'as if by the hand of their φίλοι'. If the text is right, the conditional form in which Cassandra expresses herself reflects remaining inclarities in the vision which is gradually coming into focus. West conjectures οὐ for τῶν. ὡσπερεί usually introduces a clause, but is probably defensible.

1220. κρεῶν is partitive genitive after a verb of filling, with οἰκείας βορᾶς in apposition. οἰκεῖος may simply be 'their own' (e.g. Sophocles *Ant.* 1176), in which case the phrase would mean 'food of themselves (for someone else)'. But the interpretation 'a meal from within the household' is perhaps simpler.

1221–2. The vision is now in full focus: they are clearly (πρέπουσι) holding other edible body-parts besides flesh: the organs like the heart and liver which were normally tasted at sacrifices (σπλάγχνα), and intestines (ἔντερα) which were less often eaten but which are here mixed in. To carry such a 'load' is particularly pitiful, especially since Thyestes had had a taste of it all (ὧν: partitive genitive).

1223–5. Thyestes' meal is not connected to the present horrors just by location, but also causally: someone is plotting revenge for it.

This is the play's first clear reference to Aegisthus, who is a 'cowardly lion, roaming' not amid the wildernesses, but 'in bed'; the verb hints at adultery. The oxymoron is varied in 1259 where Aegisthus is a wolf who contrasts with the real lion Agamemnon. Here, the lion comparison may recall the fable of the cub (717–36) who grew up to wreak havoc: Aegisthus was saved from death as an infant, and grew up to wreak vengeance on Agamemnon (S. West 2003). Aegisthus is also an οἰκουρός, a feminine or servile role of guarding the house while the master is absent, and suggestive of a 'stay-at-home' who got out of going on campaign (cf. 1625–6). δεσπότηι: indirect object after βουλεύειν, rather than with οἰκουρόν.

1226. The line interrupts the flow and could well be interpolated.

1228–30. The beginning of Cassandra's description of Clytemnestra as a bitch—the paradigm of shamelessness (see Intro. § 9.2)—is greatly vexed, and several approaches are available.

(1) D–P translate the OCT reading '(He) does not know what kind of detestable bitch's tongue, having spoken and with cheerful disposition having prolonged her plea, shall strike by evil chance the target of secret destruction.' The two main problems are that Clytemnestra's speech at 855–913 is not primarily a piece of self-justification, and that the natural sense of ἄτης τεύξεται would be 'will meet with ruin' not 'will successfully ruin'.

(2) Keep the emendation κἀκτείνασα (the manuscripts' καὶ κτείνασα is unintelligible), but punctuate before δίκην and interpret τεύξεται not as the future of τυγχάνω but as the future middle of τεύχω. '(He) does not know what sort of hateful bitch's tongue, after speaking and with a cheerful disposition drawing out [sc. her speech], will by an evil chance wreak for herself retribution consisting in stealthy ruin.' Fraenkel roughly adopts this approach, but takes δίκην as 'like', governing ἄτης; this seems weaker. A problem now is to find parallels for the middle τεύχομαι carrying a nuance of self-interested action.

(3) Transpose 1230 to follow 1227, so that Agamemnon becomes the subject of τεύξεται, parsed more simply as the future of τυγχάνω, 'meet with'; this also forges an attractive link between the verb and τύχηι. But now the indirect question lacks a main verb, so one must posit a lacuna after 1229 (which might account for the misplacement of 1230), or emend 1229 more drastically: see M. West (1990a), 212–14, who prints λείξασα κἀγκλίνασα φαιδρὸν οὖς, δάκνει (similarly Sommerstein).

1231. θῆλυς ἄρσενος φονεύς: paradoxical, as in the oracle in Hdt. 6. 77. 2 ὅταν ἡ θήλεια τὸν ἄρσενα νικήσασα ἐξελάσῃ. θῆλυς can occasionally be two-termination (see LSJ).

1232. ἔστιν: if this word belongs with the previous line, its position in the first foot with a stop following is too emphatic for a copula. The preceding three words make a powerful verbless sentence. We would therefore print a stop after φονεύς, and an aposiopesis after ἔστιν, to give it a different emphasis: 'She is— What hideous beast would I be correct to call her?' For the motif of correct naming, see 681–90 (on Helen), 784–7 n., *Cho.* 997.

1233. ἀμφίσβαιναν: a legendary snake with a head at both ends. Snakes return as an important image for both Clytemnestra and Orestes in *Choephoroe*: see Garvie (1986), 107.

1233–4. For the six-headed monster Scylla see *Odyssey* 12. 85–100. (The Scylla of *Cho.* 613–22 is a separate figure.) ναυτίλων βλάβην is particularly apt since Agamemnon's command of ships and sailors has been emphasized throughout the play so far.

1235–7. Conceivably the 'mother of Hades' was a fairytale figure who is not otherwise known, but more likely the words mean a 'hellish mother' (cf. 1115 δίκτυον … Ἄιδου, 'hellish net'). She is 'raving, and breathing truceless war against kinsmen'; but θυ(ί)ω 'rave' also suggests θύω 'sacrifice', as in 1118 where Agamemnon's death was a θῦμα. The reference to motherhood suggests that Clytemnestra's cause is to avenge Iphigenia's death, which is not otherwise referred to in this scene. Similarly παντότολμος recalls 221, and suggests that Agamemnon's 'all-daring' behaviour in sacrificing his daughter will find its counterpart in Clytemnestra's revenge. The military metaphors in 1235 and 1237 make Clytemnestra intrude on Agamemnon's world, and oppose the description of Aegisthus as an οἰκουρός (1223–5 n.).

The echo of 1118 goes further. ἄσπονδον Ἄρη is similar to στάσις ἀκόρετος there, and 'How she raised a triumphal shout!' (probably referring to Clytemnestra's jubilant prayer as Agamemnon entered at 973–4, and cf. 28, 587–97) recalls the *ololygē* which the στάσις was to raise at Agamemnon's sacrifice. This line therefore repeats the implication that Clytemnestra in some sense embodies the house's στάσις (1119–20 n.). See further Zeitlin (1966), 647–53.

1238. δοκεῖ δὲ χαίρειν: cf. the Coryphaeus' warning to Agamemnon about unreliable appearances at 793–8.

1239. 'And (it is) all the same if I fail to persuade (you) of some one of these things. For what (difference could it make)?' For the elliptical idiom τί γάρ, cf. 1138–9 n.

1241. γ': omitted by e.g. West, but if right it has an exclamatory force (Denniston 130): 'you'll say with pity "How all too true a prophetess!"'

1242–5. As at 1106, the Coryphaeus has understood Cassandra's allusion to the feast of Thyestes, whom he now names for the first time; but the references to the cowardly lion and serpentine bitch and their future actions still elude him.

1243. ἀληθῶς οὐδὲν ἐξηικασμένα: a compressed way of saying 'truly (expressed, and) without any images', i.e. without the hybrid animal metaphors of 1223–38.

1245. ἐκ δρόμου πεσὼν τρέχω: the metaphor of 1184–5 is reversed. The Coryphaeus, no longer Cassandra, is a running dog who has lost the scent (literally 'fallen off the track').

1246–7. The dreadful words 'Agamemnon's death', placed in the operative positions at the beginning and end of the verse, have been spoken at last, after the careful reticence with which the Watchman, Herald, and Chorus expressed their forebodings, the malevolent ambiguities of Clytemnestra's speeches, and Cassandra's veiled prophecies from earlier in this episode. The Coryphaeus is appalled: literally 'Lull your mouth, rash woman, into well-omened speech' (εὔφημον proleptic). This typifies the important assumption in Aeschylus' dramaturgy that words have power to influence events and must be spoken with care (Intro. § 6), which here contrasts with Cassandra's focus on the fatalistic view that τὸ μέλλον ἥξει (1240).

1248–9. 'But a healer is *not* in attendance at this utterance,' i.e. Agamemnon's death will come, with or without *euphēmia*. Compare 1199 παιώνιον for 'curative' speech; Fraenkel perhaps rightly sees an underlying reference to the παιάν, a cry used proactively to avert disaster. The reading Παιών (Apollo the Healer) seems too specific for the flow of the passage, especially the Coryphaeus' characteristic response: '*If* it is going to happen it cannot be cured, but I pray that somehow it does not happen.' For the Chorus's desperate prayers, cf. Introduction at n. 76, and especially 255 which follows on a statement that τὸ μέλλον ἥξει.

1251–3. In ἀνδρός the Coryphaeus shows that he has totally missed the point, as in 1253 with the masculine τοῦ τελοῦντος. In fact,

Cassandra has repeatedly referred to the murderer as feminine. She responds: 'You have been knocked extremely far from my prophecies.' As in 1245 the metaphor seems to derive from hunting with hounds, where ἀποκοπῆναι could mean 'to lose the scent'.

1254–5. 'And yet I understand Greek speech all too well!' The earlier issue of whether Cassandra knows Greek (1060–3) recurs with an ironic twist. 'Yes, and so do the Delphic declarations, but they are still obscure.'

1256–94. The Coryphaeus' reference to Delphi provides an appropriate cue for Cassandra's final paroxysm of prophetic frenzy, where she calls once more on Apollo. In this third and final long speech, Cassandra prophesies her own death. She then divests herself of the prophet's apparel which has brought her no benefit, an action in which (as in her impending slaughter) she sees Apollo himself at work. Then from 1279 she introduces a new point which points forward to the *Choephoroe*: vengeance for herself and for Agamemnon will come in the return of a wandering exile (Orestes). Cassandra concludes with a resolve to face death, and a prayer that it will be speedy.

1256–7. The hiatuses, the rather weak ἐπέρχεται δέ μοι, and the appearance of ὀτοτοῖ in trimeters all arouse suspicion. Wilamowitz plausibly suggested that Cassandra begins with four independent exclamations:

> παπαῖ·
> οἷον τὸ πῦρ ἐπέρχεται·
> ὀτοτοῖ·
> Λύκει᾽ Ἄπολλον, οἲ ᾽γώ.

A scribe unfamiliar with such bold use of *extra metrum* interjections would have altered the text. **Λύκει᾽**: the resonance of the title is obscure—perhaps 'wolf-slayer' (cf. 1259, Soph. *El.* 6–7) or 'averter of evils' (cf. the similar contexts for the epithet at e.g. *Sept* 145, Soph. *OT* 203, *El.* 645).

1258–9. Cassandra reverts to the language of riddles. Clytemnestra is again described as a paradoxical beast, a 'two-footed lioness'. Agamemnon is therefore a noble lion. Aegisthus is now a stealthy wolf, perhaps suggested by Λύκει᾽ in 1257 (see 1223–5 n.). ἀπουσίαι (dat. sing.) expresses the temporal circumstances.

1260–3. 'As if brewing a poison, she will add into her anger a reward for me too: she boasts [ἐπεύχεται: not 'prays'], as she sharpens a sword for a man, to exact a payment consisting of murder [i.e. that of Cassandra] in return for his bringing me.' Cassandra's death is what Agamemnon will pay for bringing her home; ἐμοῦ μισθόν is ambiguous (a reward paid by, to, or for Cassandra), but clarified in ἀντιτείσεσθαι ἐμῆς ἀγωγῆς. Her murder will be an extra ingredient in Clytemnestra's wrathful retribution, which she is brewing like a witch as poison against Agamemnon. The idea of Clytemnestra pouring Cassandra's death into the mix may recall Cassandra's own image at 1137 ἐπεγχέαι. Cassandra implies that bringing home a concubine and displaying her publicly (950–5) is something for which Agamemnon must pay. However, Clytemnestra does not express sexual jealousy, nor quite imply that he must be punished for infidelity (see 1438–47); contrast the very different treatment of the same topic at Euripides *Electra* 1030–40.

κότωι: often emended to ποτῶι, but the 'drink' image is already implied in φάρμακον, and a reference to Clytemnestra's anger (especially over Iphigenia: cf. 155 Μῆνις) is apt since that is her human motivation. Her anger is metaphorically the vessel in which she is mixing her retribution. **φάσγανον:** Aeschylus gives Clytemnestra a sword (borrowed from Aegisthus: *Cho.* 1011). The audience may have expected her rather to wield a hatchet, which is her means of defending Aegisthus from Orestes in art from *c.*560 BC, and appears in a scene of Agamemnon's death on the Dokimasia Painter's crater (see Intro. § 3.3), and in later literature.

1264–7. In response to the prospect of her imminent death, and in a powerful act of sacrilege, Cassandra flings off her prophetic insignia. The details of what these are and what is happening cannot be pinned down, but such an important action cannot go unexplored. We mention three approaches:

(1) Three items are involved. (*a*) Her staff is mentioned in 1265 (poetic plural σκῆπτρα), and must have been an important element in the actor's appearance, movement, and gesture up to this point. It may be golden, like that of Apollo's priest Calchas in *Iliad* 1. 15, or wooden and adorned with laurel. (*b*) Woollen bands hang around her neck (1265). (*c*) Cassandra's χρηστηρία ἐσθής (1270) is a special robe worn over her other dress referred to by 1264 τάδε, with the first καί in 1265 meaning 'and'. Cassandra is often depicted wearing an *agrēnon*, a loose-knit (netlike) shawl. In this

case, 1266 σέ may refer to the robe which she rips off one-handed (διαφθερῶ), and then discards along with the staff and the bands (1267–8, plural imperatives). The opposition between σέ μέν and the plurals is grammatically abrupt, but probably defensible in performance where there may have been a pause after 1266 (where a full stop would be better) as the physical actions continue.

(2) No robe is involved. χρηστηρία ἐσθής is 'prophetic garb', and covers the staff and στέφη, as does 1264 τάδε; this is followed by a comma, and the first καί in 1265 means 'both'. In 1266, she snaps the staff, which must be made of a brittle wood rather than metal; the plurals in 1267–8 refer only to the στέφη. Conceivably, Euripides had this in mind when Cassandra discards her στέφη and uses ἴτε at the start of *Troades* 451.

(3) Both these interpretations assign slightly awkward stage-actions to διαφθερῶ ('destroy', not merely 'sully'). Some scholars—for instance Macleod (1975), 202–3—delete 1266 as interpolated, and so eliminate that problem. Then return to (1) or (2) according to taste.

Macleod (loc. cit.) usefully points to the contrast between Cassandra's destruction of clothing and Agamemnon's in the preceding episode.

1267. ἴτ’ ἐς φθόρον: a strong expression, like 'Go to hell!'. **πεσόντα γ’ ὧδ’ ἀμείψομαι:** 'Now that you are *lying* there, I shall pay you your due like this.' ὧδ’ suggests some physical action, such as trampling on the στέφη. We marginally prefer ἀμείβομαι (see app. crit.).

1268. ἄτης ... πλουτίζετε: 'make ... rich in ruin'. Compare πλουτεῖν + genitive, 'to be rich in'.

1269–72. After πλουτίζετε there is a pause and a change from violent anger to the pathos of realization. Cassandra recognizes the hand of Apollo in the actions she has just performed.

For †μέτα† read μέγα, 'greatly'; cf. e.g. *Eum.* 113, where it also qualifies a participle at line-end. μάτην can be defended as an adverb qualified by οὐ διχορρόπως. 'and after observing me mocked greatly even in this apparel, by friends turned foes [i.e. her Trojan kinsmen], in unambiguously futile fashion ...'. The last words imply that the Trojans were wrong to mock Cassandra's prophecies, indeed (by contrast to their ambiguities) unambiguously wrong—a neat irony.

1273–4. The participles ἐκδύων and ἐποπτεύσας are not followed by a main verb. The simplest solution (e.g. Fraenkel) is to assume an anacoluthon: after 1272 Cassandra in her troubled state breaks into a new sentence with herself as subject. 'I endured being called a wretched starveling beggar, as though I were a roaming gatherer of alms.' These lines elucidate the bitterness which lay behind 1195. For ἀγύρτρια, see the contemptuous use of ἀγύρτης to Tiresias at Sophocles *OT* 388.

1275. Cassandra switches from her previous abuse at Troy (1270–4) to what Apollo is *now* doing for her at Argos. The rhetorical juxtaposition ὁ μάντις μάντιν suggests that Apollo might have shown his ward more sympathy.

ἐκπράξας: 'having undone' (cf. LSJ ἐκπράττω II). To avoid a tautology with the following line, the point is probably that Apollo had undone her status as a prophetess.

1277–8. 'Instead of my father's altar a butcher's block awaits me, made bloody with the hot preliminary slaughter of (me) having been cut down.' Instead of assisting in sacrifices at the ancestral royal altar at Troy, Cassandra will be sacrificed herself, cut as on a humble chopping board. The πρόσφαγμα is the blood-offering to a dead person's soul before their funeral: Cassandra's blood will therefore be shed after Agamemnon's, but before his burial. The image of an ἐπίξηνον recurs significantly at *Cho.* 883, where a household slave predicts that Clytemnestra's head is about to be struck off near one.

1279. 'Yet we shall not lie dead without honour [i.e. vengeance] from the gods.' The language may evoke the legal formula ἄτιμος τεθνάτω, 'Let him die dishonoured' applied to outlawed murderers who could be killed without the killer facing a murder trial (Demosthenes 9. 44). Cassandra and Agamemnon do not have this status, so Clytemnestra and Aegisthus will not get off scot-free.

1280–1. 'For another in turn shall arrive as our avenger'; τιμάορος is predicative. Line 1281 then heralds the prophecy of Orestes' return with marked alliteration (π/φ, τ). Euripides seems to pick up the rare word ποινάτωρ at *El.* 23, 268 (also of Orestes).

1282. φυγάς is nominative singular (not the accusative plural of φυγή). Orestes' words at *Cho.* 1042 φεύγω δ' ἀλήτης τῆσδε γῆς ἀπόξενος, of his exile *after* the matricide, provide an unusually marked example of how Aeschylus refers between the plays of the *Oresteia*.

1283. κάτεισι has the specific sense 'return from exile' (LSJ s.v. II).
θριγκώσων (future participle expressing purpose) is an architectural
metaphor of completion: the θριγκός is the highest course of
bricks in a wall. Orestes' matricide will therefore be the end-point or
'coping-stone' in the structure of crime.

1284 [1291]. Hermann's transposition of this line here (it is irrele-
vant after 1290) makes sense of the infinitive ἄξειν which follows.
But a divine oath of Orestes' return is not mentioned elsewhere in
the trilogy, and one could also omit the line and read ἄξει.

1285. Literally 'that his laid-out father's supine state will bring him'.
This is how Agamemnon will be displayed after 1372.

1286. ὧδ' ἀναστένω: a reference not to the delivery of the immediately preceding lines but to 1269–78. From now on, Cassandra's tone
will be more resolute.

1288. πράξασαν: 'having fared'. See 369 n.

1288–9. 'and (since those) who captured the city are coming out of
the situation like this in the judgement of the gods'. Agamemnon
and the Herald took the gods' 'judgement' to be directed against the
Trojans, but it now redounds to Agamemnon.

1290 [1289]. ἰοῦσ' ἀπάρξω: Page's emendation of ἰοῦσα πράξω; but
ἀπάρχω ('lead, start off') usually applies to a dance or, in the middle,
to a sacrifice. Others defend the manuscripts. If πράξω means 'I will
act', the switch of meaning in πράσσω from 1288 is jarring. If it
means 'I will fare', one could understand *how* Cassandra will fare
from the echo of 1288—as Troy fared, i.e. lethally.

1291. Now or just before, Cassandra turns her back to the audience
in order to greet the house as the gates of Hades, i.e. as ones which
one cannot leave alive. This line is a possible cue for the palace doors
to be opened (see Intro. § 5.1). Cassandra probably only
begins to approach the palace at 1295. The length of the walk, though
interrupted at least twice, suggests that she starts from well forward
in the *orchēstra*. For the details of her movements see Taplin (1977),
320–1 and the notes below. Her walk can be compared and contrasted with Agamemnon's over the purple garments (see e.g. 1298
πατεῖς with 957 πατῶν): his steps were taken in hubris and in
ignorance of his impending fate; Cassandra faces her own death with
the humility of a victim willingly advancing to be sacrificed.

1292–4. Cassandra prays for a well timed and well aimed (καίριος)
blow, which will kill her instantly, ' . . . so that I may close this eye of
mine without a struggle, as the blood flows in an easy death'.

ἀσφάδαιστος is used similarly at Sophocles *Ajax* 883. αἱμάτων is, unusually for this noun, plural for singular.

1295–8. Now Cassandra moves slowly towards the palace 'like a god-driven cow', a term for a sacrificial victim who approaches the altar without human compulsion. **μακρὰν ἔτεινας**: the echo of 916 μακρὰν γὰρ ἐξέτεινας prompts us to compare and contrast the different types of impressive speech exhibited by Cassandra and Clytemnestra (see Intro. at n. 93). **εὐτόλμως**: this apt description is picked up by the emphasis in 1302.

1299. Cassandra may by now have reached the steps up to the stage, assuming they existed at this date (Intro. § 5.1). She probably turns back to address the Chorus. **χρόνον πλέω**: 'for more time' i.e. 'for any longer'; accusative expressing duration.

1300. The Coryphaeus picks up on Cassandra's thought and the word χρόνος. 'But the *last* moment of one's time is particularly esteemed.' For a similar use of πρεσβεύομαι compare *Cho.* 631 'Of crimes, that of Lemnos πρεσβεύεται in story'.

1303. **ἀκούει ταῦτα**: 'has this said of him'; cf. 468–9 n.

1304–5. The Coryphaeus' *gnōmē* (marked with τοι) that 'dying with glory is a χάρις' is intended to comfort. But it inspires a single line of lamentation for Priam and Cassandra's brothers, whose 'glorious' deaths have been anything but a favour. For the genitives σοῦ and τέκνων expressing the cause of the exclamation ἰὼ πάτερ, see Smyth § 1407.

1306. We must assume that since 1305 there has been a pause as Cassandra silently turns to approach close to the palace doors, then suddenly recoils in horror. It is unusual for such stage movements not to be signalled at all in the libretto. West (followed by Sommerstein, Collard 2002) therefore transposes 1313–15 to follow 1305, so that 1315 ἰὼ ξένοι motivates 1306. But those two words in their transmitted position aptly introduce Cassandra's call to the elders to witness what she is about to suffer, and should remain there along with 1313–14 (see the note). We would rather welcome the unconventional nature of the transmitted text, which would make the stage business all the more striking. However, there is the further possibility that a cry such as ἔα has fallen out before 1306.

1307–12. The Coryphaeus assumed that Cassandra was afraid (1306), but her exclamation is rather of disgust at the reek of dripping blood (1309, 1311); scholars such as West and Sommerstein who read φῦ φῦ and ἔφυξας are probably correct. The Coryphaeus takes the smell as normal at animal sacrifices, but for Cassandra it is like the noxious vapour from a tomb. The Coryphaeus' response is grimly understated: 'It is not Syrian splendour for the house that you are describing', i.e. not the frankincense which might accompany a splendid sacrifice.

1313–14. The words fit excellently after the preceding lines— Cassandra will overcome her repulsion and enter the charnel house. She moves right up to the doors, then turns back one last time.

1315–19. The appeal ἰὼ ξένοι is like the cry to bystanders which was required by Attic law at the time of a violent action, in order to secure evidence of it later in a court. Cassandra calls on the elders to witness that she is not making a fuss about nothing, and that she is presently to be killed; 1317 τόδε refers to her present ill-treatment as a whole. In 1317–19 she envisages a future trial of Orestes (which will be staged in *Eumenides*, though not in Argos), where he must answer for his violence after matching the deaths of Cassandra and Agamemnon with those of Clytemnestra and Aegisthus. The Chorus's testimony will be relevant in justifying Orestes' homicides.

1316. The meaning of δυσοΐζω is uncertain—perhaps just 'be distressed at', or more specifically 'screech οἲ in terror'. In the latter case, θάμνον ὡς ὄρνις may be attached rather loosely as if δυσοΐζω were transitive, which would be possible if the comparison were proverbial. The bird appears to be fearful that a bush which is in fact harmless contains a predator or trap.

1319. δυσδάμαρτος: genitive, not nominative.

1320. ἐπιξενοῦμαι ταῦτα: another verb of uncertain meaning, but probably 'I make this claim of guest-friendship on you'.

1321. μόρου is genitive expressing cause of an emotion (cf. 1117–18 n.). The Coryphaeus' last words to Cassandra echo his first (1069–71) and pity is the keynote of the scene's conclusion. The ancient *hypothesis* to the play (lines 13–14 as printed in the OCT) records that critics following the principles of Aristotle's *Poetics* admired the whole scene with Cassandra 'as containing shock and a good deal of pity'.

1322–3. The emphasis in ἐμὸν τὸν αὐτῆς makes the point that Cassandra is in the unusual position of having to chant her own funeral lament, since there will be nobody else to do it for her.

1323–4. The sun is also invoked by characters who are about to die at Soph. *Ajax* 845–51, Eur. *Iph. Aul.* 1506–9.

1324–5. The emendations in the app. crit. yield a good sense: δεσποτῶν τιμαόροις | ἐχθροὺς φόνευσιν τὴν ἐμὴν τίνειν ὁμοῦ, 'that my enemies pay my master's avengers [with δεσποτῶν a poetic plural] for my murder at the same time'. Distinguish φόνευσιν (acc. of φόνευσις) from φονεῦσιν (dat. pl. of φονεύς).

1326. εὐμαροῦς χειρώματος: 'an easy conquest', in apposition to the general idea of δούλης θανούσης.

1327–30. These beautiful lines are Cassandra's lament for humanity in general. Success in life (such as Agamemnon's) can only be likened to an insubstantial shadow, while misfortune (such as Cassandra's) is suddenly closed by total annihilation—'a wet sponge with its strokes destroys the drawing'. σκιᾶι τις ἂν πρέψειεν: a sensible emendation for the manuscripts' σκιά τις ἀντρέψειεν. πρέπω 'liken' fits the artistic metaphor in 1329, unlike Porson's more conservative emendation σκιά τις ἂν τρέψειεν, 'a shadow might divert'. εἰ δὲ δυστυχῆι: for εἰ + subjunctive replacing ἐάν + subjunctive in verse, cf. e.g. 1338, 1340.

1330. καὶ ταῦτ᾽ ἐκείνων: the two pronouns might be referred to the preceding δέ- and μέν-clauses respectively, i.e. Cassandra pities the annihilation of the unfortunate more than the insubstantial nature of success. But a more telling alternative is that ταῦτα refers to the whole human predicament, and ἐκείνων to her fate and Agamemnon's as described before. Then Aeschylus would end this scene with a line which represents his tragedy as a universal situation, not just concerned with particular heroes of the legendary past (cf. the thought in 1341–2).

Choral Anapaests (1331–42): The catastrophic moment of Agamemnon's death has all but arrived. The transition between Cassandra's exit and the king's cries from within the palace is marked by a short passage of anapaests, as immediately before the murder of Aegisthus at *Cho.* 855–68. The argument runs: 'No man can have enough of prosperity and success, and Agamemnon has returned home with great success; but if in so doing he has become involved in a chain of crime and punishment, what human could boast of a destiny that is free from harm?' The question amounts to a protest of despair against Agamemnon's imminent death and the tragic situation which it exemplifies.

1331–2. 'For all mortals, faring well is insatiable in nature,' i.e. no human is ever content with the prosperity they have. For ἀκόρεστον compare 1002. ἔφυ is gnomic aorist.

1332–3. δακτυλοδείκτων ... μελάθρων: describing the kind of prosperous house which people point out with their fingers. The genitive with εἴργει expresses separation. ἀπειπών: 'saying "No"'.

1334. "μηκέτ᾽ ἐσέλθῃς τάδε" φωνῶν: 'saying "Don't come in here [τάδε] again!"'. But we prefer to end the speech at ἐσέλθῃς, and take τάδε to refer back to the words slightly redundantly, as in *Cho.* 313–14 "δράσαντι παθεῖν" τριγέρων μῦθος τάδε φωνεῖ.

1335. καὶ τῶιδε: the focus returns to Agamemnon, who illustrates the general truth just enounced.

1338–40. The different events of the series articulated by Cassandra are incorporated in just three lines. προτέρων refers to Thyestes' children whom Atreus killed, and thus Agamemnon's inherited guilt in Aegisthus' eyes. In τοῖσι θανοῦσι θανών, 'dying for those who have died', the past dead are most obviously taken as the innocent victims of the Trojan war, of whom Iphigenia is the prototype; this is Agamemnon's self-inflicted guilt. His death in turn must ordain 'retribution consisting of other deaths', i.e. those of Clytemnestra and Aegisthus.

1341–2. τίς ... βροτῶν ... φῦναι: ring composition with 1331–2 ἔφυ πᾶσι βροτοῖσιν. δαίμονι: here personifies a man's πότμος or τύχη which follows him through life. τάδ᾽ ἀκούων: the participle emphasizes the importance of the verbal, audible medium of this story, as is apt for the tragedy. But τάδε also looks forward: after their anguished question, the Chorus at once *hear* Agamemnon's death-cries.

Fifth Episode (1343–1576), including *epirrhēma* (1407–1576):
1343–71. Agamemnon cries out from inside the stage-building. Again Aeschylus is putting the relatively new theatrical architecture to good use; these may or may not have been the first offstage cries, but they were memorable enough for Sophocles to allude to them at *Electra* 1415–16, where Clytemnestra dies.

That a king's blood should be shed by his own wife marks disharmony in the order of nature and society. Aeschylus dramatizes this shattering moment by disrupting the corporate personality of the Chorus which has played such a crucial part in the play so far (Intro. § 7); it is quite exceptional for a chorus to speak as individuals in disagreement. We now see and hear twelve old men, no longer a united body but debating agitatedly between themselves. Choreographically, the ordered symmetry of the parodos and first three stasima is now probably replaced with less formal movement.

The reactions in 1344 and 1346–7 are marked off by being in trochaic tetrameters, whose headlong rhythm ($-\cup-\times$) effectively conveys excitement and agitation. We can assume that they were spoken by the Coryphaeus. The iambic couplets which follow at 1347–71 will have been delivered by each of the twelve choreuts, the final one by the Coryphaeus again in a call to order. The elders are, broadly speaking, torn between breaking in at once to confront the murderers *in flagrante delicto*, or a more cautious approach.

1343–4. καιρίαν: the stem is repeated in the following line. As at 1292 it suggests a well-aimed and so mortal blow; but it also marks that this is a critical moment of action. See also 1372. **ἔσω**: probably 'deep inside me', but West obelizes, and an alteration such as Weil's **πλευρῶν ἔσω** 'inside my ribcage' produces a more common use of the word. **πληγὴν ... οὐτασμένος**: 'wounded by a blow'; an example of a passive verb being able to govern a cognate accusative.

1345. δευτέραν: sc. πληγήν.

1346. οἰμώγμασιν: causal dative, 'to judge by the groans'.

1348. τὴν ἐμὴν γνώμην: the noun is used of a 'motion' or formal proposal.

1349. κηρύσσειν βοήν: 'to proclaim a shout' to gather public help.

1351. σὺν νεορρύτωι ξίφει: 'while the sword is freshly flowing', sc. with blood.

1353. μὴ μέλλειν δ᾿ ἀκμή: '(It is) a moment to avoid delay.'

1354–5. 'It is easy to see (what is happening): their prelude is that of people enacting signs of tyranny for the city.' This elder, like the speaker of 1362–3, assumes that there are several conspirators.

1356–7. Literally 'Of course, since we are lingering: but those who trample the repute of delaying on the ground [locative πέδοι] are not asleep with their (right) hand.' The reputation of procrastination derives from proverbial wisdom such as **σπεῦδε βραδέως** (so Sommerstein), or our 'Look before you leap'. The conspirators have 'trampled' such principles by seizing their opportunity, whereas the Chorus is not doing so.

1358–9. 'I do not know what plan I should hit on and speak. It is the part of the doer also to arrive at a plan', i.e. 'If we are going to act, we need to have arrived at a plan, and I have not.' λέγω is a deliberative subjunctive. The aorist τὸ βουλεῦσαι denotes the moment of decision, as distinct from the process of taking counsel.

Auratus' emendation πάρος ('beforehand') is easier than πέρι (adverbial: 'about the matter').

1360–1. 'I too am of this opinion': if they rush in armed only with words, it will not bring Agamemnon back to life (this being a caricature of the ambitious attitude of the second, third, and fifth speakers). Compare 1018–21 for the important idea that bloodshed is irremediable.

1362–3. 'Are we really going to prolong our lives and yield like this to these disgracers of the house as our rulers?' ἡγουμένοις is predicative. The suggestion is that they risk life and limb by rushing indoors.

1365. 'For death is less bitter [literally 'riper'] than tyranny.'

1366–7. 'Shall we really then divine by evidence from *groans* that the man has perished?' The genitive absolute, unusually, represents ὅτι ὁ ἀνὴρ ὄλωλεν. The scepticism about whether the signal is clear evidence reminds one of 479–82, and possibly the same choreut spoke both; see also Goldhill (1984*a*), 88. The thought is echoed by the next speaker.

1370–1. The Coryphaeus sums up the discussion: they need a plan before they can act, and knowledge before they can plan, so their first move should be to investigate the actual state of affairs.

ταύτην: sc. γνώμην. **πάντοθεν πληθύνομαι:** an obscure phrase, though the basic point is clear. πληθύνομαι should mean 'I am filled' or 'I am multiplied'. The former could be a metaphor from a voting urn representing a particular opinion, which is filled from all sides when there is consensus. The latter might suggest that people on all sides are duplicating his opinion. On either interpretation, the Coryphaeus assumes a consensus which does not in fact seem to exist. Alternatively, either sense of πληθύνομαι may (*pace* D–P) be interpreted via the Herodotean phrase πλεῖστός εἰμι τὴν γνώμην, 'My preferred opinion is . . .' (e.g. 1. 120. 4), after which πάντοθεν could mean 'for every reason'. **κυροῦνθ' ὅπως:** if this is equivalent to the indirect question ὅπως κυρεῖ, it is unparalleled. Sommerstein's explanation (see n. 291 to his edition) is attractive: the Coryphaeus begins to say 'to know that he is dead', but euphemistically stops short: 'to know that he is—however'.

The text does not imply a stage direction, but we might imagine the Chorus-members leaving their irregular grouping in the *orchēstra* to form up in a horizontal line, facing the steps of the palace. They start to advance but are forced to a halt as, in contrary motion, the doors are opened and the *ekkyklēma* is rolled out on to the raised platform in front of the *skēnē* (Intro. § 5.1). Now we see Clytemnestra triumphantly standing, sword in hand, over the corpses of Agamemnon and Cassandra. (The *ekkyklēma* convention simply blurs over the question of whether we are indoors or outdoors for the remainder of the play.) Agamemnon's body lies in a low narrow trough (1540 δροίτη), shrouded in a blood-stained covering which is described in 1382 as a 'limitless net' and in *Cho.* 999, where the same prop must be used again, as a κατασκήνωμα. The latter suggests 'the vast tent-like ceremonial robe which Agamemnon would expect to put on after the bath to wear at the banquet' (Garvie 1986, 328). The tableau may well suggest a perverted lying-in-state (πρόθεσις), with the bloodstained robe in place of a clean shroud, and the trough in place of a bier: see Seaford (1984) on this connection.

1372–98. In this *rhēsis* of triumphant defiance Clytemnestra renounces further pretence and describes her killing of Agamemnon. Such gory detail is normally associated with messenger-speeches in Greek tragedy, but Clytemnestra delivers them herself, like one possessed as she relives her blows and even her joy at the blood spurting onto her from her husband's wounds.

1372–3. καιρίως: for καίριος speech see 1030–3 n., and for the stem applied to Clytemnestra's actions see 1343, 1344. Her earlier speeches have included not only her insincere professions of love and loyalty, but also the loaded language which she has malevolently deployed against Agamemnon throughout. Now she will feel no shame in 'saying the opposite' of those professions and ambiguities.

1374–6. 'How else, when pursuing enmity against foes supposed to be friends, could one set the nets of harm around, (at) a height too great to leap out of?' ὕψος is loosely apposed to ἀρκύστατ'. At 358–9 Zeus used Night as a 'covering' net for the capture of Troy, with similar language; here, Clytemnestra makes it clear that *words* have been her prime weapon in the entrapment of Agamemnon.

1377–8. Clytemnestra has thought long (πάλαι ... παλαιᾶς emphatically repeated) and hard about the final struggle (ἀγών) of her feud arising from the sacrifice of Iphigenia, but the moment has come in the end. For γε μήν see Denniston 347.

1380–1. οὕτω . . . ὡς + infinitive is a consecutive clause, with 'this too I shan't deny' parenthetical.

1382. ἄπειρον ἀμφίβληστρον: the noun describes a net which ἀμφιβάλλεται—a verb regularly used of clothing too. The adjective suggests 'inescapable' rather than 'limitless' in size. In *Od.* 8. 340 δεσμοὶ ἀπείρονες is used to describe the net used by Hephaestus to entrap Ares and Aphrodite; and Agamemnon's death-robe is a χίτων ἄπειρος in Sophocles fr. 526. In some sources Clytemnestra used a robe without holes for arms or neck (see Intro. § 3.3 for one example), but Aeschylus does not describe it so precisely.

1383. περιστιχίζω: 'I hang round about'—a term from hunting with nets. After the true aorists of 1379–80, Clytemnestra switches to five historic presents mixed with only one aorist (1383 μεθῆκεν), which contributes to the vividness of the account. The verb should be spelled περιστοχίζω (M. West 1979, 107). **πλοῦτον εἵματος:** 'richness of raiment', implying that the robe was splendidly dyed, skilfully woven in several colours, or heavily embroidered.

1384. παίω δέ νιν δίς: the actor can very effectively mime the blows to the rhythm of these punchy words.

1385. αὐτοῦ: 'on the spot', not 'his'.

1386–7. Clytemnestra's third and extra blow is like the third libation to Zeus the Saviour at a feast. We may recall the feasts where Iphigenia sang the τριτόσπονδος paean at her father's table (246). In a ghastly parody of this, Clytemnestra pays her thank-offering (εὐκταίαν χάριν) to the 'underworld Zeus', i.e. Hades, in the form of a libation of blood. There is also an implication that the libation accompanies a prayer (εὐχή), that the νεκρῶν σωτήρ will keep Agamemnon's soul safely removed from the living. The nexus of ideas is followed up in *Choephoroe*, to Clytemnestra's detriment: the spirit of Agamemnon is formally conjured up to return from the dead; and the third 'libation' of blood is in fact Orestes' matricide (577–8; cf. 1073 where the Chorus describes Orestes as a τρίτος σωτήρ).

1388. ὁρμαίνει: if the reading is right, the verb must mean that Agamemnon 'makes his own soul speed forth', in agonizing gasps. But Hermann's ὀρυγάνει, 'belches out', is attractive.

1389–90. σφαγήν is used unusually in the sense of a 'spurt' of blood of the kind which follows on σφάξις. Then ἐρεμνῆι ψακάδι, 'with a dark spray', is peculiarly gruesome; ψακάς (normally 'drizzle') sets up the following image.

The lines made a strong impression: Sophocles imitated them in describing Haemon's death at *Ant.* 1238–9: καὶ φυσιῶν ὀξεῖαν ἐκβάλλει ῥοὴν | λευκῆι παρειᾶι φοινίου σταλάγματος. Ps.-Euripides *Rhesus* 790–1 may be a less thoroughgoing reminiscence.

1391–2. 'as I rejoiced no less than the sown corn (rejoices) at the Zeus-given γάνος [i.e. rain] during the labour of the bud', i.e. when the grain is about to burst from its sheath. γάνος is something bright, particularly a liquid (see LSJ), and a *mot juste* here because related to γάνυμαι, 'I rejoice'.

The magnificently luxuriant image may have been inspired by *Iliad* 23. 597–9 'And his heart was warmed, like dew on the ears of a ripening crop,' but goes well beyond it. Agamemnon's blood, like rain, is owed to Zeus' benevolence. Clytemnestra compares herself to a husk of corn about to 'give birth', with reference to the motherly rage at the root of her action. Personally, we would hesitate about the further step of interpreting the image in terms of ejaculation (Moles 1979).

1393–4. We do not think West's grounds for transposing these two lines to follow 1398 are sufficient. In delivery, 1393–8 work well as they stand: after the ecstatic climax in 1392, Clytemnestra involves the Chorus in her triumph, before a final build-up towards 1398 in vindictive self-justification. πρέσβος Ἀργείων τόδε: see 855 n. χαίροιτ' ἄν, εἰ χαίροιτ': a scornful parody of the Coryphaeus' politeness at 1049 (see n.).

1395–6. 'If it were possible to pour a libation over a corpse appropriately, these things [acts of bloodshed] would be just—no, more than just.' The first ἦν = ἐξῆν. For δικαίως ἦν instead of δίκαιον ἦν, cf. *Iliad* 7. 424 διαγνῶναι χαλεπῶς ἦν. For corrective μὲν οὖν, see 1090. Clytemnestra returns to the image of blood as libation from 1386–7. Her point is that libations directly over corpses are not usual. In fact, the appropriate ones, poured over the corpse's tomb, are made for Agamemnon in the first part of *Choephoroe*. There may also be an allusion to a libation after an animal sacrifice, given that Clytemnestra has 'sacrificed' Agamemnon: see O'Daly (1985), 11–12.

1397–8. The libation image now leads on to that of the mixing-bowl from which libations were poured before the guests at a feast themselves drank. Agamemnon has filled a κρατήρ with 'enormous [τοσῶνδε, describing size more than quantity here] and accursed crimes'. ἀραίων, like the image of the third libation (1386–7 n.), recalls Iphigenia from the parodos: see 237 φθόγγον ἀραῖον. But Agamemnon has had to drain the whole mixing-bowl of curses himself, rather than returning to a feast of celebration.

1399–1400. The Coryphaeus' first reaction is one of amazement at Clytemnestra's boldness of *speech*, not yet at what she has done. For the principle that 'It is not right to boast over dead bodies' see *Odyssey* 22. 412.

1401. 'You make trial of me, supposing that I am a thoughtless woman.' As in e.g. 278 and 348, Clytemnestra reacts defensively against the Chorus's sexism, i.e. their particular horror that a wife should gloat over a husband like this. She may be a γυνή, but she is not ἀφράσμων and can still be fearless (1402) and define the situation (1404–6).

1403–6. The four consecutive lines with enjambment, each followed by a pause after the first foot, contribute to the build-up of the sentence.

1403. Understand a first εἴτε before αἰνεῖν (cf. 532–3 n.). Clytemnestra denies any verbal power to the Chorus's denunciations, although in the ensuing lyric exchange her attitude does yield to its pressure.

1406. δικαίας τέκτονος: cf. Calchas' prophecy of a νεικέων τέκτονα ... οὐ δεισήνορα in 151–3.

1407–1576. There follows an *epirrhēma*, a dialogue (often, as here, quite confrontational) where the Chorus sings agitatedly, while an actor speaks. The Chorus attacks Clytemnestra and laments Agamemnon. Its attempt to assign blame for the murder elicits a succession of responses from Clytemnestra, during which, in a remarkable passage of psychological development, her mood of triumph gradually cedes to a frightened realization that she will have to pay in turn for her own crime. For further summary of the train of thought, see the introductory comments on each turn in the dialogue. There is an interesting interpretation in Foley (2001), 202–34.

Clytemnestra first has two iambic speeches, answering the Chorus's first strophic pair. Then from 1448 the structure of the interchange becomes more complex. The Chorus is given three strophic pairs, but each also contains a largely anapaestic ephymnion

immediately after the strophe. All three ephymnia start with ἰώ
by way of lamentation, and the second (the lament for Agamemnon)
is given centrality in the sequence by being repeated after its
antistrophe too. Clytemnestra's responses also change form after
1448, switching to recited anapaests. For detail on the Chorus's
rhythms see Appendix § 5; the leitmotif of syncopated iambics as a
vehicle for the theme of sin and retribution becomes more and more
insistent as Clytemnestra advances towards her appreciation of what
lies ahead.

As a possible staging, Clytemnestra may initially remain on or
close to the *ekkyklēma* while the Chorus denounces her; it may
be grouped on either side of the rear of the *orchēstra*. The second
strophic pair and Clytemnestra's switch to anapaests suggest a
change of arrangement: the Chorus moves down the *orchēstra*
at 1448 for a more personal wish for death, and Clytemnestra
joins it for her rebuttal at 1462; at this point the visual pattern
would be broadly similar to the *kommos* with Cassandra (1072–
1177). For the staging at the movement's conclusion, see after
1570–6 n.

1407–11. In agitated dochmiacs, the Chorus suggests that
Clytemnestra must have been driven mad to 'take this sacrifice
upon yourself', by eating a poisonous plant or (apparently)
drinking seawater. They declare that she deserves exile (see
Intro. § 4.1).

1409–10. The OCT implies that the 'people's curses' occurred in the
past. It is more convincing to remove the comma after θύος and
place the question-mark after ἀράς. The (future) curses become a
second object of ἐπέθου, and the three ἀπο- compounds belong
together in a second sentence. The resulting asyndeton between 1409
and 1410 balances that between 1428 and 1429 in the antistrophe.
ἀπέδικες ἀπέταμες 'You have cast away, you have severed' then has
no object expressed, but something like 'civic order' is suggested
by the context and the following ἀπόπολις. On public curses see
456–8 n.

1411. 'a mighty source of loathing to the citizens', in apposition to
'you'. The loathing has a religious element of 'abomination':
Clytemnestra's action bears a horrific pollution, which causes their
determination to exile her (cf. 1485).

ὄβριμον is rather unexpected: the adjective normally refers to
military might.

1412–25. Clytemnestra first asks why she should be punished by exile, when Agamemnon was not for the reckless sacrifice of Iphigenia. Then she defiantly warns the elders not to expect her to be a pushover; she is ready to respond.

1413. The queen sarcastically picks up the threats from 1410–11. δημόθρους also recalls 883, where she appeared to consider the *vox populi* powerful; now she is dismissive of it.

1415–17. 'who, giving it no special value, as if it were the death of an animal from his sheep which abound in fleecy flocks, sacrificed his own daughter'. μόρον is probably accusative in apposition to the idea of sacrifice in the main clause (cf. 225–6 n.). μήλων φλεόντων could be a partitive genitive as in the gloss, or genitive absolute.

Although Iphigenia has often been a submerged presence during the play, this is the first open reference to her death since the parodos.

1418. ἐπωιδὸν Θρηικίων ἀημάτων: 'a spell for Thracian puffs'. Clytemnestra bitterly downplays the relevance of Artemis' anger and Agamemnon's military obligations, to make his treatment of Iphigenia as far removed as possible from her feelings as a mother: the sacrifice was an absurd spell on impersonal winds, and ones all the way from Thrace.

1420. μιασμάτων: killing one's daughter incurs a religious pollution which is potentially contagious to one's kin and associates. In myth, such pollution is commonly treated by exile to a different state where it becomes open to purification. Thus Agamemnon should have been exiled *in absentia*, for the good of Argos. On the logic, see R. Parker (1983), esp. 118. However, as soon as 1432 Clytemnestra will revert to the view that full justice for Iphigenia's death was only achievable by the death penalty.

1420–1. For the courtroom image of δικαστής see Introduction § 4.1. ἐπήκοος has a rather elevated register, and is also used in legal contexts at *Cho.* 980, *Eum.* 732.

1421–5. The OCT should probably be construed 'And I tell you, make such threats in the knowledge that (I am) equally prepared for (someone) who wins by force to rule over me, but if the god ordains the reverse, you will be taught—though late in the day—to recognize good sense.' ὡς introduces a genitive absolute, sc. μου, and τινά or σε must be understood as the referent of νικήσαντα. ἐκ τῶν ὁμοίων introduces two possible outcomes for which Clytemnestra is equally ready (being defeated, or defeating and punishing them), and which are expressed in clauses which do not balance precisely.

However, the accusative and infinitive after $\pi\alpha\rho\epsilon\sigma\kappa\epsilon\upsilon\alpha\sigma\mu\acute{\epsilon}\nu\eta\varsigma$ is difficult, so Sommerstein posits a lacuna there, and repunctuates so that $\acute{\epsilon}\kappa\ \tau\hat{\omega}\nu\ \acute{o}\mu o\acute{\iota}\omega\nu$ is taken with $\nu\iota\kappa\acute{\eta}\sigma\alpha\nu\tau$': 'having won from equal terms', i.e. in a fair fight.

1426–30. The Chorus continues to attribute Clytemnestra's proud thinking and arrogant words to mental derangement, but this time warns that she will have to pay for blow with blow, i.e. it foresees a lethal retribution rather than a penalty of exile (contrast 1407–11).

1426. $\mu\epsilon\gamma\alpha\lambda\acute{o}\mu\eta\tau\iota\varsigma$: a *hapax* of uncertain meaning, probably in the range 'of outrageous, proud, ambitious plots'. Sommerstein's 'of great cunning' fits poorly with the reference to madness which follows immediately. $\pi\epsilon\rho\acute{\iota}\phi\rho o\nu\alpha\ \delta$' $\acute{\epsilon}\lambda\alpha\kappa\epsilon\varsigma$: Clytemnestra's hectoring words ($\lambda\acute{\alpha}\sigma\kappa\omega$: cf. 614 n.) attract comment as well as her $\mu\hat{\eta}\tau\iota\varsigma$. They are $\pi\epsilon\rho\acute{\iota}\phi\rho o\nu\alpha$, which here means 'haughty' (not 'sensible', as often of Penelope in the *Odyssey*).

1427–8. Literally 'Just as your mind is mad with the circumstance involving dripping gore, the drop of blood is conspicuous on your eyes.' Clytemnestra's bloodshot eyes bear witness to her frenzy, which also involves dripping blood. Bloodshot eyes are also a symptom of madness in e.g. Euripides *Heracles* 933, Hippocrates *Sacred Disease* 15, Vergil *Aeneid* 4.643.

1429–30. The theme of retribution is strikingly sounded in the alliteration of τ through these two lines, and the prominent position of $\acute{\alpha}\nu\tau\iota\tau o\nu$ (which could be construed with $\sigma\epsilon$ or $\tau\acute{\upsilon}\mu\mu\alpha$, without affecting the general sense). For the thought cf. *Cho.* 312–13 $\acute{\alpha}\nu\tau\grave{\iota}\ \delta\grave{\epsilon}$ $\pi\lambda\eta\gamma\hat{\eta}\varsigma\ \phi o\nu\acute{\iota}\alpha\varsigma\ \phi o\nu\acute{\iota}\alpha\nu$ | $\pi\lambda\eta\gamma\grave{\eta}\nu\ \tau\iota\nu\acute{\epsilon}\tau\omega$.

1431–47. Clytemnestra now affirms that she is not 'bereft of friends', and has nothing to fear while Aegisthus—whose name is now unveiled for the first time in the play—presides in her house. Fraenkel (p. 678) may well be right to suggest that she is protesting too much, and trying by force of words to paper over her first feelings of nervousness.

The open reference to her own adultery leads abruptly at 1438 to her view of Agamemnon's relationships with women whom he enslaved. Her focus is more on how Cassandra's demise gave her a peculiar satisfaction, than on how she felt especially hurt (let alone jealous) of another woman's presence in the bed which she despised.

1431. Here Clytemnestra expresses herself with peculiar solemnity. The use of indicative $\acute{\alpha}\kappa o\acute{\upsilon}\epsilon\iota\varsigma$ is even more assertive than an

imperative would be. Similarly, θέμιν implies the religious right-
eousness of the oath which follows. The word ὅρκιον is particularly
used of oaths following on a sacrifice: cf. 1433 ἔσφαξα.

1432–3. Clytemnestra swears by personifications of Justice and Atē,
and an Erinys who is evidently the spirit which demanded retaliation
for Iphigenia's sacrifice. Unlike the girl herself, the Justice for
Iphigenia is personified as τέλειος—fully grown, i.e. perfectly fulfilled. In Atē, Clytemnestra refers specifically to the spirit embodying
Agamemnon's ruin; on this see Introduction § 4.3.3. Clytemnestra
does not yet see that Justice and the Erinys for Agamemnon will
presently assail her in turn. αἷσι: probably instrumental, 'through
whose agency'. Alternatively, it could mean 'for whom', and present
the three personifications as the recipients of Clytemnestra's
'sacrifice' of Agamemnon.

1434–6. ἑστίας suggests that μέλαθρον is to be taken literally: 'The
expectation of fear in no way treads my hall, while on my hearth
Aegisthus kindles the fire,' i.e. performs the family sacrifices as the
lord of the household. However, the word-order suggests taking
φόβου with μέλαθρον not ἐλπίς (see Fraenkel pp. 827–8), so a
different interpretation of 1434 should at least be considered: 'My
expectation in no way treads the hall of fear.'

   Aegisthus' name, revealed here at last, is emphatically delayed to
the end of its clause in enjambment.

1437. Aegisthus' behind-the-scenes role is developed in an image
which is suggestive about their relationship: he is a shield, a tool for
securing Clytemnestra's warlike courage.

1438–9. The transition to Agamemnon is very abrupt, and possibly a
line or two has dropped out. λυμαντήριος is applied to Aegisthus
at *Cho.* 764, and its cognates suggest a rapist or seducer (Euripides
Hipp. 1068, *Bacch.* 354). γυναικὸς τῆσδε therefore refers to
Cassandra not Clytemnestra herself, and would have been
clarified with a gesture (cf. 1440 ἥδε, 1441 τοῦδε for such deictics).
Agamemnon is also called (literally) the 'thing which soothed
the Chryseides at Troy'. The plural implies that there were many
concubines who were just like Chryseis. Aeschylus may be recalling
the *Iliad*'s only reference to Clytemnestra, which occurs when
Agamemnon expresses his preference for Chryseis at 1. 113.

1440–7. Clytemnestra's contemptuous abuse of Cassandra has
three targets: her concubinage, her role as a prophetess, and her
servility.

1443. ἰσοτριβής: a conjecture for the manuscripts' ἰστοτρίβης: Cassandra 'wore out' the ships' benches 'equally' with Agamemnon. However, the word is not especially abusive, and ἰσο- is not elsewhere compounded with verbs, so one is better off trying to interpret the manuscripts' reading. The mention of ships' benches suggests ἱστός 'mast', which is used as slang for an erect penis at Strabo 8. 6. 20. An obscene pun, 'his mast-rubber', would be most unusual in Greek tragedy and especially shocking from female lips, but fits the sexual context, and the word's position at the climax of a sentence of abuse. For others this breakdown of tragic register is too extreme: for example M. West (1990a), 220–1 interprets the adjective instead as 'one who must spend time at the loom' (LSJ ἱστός II)—a contemptuous reference to her servile status, like αἰχμάλωτος. See further Introduction § 9.1, Borthwick (1981), Sommerstein (2002), 151–7.

ἄτιμα δ' οὐκ ἐπραξάτην: the verb is dual. The pair slept together in life, and have now paid for their actions by lying together in death (cf. *Cho.* 975–6). One might hear an ironic echo of 1279, where Cassandra said that she and Agamemnon would not die ἄτιμοι, i.e. that their deaths would be avenged.

1444–5. Clytemnestra refers to the idea that a swan only breaks into song just before its death, and perhaps harks back to the prophetess' earlier silence during 1035–70. This is the last of a long series of animal-comparisons for Cassandra: see 1050–2 n.

1446. φιλήτωρ: strikingly applied here not to a man as (in the Greek view) the active participant in sex, but to Cassandra. As in the use of the neuter μείλιγμα in 1439, Clytemnestra is presenting Agamemnon as unmanly and passive.

1446–7. 'And for *me* she has brought along a side-dish to the luxuriance of *my* bed.' In other words, Clytemnestra will relish sex with Aegisthus all the more now that she has the satisfaction of having murdered Agamemnon's πιστὴ ξύνευνος (1442). Clytemnestra is nowhere else as explicit about the physicality of her adultery. The word παροψώνημα is particularly apt, since it can mean a 'bit-on-the-side', i.e. a lover (see Aristophanes fr. 191 παροψίς): Agamemnon intended Cassandra as his παροψώνημα in that sense, but Clytemnestra has reclaimed her as a source of pleasure for her *own* bed. See Pulleyn (1997).

Fraenkel, followed by West and Sommerstein, preserves the manuscripts' χλιδῆς, and assumes that εὐνῆς is a marginal gloss which displaced another word (e.g. τερπνόν). Clytemnestra's χλιδή might then be her luxuriating in revenge, rather than having a sexual connotation.

1448–1576. For the change in form and staging at this point of the *epirrhēma*, see 1407–1576 n.

1448–61. The Chorus turns from denouncing Clytemnestra and prays for death, since its φύλαξ εὐμενέστατος has 'lost his life at a woman's hands, after enduring many things through a woman's doing'. That woman is Helen; cf. 448 ἀλλοτρίας διαὶ γυναικός. The sisters Clytemnestra and Helen are thus aligned as destructive forces, and the words set up the ephymnion where Helen is related to a personified Discord in the house, and Agamemnon's death is seen as her crowning achievement.

1448–51. The question with ἄν basically expresses a wish: 'May some fate come.' Cf. 622–3 n. **δεμνιοτήρης:** here implying a slow death where people watch at the bedside. **φέρουσ᾽ ἐν ἡμῖν:** ἐν with φέρουσα is very odd. Weil's φέρουσα χἠμῖν, 'bringing to me too' (as well as to Agamemnon), or Emperius' φέρουσ᾽ ἂν ἡμῖν (repeating the ἂν in 1448) are attractive emendations.

1455. **ἰώ:** West reads ἰώ <ἰώ>, scanned as four longs as at 1489. This produces a more powerful dimeter, and the other ephymnia both begin with a doubled cry.

1456–7. πολλὰς ψυχάς: inspired by *Iliad* 1. 3 πολλὰς δ᾽ ἰφθίμους ψυχάς, though there the warriors at Troy are killed by Achilles' anger rather than Helen.

1458–61. 'Now you have crowned yourself with a final [or 'perfect'], memorable crown, because of [Agamemnon's] uncleansable blood. To be sure, there was back then a strong-built spirit of discord in the palace, a source of misery for a man [or 'husband': Menelaus].' The simplest emendation of the unmetrical δὲ τελείαν is Wilamowitz's τελέαν; for the construction of the feminine adjectives, see 219–21 n. With the OCT's ἧ τις, Helen is closely linked to the discord in the house, but the manuscripts' ἥτις (after a comma) makes Helen *personify* discord, and may be stronger.

    ἐν δόμοις Ἔρις ἐρίδματος: the double wordplay suggests that the *hapax* ἐρίδματος is related to δεμ-/δομ- ('strongly built'), not to δαμ- ('strongly destroying'). A comma should separate the phrase from ἀνδρὸς οἰζύς, which is in apposition.

1462–7. Clytemnestra responds that the elders do not need to pray for death or to turn their wrath on Helen and call her a 'destroyer of men' (Clytemnestra quotes their words from 1456–7; cf. 1413).

1465. ὥς: an indirect statement can follow because angry *words* are implied in the phrase 'divert your anger'.

1467. ἀξύστατον ἄλγος: literally 'a pain that does not stand together', [~ ξυνίστημι] i.e. a painful wound that will not close.

1468–74. Clytemnestra did not respond to the Chorus's allusion to an Ἔρις in the house (1461). It now expands on a closely related idea, that one cause of Agamemnon's murder is the δαίμων of the house (Intro. § 4.3.4), which has assailed the two sons of Atreus, working through their wives. This pains the elders (καρδιόδηκτον ἐμοί). They imagine the spirit, embodied in Clytemnestra, to be like a raven: it stands over Agamemnon's body (like a raven scavenging) and squawks a tuneless hymn of triumph. The description in 1468 recalls that of Cassandra's personal δαίμων in 1175.

1468–9. διφυίοισι Τανταλίδαισιν: 'the two-natured offspring of Tantalus'—Agamemnon and Menelaus, of whom Tantalus was a great-grandfather. For 'two-natured' see 122 δύο λήμασι δισσούς.

1470–1. Literally 'are exercising equal-souled power from women', i.e. working through women whose souls are equally wicked or bold (ἰσόψυχος could imply either quality). ἰσό-ψυχον contrasts with δι-φυίοισι: the brothers were different but the sisters were alike (cf. 1448–61 n.).

1473–4. It is probably better to read the masculine σταθείς, since the change of subject to Clytemnestra is very abrupt. The Chorus switches (as often happens) from addressing the δαίμων to describing it in the third person (cf. ἐπεύχεται); they perceive Clytemnestra, who is the one actually standing and 'crowing' over the body, as its human vehicle. ἐκνόμως: for the motif of 'tuneless song' compare in particular 1142, 1187. ἐπεύχεται: the verb was also used of Clytemnestra's 'glorying, boasting' at 1262 and 1394.

At the end, an iambic word has dropped out. Plausible suggestions include Kayser's δίκας and Sommerstein's χαρᾶς, both defining ὕμνον.

1475–80. Clytemnestra, now more on the defensive, eagerly seizes on the idea of the family's δαίμων in an attempt to shift responsibility away from Helen and herself.

1475. ὤρθωσας: contrast the idea of 'turning off course' in 1464 ἐκτρέψῃς.

1476. τριπάχυντον: 'thrice-fattened', presumably with reference to the blood of Thyestes' children, Iphigenia, and Agamemnon. In *Cho.* 577–8 and 1065–7 an alternative triple succession elides Iphigenia but includes the murder of Clytemnestra and Aegisthus as the climactic horror.

1478–80. The δαίμων is the source of 'lust of lapping blood', which (like τριπάχυντον) recalls the picture of the blood-drinking Erinyes in 1188–9. The emendation νείραι, if correct, would be locative dative: the desire is nurtured 'deep in the belly' of the family-members—a poetically rather than physiologically apt location for a thirst. The construction of νέος ἰχώρ is unusual, since γίγνεται rather than ἐστί must be supplied: 'new pus arises'. ἰχώρ is strictly the 'serum' which seeps from an open or purulent wound, rather than 'blood' (LSJ).

(Other scholars prefer to change νείραι into a verb, and to punctuate before τρέφεται rather than after: West suggests τείρει or νεῖται, 'comes'.)

1481–8. The Chorus despairingly reaffirms the power of the δαίμων and traces it to Zeus, the cause and worker of all. Chthonian and Olympian deities are working to the same end, as usual in *Agamemnon* and *Choephoroe* (Intro. § 4.2).

1481. ἦ μέγαν †οἴκοις τοῖσδε†: the metre does not correspond with 1505. We are attracted by Weil's ἦ μέγαν <ἦ μέγαν> οἴκοις, with ὡς μὲν ἀναίτιος εἶ <σύ> in the antistrophe. The doubling in Weil's reconstruction, and repeatedly below (1483, 1485, 1489, 1494), is a typical feature of Greek laments.

1482–4. αἰνεῖς must mean 'tell of' here, rather than 'praise'. αἶνον then follows as an accusative in apposition to the idea of the preceding clause. However, West's reading δαίμονα ... αἰνεῖς—φεῦ φεῦ, κακὸν αἶνον—ἀτηρᾶς τύχας ἀκόρεστον yields a better sense: 'You tell of the *daimōn* (alas—an awful tale) who cannot be sated with ruinous misfortune.'

1486. πανεργέτα: Doric genitive ending in -ā (Attic would have -ου).

1489–96. The second ephymnion (repeated after the antistrophe at 1513–20) shows the Chorus leaving its focus on the δαίμων and Zeus as the divine sources of what has happened, and confronting its emotions in a lament for Agamemnon which shows its φιλία (1491). Their questions in 1489–91 are a typical start for a Greek threnody. The robe in which Agamemnon is lying is a 'spider's web' prepared by Clytemnestra. They denounce his death as ἀσεβής and δόλιος.

1490. δακρύσω: deliberative aorist subjunctive, not future indicative (cf. 1491 εἴπω).

1494. κοίταν τάνδ' ἀνελεύθερον: internal accusative after κεῖσαι— literally 'You lie in this unfree lying'. ἀνελεύθερος suggests both the physical restraint of the robe, and the change in status from noble to subjected.

1496. ἐκ χερός: rather vague, and Enger's suggestion to add <δάμαρτος> at the end of 1495 would strengthen the meaning and motivate Clytemnestra's response at 1497–9 more clearly, but see Appendix ad loc. **βελέμνωι:** normally a missile, but the audience can surely see Clytemnestra's sword which she still holds (cf. 1379). The effect is therefore rather different from Cassandra's riddling reference to the same object as a δόρυ in 1149.

1497–1504. Clytemnestra introduces the ἀλάστωρ, another figure similar to the house's δαίμων and spirit of ἔρις: she presents Agamemnon's death as the due exacted for the Thyestean banquet by the 'the ancient fierce avenging spirit, taking the likeness of the wife of this corpse'. Clytemnestra does not even say 'taking my likeness': she is detaching herself as far as possible from the murder (contrast 1404–6), and stresses not her main personal motive—the sacrifice of Iphigenia—but the guilt which Agamemnon inherited from Atreus.

1497–9. αὐχεῖς: 'you confidently imagine'; see 506 n. **τῆιδ' ἐπιλεχθείς:** we would read μηδ' ἐπιλεχθῆις, which is what the manuscripts suggest: 'But do not take into account the idea that I am Agamemnon's wife.' Since μηδέ only rarely connects a prohibition to a positive statement, something like <μὴ τοῦτ' εἴπηις> may have dropped out before it. With this reading, it may also be better to punctuate 1497 as a question.

At first sight Clytemnestra's point seems to be 'You are wrong to think that I am Agamemnon's wife; rather, I am the ἀλάστωρ in the form of Agamemnon's wife,' which raises the absurd question 'So where is the real Clytemnestra?' But a better interpretation of the logic is available: 'You are wrong to treat it as *important* that I am Agamemnon's wife—what is important is that the ἀλάστωρ invaded this body.' This still suggests exculpation, which is how the Chorus takes Clytemnestra's words at 1505, and expresses her resistance to the Chorus's preceding words, in particular the charge that Agamemnon's death was ἀσεβής.

(The OCT and D–P give Page's emendation τῆιδ' ἐπιλεχθείς, 'reckoning in this way, viz. that . . .'. But we agree with Fraenkel that ἐπιλέγομαι should mean 'take into account the idea that' rather than 'reckon that'; cf. Hdt. 7. 49. 5, 52. 2.)

1503–4. The ἀλάστωρ of Atreus 'offered this man in requital, by sacrificing [aspectual aorist] an adult in addition to [ἐπι-] young ones', i.e. Agamemnon in addition to Thyestes' children. The allusive antithesis in τέλεον νεαροῖς adds a final distancing touch to Clytemnestra's self-defence.

1505–12. The Chorus insists that Clytemnestra herself must still accept responsibility, while conceding that 'The ἀλάστωρ inherited from his father might have been your accomplice.' Slaughter in revenge for Atreus' crime is (still) on the march.

1505. For the text see 1481 n., where we supported the addition of <σύ> at the end of this line: the emphatic pronoun emphasizes the Chorus's point.

1507. πῶ πῶ: for πόθεν, 'How could that be?' The adverb is characteristic of Western Greek dialects (D–P).

1509–12. 'Black Ares is forcing his way with additional [ἐπι-] streams of kindred blood, to wherever in his advance he will provide justice for the clotted blood [πάχναι] of devoured boys.' Ares is the god of slaughter, black with the μέλαν αἷμα of a fatal wound (cf. 1020). The future παρέξει makes it clear that the inherited liability for the Thyestean banquet, embodied in the ἀλάστωρ, will not stop with vengeance on Agamemnon, but will be extended to the further horror of Orestes' matricide.

1513–20. The repetition of the ephymnion reinforces the Chorus's sense of personal grief.

1521–9. Motivated, perhaps, by the menacing implications of the Chorus's words at 1509–12, Clytemnestra starts to justify herself at a more personal level. Her bitter tone here and at 1551–9 suggests a shift of emphasis from her as the embodiment of the δαίμων to a person of womanly instincts with a renewed sense of injury as a mother. As her previous response to the ephymnion seemed to focus on the word ἀσεβής, here she more clearly focuses on the phrases κοίταν ἀνελεύθερον and δολίωι μόρωι. She does not think that Agamemnon's death was 'unworthy of a free person'; and he himself perpetrated a 'treacherous act of ruin' when he killed the innocent Iphigenia; he has duly paid the price for his crime.

1522b. A lacuna is implied by the absence of a second οὔτε-clause (presumably about δόλος) and the metrically unwarranted hiatus between γενέσθαι and οὐδέ. For possible supplements, see app. crit., and M. West's <δόλιόν τε λαχεῖν μόρον οὐκ ἀδίκως·> (1990a, 222–3).

1523–4. οὐδὲ γὰρ οὗτος: 'For did not he *too* . . . ?' **δολίαν**: an allusion to the story (e.g. *Cypria*, Eur. *Iph. Aul.*) that Agamemnon summoned his daughter to Aulis on the false pretext of marrying Achilles. See also 227 n.

1525. ἀλλ᾽: the particle signals the logic that Agamemnon practised δόλος, so has no right to boast. **ἐμὸν ἐκ τοῦδ᾽ ἔρνος ἀερθέν**: ἀείρω may have its normal sense 'lift up', whose relevance would be clarified by the echo of 234 ἀερδήν during the description of Iphigenia's sacrifice: Agamemnon acted unfairly towards her while she was raised aloft. Other editors assign ἀείρω a very unusual sense—either 'conceive' (Fraenkel, Sommerstein) or 'rear' (D–P).

1526–7. Page's text makes sense; the rhythm is unusual for anapaests, but this may be significant (see Appendix § 5). Fraenkel, West, and Sommerstein prefer ἄξια δράσας ἄξια πάσχων as an independent clause, where the underlying idea would be 'his deeds deserved his suffering' (not 'his deeds and his suffering were both worthy'). However, there are not close parallels for this use of doubled ἄξιος. If the first ἄξια were correct, one would need a lacuna after Ἰφιγένειαν, including a main verb. In any case, Iphigenia is named for the first time in the play in this personal context.

1527–8. For ἐν + genitive, 'in (the house) of', see LSJ s.v. I 2. Agamemnon should not vaunt himself in the underworld as a blameless king. See by contrast *Cho.* 355–62, where in the *kommos* conjuring up Agamemnon's shade the Chorus envisages his prominence and friendship with the shades of those who died gloriously.

1529. ἅπερ ἦρξεν: 'the start which he made'. The sacrifice of Iphigenia is the crime by which Agamemnon initiated events. However, West and others prefer Bourdelot's emendation ἔρξεν, 'did' (from ἔρδω), and this produces the appealing chiastic pattern δράσας/πάσχων, τείσας/ἔρξεν.

1530–6. In the final strophic pair, the syncopated iambic trimeter which has been associated with sin and retribution (Appendix § 4.4) comes to predominate as the Chorus in ἀμηχανία contemplates the bloody future with a series of forceful metaphors.

1530–1. φροντίδος στερηθεὶς ... μέριμναν: here στερέω governs the accusative, which has a subjective genitive: 'deprived of thought's resourceful care' (D–P).

1533–4. Literally 'I fear this [τόν has a demonstrative nuance] bloody, house-shaking beat of rain; the drizzle is ceasing.' Bloodshed in the house is turning from a drizzle into a noisy cloudburst and, like a very severe rainstorm, makes the house totter.

1535–6. We prefer the alternative restoration quoted in the app. crit.: δίκαν ... θηγάνει ... Μοῖρα: 'Moira is sharpening justice on other whetstones for another deed of harm.' Justice is metaphorically a sword; βλάβας is Doric gen. sing. (and might be construed with θηγάναισι, though the colometry rather suggests it goes with πρᾶγμα, as in the gloss). The phrasing then accords closely with the expression of the same basic idea at *Cho.* 646–7: Δίκας δ' ἐρείδεται πυθμήν, προχαλκεύει δ' Αἶσα φασγανουργός, 'The anvil of Justice is firmly set, and sword-making Aisa [=Moira] is forging bronze in preparation.' For Moira as a spirit of retribution, see Introduction at n. 43.

1537–50. The idea of burial unites the thought of the Chorus's third ephymnion. It first invokes the earth into which it would have wished to pass before witnessing the sight of Agamemnon lying dead in a bathtub. This leads on to the question of the king's funeral rites. Who will perform these? It would naturally fall to the family-members, but from his murderers they would be a meaningless and insincere tribute. At *Odyssey* 11. 424–6, Agamemnon's shade mentions that Clytemnestra did not tend his corpse at all after his death. Aeschylus specifies at *Choephoroe* 429–39 that Clytemnestra mutilated the corpse and had it buried in secret.

1540. δροίτας κατέχοντα χάμευναν: Agamemnon occupies the lowly couch (χάμευνα: literally 'bed-on-the-ground') of a δροίτη, which seems to indicate a low, narrow tub, but can also mean 'coffin'. κατέχω is also appropriate to occupying a grave (as in 454). This is certainly an ἀνελευθέρα κοίτη (1518) compared with the raised bier appropriate to a royal πρόθεσις.

1544. ἀποκωκῦσαι: to 'wail aloud', in a formal threnody.

1545–6. 'and to perform to his spirit a tributeless tribute, in return for his mighty deeds'. Compare *Cho.* 42 χάριν ἀχάριτον, used very similarly of Clytemnestra's libations to Agamemnon's shade. Her tributes lack χάρις both because they are insincere, and because Agamemnon's soul gets no joy from them. ἀντ' ἔργων μεγάλων recalls the language of Greek epitaphs.

1547–50. 'Who, sending [i.e. uttering] with tears a grave-side eulogy for a godlike man, will labour in truth of mind [i.e. sincerely]?' θείωι suggests the grandeur of a Homeric hero. The 'grave-side eulogy' seems to be part of the general lament at a heroic funeral, like Andromache's speech at Hector's funeral (*Iliad* 24. 723–46).

1551–9. 'No business of yours', retorts Clytemnestra. Agamemnon *will* be buried by those who killed him, but without the lamentation of those from his house. (For this event, see *Cho.* 429–33, 439.) Instead—returning to the emphasis on her daughter from 1525–9—Iphigenia will meet her father at the ferry into the underworld, and welcome him with an embrace.

1551–2. τὸ μέλημ' ἀλέγειν τοῦτο: 'to have this care as your concern'. μέλημα is internal accusative with ἀλέγειν (an epic word which normally governs a genitive).

1553. For the vigorous 'homoeoarchon' cf. 1410.

1554. 'not to the accompaniment of wailings of those in his house'. This probably anticipates *Cho.* 444–9, where Agamemnon's other daughter Electra complains that she was excluded from her father's burial rites. Electra and Orestes do perform a belated ἐπιτύμβιος θρῆνος (*Cho.* 334–5) in the great *kommos* of the second play.

1556. θυγάτηρ, ὡς χρή: heavily ironical. It is unclear what an Athenian audience might have taken as the 'required' role of a daughter at her father's funeral in the mythical world, but the tribute which Iphigenia will pay is certainly very different: the normal honours paid by the living kinsfolk are withheld, and she will give him a 'loving' welcome on his entry to the underworld. See Fraenkel pp. 735–6 for references to Attic vases which depict such δεξίωσις by one's former companions.

1558. πόρθμευμ' ἀχέων: 'the ferry of sorrows' alludes to the river Acheron.

1559. περὶ χεῖρα βαλοῦσα φιλήσει: περι-βαλοῦσα is in tmesis. The phrase is an epicism: see Introduction § 9.1. The powerfully intimate φιλήσει ('kiss' not 'love') is left for the climactic word.

1560–6. The Chorus now accepts that Clytemnestra may have a point about Agamemnon's guilt, but the thought of the law of retribution leads them straight back to a further cry of despair in their final two lines, about the long-term future of the family.

1560–1. 'This taunt comes for taunt, and judging is a hard struggle.' Clytemnestra's taunt about Iphigenia welcoming Agamemnon to the underworld, and the denunciation this implies, *is* some form of justification which balances the Chorus's attempts to shame Clytemnestra by denouncing her guilt. This leaves it in an impasse about how to judge the case.

1562. φέρει φέροντ': a way of saying φέρει τις τὸν φέροντα with maximum focus on the balance of action and reaction. φέρω means 'despoil, plunder' (LSJ s.v. A VI 2).

1563–4. The Chorus reaffirms the ordinance (cf. θέσμιον) 'that the doer suffers'—for which see Introduction § 4.1. This, they believe, 'remains as long as Zeus remains on his throne', i.e. it is eternal and sanctioned by Zeus. Unlike the doublings of ὄνειδος and φέρω which expressed balance (in arguments about guilt and in violent acts respectively), the doubling of μίμνω emphasizes the stability of the ordinance.

1565–6. γονὰν ἀραῖον: 'the seed of the curse'. It is not enough to remove certain accursed individuals: the curse reproduces itself within the family by seeding, and could spring up again in the future. κεκόλληται: a vivid metaphor, whether it means 'is glued fast' (as in carpentry), 'is soldered fast' (as in metalwork), or 'is clamped fast' (as in the bracketing of masonry). The last option seems most attractive given the focus on the house.

1567–76. Clytemnestra is now worried. In a moving conclusion to the *epirrhēma* she acknowledges the implication of the Chorus's affirmation: *she* will be the *daimōn*'s next victim. She no longer embodies the *daimōn* herself as she has appeared to do in her speech of triumph at 1372–98 (and cf. 1472–4, 1497–1504). Rather, she wishes to make a sworn pact with it, at any material price, to let the crazed present situation be and go away to haunt another family.

1567–8. 'You have entered on this χρησμός with truth on your side.' In a remarkable admission for one who has been so defiant, Clytemnestra invests the predictions of the Chorus with the authority of an oracle.

1568–76. ἐγὼ δ' οὖν: the familiar particles once again introduce a hope against hope (34–5 n.), and the emphatic ἐγώ suggests that the δαίμων may not be so ready to bargain: 'Well, at any rate, I . . .' Thereafter, construction and interpretation are vexed.

(1) As the text stands, στέργειν must be prolative: '*I* am willing, after laying down oaths for [i.e. in a pact with] the *daimōn* of the

sons of Pleisthenes, to acquiesce in *these* things, though they are δύστλητα, and as for what (is) in the *future* [ὃ δὲ λοιπόν, adverbial] (I wish) that he leaves ...' Then δύστλητα must mean 'hard to bear', but it is hard to see how Clytemnestra can 'acquiesce' in Agamemnon's death or find it hard to bear. Furthermore the change of construction at ἰόντα is uncomfortably abrupt.

(2) Both these problems are eased if ἐθέλω is replaced by αἰνῶ. The δαίμων becomes the subject of στέργειν, and δύστλητα means 'dreadful to dare' (cf. 408 ἄτλητα). 'I recommend to the *daimōn* of the sons of Pleisthenes, laying down oaths for him, to acquiesce in *these* things though they were dreadful to dare, and as for what lies in the *future* (I recommend) that he leave this palace and wear down a different family with deaths of kindred murder.' Aeschylus also uses αἰνῶ + dative + infinitive at *Cho.* 715. Aeschylus may have recalled his words at *Pers.* 642–3 δαίμονα ... ἰόντ᾽ αἰνέσατ᾽ ἐκ δόμων. Since αἰνέω there means 'assent to' and is glossed by θέλω (Schol._B), one can imagine how ἐθέλω could have got into our passage.

Pleisthenes is another ancestor, also mentioned at 1602, to go with Tantalus (1469) and Pelops (1600). Aeschylus leaves his position in the family tree vague (for other sources see Gantz 1993, 552–5).

1570–6. The *daimōn*'s side of the bargain is to leave matters where they are and not to punish Clytemnestra in turn. Her side will be to sacrifice any amount of her possessions—'anything' will suffice once she has 'removed the madness of mutual murder from the palace'. She apparently wants to resolve the blood-feud by putting down a sum of money in compensation, but in the world of Aeschylus' trilogy, this is a forlorn hope (cf. 1008–21, Intro. § 4.1).

Clytemnestra, now a spent force in comparison with her assertive entrance on the *ekkyklēma*, probably now turns away from the Chorus and, before Aegisthus enters, adopts a visible but less conspicuous position, so that her presence can be ignored until 1654 without too much artificiality. This position may be near the *skēnē* but to one side.

Exodos (1577–1673): The closing scene of *Agamemnon* prepares for *Choephoroe*. Aegisthus enters not from the house but from a distance, down one of the *eisodoi*; he is attended by a group of armed guards. After the minimal attention paid to him in the play so far, his entry comes as something of a surprise. However, his presence in the palace as a usurper needs to be established firmly before Orestes returns both to avenge his father and to recover his patrimony (*Cho.* 301). And the lateness of Aegisthus' entrance is also central to his characterization, as cowardly behind his vindictive and bullying bluster (see Intro. § 3.4). Where we may after the *epirrhēma* feel some pity for Clytemnestra, in Aegisthus' case retribution will be humanly warranted as well as inevitable.

After he has delivered a *rhēsis* of personal victory, he is challenged by the Coryphaeus, who in this scene is treated more as a character in his own right (and who twice has speeches longer than the four lines to which chorus-leaders tend to be limited: 1612–16, 1643–8). After an altercation, Aegisthus calls on his guards, who are about to come to blows with the elders when, in another dramatic surprise, Clytemnestra intervenes to prevent it. There are no concluding lines to cover the Chorus's exit, which lends an appropriate note of incompleteness to the end of the first play (see final n.).

1577–1611. Aegisthus claims justice both in his opening line and in a series of words related to δίκη towards the end of his speech (1601, 1604, 1607, 1611), and his gruesome description of the quarrel between his father and Agamemnon's shows how he became involved in the chain of crime and punishment. As far as Aegisthus is concerned, Agamemnon has paid for the sins of the father, and in 1608–9 he proudly claims the main credit for the murder. However, there is a splendid irony in Aegisthus' failure to appreciate the consequences that await himself; he lacks the insight which Clytemnestra has acquired into the future implications of Agamemnon's murder.

1577. Aegisthus' grandiloquent exclamation echoes Clytemnestra's opening lines. In particular, the sinister associations of εὔφρων in the play (264–7 n.) may rub off on him.

1578. ἤδη νῦν: 'now at any rate'.

1579. γῆς: better taken as qualifying ἄχη, rather than with ἄνωθεν.

1580. πέπλοις Ἐρινύων: the clothing in which Agamemnon has been trapped is the 'robe of the Erinyes', since they are the agents of just retribution. Compare the Herald's similar oxymoron παιᾶνα τόνδ' Ἐρινύων (645). Sophocles *Trach.* 1051–2 Ἐρινύων ἄφαντον ἀμφίβληστρον echoes this line and 1382, in referring to the poisoned robe which Deianira accidentally sent to Heracles at the prompting of the vengeful Nessus.

1581. φίλως ἐμοί: the point would be clearer with a comma after κείμενον.

1583–4. Ἀτρεὺς γὰρ ... Θυέστην: the chiasmus rhetorically figures the opposition of the two brothers. The pattern is repeated in 1590–2, τοῦδε πατὴρ ... πατρὶ τὠμῶι.

1584. ὡς τορῶς φράσαι: the phrase would be otiose were it not that it draws attention to the partiality of Aegisthus' account. He is not speaking τορῶς, since he suppresses his father's prior adultery (1193).

1585. ἀμφίλεκτος: 'disputed', 'challenged'; cf. 881 n.

1587. ἑστίας: objective genitive with προστρόπαιος, 'supplicating the hearth'. For the importance of the hearth in supplications, as a sacred place within the house, see Gould (1973), 97–8.

1588. ηὕρετ': middle, 'found for himself'.

1589. The infinitive phrase is in apposition to μοῖραν, and explains the limited extent to which that was ἀσφαλής.

1590–3. For the four consecutive enjambed lines compare 1403–6 n. A complementary effect is the long suspense between the innocuous initial word ξένια and the horrendous final phrase apposed to it— δαῖτα παιδείων κρεῶν.

1590. αὐτοῦ: 'where he was', but Blomfield's αὐτός has a great deal more force.

1591. πατρί: perhaps remove the comma after φίλως and take πατρί with the preceding adverbs rather than as indirect object of πάρεσχε: 'with more enthusiasm than love towards my father'. This change produces a correspondence with 1581 φίλως ἐμοί.

1592. κρεουργὸν ἦμαρ: 'a day of meat-making'—ostensibly a traditional form of reconciliation involving animal sacrifices and a banquet. But κρεουργός is a sinister adjective, which does not specify what κρέας is to be eaten; Herodotus similarly uses κρεουργία in contexts of humans being 'butchered' at 3. 13. 2, 7. 181. 2.

1594–7. A corrupt passage which has been variously emended.

(1) We suggest reading ἄπωθεν, and καθημένου followed by a comma: literally, Atreus 'minced up the foot-parts and the outlying combs of the hands away from the man sitting at his own table; then he [Thyestes] in ignorance at once picked up the signless parts of them [the children, easily understood from 1593 παιδείων] and ate them—a meal (as you can see) which brought no safety to the family'. The μὲν ... δέ antithesis suggests that the obviously human parts (the hands and feet—there is no mention of the heads) have to be specially prepared out of Thyestes' sight; he is then served their mince and the rest of his children's flesh, which is not identifiably human. The victims' fingers and palms are ghoulishly described as

'combs' (κτένας, acc. pl. of κτείς). ἔσθει, like ἀμπίπτει and ἐπεύχεται below, is a historic present: see 1383 n. Finally, ἄσωτον γένει is a litotes: the meal has now caused destruction for Agamemnon.

(2) The unmarked change of subject to Thyestes seems comprehensible from the context, but some scholars have followed Dindorf's emendation ἄσημ'· ὁ δ'. In this case ἄσημ' is proleptic: Atreus minced the feet and hands 'so that they did not give a sign'. (Or he hid them, reading ἔκρυπτ'. But this is blander and presupposes an unlikely corruption.) Sommerstein also adds a lacuna before ἔθρυπτε, which he uses to assimilate the passage to Herodotus' account of the banquet of Harpagus (1. 119; see Sommerstein n. 331). But although Herodotus does model his story on the myth of Thyestes' banquet, the mild similarities of phrasing do not persuade us that he was imitating this passage of Aeschylus.

ἀνδρακάς: Thyestes is made to sit at a separate table to avoid inflicting cannibalism on the other guests. But the arrangement may also have suggested to the Athenian audience the Choes ritual on 12 Anthesterion, when they drank together, but unusually sat at individual tables. The aetiology of this ritual (i.e. the myth explaining its origin) interestingly relates it to the story of Orestes: when he arrived at Athens, still seeking purification, king Demophon accorded him hospitality but made him sit at a separate table and drink from an individual pitcher. See Euripides *Iph. Taur.* 947–60, Bowie (1993), 23–4. *Eumenides* gives a different account of Orestes' welcome, which writes out Demophon and emphasizes law and the Areopagites. But there could still be a resonance of the alternative story here.

1598. Aegisthus need not explain how Thyestes came to realize what he had done: the story is horrific enough already.

1599. ἀπὸ . . . ἐρῶν: tmesis, 'vomiting forth' (LSJ s.v. ἐράω B).

1600. Πελοπίδαις: Pelops is the father of Atreus and Thyestes.

1601–2. Thyestes prayed, 'while giving the table a kick as an associate in justice with his curse, that just so the race of Pleisthenes might be destroyed completely'. The point of οὕτως is that the family will be overthrown as the table is. This helps explain ξυνδίκως: the kick and curse are simultaneous and connected, and concern δίκη. Thyestes interestingly cites the race of Pleisthenes (on whom see 1568–76 n.), which includes himself and Aegisthus. This generates irony since Aegisthus, with his triumphalist tone, seems to ignore that he too must be implicated in the 'complete' destruction.

1603. σοι: best taken with πάρα (= πάρεστι): 'it is possible for you'. The Coryphaeus was also addressed in 1597 ὡς ὁρᾷς.

1604. κἀγὼ ... ῥαφεύς: Aegisthus arrogantly claims the credit (whether truly or not) for planning Agamemnon's murder. Whereas Clytemnestra claimed in 1406 that her hand was the δίκαιος 'builder' of the deed, Aegisthus claims to be the δίκαιος 'stitcher' of the plot. According to *Choephoroe* he is φόνου μεταίτιος (134), and lent his sword to Clytemnestra (1011).

1605. †ἐπὶ δέκ'†: some scholars accept this as a true reading: Aegisthus was the third child 'in addition to ten', i.e. Thyestes' thirteenth child. Others think that cooking twelve children is excessive and emend, e.g. τρίτον γὰρ ὄντα μ' ἔλιπε, κἀθλίωι πατρί. In most other sources, three children are killed rather than two or twelve (Gantz 1993, 550–2).

1607. This is just what we know will happen to Orestes (whose 'swaddling' is also mentioned, at *Cho.* 755).

1608–9. Aegisthus was θυραῖος, 'away from home', at Agamemnon's murder, yet he 'fastened his grip [ἡψάμην]' on him, 'after fastening together [ξυνάψας] the whole contrivance of bad counsel'. The wordplay on ἅπτω/ἅπτομαι draws attention to the carefully related series of images. ξυνάπτω is often used of knotting together threads, while in 1604 Aegisthus 'stitched' up the plot. The instrument of assassination was a piece of clothing which was woven (1580) but is metaphorically a 'net' (1611) and so knotted together. Detienne and Vernant (1978, 292–305) give an interesting exploration of the frequent connections between knots, nets, weaving, and cunning in Greek thought. **δυσβουλίας:** Aegisthus means 'of malign counsel', but the noun usually means 'ill-advised counsel'. Another touch of irony (cf. 1601–2 n., next n.).

1610. An excellent *klēdōn* (Intro. § 6). Aegisthus uses a formula for expressing unalloyed joy at achieving one's goals, by wishing for death (cf. 539). But his narrative has contained the seeds of his own downfall.

1612. 'Aegisthus, I do not revere one who behaves insolently in a bad situation.' Understand τινα with ὑβρίζοντα. (The manuscripts' ὑβρίζειν would require a different sense of σέβω: 'I do not proudly practice insolence in a bad situation.' But the more antagonistic tone is wanted.)

1613–16. After the preceding statement of his general attitude, the Coryphaeus homes in on the current situation with the emphatic σὺ ... φῄς, which is contrasted with οὔ φημι: 'You declare ... ; well, I declare ...'. The Coryphaeus threatens 'curses which bring stoning, hurled by the populace'. Compare the threat of δημο-θρόους ἀράς directed at Clytemnestra in 1409; here δημορριφεῖς nicely suggests the hurling of both stones and curses. For λεύσιμος cf. 1118. The Coryphaeus repeatedly emphasizes Aegisthus' admission in 1609 that he planned Agamemnon's murder alone (cf. 1627, 1634) and warns him of the consequences ἐν δίκηι, 'in the hour of justice'. For Athenians 'the planner is treated the same as the person who committed a crime with their hand' (Andocides 1. 94).

1617–18. 'Do *you* say that—you who sit at the lower oar, when those on the bridge command the ship?' The emphatic σύ here (and in 1625) marks the scornful tone. δορός seems better taken with κρατούντων rather than ζύγωι, and means 'ship' rather than 'plank'. Aegisthus compares the Coryphaeus to a rower challenging the helmsman who sits higher up on the stern-deck and gives orders. The metaphor of a governor of a state as the helmsman of a ship is a commonplace (cf. the derivation of 'governor' via Latin from κυβερνήτης, 'helmsman').

1619–20. Contrast 584; even Clytemnestra's threat of the 'school of hard knocks' in 1421–5 came with the alternative that they might defeat her instead (see also Intro. § 4.4). Aegisthus' intolerance of dissent contrasts with the Athenians' pride in their freedom of speech (παρρησία), and characterizes him as tyrannical. σωφρονεῖν εἰρημένον: accusative absolute, 'when showing sense is the stated task'.

1621–3. Aegisthus threatens that a hungry spell in prison will teach them to be quiet, if nothing else will. δεσμόν is nominative neuter, unusually (the usual singular is δεσμός, though δεσμά is common in the plural). This and the δύαι are 'healer-seers of the mind, most excellent at teaching even old age': καὶ τὸ γῆρας is the object of διδάσκειν rather than another subject. Apollo is an ἰατρόμαντις at *Eum.* 62. By contrast, Aegisthus' use is ironic, almost blasphemous: prison and starvation will be a 'seer' in making the Coryphaeus aware of his folly, and a 'doctor' in curing it.

1624. πρὸς κέντρα μὴ λάκτιζε: proverbial, as 'Don't kick against the pricks' is in English. Possibly the further commonplace, following on the stock metaphor of 1617–18, characterizes Aegisthus' domineering attitude.

1625. γύναι: addressed as a taunt to Aegisthus, as the stay-at-home adulterer, whereas Agamemnon is twice referred to as an ἀνήρ in 1626–7. Compare *Cho.* 304, where Orestes speaks of Argos as subject to 'two women'. **μένων:** the manuscripts' νέον, 'recently', is acceptable. It involves a mild anacoluthon whereby τοὺς ἥκοντας is changed to ἀνδρὶ στρατηγῶι when the main verb is finally chosen; there is a similar shift in e.g. Xenophon *Cyr.* 4. 3. 19, αὐτῶν apposed to πολλοῖς. (West's addition of commas after οἰκουρός and ἅμα is a useful clarification of the flow.)

1629–32. Aegisthus makes a menacing joke. Orpheus miraculously *led on* animals, trees, and rocks 'joyfully, by means of [ἀπό] his voice'—a popular myth also alluded to at e.g. Euripides *Bacch.* 561–4. By contrast, the Coryphaeus' 'silly yapping' does 'stir up' Aegisthus (understand με after ἐξορίνας), but will cause him to be *led off* to prison. Orpheus tamed wild animals; defeat will tame the Chorus. **ἄξηι:** future middle indicative, with a passive sense: cf. 170 λέξεται.

1633. ὡς δή: with this idiom the main verb has to be understood from context: '(You speak) as though . . .' The tone of δή is indignant or sceptical: Denniston 229.

1634–5. οὐκ . . . οὐκ: reinforcing the negation.

1636–7. 'Of course: the trick was clearly the woman's part.' This seems to be explained in what follows: the ancient feud with Agamemnon would instantly have put Aegisthus under suspicion. The general connection made by Greeks between women and trickery is in the background, but not (*pace* Sommerstein) the main point of 1636.

1638–42. Far from rejecting the charge of tyranny, which most fifth-century Athenians regarded with constant horror, Aegisthus announces his intention to buy support and to consign dissenters to an unlit cell (cf. 1621–3).

1640. ζεύξω βαρείαις: sc. ζεύγλαις, 'I will yoke them with heavy yoke-straps.' The ship of state (1617–18) is now a chariot of state, and its disobedient citizens will be subjugated.

1640–1. 'in no way at all a barley-fed tracehorse'. οὐ μή as an expression of strong denial is otherwise used with finite verbs, so many scholars prefer μήν or δή to μή. For trace-horses see 841–4 n.; one of their functions was to give an extra spurt at the turn in a chariot race, so they were specially fed on barley. This point paves the way for the contrast with λιμός which follows.

1643–8. Undeterred, the Coryphaeus returns to his taunt that Aegisthus was too cowardly to kill Agamemnon himself, and adds that the whole city has been polluted because Clytemnestra did it instead. Wondering how that can be put to rest, he asks whether Orestes is alive to return from exile and murder them both. Orestes' return, though predicted allusively by Cassandra at 1280–4, is now mentioned openly and explicitly for the first time. This is further preparation for *Choephoroe*, where Orestes enters at the very beginning of the following play.

1644. σύν: adverbial, 'together with you'.

1645. The line could be in apposition to γυνή (just as Clytemnestra will be called a μίασμα at *Cho.* 102) or to the general idea of γυνή ... ἔκτεινε. Either way, the point seems to be that the pollution of a wife killing a husband is worse than that of cousin killing cousin. Greek attitudes to 'degrees of pollution' in homicide were not consistent: see R. Parker (1983), ch. 4.

1646–8. Here the Coryphaeus turns away from Aegisthus (cf. the third-person reference to him in 1648), with a question addressed to the heavens. The name of Orestes displaces ἆρα from the head of the question, and thus has special emphasis. (The sentence should have a question-mark at the end.) παγκρατής: 'all-victorious', rather than the normal sense 'all-powerful' (of gods). The Coryphaeus is responding to Aegisthus' assertions of his κράτος, namely 1618 κρατούντων and 1632 κρατηθείς (Lavery 2004*b*, 64).

1649–53. The change to trochaic tetrameters marks a faster pace of delivery and mounting tension in response to the mention of Orestes (see Appendix § 2.2). Line 1649 would also be a suitable moment for the *ekkyklēma* with the corpses to be withdrawn, to leave the doorway clear for the final exit.

The distribution of 1650–3 between Aegisthus and the Coryphaeus has been disputed, but the OCT's arrangement is very satisfactory. The Coryphaeus cannot speak 1651, since the elders of the Chorus are not sword-wearers, and it is difficult to envisage that the Coryphaeus is raising a general shout for sword-wearing bystanders to rush up. The Coryphaeus can, however, speak 1650 and 1652 (retaining πρόκωπος): in both λοχῖται and πρόκωπος, he girds the other elders to fight by using military terms which are more easily applicable to their opponents. Thus Aegisthus' guards are called on to hold their swords 'hilt-forward', i.e. ready to draw (1651 πρόκωπον); in response, the Coryphaeus is also 'at the ready' as he (followed by the other elders) presents his stave forwards, in a rather futile demonstration of boldness. The contrast with 72–82, where the Chorus expressed its sense of physical weakness with reference to its walking sticks, is effective.

(Sommerstein n. 341 denies that the Coryphaeus could call his colleagues λοχῖται, and attributes 1650 to Aegisthus and 1651 to the leader of the bodyguards, who repeats Aegisthus' instruction slightly more clearly. But breaking the regular stichomythic pattern, and introducing a new speaker to utter a repetitive line, does not seem plausible.)

1649. δοκεῖς: 'you think fit', not 'you seem'; cf. 16. **ἔρδειν:** Aegisthus exaggerates the extent of the Chorus's resistance, which has been purely verbal. **γνώσηι τάχα:** a formulaic threat where the object is left menacingly vague. Fraenkel gives several parallels.

1650. εἶα δή: a vigorous 'Come on, now!'

1653. δεχομένοις λέγεις θανεῖν γε: literally ' "To die", at least, you say to people who accept it (as an omen).' Most of the Coryphaeus' words have irked Aegisthus, but he welcomes his readiness to die, and treats it as a *klēdōn* which will be translated into fact (Intro. § 6). For δέχομαι as a response to an omen, see LSJ s.v. I 2b.

(West retains the manuscripts' σε in place of γε. This may be possible, though τό would be expected with θανεῖν: 'the idea that you should die'. Perhaps compare Euripides *El.* 685 προφωνῶ ... Αἴγισθον θανεῖν, 'I declare Aegisthus' death,' though there too the text is debated.)

τὴν τύχην δ' αἱρούμεθα: 'and we choose that event', i.e. the particular outcome signified by the omen. This suggests a gesture from Aegisthus to his guards to draw their swords.

1654–6. As the guards and the Chorus are about to engage, Clytemnestra advances from the lonely background position where she has remained in silence (1570–6 n.), to address her 'dearest' Aegisthus in a moving appeal: 'Let us do no other horrors. No—even these things [i.e. the present events] are many to reap, a grievous harvest. *Enough* sorrow [partitive genitive] is already with us.' The words κακά, δύστηνον, and πημονῆς do not imply that she sees the assassination of Agamemnon as morally wrong, but she does now see the danger of retribution, and the distaste which attaches to any murder. μηδέν: might well be emended to μήκεθ', 'Let us not bloody our hands further.' Otherwise the clause would jar, since Clytemnestra has spoken of being sprayed with Agamemnon's blood (1389–90).

1657–8. Reconstruction of these two corrupt lines can only be very tentative. We suggest

στείχετ', αἰδοῖοι γέροντες, πρὸς δόμους, πεπρωμένοις
πρὶν παθεῖν εἴξαντες. <
                    > καιρόν· χρῆν τάδ' ὡς ἐπράξαμεν.

'Go home, reverend elders, and yield to fate before you suffer. <All things require their> moment: these things were necessary, as we performed them.' (And, by contrast, this is *not* the moment for the Chorus to try to be heroic.)

(1) αἰδοῖοι is palaeographically plausible, and would mark Clytemnestra's greater humility now that she has begun to presage retribution—a humility also seen in her desire to engage in diplomacy with the δαίμων (1568–76), and in 1654–6. Finally, αἰδοῖοι might form a contrast with her ironic use of αἰδοῖον πόσιν in 600. (2) The stem of πεπρωμένους is suited to appear near χρῆν, but the participle cannot qualify δόμους. Madvig's πεπρωμένοις | πρὶν παθεῖν εἴξαντες, 'and yield to fate before you suffer', is attractive: plausibly, a scribe slipped because of being reminded of παθεῖν τὸν ἔρξαντα (1564), but this important theme applies to far more serious crimes than the Chorus's taunts. (3) Metre requires the deletion of τούσδε. (4) The lacuna was posited by M. West (1990*a*), 227–8. Others emend καιρόν rather arbitrarily to an infinitive of their choice, e.g. Fraenkel's αἰνεῖν: 'You should accept these things, as we have performed them.'

1659. †ἅλις γ' ἐχοίμεθ' ἄν†: read ἅλις, δέχοιμεθ' ἄν. ἅλις is controversial, but picks up 1656 πημονῆς ἅλις and can plausibly be retained (so Fraenkel). Phrases like ἅλις τούτων are widespread as a way of calling for an end to something. This idiom is incorporated in the conditional clause: literally 'If enough-of-these-toils were to come about [i.e. if someone were to call a stop to them], then we should welcome it.' West and Sommerstein read ἄκος instead.

1660. χηλῇ: 'hoof' or 'talon', with the δαίμων envisaged as a warhorse or bird of prey respectively. πεπληγμένοι perhaps favours the former interpretation.

1661. This final line of Clytemnestra's speech is a striking climb-down from the almost feminist self-assertiveness of 348, 614, and 1401. There is pathos in the sincere humility of εἴ τις ἀξιοῖ μαθεῖν.

1662. The accusative-and-infinitive phrases here and below are used as indignant exclamations: see Smyth § 2015. †ἀπανθίσαι†, 'to pluck the flower of', is an odd metaphor to use with ματαίαν γλῶσσαν. Editors cite Blomfield's ἀκοντίσαι, 'to cast (like a javelin)', without much confidence.

1663. δαίμονος πειρωμένους: 'putting their *daimōn* [i.e. their luck: cf. 1341–2] to the test'. Aegisthus is, however, unaware that he and Clytemnestra will presently make trial of the house's δαίμων. Similarly in the following words he ironically criticizes the elders' lack of σωφροσύνη, when in comparison to Clytemnestra he lacks it himself.

1664. The manuscripts have the meaningless ἁμαρτῆτον, and lack three syllables at the end of the verse. Casaubon's ἁμαρτεῖν τόν plus Blomfield's <θ᾿ ὑβρίσαι> give reasonable sense, and it would be attractive for the verse to include the three common ethical concepts σωφροσύνη, ἁμαρτία, and ὕβρις.

1665–73. Aegisthus accepts that there will be no fighting today (1666) but the battle of words resumes until Clytemnestra's closing intervention.

1667. The Coryphaeus boldly names Orestes again. Though δαίμων can be used for a god whose identity is unknown (634–5 n.), it is more tempting here to see it as the guardian spirit of the house, mentioned in 1660 and brought to mind in 1663, who directs Orestes home as the next agent of retribution.

1668. 'I know well that men in exile feed (only) on hopes.' Aegisthus is mockingly alluding to a proverb: cf. Euripides *Phoen.* 396 αἱ δ᾿ ἐλπίδες βόσκουσι φυγάδας, ὡς λόγος.

1669. The Coryphaeus returns Aegisthus' mockery. The alliteration of π and the assonance in πιαίνου μιαίνων reinforce the defiant tone. πρᾶσσε is approximately 'Carry out what you've started'. Then πιαίνου, 'fatten yourself', picks up Aegisthus' taunt about Orestes' hunger, and taunts him with greed in return; it may also be relevant that the Greeks connected gluttony and a tendency to utter insults (Steiner 2002). Finally μιαίνων τὴν δίκην asserts that Aegisthus is *polluting* justice when he has claimed to champion it.

1671. ἀλέκτωρ ὥστε θηλείας πέλας: 'like a cock beside his hen'. The Coryphaeus is allowed the concluding insult, which is targeted at Aegisthus' pretension and belligerence towards other males.

1672–3. The last two lines of the play are Clytemnestra's desperate attempt to put a bold face on an extremely bleak outlook. After her failed attempt in 1657–61 to mollify the elders, she dismisses the Coryphaeus' jibes as 'futile barkings' (cf. 1631). She thus portrays him as a dog (see Intro. § 9.2), after he has just portrayed her and Aegisthus as hen and cock. Finally, she reasserts her own and Aegisthus' sovereignty.

A word of two syllables has fallen out at the end of each line (cf. the damaged ends of 1657, 1662, 1664). <ἐγώ> is certain, given καὶ σύ. <καλῶς> is derived from the scholiast's paraphrase. In 1673, it is also desirable to give θήσομεν an object: thus Fraenkel, who also suggests transposing to give a stronger word-order, reads <ἐγώ> | καὶ σὺ δωμάτων κρατοῦντε πάντα θήσομεν <καλῶς>. This latter leaves us admirably on the motif of a hope against hope (Intro. at n. 76), though Clytemnestra simply uses the future indicative. 'You and I, masters of this house, will manage everything—*well*.'

Final exit: the stage business can only be conjectured. Perhaps Aegisthus gives a further signal to his guards and the Chorus retreats before their swords, to exit down an *eisodos* in sullen silence. The guards might even follow them at close quarters, or they could stay on while the old men file off with the aulete in a more orderly manner. More important, however, is that we do not get the usual anapaests to see the Chorus out after the main actors have left the stage. It is therefore tempting to imagine the Chorus leaving the *orchēstra* while Clytemnestra and Aegisthus are still present in a dominant position onstage. After they have disappeared, Clytemnestra could lead Aegisthus (followed by the guards?) into the palace through the open doors, which would then be closed from within. The usurpers are in control, but we know that this is not the end of the story.

APPENDIX

Sound and Rhythm

1 Introductory

The music of poetry is part of its meaning, and the *Agamemnon* was composed to be heard, not read. To appreciate Aeschylus to the full, some sense of the grand sonorities of his verse and of its varied rhythms is essential. We urge readers to develop a skill in reciting the text aloud, so as to experience its musical dimension. Attention to the metres of the choral songs is particularly rewarding. Though their melodic line is irretrievably lost, one may attempt to recover a rhythmical 'score' with an emotive power and significance of its own.

Greek metre is based on the 'quantity' of syllables, long (−) or short (∪). This appendix assumes a knowledge of the basic rules of quantity, a useful guide for which is Raven (1962), 22–4. For pronunciation see Allen (1987), especially 177–9, and for the effects of accentuation on pitch, which can be expressive, see Probert (2003), 15–18. For much more detailed guides to Greek metre see Raven (1962), M. West (1982).

Greek tragedies are segmented according to three distinctive modes of performance, which form the basis for the next three sections: (§ 2) declamation without music; (§ 3) declamation to the accompaniment of the double *aulos* (a pipe, somewhat like an oboe); (§ 4) singing with *aulos* accompaniment.[1] As outlined below, the first two are associated with particular metres, whereas the third is more varied. § 5 then gives a line-by-line analysis of the rhythms of the play.

2 Declamation without Music

2.1 Iambic Trimeter

This was the normal medium for the spoken parts of the play, whether in the form of long speeches (*rhēseis*) or dialogue allotted to the solo actors and chorus-leader. Single lines in alternation between speakers ('stichomythia') is a common form of the latter.

---

[1] Though the last are normally referred to as 'lyric', they were accompanied by the *aulos* rather than by the lyre. For more on the *aulos* see M. West (1992), 81–107.

The trimeter consists essentially of three iambic metra in the form × – ∪ –, where '×' indicates an 'anceps' position, i.e. one which can be occupied by a short or a long syllable. Trimeters are practically always broken by a 'caesura' (word-break) in the second metron which yields two phrases of unequal length (5+7 syllables or 7+5).[2] For example:

∪ –   ∪ – – ‖ –   ∪ – ∪ –   ∪ –   (5+7)

1   θεοὺς μὲν αἰτῶ τῶνδ' ἀπαλλαγὴν πόνων

∪ – ∪ – ∪ – ∪‖– – – ∪ –   (7+5)

11   γυναικὸς ἀνδρόβουλον ἐλπίζον κέαρ

As in the dactylic hexameter, even a syllable which is short according to the rules of quantity may occupy the final ('long') position in the line. Aeschylus sometimes 'resolves' a long position into two shorts. In *Agamemnon* this occurs most frequently in the middle of the second metron (e.g. 270 χαρά μ' ὑφέρπει δάκρυον ἐκκαλουμένη). The first anceps may also be replaced with two shorts, especially if it involves a proper name: cf. 26, 28.

In practising delivery, it is important to sense the flow of the two main patterns above, and to observe the variety afforded by the frequent 'enjambments' where sense runs through into the next verse.[3]

2.2 Trochaic Tetrameter Catalectic

This metre appears briefly in *Agamemnon* at Agamemnon's murder (1344, 1346–7), and at the very end in 1649–73. Its effect is to quicken the tempo at moments of high tension. The line consists of four trochaic metra (– ∪ – ×) with word-break after the second, and 'catalexis', i.e. the removal of one syllable at the end:

–̆ ∪ –   – – ∪– –‖– ∪– – –   ∪ –

1344   σῖγα· τίς πληγὴν ἀυτεῖ καιρίως οὐτασμένος;

3 Declamation with Music (Anapaests)

These sections can be seen as intermediate in linguistic and musical register between the other two performance modes. Probably the delivery was closer to speech than to song, but the rhythm in these was more sharply defined than in the fluid spoken iambic verse.[4] The metre was originally associated

---

[2] A 'quasi-caesura', entailing an elision at the end of the third foot, is also found very occasionally, as at 605 ἥκειν ὅπως τάχιστ' ἐράσμιον πόλει. See also 943 n.

[3] For lyric iambics see below, § 4.3.1.

[4] Sung anapaests are also found. Like all sung parts of tragedy, these are distinguished by the use of a patina of Doric vowels, in particular ᾱ for η and -ᾶν for -ῶν (first declension genitive plural).

with marching songs and is used by Aeschylus in the *Agamemnon* (as in *Persae* and *Supplices*) to accompany the entrance of the chorus (40–103).

Most anapaestic lines are in dimeters with the basic scheme:

$$∪∪\acute{-}∪∪\acute{-}\;∪∪\acute{-}∪∪\acute{-}$$

(Accents mark the first syllable of the *thesis*, the 'footfall' or beat.) However, 'contraction', whereby ∪ ∪ is replaced by one long, is common. Moreover, ∪ ∪ – can be replaced with – ∪ ∪ providing that the following syllable is long. This effect, called 'dactylic substitution', gives the rhythm a backward swing while the march continues steadily, as in:

$$∪∪\acute{-}∪∪\acute{-}\;–\;\acute{∪}∪–\;\acute{-}$$
42 Μενέλαος ἄναξ ἠδ' Ἀγαμέμνων

This offers variety and often lends a special emphasis to the 'out-of-sync' words, as in the example, and repays careful attention throughout.

Each line ends with a word break, and indeed most individual metra do. A run of anapaests normally ends with a catalectic form (the 'paroemiac'), where the final syllable is removed, to provide a cadence and a rest for the voice (marked '∧'):

$$∪∪\acute{-}∪∪\acute{-}∪∪\acute{-}–\acute{∧}$$

Sometimes catalectic lines seem to be deliberately placed to articulate the argument (as in 783–809), and this too repays attention.

4 Singing with Musical Accompaniment

4.1 Structure

The main unit of composition in the sung movements of tragedy was the stanza or 'strophe'.[5] In Aeschylus, most strophes are paired with a musically corresponding 'antistrophe'. Occasionally the structure is more complex. For example, at 104–59 the pair is crowned with an 'epode' to form a triad (a common structure in choral lyric outside drama); in the fourth and fifth episodes strophic pairs are divided by iambic or anapaestic responses, and so on. Strophes are as a rule syntactically complete and one might assume an interval of, perhaps, two or four 'beats' between them, although there is a remarkable instance of runover in 237–8 (see commentary).

---

[5] Literally 'turn' (στροφή), probably referring to a notional choreographic sequence where the chorus moved around the altar or other central point in the dancing space.

A strophe consists of a succession of 'metra' (e.g. iambic, trochaic, dactylic) or 'cola'. A colon (literally 'limb') is a longer unit from the stock of common metrical patterns, to many of which names were attached by ancient metricians (see § 4.3). Strophes may also be subdivided into groups of cola, known as 'periods', within which the rules of quantity apply normally at the breaks between cola ('synaphaea'), and where a single word may run over the breaks ('dove-tailing', marked in the OCT by indentation).

Often a metrical structure can be analysed into cola in different ways (such analysis is called 'colometry'). Since line-divisions were not shown in the earliest Greek texts of choral lyric, there is no authoritative source for Aeschylus' 'original' colometry. The question is not merely one of labelling: as explained in the following subsection, different colometries may imply different rhythmic effects which the reader can choose between. But first we must confront a broader problem about the relationship of metre and rhythm.

4.2 Rhythm

The analysis in § 5 below will present the scansion of each line of lyric in *Agamemnon*. But metrical analysis should be more than a matter of identifying long and short syllables and labelling the different patterns with the appropriate jargon. A lyric strophe was a musical composition, designed for dancing as well as singing, and one would like to identify the syllables which define the rhythm and correspond, at least in principle, with the fall of a foot (θέσις) in the choreography.[6] In what follows these are called the 'primary syllables', and are marked with an accent.

The 'beat' of anapaests (§ 3 above) is known from ancient sources. But how should we mark the rhythm of, for example, the very common 'glyconic' colon, which scans $- \times - \cup \cup - \cup -$? Here we encounter a major point of debate. According to most scholars today, Greek metre was essentially quantitative: with limited exceptions, long syllables were equally long and short syllables were equally short. Thus in the above glyconic, the time-gap between the first and second long positions may vary, as the intervening position is anceps; and the $\cup \cup$ between the second and third long positions will cover a longer interval than the $\cup$ between the third and the fourth. Therefore the stresses on the four long syllables in $- \times - \cup \cup - \cup -$ would not produce four regular beats.

---

[6] In practice, it may be better not to assume that the chorus was on the move throughout every stanza.

Martin West (1982), 23–5 maintains that an irregular beat is what gives such Greek metres their musical characteristics. Another view is that this kind of rhythm would have been impossible for non-professional choruses to dance (as opposed merely to sing), and that regularity should be restored by allowing (for example) – ∪ to occupy the same duration as – ∪ ∪ or – –. The two syllables of the trochee would maintain the 2:1 ratio of their lengths, but would each last slightly longer than the corresponding syllables in the dactyl.[7] This theory was championed in particular by Pearson, who found evidence in the earliest Greek theorist of rhythm, Aristoxenus of Tarentum.[8] Aristoxenus certainly distinguishes between words (λέξις) and rhythm (ῥυθμός), and suggests that there were various ways to set a given sequence of long and short syllables to different rhythms, i.e. that the rules of quantity did not alone determine the rhythm. Unfortunately, his remains leave many questions unanswered, Pearson's interpretations have not been widely accepted, and conclusive evidence from ancient rhythmical theory and from our fragments of ancient Greek music is lacking.

Any attempt to deliver the choruses of Greek tragedy will be affected in practice by our own sense of rhythm. The rhythmical interpretations in the remainder of this Appendix are premised on the existence of a regular pulse in most metres other than the dochmiac. They lay no claim to historical certainty, but they will nevertheless justify themselves if they encourage students to practise reading aloud and to pay attention to effects of sound, which are an aspect of Aeschylus' artistry.

Given this background, let us return to the question of different colometries mentioned at the end of the preceding section, with a preliminary example. The colon – ∪ ∪ – ∪ – can be analysed as belonging to either of two systems, aeolic or dochmiac.[9] According to the interpretation followed here, aeolic cola did have a regular pulse (which will be marked by acute accents) whereas dochmii had an irregular one, based strictly on quantity (marked by grave accents). The two interpretations of the colon are then:

(1) ´– ∪ ∪ ´– ∪ ´–   dodrans (aeolic)
(2) – ∪ ∪ `– ∪ `–   dochmius

[7] In our notation, they would form a minim + crotchet triplet in contrast to a crotchet + two quavers.
[8] Aristoxenus was a pupil of Aristotle in the late fourth century BC. See Pearson (1990, 1974), on the more complicated 'dactylo-epitrite' metres found in e.g. Pindar. M. West (1992), ch. 5 discusses a broader range of ancient sources on rhythm.
[9] These types of colon will be introduced more fully below: §§ 4.3.4, 4.3.6.

In (1), the long and short syllables do not all occupy the same durations, so that the beats are evenly spaced. In (2), the two groups do occupy the same durations.

Another important detail of rhythm, normally omitted from metrical analysis, is the position of 'rests' (κενοὶ χρόνοι), where the singer takes a breath while the rhythm and music continue. Ancient sources say that rests could cover one or two beats. They are most naturally placed at syntactical breaks, and are indicated here by the caret (∧). We met one at the end of the catalectic form of anapaestic dimeter (above, § 3). Similarly with other catalectic cola used as cadences, in *Ag.* particularly the aristophanean (‒ ∪ ∪ ‒ ∪ ‒ ‒ ∧, e.g. 257). A beat in between a pair of cola can also be detected where the former colon is 'pendant' (i.e. its final beat falls on its penultimate syllable), and the latter has an 'upbeat' (i.e. the first beat falls after the first syllable). This may be associated with a change of metre within a strophe; see § 5 *ad* 120, 689. Conversely, when one colon ends with a primary syllable (or is 'blunt') and the next begins with a primary syllable, some extra time would have been taken to keep the rhythm regular. However, this could have involved a prolonged note rather than a rest, and no special indication is given in the analysis below.

4.3 The Main Lyric Metres of Agamemnon

4.3.1 Iambi

The basic metron is, as with spoken iambics, × ‒ ∪ ‒ (§ 2.1). However, the anceps is generally short, lines are not always trimeters, there is no main caesura, and there is often 'syncopation'. This term refers to the suppression of one or more short positions in the line (marked by '•'), combined with protraction of a neighbouring syllable.[10] Examples are:

        ∪ ‒   ∪ ‒ •   ‒   ∪ ‒   ∪ ‒ • ‒

192   πνοαὶ δ᾽ ἀπὸ Στρυμόνος μολοῦσαι

        ∪ ‒ •   ‒ • ‒   ∪ ‒   ∪   ‒ • ‒

367   Διὸς πλαγὰν ἔχουσιν εἰπεῖν

Ancient sources provide good evidence for a regular pulse in this metre, and the result is an exciting tautness. The importance of this syncopated rhythm in *Agamemnon* is discussed in § 4.4.

---

[10] See Raven (1962), 39 on the question of which neighbouring syllable was protracted. The ancient meaning of 'syncopation' should not be confused with the modern one.

4.3.2 Trochees

The basic metron is $-\cup-\times$. Often cola end with catalexis, i.e. just $-\cup-$. The most important trochaic line for the *Oresteia* is the catalectic dimeter known as the 'lecythion', which is discussed further in § 4.4 below:

$$\acute{-}\cup\ \acute{-}\ \cup\ \acute{-}\ \cup\acute{-}$$

975   τίπτε μοι τόδ' ἐμπέδως.

4.3.3 Dactyls

The basic foot is $-\cup\cup$. Runs of these produce lines of varying length (not just the hexameter, which will be familiar from Homer). Contraction of $\cup\cup$ into a long is fairly frequent, though less so than in Homer.

4.3.4 Aeolic[11]

The choriambus ($-\cup\cup-$) may appear in series in triple time, as at 201–3/ 214–16 ($\acute{-}\cup\cup-\ \acute{-}\cup\cup-\ \acute{-}\cup\cup-\ \ldots$). But it more often appears as the basis for a variety of cola which together fall under the heading 'aeolic'. Nine cola used repeatedly in *Agamemnon* are laid out in Table 1, arranged so as to draw attention to key points of variation: the number of syllables besides the choriambus; the position of the latter at the beginning, middle, or end of the colon; and pairs which are identical except for catalexis, so that in one the last primary syllable is in penultimate place ('pendant') while in the other it is in last place ('blunt').[12]

The interpretation of a further trio of cola in *Ag.* is disputable. They resemble aeolic cola with the choriambus in first place, but with a rest replacing the first syllable (see Raven 1962, 76); alternatively, they could be seen (without the rest) as variations on ionic cola, which would suggest a different beat (see § 4.3.5 below). They are:

1495 $\wedge\cup\cup-\cup-\cup-$ (~ glyconic B)
451    $\wedge\cup\cup-\cup--$ (~ aristophanean)
449    $\wedge\cup\cup-\cup-\cup--$ (~ hipponactean B)

All are discussed further below ad locc., as are two other cola which appear once each in aeolic contexts (748/761 and 1481/1505).

4.3.5 Ionics *a minore*

The basic foot is $\cup\cup--$, usually in dimeters to give a triple-time rhythm: $\cup\cup\acute{-}-\ \cup\cup\acute{-}-$. There is also an 'anaclastic' form, with the middle two syllables transposed, known as the 'anacreontic': $\cup\cup\acute{-}\cup-\cup\acute{-}-$.

---

[11] L. Parker (2007), pp. lxxvi–lxxviii distinguishes between 'Iambo-choriambic' and 'Aeolo-choriambic'; it seemed simpler for the purposes of this Appendix to use a single term.

[12] For a fuller range of cola see Raven (1962), 74–6 with the folding table.

Table 1: The main aeolic cola used in *Agamemnon*

	Scansion	Example	Conventional name
(a)	××[a] – ∪∪ – ∪ –	383 λακτίσαντι μέγαν Δίκας	glyconic
(b)	××[a] – ∪∪ – –	384 βωμὸν εἰς ἀφάνειαν	pherecratean (= (a) with catalexis)
(c)	– ∪∪ – ∪ – ∪ –	705 πρασσομένα τὸ νυμφότι-	glyconic B, or 'choriambic dimeter'
(d)	– ∪∪ – ∪ – –	212 πῶς λιπόναυς γένωμαι	aristophanean (= (c) with catalexis)
(e)	××[a] – ∪∪ – ∪ – –	143 θηρῶν ὀββρικάλοισι τερπνά	hipponactean (= (a) + a long)
(f)	– ∪∪ – ∪ – ∪ – –	706 -μον μέλος ἐκφάτως τίοντας	hipponactean B (= (c) + a long)
(g)	– ∪∪ – ∪∪ – ∪ – –	1482 δαίμονα καὶ βαρύμηνιν αἰνεῖς	aeolic 10-syllable (an extension of (e))
(h)	× – ∪∪ – ∪ – –	1483 φεῦ φεῦ, κακὸν αἶνον ἄτη-	hagesichorean (= decapitated (e))
(i)	– ∪∪ – ∪ –	1448 φεῦ τίς ἂν ἐν τάχει	dodrans

[a] The first two syllables in glyconics, pherecrateans, and hipponacteans cannot both be short (you may see pairs of anceps positions with this stipulation notated 'o o'). In fact, the first syllable of glyconics and pherecrateans is always long in *Ag.* except at 717/727.

4.3.6 Dochmii

A metre used in moments of high agitation or pathos. In *Agamemnon* Aeschylus uses two main forms of dochmius, namely ∪ – – ∪ – and – ∪ ∪ – ∪ –. These may be felt to have slightly different effects. They can correspond, as at 1164/1175, 1409/1429, *Cho.* 960/971. Forms with resolution of long positions into two shorts are common, particularly ∪ ∪∪ – ∪ –.

The position of the beat is debated. That the two basic forms can correspond may suggest: ∪ – $\overset{\backprime}{-}$ ∪ $\overset{\backprime}{-}$ / – ∪ ∪ $\overset{\backprime}{-}$ ∪ $\overset{\backprime}{-}$.[13] The metre's name (cf. δόχμιος, 'aslant') suggests an irregular beat, and the patterns produce an appropriate jerky, forward-leaning effect if delivered strictly according to quantity. If the suggestion is correct that other metres including aeolic cola did have a regular beat, the effect of dochmii would have been all the more striking.

4.4 *Lyric Rhythm and Subject Matter*

Several scholars have drawn attention to the unifying effect in the *Oresteia* of Aeschylus' repeated use of two metres in distinctive contexts. See in particular Kitto (1955), Scott (1984). Such a use of rhythm could be compared to Wagner's employment of the melodic leitmotif as a unifying element in his music-dramas.

Syncopated iambics appear particularly associated with the central tragic theme of retaliatory justice. They dominate the parodos from 192, the passage describing Iphigenia's slaughter for which Agamemnon later pays. They also dominate the whole first stasimon, with its focus on Paris' come-uppance, gradually ceding to uneasy thoughts about Agamemnon (see introductory comment to 355–487). Syncopated iambics reappear in the third strophic pair of the second stasimon, in preparation for their dominance of the final (fourth) pair, as the discussion of hubris regenerating itself and of Justice abandoning the rich sinner builds up to the entrance of Agamemnon. Finally, they gradually come to the fore during the Chorus's utterances in the *epirrhēma* with Clytemnestra, as they force her to an awareness of the retribution which awaits her.[14]

---

[13] The writer's (D.A.R.'s) experience in delivering Greek suggests that this rhythm is effective. Admittedly, later Greek sources place the *thesis* on the shorter form differently: ∪ $\overset{\backprime}{-}$ – $\overset{\backprime}{∪}$ –.

[14] For syncopated iambics in the other plays, see esp. *Cho.* 456–65, *Eum.* 381–3 = 389–91.

The other characteristic rhythm is the trochaic, which appears especially in the form of lecythia. It is introduced in the Hymn to Zeus in the parodos, where the Chorus seek a divine significance behind the events it is narrating (160–91). A trochaic sequence next appears at the beginning of the second stasimon, where the Chorus is grasping after which mysterious power made the words Ἑλένη and κῆδος so significant. The rhythm pervades the third stasimon, where the Chorus is seeking to realize the sense behind its premonitions. (The optimistic spirit in which the rhythm first appeared in the Hymn to Zeus has thus been reversed.) The rhythm appears to reflect a concern to understand the order and ultimate significance of the events being realized in the drama.[15]

This aspect of rhythm in *Agamemnon* is explored further in the analyses which follow, as in the commentary.

5 Analysis of Choral Movements

Conspectus of symbols and abbreviations

Metre

−	long syllable
∪	short syllable
×	anceps (i.e. long or short) position
∪∪	resolved long position
∩	*brevis in longo* (short syllable in a long position at line-end)

Where two of these symbols appear one on top of the other (e.g. ∪̄, ∪̄, ∪∪̄), the upper symbol describes the strophe and the lower the antistrophe.

•	short syllable absorbed in syncopation
|	junction between different metres within a line[16]

Rhythm

´	primary syllable (or rest) where rhythm is regular
`	primary syllable where rhythm is irregular
∧	vocal rest of one beat between cola
∧²	vocal rest of two beats between cola

---

[15] For trochees and lecythia in the other plays, see esp. *Cho.* 783–9, 794–9, *Eum.* 997–1002 = 1015–20. Their relevance is discussed by Chiasson (1988), with a rather different interpretation.

[16] Distinguish this use from West's in the metrical analysis in the appendix of his Teubner, where '|' is used to mark word-breaks.

Feet and metra[17]

an	anapaestic metron	∪ ∪ – ́ ∪ ∪ – ́
bac	bacchius	∪ –̀ –
cho	choriambus	–́ ∪ ∪ –
cre	cretic	–̀ ∪ –
da	dactyl	–́ ∪ ∪
doch	dochmius	∪ – –̀ ∪ –̀ or – ∪ ∪ –̀ ∪ –̀
ia	iambic metron	× –́ ∪ –́
io	ionic *a minore*	∪ ∪ –́ –
pae	paeon	∪̆∪̆ ∪ – (a resolved cretic)
tr	trochaic metron	–́ ∪ –́ ×

Cola

aeo₁₀	aeolic 10-syllable	–́ ∪ ∪ –́ ∪ ∪ –́ ∪ –́ –
anac	anacreontic	∪ ∪ –́ ∪ – ∪ –́ –
aris	aristophanean	–́ ∪ ∪ –́ ∪ –́ –
dod	dodrans	–́ ∪ ∪ –́ ∪ –́
glyc	glyconic	–́ × –́ ∪ ∪ –́ ∪ –́
glyc^B	glyconic B	–́ ∪ ∪ –́ ∪ –́ ∪ –́
hag	hagesichorean	× –́ ∪ ∪ –́ ∪ –́ –
hem	hemiepes	–́ ∪ ∪ –́ ∪ ∪ –́
hipp	hipponactean	×́ × –́ ∪ ∪ –́ ∪ –́ –
hipp^B	hipponactean B	–́ ∪ ∪ –́ ∪ –́ ∪ –́ –
lec	lecythion	–́ ∪ –́ ∪ –́ ∪ –́
par	paroemiac	∪ ∪ –́ ∪ ∪ –́ ∪ ∪ –́ –
pher	pherecratean	–́ × –́ ∪ ∪ –́ –

Parodos (40–257)

40–103

Recited anapaests: see above (§ 3) for a guide to delivery and analysis.

104–59

Strophic triad, mostly dactylic (with iambic and, in the epode, aeolic elements); see also 104–59 n. for the use of dactyls.

---

[17] Only the basic form of each foot, metron, or colon is given. For further detail see above, §§ 2–4.

254   *Appendix: Sound and Rhythm*

Strophe α 104–21 = Antistrophe α 122–39

	–�השׁ –⏑⏑ –⏑⏑ –⏑⏑ –⏑⏑ ––	6 da
105/123	–⏑⏑ –⏑⏑ –⏑⏑ –⏑⏑ ––	5 da
	–– –– –– –⏑⏑ ––∧²	5 da
	⏑–⏑– | –⏑⏑ –⏑⏑ –⏑⏑ ––	ia + 4 da
110/128	–⏑⏑ ––	2 da
	–– –⏑⏑ –⏑⏑ –שׁ	4 da
	–⏑⏑ –– –⏑⏑ –⌒	4 da
	–– –⏑⏑ –⏑⏑ –⏑⏑	4 da
115/133	–⏑⏑ –⏑⏑ –⏑⏑ ––	+ 4 da
	⏓⏑–⏑– | –⏑⏑ –⏑⏑ –⏑⏑ ––	ia + 4 da
	–– –⏑⏑ –⌒	3 da
	–⏑⏑ –⏑⏑ –⏑⏑ –⏑⏑ –⏑⏑ ––	6 da
120/138	⏓ū–⏑– ⏑–⏑–	2 ia
	–⏑⏑ –⏑⏑ –⏑⏑ –– ––	5 da

106–7/124–5. The switch from dactyls to an iambic metron occurs at a syntactical break: a rest of two beats may be allowed.

121/139. Practise the effect of the 'dragged' ending εὖ νικάτω (four longs).

Epode (140–59)

140	⏑–⏑– ––⏑–	2 ia
	⏑–⏑– | –⏑⏑–⏑––	ia + aris
	–– –⏑⏑ –⏑⏑ ––	4 da
	––⏑⏑–⏑––	hipp
	–– –– –⏑⏑ ––	4 da
145–6	–⏑⏑ –⏑⏑ –⏑⏑ –⏑⏑ <––>	5 da
	⏓⏑–⏑– | –⏑⏑–⏑–⌒	ia + aris
	–⏑⏑ –⏑⏑ –⏑⏑ –⏑⏑	4 da
	–⏑⏑ –⏑⏑ ––	+ 3 da
150–1	–⏑⏑ –⏑⏑ –⏑⏑ –⏑⏑ –⏑⏑ –⏑⏑ ––	7 da
	–– –⏑⏑ –⏑⏑ ––	4 da
	–⏑⏑ –– –⏑⏑ –⏑⏑ –⌒	+ 5 da
155	–⏑⏑ –⏑⏑ –– –– –⏑⏑ ––	6 da
	–⏑⏑ –– –⏑⏑ –⏑⏑ –⏑⏑ ––	6 da
	–⏑⏑ –– –⏑⏑ –– –⏑⏑ ––	6 da
	–⏑⏑ –⌒	2 da
	–⏑⏑ –⏑⏑ –⏑⏑ –– ––	5 da

140. West's emendation (see n.) would give ⏑ – ⏑ – \| – ⏑ ⏑ – (ia + cho), which is a fairly common colon outside *Ag.*

145–6. Assuming <κρίνω> at end (see n.).

147. Assuming δή before καλέω (see n.). The first syllable of *Παιᾶνα* scans as short (intervocalic ι counting as a single consonantal 'y').

152. νεικέων: two longs, by synizesis of εω.

160–91

Two strophic pairs, trochaic except for one dactylic colon. For the 'leitmotif' of lecythia, see § 4.4 above.

Str. β 160–7 = Ant. β 168–75

160/168	–•–• –∪–∪–∪–	tr + lec
	–∪–∪–∪–	+ lec
	–∪–∪–∪–	lec
	–∪–∪–∪–	lec
	–∪–∪–∪–	+ lec
165–6/173–4	–∪∪ –∪∪ –∪∪ –∪∪ ––	5 da
	–∪–∪–∪–	lec

160/168. The first two syllables are protracted to give a heavy emphasis.

165–6/173–4. The dactylic colon lends power to the climax of the stanza; in both strophe and antistrophe Zeus is named in this line.

Str. γ 176–83 = Ant. γ 184–91

	–∪–∪–∪–	lec
	–∪–∪–∪–	+ lec
	–∪–∪–∪–	lec
	–•–• –∪–∪–∪–	tr + lec
180/188	–∪–• –∪–• –∪–	3 tr
	–∪–∪–∪–	+ lec
	–∪–∪ –∪–∪ –•–•	3 tr
	–∪–∪–∪–	+ lec

179–80/187–8. Protraction marks the slow heavy 'drip' of the remembered pain in the strophe, and in the antistrophe the dead weight of the delay at Aulis.

182/190. Again, the protractions on βίαι-ος and παλιρ-ρόχ- can be delivered with effect.

192–257

Three strophic pairs in syncopated iambics, yielding in each case to an aeolic close. For the association of the metre with sin and retribution, see § 4.4 above.

Str. δ 192–204 = Ant. δ 205–17

	∪⌣∪⌣ •⌣∪⌣ ∪⌣•⌣	3 ia
	∪⌣∪⌣ •⌣∪⌣ ∪⌣•⌣	3 ia
	∪⌣∪⌣	ia
195/208	‾⌣∪⌣ •⌣∪⌣ ∪⌣•⩘	+ 3 ia
	∪⌣•⌣ •⌣∪⌣ ∪⌣•⌣	3 ia
	∪⌣∪⌣ •⌣∪⌣ ∪⌣•⌣	3 ia
	•⌣∪⌣ ∪⌣∪⌣	+ 2 ia
	⌣∪∪⌣∪⌣‾	aris
200/213	⌣∪∪⌣∪⌣‾	aris
	⌣∪∪‾ ⌣∪∪‾	2 cho
	⌣∪∪‾ ⌣∪∪‾	+ 2 cho
	⌣∪∪‾ ⌣∪∪‾	+ 2 cho
	⌣∪∪⌣∪⌣‾⩘	+ aris

197–8/210–11. A more satisfying effect might be achieved, without dove-tailing, by reading Ἄργους (Hermann) for Ἀργεί-ων and πρὸ βωμοῦ (Lindau) for πέλας βωμοῦ. This would make 198/211 ⩘ ∪ ⌣ ∪ ⌣ ∪ ⌣, an iambic dimeter with a vocal rest replacing the first foot.

199/212. Here the stanza mounts in tension with a switch to two shorter aeolic cola, leading into a run of choriambs (in triple time) with a final aristophanean for clausula. See also 198–204 n.

Str. ε 218–27 = Ant. ε 228–37

	∪⌣∪⌣ •⌣∪⌣ ∪⌣•⌣	3 ia
	∪⌣∪⌣ •⌣∪⌣ ∪⌣•⌣	3 ia
220/230	∪⌣∪⌣⌣ ∪⌣∪⌣	2 ia
	∪⌣∪⌣ •⌣∪⌣ ∪⌣•⌣	3 ia
	∪⌣∪⌣ •⌣∪⌣ ∪⌣•⌣	3 ia
	∪⌣∪⌣⌣ ∪⌣•⌣ ∪⌣•⌣	3 ia
	∪⌣•⌣ ∪⌣∪⌣	2 ia
225/235	⌣∪∪⌣∪⌣∪⌣	+ glyc[B]
	⌣∪∪⌣∪⌣‾⩘	+ aris
	⌣∪∪⌣∪⌣‾⩘	aris

224–6/234–6. The dove-tailing reinforces the horror of Agamemnon's momentous decision, and the inexorable violence with which Iphigenia is lifted up for the sacrifice and gagged.

Str. ζ 238–47 = Ant. ζ 248–57

The delivery of the syncopated iambics probably becomes gentler from 239.

	∪⌣∪⌣ •⌣∪⌣ •⌣∪⌣	3 ia
	∪⌣∪⌣ •⌣∪⌣ ∪⌣•⩘	3 ia

240/250	⏑´⏑´ •´⏑´	2 ia
	•´⏑´ ⏑´⏑´ ⏑´•´	+ 3 ia
	⏑´⏑´ •´⏑´ ⏑´⏑´	3 ia
	⏑´⏑´ •´⏑´	2 ia
	⏑´⏑´ •´⏑´ ⏑´•´	3 ia
245/255	⏑´⏑´ •´⏑´ •´⏑´ •´⏑´	4 ia
	⏑´⏑´ •´⏑´ ⏑´•´	3 ia
	´⏑⏑´⏑´ – ⋏	+ aris

First Stasimon (355–487)

For the structure and metre of this ode in relation to the subject-matter, see 355–487 n.

355–66

Introductory anapaests. The highlighting effect of dactylic substitution (see § 3 above) is particularly notable in 358, where the imagery of nets is introduced in the unusual pattern ⏑ ⏑ ´ – ⏑́ ⏑ – ´⏑ ⏑ ´, with the second anapaest replaced by a dactyl.

Str. α 367–84 = Ant. α 385–402

Syncopated iambics with an aeolic clausula (380/398), leading into a four-line aeolic ephymnion, i.e. a rhythmical pattern which repeats at the end of the second and third strophic pairs.

	⏑´•´ •´⏑´ ⏑´•´	3 ia
	⏑´•´ •´⏑´ ⏑´•´	3 ia
	⏑´⏑´ ⏑´⏑´ ⏑´•´	3 ia
370–1/388–9	⏑´⏑´ •´⏑´ •´⏑´	3 ia
	⏑´⏑´ •´⏑´	2 ia
	⏑´⏑´ •´⏑´	2 ia
	⏑´•´ •´⏑´	2 ia
375/393	⏑´•´ •´⏑´	2 ia
	⏑´•´ •´⏑´ ⏑´•´	3 ia
	⏑´•´ •´⏑´ ⏑´•´	3 ia
	⏑´⏑´ •´⏑´ •´⏑´	3 ia
	•´⏑´ ⏑´•´	+ 2 ia
380/398	´⏑⏑´⏑´⌒⋏	aris
	´⏑´⏑⏑´–	pher
	´ū´⏑⏑´⌒	pher
	´⏑´⏑⏑´⏑´	glyc
	´ū´⏑⏑´⌒⋏	+ pher

Str. β 403–19 = Ant. β 420–36

Syncopated iambics followed by the aeolic ephymnion.

	⏑⏑ • ⏑ • ⏑	3 ia
	⏑⏑ • ⏑	2 ia
405/422	• ⏑ ⏑ •	+ 2 ia
	⏑⏑ ⏑⏑ ⏑⏑	3 ia
	⏑ • • ⏑⏑̆	2 ia
	⏑⏑ ⏑⏑⏑⏑ ⏑⏑	+ 3 ia
	⏑⏑ • ⏑ ⏑ •	3 ia
410/427	⏑⏑ • ⏑ ⏑⏑	3 ia
	⏑⏑ • ⏑ ⏑⏑	3 ia
	⏑⏑ • ⏑ • ⏑ ⏑⏑	4 ia
	• ⏑ ⏑⏑	+ 2 ia
	⏑⏑ • ⏑	2 ia
415/432	• ⏑ • ⏑ ⏑ •	3 ia
	– – ⏑⏑	pher
	⏑⏑⏑	pher
	⏑⏑⏑⏑	glyc
	⏑⏑ –	+ pher

412–13/429–30. The metre is adopted from the antistrophe; the strophe is corrupt.

Str. γ 437–55 = Ant. γ 456–74

Once again syncopated iambics, up to 447/466. For 448–51/467–70 alternative colometries and rhythmical interpretations are possible (discussed below). The stanza concludes with the familiar aeolic quatrain.

	⏑⏑ • ⏑ • ⏑	3 ia
	• ⏑ • ⏑ ⏑⏑	3 ia
440/459	⏑⏑ • ⏑	2 ia
	⏑⏑ • ⏑	2 ia
	• ⏑ ⏑⏑	2 ia
	• ⏑ ⏑⏑	+ 2 ia
	• ⏑ ⏑⏑	+ 2 ia
445/464	⏑⏑ ⏑⏑	2 ia
	⏑⏑ ⏑⏑	+ 2 ia
	⏑⏑ ⏑⏑	2 ia
	⏑⏑⏑⏑	+ glyc^B
	⏑⏑⏑⏑	+ glyc^B
450/469	⏑⏑⏑⏑	+ glyc^B
	⏑⏑⏑ –	+ aris

	´ – ´∪∪´ –	pher
	´ – ´∪∪´ –	pher
	´ – ´∪∪´∪´	glyc
455/474	´∪´∪∪´∩∧	pher

448–51/466–9. The OCT colometry is given above, but the repetition of glyconic B with dove-tailing sounds flat in the menacing context, and necessitates awkward quick breaths in mid-colon. Fraenkel and West prefer this line division, so that cola end at word-breaks:

	ἀλλοτρίας διαὶ γυναικός·	´∪∪´∪´∪´ –	[18]
	τάδε σῖγά τις βαΰζει	∪∪´∪–∪´ –	anac
450	φθονερὸν δ' ὑπ' ἄλγος ἔρπει	∪∪´∪–∪´ –	anac
	προδίκοις Ἀτρείδαις	∪∪´∪–´	ionic clausula[19]

These metrical units admit of yet another analysis if one posits vocal rests, possibly with (say) a stamp on the ground, at the start of 449, 450, and 451. The two cola 449–50 would then have the rhythm ∧∪∪´∪´∪´ –, and be equivalent to the hipp[B] which precedes. 451/469 would have the rhythm ∧∪∪´∪´ – ∧, like an aristophanean.[20] These decapitated forms seem to produce a tension more suited to the denunciatory context at the climax of the ode. Ionic cola, on the other hand, are commonly associated with the East, and may be languid (as at 690–5), or frenetic (as in Euripides *Bacchae*), neither of which is quite suitable here.

Students are encouraged to practise the three rhythmical interpretations and to decide for themselves which effect they prefer.

Epode (475–87)

Syncopated iambics again, possibly in a faster, more relaxed tempo as emphasized metrically by the resolutions in 485–6.

475	∪´∪´ • ´∪´	2 ia
	∪´∪´ • ´∪´	2 ia
	• ´∪´ ∪´∪´	2 ia
	∪´∪´ ∪´∪´ ∪´∪´	3 ia
	∪´∪´ ∪´∪´ ∪´∪´	3 ia
480	∪´∪´ • ´∪´	2 ia
	∪´∪´ • ´∪´ ∪´∪´	3 ia
	• ´∪´ ∪´∪´	+ 2 ia

---

[18] Fraenkel pp. 184–6 analyses as hipp[B], West as – + anac.
[19] Also found after a run of ionics in Euripides *Bacchae* 385–6, 401–2.
[20] See also § 4.3.4 above.

	⏑–⏑– •–⏑–		2 ia
	⏑–⏑– •–⏑– ⏑–⏑–		3 ia
485	⏑⏕⏑– ⏑–⏑⏕ ⏑⏕⏑–		3 ia
	⏑⏕⏑– ⏑⏕⏑–		2 ia
	⏑–⏑– •–⏑– ⏑–⏑⏗		3 ia

Second Stasimon (681–781)

This ode, at least in its first three strophic pairs, combines a more complex variety of rhythms within single stanzas. These alternations mirror the content, which has much to do with changeable situations. Each stanza ends with an aeolic clausula. A sense of rising tension can be felt in the general decrease in the length of each strophic pair; they have sixteen, ten, twelve, and nine cola respectively.

Str. α 681–98 = Ant. α 699–716

The opening trochaic cola (681–5/699–704) again reflect the Chorus's search for deeper significance—here through Helen's name and the double sense of κῆδος (see above § 4.4; 681–781 n.). A rare colon at 688–9/706–7 links the choriambs in the two preceding cola and the ionics which follow (690–5/708–13). These take the rhythm off into triple time. In the strophe, this is particularly apt for the description of Helen's flight. In the antistrophe it marks the change from wedding-hymn to dirge. In the last three cola the song and choreography steady down to an aeolic rhythm in common time.

	–⏑–⏑–⏑–	lec
	–⏑–⏑–⏑–	+ lec
	–⏑–⏑ –⏑– • –⏑–	3 tr
	–⏑–⏑–⏑–	+ lec
685/703	–⏑–⏑–⏑–	lec
	–⏑⏑–⏑–⏑–	glyc^B
	–⏑⏑–⏑–⏑– –	+ hipp^B
	⏗⏑⏑–⏑–⏑⏑–	(transitional—see above)
690/708	⏑⏑–– ⏑⏑––	+ 2 io
	⏑⏑–⏑–⏑––	anac
	⏑⏑–⏑–⏑––	anac
	⏑⏑–– ⏑⏑–⏑–⏑––	io + anac
695/713	⏑⏑–⏑–⏑––	+ anac

´ – ´∪∪´∪´	glyc
´∪∪´∪´–	+ aris
⌣∪´∪∪´∩ ʌ	pher

688–9/706–7. A rest is needed here between pendant ending and upbeat.

696–8/714–16. Antistrophe corrupt (see 714–16 n.); the strophe gives the metre.

Str. β 717–26 = Ant. β 727–36

For the lion-cub fable Aeschylus uses a variety of metrical patterns: aeolic, dactylic, trochaic, then ending with aeolic, as in Str. α. The effect is beguiling first time through, sinister in the antistrophe.

	∪´´∪∪´∪´	glyc
	´∪´∪∪´∪ ´	+ glyc
	´∪´∪∪´∩	+ pher
720/730	´∪∪ ´∪∪ ´–	3 da
	´∪∪ ´∪∪ ´∩	3 da
	´∪∪ ´∪∪ ´–	3 da
	⌣∪´∪´∪´	lec
	⌣∪´∪´∪´	lec
725/735	´ū´∪∪´∪´	glyc
	´∪´∪∪´– ʌ	+ pher

717. Attention is drawn to the start of the fable by the glyconic beginning in ∪ – rather than the more usual – ×.

720–2/730–2. The repeated dactylic cola have an appealing tenderness in the context of the harmless cub in the strophe. In the antistrophe, by contrast, the repetition may emphasize the relentless havoc wrought by the adult lion.

Str. γ 737–49 = Ant. γ 750–62

The stanza is clearly divided into two halves, each ending with two aeolic cola. The first half begins with the 'retribution motif' of syncopated iambics (§ 4.4). The second half switches to triple-time ionics. This point mirrors the change in the content of both strophe and antistrophe—the changed implications of Helen's presence for Troy, and the declaration of a different attitude to ethical dangers. In the last two cola the rhythm steadies in a firm aeolic clausula; in the strophe this accompanies the final revelation of Helen as an Erinys (see commentary on 744–9).

∪´∪´ • ´∪´ ∪´∪´	3 ia
∪´ • ´ ∪´∪´	2 ia

740/753	• –́υ–́ υ–́•–́	+ 2 ia
	υ–́•–́ •–́υ–́ υ–́•–́	3 ia
	–́υυ–́υ–́υ–́	glyc[B]
	–́υ–́υυ–́υ–́–∧²	hipp
	υυ–́– υυ–́–	2 io
745/758	υυ–́υ–υ–́–	+ anac
	υυ–́– υυ–́–	2 io
	υυ–́– υυ–́–	2 io
	∧––́υ–́υυ–́	(see below)
	–́υ–́υυ–́–∧	pher

740–1. The protracted syllables in γαλ*ά*ν*ας* ἀκ*ασ*κ*αῖ*ον <δ'> are particularly sensual.

743–4/756–7. A two-beat rest is posited to smooth the change to ionics and allow a good breath.

748/761. A rare colon used transitionally (compare 688–9/706–7).[21]

Str. δ 763–71 = Ant. δ 773–81

Syncopated iambics reassert themselves forcefully in solid dimeters as, in the final build-up to Agamemnon's entrance, the Chorus proclaims the laws of generative hybris and Justice's rejection of wealth.

	υ–́υ–́ •–́υ–́	2 ia
	•–́υ–́ •–́υ–́	+ 2 ia
765/775	•–́υ–́ υ–́υ–́	+ 2 ia
	υ–́υ–́ υώυ–́	2 ia
	υ–́υ–́ υ–́υ–́	+ 2 ia
	–ώυ–́ υώυώ	2 ia
	υώυ–́ υ–́υ–́	+ 2 ia
770/780	–́υυ–́υ–́–∧	+ aris
	–́υυ–́υ–́ₒ∧	aris

768–9/778–9. The resolutions in these iambic cola, combined in the strophe with alliteration of μ, add to the insistence of the rhythm which emphasizes the dark and inexorable fate awaiting Agamemnon. For the text of the antistrophe see 773–9 n.

770–1/780–1. By positing vocal rests after each aristophanean, one reaches a potent musical scheme with four beats to every colon. These rests also set

---

[21] West labels it a type of telesilleion. The more common form is × – υ υ – υ – (= decapitated glyconic), which does not occur in *Ag.*

771/781 apart; this would be particularly effective in the antistrophe, where 781 (see n.) is an extremely powerful cue for Agamemnon's entry.[22]

Anapaests (783–809)

See the suggestions above, § 3.

Third Stasimon (975–1034)

The Chorus's song of fearful anticipation metrically recalls 160–91 in its use of trochees (especially lecythia) with occasional dactylic cola. For the significance of this echo see 975–1034 n. Alien elements intrude in a remarkable effect at the beginning of the second strophic pair.

Str. α 975–87 = Ant. α 988–1000

975/988	$- \cup - \cup - \cup -$	lec
	$- \cup - \cup - \cup -$	lec
	$- \cup - \cup \ - \cup - \cup \ - \bullet - \bullet$	3 tr
	$- \cup\cup \ - \cup\cup \ - \cup\cup \ - \cup\cup \ - -$	5 da
980/993	$- \cup - \cup - \cup -$	lec
	$- \cup - \cup - \cup -$	lec
	$- \cup - \bullet \ - \cup - \bullet$	2 tr
	$- \cup - \cup - \cup -$	+ lec
	$\cup - \cup - \ - - \cup - \ \cup - \cup -$	3 ia
985/998	$- \cup - \bullet \ - \cup - \bullet$	2 tr
	$- \cup - \cup - \cup \widehat{-}$	+ lec
	$- \cup - \cup - \cup -$	lec

977/990. The protractions in ποτᾶται / ὑμνῳδεῖ make a fine effect. The upsilon of ὑμνῳδεῖ is short, though μν more often lengthens the preceding syllable.

984/997. The iambic line barely interrupts the prevailing trochaic feel. (The text of 984–5 is reconstructed from the metre of the antistrophe: see 984–7 n.)

Str. β 1001–17 = Ant. β 1018–34

The Elders' uneasiness is strikingly expressed in three paeons in the opening colon, followed by a single ionic metron, then a short run of anapaests. This strange effect leads back to a steadier alternation between the two metres of the first strophic pair—dactyls and trochees.

---

[22] A modern director might introduce a great cymbal clash preceding the words 'She [Justice] guides everything to its end.'

	‿‿∪− ‿‿∪− ‿‿∪−	3 pae
	∪∪‑−∣∪∪‑∪∪‑	io + an
	‾∪‾∪‑∪∪‑ ∪∪‑−⋏	+ par
1005/1022	‑∪∪‑∪∪‑	hem
	‑∪∪‑∪∪‑	hem
	‑∪∪‑∪∪∣‑∪‑◠	2 da + tr
	‑∪‑∪‑∪‑	lec
	‑∪‑∪‑∪‑	lec
1010/1027	‑∪‑∪‑∪‑	lec
	‑∪‑∪‑∪‑	lec
	‑∪‑∪‑∪‑	lec
	‑∪‑∪‑∪‑	lec
1014–15/1031–2	‑− ‑∪∪ ‑∪∪ ‑∪∪	4 da
	‑∪∪ ‑∪∪ ‑∪∪ ‑−	+ 4 da
	‑∪‑∪‑∪‑	lec

1001–4/1018–21. For the text in the strophe, see commentary. If Page's colometry is right, one has three bars of 5/8 time, followed by a colon whose rarity would contribute to the nervous atmosphere.[23]

1006–7/1023–4. For the text in the strophe, see 1005–7 n. The trochaic metron at the end of 1007/1024 provides the transition from the preceding dactyls to the lecythia that follow. (Contrast the same metrical pattern in an aeolic context at 1451.)

1008–13/1025–30. Aeschylus allots the Elders a long, measured sequence of lecythia as they voice their *gnōmai* on cautious jettison and their deep concerns about conflicting μοῖραι.

1014–16/1031–3. The run of dactyls at the climax of the strophe includes a reference to Zeus—compare 165/174. In the antistrophe, the series elegantly reflects the metaphor of 'winding off'.

Kommos (1072–1177)

For the general dynamics of this passage, whereby Cassandra begins in wilder song and gradually moves towards speech, while the Coryphaeus begins with speech and the whole Chorus gradually joins in with song as it catches her agitation, see introductory note to 1035–1330. The predominant metrical feature is the irregular dochmius (∪ − ‑ ∪ ‑), which expresses both agitation and pathos. It is combined particularly with the iambic metron, the bacchius and the cretic.

---

[23] The traditional line-numeration is: 1001/1018 2 pae; 1002/1019 pae + io; 1003/1020 an; 1004/1021 par.

Str. α 1072–5 = Ant. α 1076–9

     Κα.   ∪∪́∪∪◡́ ∪◡́•◡́   2 ia
             ◡́•◡́∪ ◡́•◡́∪   2 tr(?)
     Χο.   two iambic trimeters

1073/1077. Details of the text and metre of this anguished invocation of
Apollo are uncertain. The OCT reading probably sounds best as a syncopated trochaic dimeter, with both omegas prolonged.

Str. β 1080–4 = Ant. β 1085–9

1080/1085 *Κα.*   ◡́•◡́∪ ◡́•◡́∪   cf. 1073/1077
                ∧∪−−∪−−∪∩   (see below)
                iambic trimeter
       Χο.   two iambic trimeters

1081/1086. Metrical description is difficult. It is perhaps best to take *ἀγυιᾶτ’*
as the first three syllables of a dochmius, after which *ἀπόλλων ἐμός* is a full
dochmius. Thus: ∪−◡̲ ∪−◡̲∪∩ [24]

Str. γ 1090–4 = Ant. γ 1095–9

     Κα.   ᾱ̂ ᾱ̂   *extra metrum*
1090/1095   −∪∪◡̲∪◡̲ −∪∪◡̲∪∩̲   2 doch
           −∪́∪∪∪́ ∪◡́∪∩́   2 ia
           iambic trimeter
     Χο.   two iambic trimeters

1090. See 1090 n. on ᾱ̂ ᾱ̂. This is the first appearance of the longer dochmius
(§ 4.3.6), with its slightly different effect from the more common form.

1091/1096. The text in the strophe is corrupt: see 1090–1 n.

Str. δ 1100–6 = Ant. δ 1107–13

1100/1107 *Κα.*   ∪◡́∪◡́ | ∪∪̲◡̲∪◡̲   ia + doch
               ∪́∪∪∪̲∪◡́∪∩́   lec (?)
               ∪̲◡́∪◡́ ∪̲◡́∪◡́ ∪◡́∪◡́   3 ia
               ∪◡̀− ∪◡̀− ∪◡̀− ∪◡̀−   4 bac
               ∪∪∪◡̲◡̲∪◡́   + doch
1105/1112 *Χο.*   two iambic trimeters

---

[24] Contrast the analysis bac + doch: ∪◡̀−∪−◡̲∪∩̀ .

1101/1108. With the OCT, the colon is a resolved lecythion. But the first seven syllables form a dochmius, so there is a case for excising μέγα and πόσιν (Enger).

1103–4/1110–11. The movement of four bacchii running into the closing dochmius is extremely sinister.[25]

Str. ε 1114–24 = Ant. ε 1125–35

	Κα.	∪∪∪‿∪‿ ∪∪∪‿∪‿	2 doch
1115/1126		‒‿∪‿ ∪‿•‿	2 ia
		⏗‿∪‿ ∪‿∪‿ ∪‿∪⏗	3 ia
		∪‿∪‿│∪∪∪‿∪‿	ia + doch
		∪∪‿∪‿│‿∪‒ ‿∪‒	doch + 2 cre
	Χο.	two iambic trimeters	
1121/1132		∪∪∪‿∪‿ ∪∪∪‿∪‿	2 doch
		∪‒‿∪‿ ∪‒‿∪‿	2 doch
		∪∪∪‿∪‿│‿∪‿‒	doch + tr
		∪‿∪‿ •‿∪‿	2 ia

1114/1125. The lines begin with two cries, scanning ∪ ∪. In ἒ ἒ there is hiatus; in ἆ ἆ the long vowels are shortened by correption.

1115/1126. During the second metron, the protractions in Ἅ̲ι̲δ̲ο̲υ̲ / π̲έ̲π̲λ̲ο̲ι̲σ̲ιν may lend the words a sinister emphasis.

1118/1129. The last six syllables could also be taken as 2 tr, with a different rhythm (‿∪‿• ‿∪‿).

1123–4/1134–5. The OCT colometry implies the description 'doch + tr, 2 ia'. However, West divides the cola *before* δύντος αὐγαῖς / θεσπιωιδῶν, to produce:

∪∪∪‿∪‿	doch
‿∪‒ ‿∪‒│∪‒‿∪‿	2 cre + doch

This sounds good and offers a similar (but reversed) pattern to 1118/1129.

Str. ζ 1136–45 = Ant. ζ 1146–55

Cassandra begins to contemplate her own death; her dochmii express more pathos than frenzy, and start to yield to iambic trimeters (see 1136–77 n.).

	Κα.	∪‿∪‿ ∪‿•‿‿│∪∪∪‿∪‿	2 ia + doch
		∪∪∪‿∪‿ ∪∪∪‿∪‿	2 doch
		two iambic trimeters	

---

[25] Contrast the rhythm of syncopated iambics: ∪‿•‿‿ ∪‿•‿‿ ∪‿•‿.

1140/1150	*Xo.*	⏑⏑⏑⏤⏑⏤ ⏑⏑⏑⏤⏑⏤	2 doch
		⏑⏤⏤⏑⏤	+ doch
		⏑⏑⏑⏑̆ ǀ ⏤⏑⏤⏤⏤	(see below)
		⏑⏑⏑⏤⏑⏤ ǀ ⏤⏑⏤ ⏤⏑⏠	doch + 2 cre
		⏑⏑⏑⏤⏑⏤ ⏤⏑⏑⏤⏑⏤	2 doch
1145/1155		⏑⏤⏤⏑⏠	doch

1136/1146. The second syllable could scan short by correption, which would give ⏝⏑⏤⏑⏤ ǀ ⏤⏑⏝ ⏤⏑⏤ (doch + 2 cre). But this loses the effective protractions in ταλαίνας / λιγείας.

1142/1152. Difficult to analyse, but the rhythm given seems most effective. For the incomplete dochmius at the beginning compare 1081/1086; the last five syllables are perhaps to be related to the 'hypodochmius' ⏤ ⏑ ⏤ ⏑ ⏤ (see M. West 1982, 110 n. 92). In his edition, West interprets the colon as ⏝ ⏑ ⏝ ⏤ ⏑ ⏤ ǀ • ⏤ • ⏤ (2 cre + ia).

Str. η 1156–66 = Ant. η 1167–77

The longer form of dochmius features more prominently in this final strophe of the lyric dialogue. The Chorus's dochmii undergo a great deal of resolution to reflect their extreme agitation.

	Ka.	⏑⏤⏑⏤ ⏑⏤⏑⏑̆ ǀ ⏑⏑⏑⏤⏑⏤	2 ia + doch
		⏑⏤⏑⏤ ǀ ⏤⏑⏑⏤⏑⏤	ia + doch
		⏑⏑⏑⏤⏑⏤ ⏤⏑⏑⏤⏑⏤	2 doch
1160/1171		⏤⏑⏑⏤⏑ ⏤	+ doch
		two iambic trimeters	
	Xo.	⏑⏑⏑⏑̆⏑⏑⏤ ⏑⏑⏑⏤⏑⏤	2 doch
		⏟⏤⏑⏝⏑⏤⏑⏤	2 ia
1164/1175		⏑⏤⏤⏑⏤ {⏤⏑⏑⏤⏑⏤ / ⏑⏤⏤⏑⏤}	+ 2 doch
1165/1176		⏑⏤⏤⏑⏤ ⏑⏑⏑⏑̆⏑⏑⏝	2 doch
		⏤⏑⏑⏤⏑⏤	doch

1164/1175. For the correspondence of the two different types of dochmius, see § 4.3.6.

Anapaests (1331–42)

See § 3 above.

Epirrhēma (1407–1576)

For general comments on the structure of this movement, see 1407–1576 n. The Chorus begins with confused and agitated dochmiacs, but gradually moves towards the insistence of syncopated iambics, which dominate its final strophic pair. This movement reflects the increasing clarity of the fact that Clytemnestra will have to suffer retribution in her turn. In the ephymnia, the prevailing aeolic and iambic cola are introduced by a run of anapaests.

Str. α 1407–11 = Ant. α 1426–30

	⏑⏑⏑⏠⏑⏠	doch
	⏑⏓⏑⏑⏑⏓ ⏑⏠⏑⏠	2 ia
	⏑⏑⏑⏠⏑⏠ −⏑⏑⏑⏑⏑⏠	2 doch
	⏑⏑⏑⏠⏑⏠ −⏑⏑⏠⏑⏠	2 doch
1410/1429	⏑⏑⏑⏑⏑⏑⏑⏑ }⏑⏑⏑⏠⏑⏠ −⏑⏑⏑⏑⏑⏠	2 doch

1408–9/1427–8. The two main forms of dochmiac are contrasted.

1410/1429. The fully resolved dochmius in 1410 is particularly striking. Then the other form of dochmius corresponds to it in 1429 (cf. 1164/75).

Str. β 1448–54 = Ant. β 1468–74

The Chorus's attack continues in a mixture of aeolic and iambo-trochaic cola.

	⏠⏑⏑⏠⏑⏠ ⏠⏑⏑⏠⏑⏠	2 dod
	⏠⏑⏠⏑⏑⏠−⏗	+ pher
1450/1470	⏑⏠⏑⏠ •⏠⏑⏠ ⏑⏠•⏠	3 ia
	⏠⏑⏑⏠⏑⏑⏠⏑⏠−	aeo₁₀
	⏑⏑⏑⏠⏑⏠⏑⏠	lec
	⏑⏑⏑⏑− ⏠⏑− ⏠⏑−	3 cre
	⏠⏑−	⏠⏑⏠⏑⏠⏑⏠	cre + lec

1448/1468. Or 2 doch, but the steadier dodrans, with its pulse on the first syllable, fits the other aeolic cola in the stanza (for the difference, see above, end of § 4.2).

1452–4/1472–4. These three cola could also be rhythmized as eight syncopated iambics. If cretics are right, there is a forceful effect to be heard in a succession of four bars in 5/8 time. For the text of 1474 see 1473–4 n.

Ephymnion 1 (1455–61)

A run of anapaests followed by the same types of cola (aeolic and iambic) as the preceding strophe.

1455	$--\acute{}<-\acute{}>\ \cup\cup\acute{}\cup\cup\acute{}$	2 an
	$\cup\cup\acute{}--\acute{}\ -\acute\cup\cup-\acute{}$	2 an
	$--\acute\cup\cup\acute{}\ \cup\cup\acute{}-\acute\curlywedge$	par
	$\acute\cup\cup\acute\cup\acute{}\ \acute\cup\cup\acute\cup\acute{}$	2 dod
1459–60	$\cup\acute\cup\acute{}\ \cup\acute\cup\acute{}\ \cup\acute\cup\acute{}$	3 ia
	$\bullet\acute\omega\cup\acute{}\ \bullet\acute{}\cup\acute{}\ \cup\acute{}\bullet\acute{}$	3 ia[26]

1455. For text see 1455 n.

1458–60. For text see 1458–61 n. For the metre compare 1448.

1462–7. Anapaests for Clytemnestra (see § 3).

1468–74 ~ 1448–54.

1475–80. Anapaests for Clytemnestra (see § 3).

Str. γ 1481–8 = Ant. γ 1505–12

	$\acute\cup\cup\acute\cup\cup\acute\frown$	(see below)
	$\acute\cup\cup\acute\cup\cup\acute\cup\acute{}-$	aeo$_{10}$
	$\acute\curlywedge-\acute\cup\cup\acute\cup\acute{}-$	hag
	$\acute\cup\acute\cup\cup\acute{}-\curlywedge$	+ pher
1485/1509	$\cup\acute\cup\acute{}\ \cup\acute\cup\acute{}$	2 ia
	$\cup\acute\cup\acute{}\ \cup\acute\cup\acute{}$	2 ia
	$\cup\acute\cup\acute{}\ \cup\acute\cup\acute{}\ \cup\acute{}-\curlywedge$	3 ia catalectic
	$\cup\acute{}\acute\cup\cup\acute\cup\acute\frown$	hipp

1481/1505. For readings at both these lines, see commentary. The colon could be described as three dactyls, but this obscures its link to the following colon: one might use a label such as 'aeolic 8-syllable'.

1487/1511. The third metron sounds better if taken as above, rather than as syncopated ($\cup\ \acute{}\bullet\acute{}$).

Ephymnion 2 (1489–96 = 1513–20)

	$-\acute{}-\acute{}\ \cup\cup\acute\cup\cup\acute{}$	2 an
1490/1514	$-\acute\cup\cup-\acute{}$	an
	$\cup\cup\acute\cup\cup\acute{}\ \cup\cup\acute{}-\curlywedge$	par
	$-\acute\cup\cup\acute{}\ \cup\cup\acute\cup\cup\acute{}$	2 an
	$\cup\ \cup\acute\cup\ \cup\acute{}\ \cup\cup\acute{}-\curlywedge$	par
	$-\acute{}\bullet\acute{}\mid\acute{}--\acute\cup\cup\acute\cup\acute{}$	ia + glyc
1495/1519	$\curlywedge\cup\cup\acute\cup\acute\cup\acute{}$	(see below)
	$\acute\cup\cup\acute\cup\cup\acute\cup\acute{}-$	aeo$_{10}$

---

[26] Or the first metron could be rhythmized $\cup\ \acute\omega\cup\bullet\acute{}$, if the succeeding syllable was protracted in syncopation: see above, n. 10.

1493/1517. ἐκπνέων: two syllables, by synizesis of εω.

1495/1519. This unusual colon may be interpreted as a decapitated version of glyc^B (compare 459–61, and § 4.3.4 above). In 1495 the vocal rest on the initial syllable might suggest the chop of Clytemnestra's sword, which is described in the following words.

1497–1504. Anapaests for Clytemnestra (see § 3).

1505–12 ~ 1481–8.

1513–20 = 1489–96.

1521–9. Anapaests for Clytemnestra, with a noteworthy number of dactylic substitutions, especially around the mention of Iphigenia.

Str. δ 1530–6 = Ant. δ 1560–6

Syncopated iambic trimeters now prevail almost throughout.

1530/1560	u‒u‒ • ‒u‒u‒ • ‒	3 ia
	‒uu‒u‒∩⋏	aris
	u‒u‒ • ‒u‒ u‒ • ‒	3 ia
	u‒u‒ • ‒u‒ u‒u‒	3 ia
	u‒u‒ • ‒u‒ u‒ • ‒	3 ia
1535/1565	u‒u‒ u‒u‒ u‒u‒	3 ia
	u‒ • ‒ • ‒u‒ u‒ • ‒	3 ia

1531/1561. For the use of an aristophanean within syncopated iambics compare 247, 380.

1535–6/1565–6. The final two cola juxtapose unsyncopated and syncopated metra with striking effect. The latter is a final recapitulation of the 'retribution motif' (see above, § 4.4; also below on 1550).

Ephymnion 3 (1537–50)

	‒‒‒‒ ‒uu‒‒	2 an
	‒‒uu‒ ‒uu‒‒	2 an
1540	‒‒uu‒ uu‒‒⋏	par
	uu‒‒‒ uu‒‒‒	2 an
	‒uu‒‒ ‒‒‒‒	2 an
	‒uu‒‒ uu‒‒‒	2 an
1545	‒‒uu‒ uu‒‒‒	2 an
	uu‒uu‒ uu‒‒⋏	par
	‒uu ‒uu ∣ ‒uu‒u‒‒	2 da + aris
	‒uu‒u‒‒⋏	aris
1550	u‒ • ‒ • ‒u‒ u‒ • ‒	3 ia

1547–8. The description given shows the relationship with the following colon.

1550. The final line of the ephymnion matches exactly the syncopation in the final line of strophe and antistrophe (1536/1566).

1551–9. Anapaests for Clytemnestra. There are a large number of dactylic substitutions in 1551–4, ceding markedly to uninterrupted forward motion for the lines describing Iphigenia coming to meeting Agamemnon on the banks of the Acheron.

1560–6 ~ 1530–6.

1567–76. Anapaests for Clytemnestra (see § 3).

D.A.R.

Works Cited

Allen, W. S. (1987), *Vox Graeca: A Guide to the Pronunciation of Classical Greek* (3rd edn.; Cambridge: Cambridge University Press).

Austin, C. A., and Olson, S. D. (2004), *Aristophanes: Thesmophoriazusae* (Oxford: Oxford University Press).

Austin, J. L. (1962), *How to Do Things with Words* (Oxford: Oxford University Press).

Badian, E. (1988), 'Towards a Chronology of the Pentekontaetia down to the Renewal of the Peace of Callias', *Echos du Monde Classique* 32: 289–320.

Bain, D. (1977), '*Electra* 518–44', *BICS* 24: 104–16.

Barber, E. J. W. (1992), 'The Peplos of Athena', in J. Nelis, ed., *Goddess and Polis: The Panathenaic Festival in Ancient Athens* (Princeton: Princeton University Press), 103–18.

Barrett, W. S. (1964), *Euripides: Hippolytus* (Oxford: Clarendon).

Beattie, A. J. (1954), 'Aeschylus, *Agamemnon* 281–316', *CR* 4: 77–81.

Betensky, A. (1978), 'Aeschylus' *Oresteia*: The Power of Clytemnestra', *Ramus* 7: 11–25.

Biles, Z. P. (2006–7), 'Aeschylus' Afterlife: Reperformance by Decree in 5th c. Athens?', *ICS* 31–2: 206–42.

Bollack, J., and Judet de la Combe, P. (1981–2), *L'Agamemnon d'Eschyle: Le Texte et ses interprétations*, 2 vols. (Lille: Presses Universitaires de Lille). *See also* Judet de la Combe (2001).

Borthwick, E. K. (1976), 'The "Flower of the Argives" and a Neglected Meaning of *ΆΝΘΟΣ*', *JHS* 96: 1–7.

—— (1981), '*Ἱστοτρίβης*: An Addendum', *AJPh* 102: 1–2.

Bowie, A. M. (1993), 'Religion and Politics in Aeschylus' *Oresteia*', *CQ* 43: 10–31.

Browning, R. (1877), *The Agamemnon of Aeschylus, Transcribed* (London: Smith Elder).

Burkert, W. (1985), *Greek Religion: Archaic and Classical*, trans. J. Raffan (Oxford: Blackwell).

Campbell, D. A. (1991), *Greek Lyric*, iii (Cambridge, Mass.: Harvard University Press).

Carter, D. M. (2007), *The Politics of Greek Tragedy* (Bristol: Phoenix).

Chiasson, C. C. (1988), 'Lecythia and the Justice of Zeus in Aeschylus' *Oresteia*', *Phoenix* 42: 1–21.

Citti, V. (1994), *Eschilo e la lexis tragica* (Amsterdam: Hakkert).

Collard, C. (2002), *Aeschylus: Oresteia* (Oxford: Oxford University Press).

—— (2005), 'Colloquial Language in Tragedy: A Supplement to the Work of P. T. Stevens', *CQ* 55: 350–86.

Conacher, D. J. (1976), 'Comments on an Interpretation of Aeschylus, *Agamemnon* 182–183', *Phoenix* 30: 328–36.

—— (1983), review of P. Smith (1980), in *Phoenix* 37: 163–6.

—— (1987), *Aeschylus' Oresteia: A Literary Commentary* (Toronto: University of Toronto Press).

—— (2000), 'Aeschylus' *Oresteia* and Euripides' *Bacchae*: A Critique of Some Recent Critical Approaches', *Echos du Monde Classique* 44: 333–49.

Csapo, E., and Slater, W. J. (1994), *The Context of Ancient Drama* (Ann Arbor: University of Michigan Press).

Davidson, J. (2005), 'Theatrical Production', in Gregory (2005), 194–211.

Detienne, M., and Vernant, J-P. (1978), *Cunning Intelligence in Greek Culture and Society*, trans. J. Lloyd (Hassocks: Harvester).

Dietrich, B. C. (1965), *Death, Fate, and the Gods: The Development of a Religious Idea in Greek Popular Belief and in Homer* (London: Athlone).

Dodds, E. R. (1973), *The Ancient Concept of Progress* (Oxford: Clarendon).

Dover, K. J. (1987), 'The Red Fabric in the *Agamemnon*', in *Greek and the Greeks: Collected Papers*, i. *Language, Poetry, Drama* (Oxford: Blackwell).

Doyle, R. E. (1970), '*Ὄλβος, κόρος, ὕβρις* and *ἄτη* from Hesiod to Aeschylus', *Traditio* 26: 293–303.

Earp, F. R. (1948), *The Style of Aeschylus* (Cambridge: Cambridge University Press).

Easterling, P. E. (1973), 'Presentation of Character in Aeschylus', *G&R* 20: 3–19.

—— and Hall, E. (2002), *Greek and Roman Actors: Aspects of an Ancient Profession* (Cambridge: Cambridge University Press).

Ewans, M. (1995), *Aeschylus: The Oresteia* (London: Dent).

Finglass, P. J. (2007), *Pindar: Pythian 11* (Cambridge: Cambridge Universtiy Press).

Finkelberg, M. (2000), 'The *Cypria*, the *Iliad*, and the Problem of Multiformity in Oral and Written Tradition', *CPh* 95: 1–11.

Foley, H. P. (2001), *Female Acts in Greek Tragedy* (Princeton: Princeton University Press).

—— (2003), 'Choral Identity in Greek Tragedy', *CPh* 98: 1–30.

Fornara, C. W. (1983), *Archaic Times to the End of the Peloponnesian War* (2nd edn.; Cambridge: Cambridge University Press).

Fowler, B. H. (1967), 'Aeschylus' Imagery', *Classica et Medievalia* 28: 1–74.

Frazer, J. G. (1921), *Apollodorus: The Library*, 2 vols., Loeb Classical Library (Cambridge, Mass.: Harvard University Press).

Furley, W. D. (1986), 'Motivation in the Parodos of Aeschylus' *Agamemnon*', *CPh* 82: 109–21.

Gagarin, M. (1976), *Aeschylean Drama* (Berkeley: University of California Press).

Gannon, J. F. (1997), 'A Note on Aeschylus, *Agamemnon* 403–5/420–2', *CQ* 47: 560–4.

Gantz, T. (1983), 'The Chorus of Aeschylus' *Agamemnon*', *HSPh* 87: 65–86.

—— (1993), *Early Greek Myth: A Guide to Literary and Artistic Sources* (Baltimore: Johns Hopkins University Press).

Garner, R. (1990), *From Homer to Tragedy: The Art of Allusion in Greek Poetry* (London: Routledge).

Garvie, A. F. (1986), *Aeschylus: Choephoroe* (Oxford: Clarendon).

—— (2009), *Aeschylus: Persians* (Oxford: Oxford University Press).

George, L. R. (2001), 'The Conjecture of a Sleeping Mind', *Eranos* 99: 75–86.

Goette, H. R. (2007), 'An Archaeological Appendix', in P. J. Wilson, ed., *The Greek Theatre and Festivals* (Oxford: Oxford University Press), 116–21.

Goldhill, S. (1984*a*), *Language, Sexuality, Narrative: The Oresteia* (Cambridge: Cambridge University Press).

—— (1984*b*), 'Two Notes on τέλος and Related Words in the *Oresteia*', *JHS* 104: 169–76.

—— (1986), *Reading Greek Tragedy* (Cambridge: Cambridge University Press).

—— (1990), 'The Great Dionysia and Civic Ideology', in J. J. Winkler and F. I. Zeitlin, eds., *Nothing to do with Dionysus?: Athenian Drama in its Social Context* (Princeton: Princeton University Press), 97–129.

—— (2000), 'Civic Ideology and the Problem of Difference: The Politics of Aeschylean Tragedy, Once Again', *JHS* 120: 34–56.

Gould, J. (1973), '*HIKETEIA*', *JHS* 93: 74–103.

—— (1978), 'Dramatic Character and "Human Intelligibility" in Greek Tragedy', *PCPhS* 24: 43–63.

Goward, B. (2005), *Aeschylus: Agamemnon* (London: Duckworth).

Gregory, J. (2005), *A Companion to Greek Tragedy* (Oxford: Blackwell).

Griffith, M. (1977), *The Authenticity of the Prometheus Bound* (Cambridge: Cambridge University Press).

—— (2002), 'Slaves of Dionysos: Satyrs, Audience, and the Ends of the *Oresteia*', *ClAnt* 21: 195–258.

—— (2009), 'The Poetry of Aeschylus (in its Traditional Contexts)', in Jouanna and Montanari (2009), 1–55.

Gruber, M. A. (2009), *Der Chor in den Tragödien des Aischylos: Affekt und Reaktion* (Tübingen: Narr).

Guthman, E. O., and Allen, C. R. (1993), *RFK: Collected Speeches* (New York: Viking).

Hall, E. (1989), *Inventing the Barbarian: Greek Self-Definition through Tragedy* (Oxford: Clarendon).

—— (2005), 'Aeschylus' Clytemnestra versus her Senecan Tradition', in Macintosh et al. (2005), 53–75.

Harriot, R. M. (1982), 'The Argive Elders, the Discerning Shepherds, and the

Fawning Dog: Misleading Communication in the *Agamemnon*', *CQ* 32: 9–17.

Headlam, W. G. (1904), *Aeschylus: The Agamemnon* (London: G. Bell).

Heath, J. (1999), 'Disentangling the Beast: Humans and Other Animals in Aeschylus' *Oresteia*', *JHS* 119: 17–48.

—— (2001), 'The Omen of the Eagles and Hare (*Agamemnon* 104–59): From Aulis to Argos and Back Again', *CQ* 51: 18–22.

Heath, M. (2006), 'The "Social Function" of Tragedy: Clarifications and Questions', in D. Cairns and V. Liapis, eds., *Dionysalexandros: Essays on Aeschylus and his Fellow Tragedians in Honour of Alexander F. Garvie* (Swansea: Classical Press of Wales), 253–81.

Heirman, L. J. (1975), 'Kassandra's Glossolalia', *Mnemosyne* 28: 257–67.

Helm, J. J. (2004), 'Aeschylus' Genealogy of Morals', *TAPhA* 134: 23–54.

Herington, J. (1985), *Poetry into Drama: Early Tragedy and the Greek Poetic Tradition* (Berkeley: University of California Press).

Hershbell, J. P. (1978), 'The Ancient Telegraph: War and Literacy', in E. A. Havelock and J. P. Hershbell, eds., *Communication Arts in the Ancient World* (New York: Hastings House), 81–94.

Housman, A. E. (1888), 'The *Agamemnon* of Aeschylus', *Journal of Philology* 16: 244–290, repr. *The Classical Papers of A. E. Housman: Volume I 1882–1897*, ed. J. Diggle and F. R. D. Goodyear (Cambridge: Cambridge University Press, 1972), 55–90.

—— (1997), *The Poems of A. E. Housman*, ed. A. Burnett (Oxford: Clarendon).

Hutchinson, G. O. (1984), *Aeschylus: Septem contra Thebas* (Oxford: Clarendon).

Jackson, P., dir. (2003), *The Lord of the Rings: The Return of the King* [film] (USA and New Zealand: New Line).

Jameson, M. H., Jordan, D. R., and Kotansky, R. D. (1993), *A Lex Sacra from Selinous* (Durham, NC: Duke University Press).

Jebb, R. C. (1898), *Sophocles: The Plays and Fragments*, iv. *The Philoctetes* (2nd edn.; Cambridge: Cambridge University Press).

Jouanna, J., and Montanari, F. (2009), *Eschyle à l'aube du théâtre occidental*, Entretiens Hardt 55 (Vandœuvres: Fondation Hardt).

Judet de la Combe, P. (2001), *L'Agamemnon d'Eschyle: Commentaire des dialogues*, 2 vols. (Villeneuve-d'Ascq: Presses Universitaires du Septentrion).

Kitto, H. D. F. (1955), 'The Dance in Greek Tragedy', *JHS* 75: 36–41.

—— (1956), *Form and Meaning in Drama: A Study of Six Greek Plays and of Hamlet* (London: Methuen).

Knoepfler, D. (1993), *Les Imagiers de l'Orestie: Mille ans d'art antique autour d'un mythe grecque* (Kilchberg: Akanthus).

Knox, B. M. W. (1952), 'The Lion in the House (*Agamemnon* 717–36)', *CPh* 47: 17–25.

Works Cited

Knox, B. M. W. (1972), 'Aeschylus and the Third Actor', *AJPh* 93: 104–24.

Kovacs, D. (1987), 'The Way of a God with a Maid in Aeschylus' *Agamemnon*', *CPh* 82: 326–34.

—— (2005), 'Text and Transmission', in Gregory (2005), 379–93.

Lavery, J. F. (2004*a*), 'Aeschylus *Agamemnon* 1180–2: A Booster?', *Hermes* 132: 1–19.

—— (2004*b*), 'Clytemnestra's Negatives and the Final Line of *Agamemnon*', *BICS* 47: 57–77.

—— (2004*c*), 'Some Aeschylean Influences on Seneca's *Agamemnon*', *Materiali e Discussioni* 53: 183–94.

Lebeck, A. (1971), *The Oresteia: A Study in Language and Structure* (Washington: Center for Hellenic Studies).

Lesky, A. (1983), 'Decision and Responsibility in the Tragedy of Aeschylus', in E. Segal, ed., *Oxford Readings in Greek Tragedy* (Oxford: Oxford University Press), 13–23.

Ley, G. (2007), *The Theatricality of Greek Tragedy: Playing Space and Chorus* (Chicago: University of Chicago Press).

Lloyd, M. (1999), 'The Tragic Aorist', *CQ* 49: 24–45.

Lloyd-Jones, H. (1952), 'The Robes of Iphigeneia', *CR* 2: 132–5.

—— (1978), 'Ten Notes on Aeschylus, *Agamemnon*', in R. D. Dawe, J. Diggle, and P. E. Easterling, eds., *Dionysiaca: Nine Studies in Greek Poetry by Former Pupils, Presented to Denys Page on his Seventieth Birthday* (Cambridge: The Editors), 45–61.

—— (1979), *Aeschylus' Oresteia: Agamemnon* (2nd edn.; London: Duckworth).

Long, C. R. (1987), *The Twelve Gods of Greece and Rome* (Leiden: Brill).

Lynn-George, M. (1993), 'A Reflection of Homeric Dawn in the Parodos of Aeschylus, *Agamemnon*', *CQ* 43: 1–9.

McClure, L. (1999), *Spoken Like a Woman: Speech and Gender in Athenian Drama* (Princeton: Princeton University Press).

MacDowell, D. M. (1978), *The Law in Classical Athens* (London: Thames & Hudson).

McHardy, F. (2008), *Revenge in Athenian Culture* (London: Duckworth).

Macintosh, F. (2009), 'The "Rediscovery" of Aeschylus for the Modern Stage', in Jouanna & Montanari (2009), 435–68.

——, Michelakis, P., Hall, E., and Taplin, O. (2005), *Agamemnon in Performance, 458 BC to AD 2004* (Oxford: Oxford University Press).

Macleod, C. W. (1975), 'Clothing in the *Oresteia*', *Maia* 27: 201–3.

—— (1982), 'Politics and the *Oresteia*', *JHS* 102: 124–44.

Marshall, C. W. (2003), 'Casting the *Oresteia*', *CJ* 98: 257–74.

Mazzoldi, S. (2002), 'Cassandra's Prophecy between Ecstasy and Rational Mediation', *Kernos* 15: 145–54.

Metzger, E. (2005), 'Clytemnestra's Watchman on the Roof', *Eranos* 103: 38–47.

Mitchell-Boyask, R. (2006), 'The Marriage of Cassandra and the *Oresteia*: Text, Image, Performance', *TAPhA* 136: 269–97.

—— (2009), *Aeschylus: Eumenides* (London: Duckworth).

Moles, J. L. (1979), 'A Neglected Aspect of *Agamemnon* 1389–92', *Liverpool Classical Monthly* 4: 179–89.

Morgan, K. (1994), 'Apollo's Favorites', *GRBS* 35: 121–43.

Moritz, H. E. (1979), 'Refrain in Aeschylus: Literary Adaptation of Traditional Form', *CPh* 74: 187–213.

Nussbaum, M. C. (2001), *The Fragility of Goodness: Luck and Ethics in Greek Tragedy and Philosophy* (2nd edn.; Cambridge: Cambridge University Press).

O' Daly, G. J. P. (1985), 'Clytemnestra and the Elders: Dramatic Technique in Aeschylus, *Agamemnon* 1372–1576', *Museum Helveticum* 42: 1–19.

Olson, S. D. (1995), *Blood and Iron: Story and Storytelling in Homer's Odyssey* (Leiden: Brill).

Ostwald, M. (1988), *ΑΝΑΓΚΗ in Thucydides* (Atlanta: Scholars Press).

Owen, E. T. (1952), *The Harmony of Aeschylus* (Toronto: Clarke, Irwin).

Padel, R. (1995), *Whom Gods Destroy: Elements of Greek and Tragic Madness* (Princeton: Princeton University Press).

Parker, L. P. E. (2007), *Euripides: Alcestis* (Oxford: Oxford University Press).

Parker, R. C. T. (1983), *Miasma: Pollution and Purification in Early Greek Religion* (Oxford: Clarendon).

—— (1997), 'Gods Cruel and Kind: Tragic and Civic Theology', in Pelling (1997), 143–60.

—— (2009), 'Aeschylus' Gods: Drama, Cult, Theology', in Jouanna and Montanari (2009), 127–64.

Pearson, L. (1974), 'Catalexis and Anceps in Pindar: A Search for Rhythmical Logic', *GRBS* 15: 171–91.

—— (1990), *Aristoxenus: Elementa Rhythmica* (Oxford: Clarendon).

Pelling, C. B. R. (1990), *Characterization and Individuality in Greek Literature* (Oxford: Clarendon).

—— (1997), *Greek Tragedy and the Historian* (Oxford: Clarendon).

—— (2000), *Literary Texts and the Greek Historian* (London: Routledge).

Peradotto, J. J. (1969), 'Cledonomancy in the *Oresteia*', *AJPh* 90: 1–21.

Pfundstein, J. M. (2003), '*Λαμπροὺς δυνάστας*: Aeschylus, Astronomy and the *Agamemnon*', *CJ* 98: 397–410.

Pickard-Cambridge, A. (1988), *The Dramatic Festivals of Athens*, rev. J. Gould and D. M. Lewis (3rd edn.; Oxford: Clarendon).

Podlecki, A. J. (1966), *The Political Background of Aeschylean Tragedy* (Ann Arbor: University of Michigan Press).

—— (1983), 'Aeschylean Women', *Helios* 10: 23–47.

—— (1989), *Aeschylus: Eumenides* (Warminster: Aris & Phillips).

Poe, J. P. (1989), 'The Altar in the Fifth-Century Theatre', *ClAnt* 8: 116–39.

Pope, M. (1974), 'Merciful Heavens? A Question in Aeschylus' *Agamemnon*', *JHS* 94: 100–13.

Porter, D. H. (1986), 'The Imagery of Greek Tragedy: Three Characteristics', *Symbolae Osloenses* 61: 19–42.

Prag, A. J. N. W. (1985), *The Oresteia: Iconographic and Narrative Tradition* (Warminster: Aris & Phillips).

Pritchett, W. K. (1985), *The Greek State at War*, iv (Berkeley: University of California Press).

Probert, P. (2003), *A New Short Guide to the Accentuation of Ancient Greek* (Bristol: Bristol Classical Press).

Pulleyn, S. (1997), 'Erotic Undertones in the Language of Clytemnestra', *CQ* 47: 565–7.

Quincey, J. H. (1963), 'The Beacon-Sites in the *Agamemnon*', *JHS* 83: 118–32.

Raeburn, D. A. (2000), 'The Significance of Stage Properties in Euripides' *Electra*', *G&R* 47: 149–68.

Raven, D. S. (1962), *Greek Metre: An Introduction* (London: Faber & Faber).

Rehm, R. (1992), *Greek Tragic Theatre* (London: Routledge).

Renehan, R. (1976), *Studies in Greek Texts: Critical Observations to Homer, Plato, Euripides, Aristophanes and Other Authors* (Göttingen: Vandenhoeck & Ruprecht).

Rhodes, P. J. (1972), *The Athenian Boule* (Oxford: Clarendon).

—— (1992), 'The Athenian Revolution', in D. M. Lewis, J. Boardman, J. K. Davies, and M. Ostwald, eds., *The Cambridge Ancient History*, v (2nd edn.; Cambridge: Cambridge University Press), 62–77.

Rihll, T. E. (1995), 'Democracy Denied: Why Ephialtes Attacked the Areiopagus', *JHS* 115: 87–98.

Roberts, D. H. (1984), *Apollo and his Oracle in the Oresteia* (Göttingen: Vandenhoeck & Ruprecht).

Rosenbloom, D. (1995), 'Myth, History, and Hegemony in Aeschylus', in B. Goff, ed., *History, Tragedy, Theory: Dialogues on Athenian Drama* (Austin: University of Texas Press), 91–130.

Rosenmeyer, T. G. (1984), *The Art of Aeschylus* (Berkeley: University of California Press).

Rutherford, R. B. (2010), 'The Greek of Athenian Tragedy', in E. J. Bakker, ed., *A Companion to the Ancient Greek Language* (Oxford: Wiley–Blackwell), 441–54.

Schenker, D. J. (1994), 'The Chorus' Hymn to Zeus: Aeschylus, *Agamemnon* 160–83', *Syllecta Classica* 5: 1–7.

—— (1999), 'Dissolving Differences: Character Overlap and Audience Response', *Mnemosyne* 52: 641–57.

Scott, W. C. (1969), 'The Confused Chorus: *Agamemnon* 975–1034', *Phoenix* 23: 336–46.

—— (1984), *Musical Design in Aeschylean Theatre* (Hanover, NH: University Press of New England).

Scullion, S. (1994*a*), *Three Studies in Athenian Dramaturgy* (Stuttgart: Tuebner).

—— (1994*b*), 'Olympian and Chthonian', *ClAnt* 13: 75–119.

—— (2002), 'Nothing to do with Dionysus: Tragedy Misconceived as Ritual', *CQ* 52: 102–37.

Seaford, R. S. (1984), 'The Last Bath of Agamemnon', *CQ* 34: 247–54.

—— (1987), 'The Tragic Wedding', *JHS* 107: 106–30.

—— (2003), 'Aeschylus and the Unity of Opposites', *JHS* 123: 141–63.

Seidensticker, B. (2009), 'Charakter und Charakterisierung bei Aischylos', in Jouanna and Montanari (2009), 205–56.

Sens, A. (2011), *Asclepiades of Samos: Epigrams and Fragments* (Oxford: Oxford University Press).

Sewell-Rutter, N. J. (2007), *Guilt by Descent: Moral Inheritance and Decision Making in Greek Tragedy* (Oxford: Oxford University Press).

Sideras, A. (1971), *Aeschylus Homericus: Untersuchungen zu den Homerismen der aischyleischen Sprache* (Göttingen: Vandenhoeck & Ruprecht).

Silk, M. S. (1983), 'LSJ and the Problem of Poetic Archaism: From Meaning to Iconyms', *CQ* 33: 303–30.

—— (1996), *Tragedy and the Tragic: Greek Theatre and Beyond* (Oxford: Clarendon).

Simon, E. (1982), *The Ancient Theatre*, trans. C. E. Vafopoulou-Richardson (London: Methuen).

Skeat, T. C. (1975), '"Ὄκνος', in J. Bingen, G. Cambier, and G. Nachtergael, eds., *Le Monde grec: Pensée, littérature, histoire, documents: Hommages à Claire Préaux* (Brussels: Éditions de l'Université), 791–5.

Smith, O. L. (1976), *Scholia graeca in Aeschylum quae exstant omnia*, i (Leipzig, Teubner).

Smith, P. M. (1980), *On the Hymn to Zeus in Aeschylus' Agamemnon* (Chico: Scholars Press).

Sommerstein, A. H. (1989), *Aeschylus: Eumenides* (Cambridge: Cambridge University Press).

—— (1995–6), 'Aesch. *Ag.* 104–59: The Omen of Aulis or the Omen of Argos?', *Museum Criticum* 30–1: 87–94.

—— (1996), *Aristophanes: Frogs* (Warminster: Aris & Phillips).

—— (2002), 'Comic Elements in Tragic Language: The Case of Aeschylus' *Oresteia*', in A. Willi, ed., *The Language of Greek Comedy* (Oxford: Oxford University Press), 151–68.

—— (2010), *Aeschylean Tragedy* (2nd edn.; London: Duckworth).

Stanford, W. B. (1940), 'Three-Word Iambic Trimeters in Greek Tragedy', *CR* 54: 8–10.

—— (1942), *Aeschylus in his Style: A Study in Language and Personality* (Dublin: University Press).

Steiner, D. T. (1995), 'Eyeless in Argos: A Reading of *Agamemnon* 416–19', *JHS* 115: 175–82.

—— (2002), 'Indecorous Dining, Indecorous Speech: Pindar's First *Olympian* and the Poetics of Consumption', *Arethusa* 35: 297–314.

Struck, P. (2004), *Birth of the Symbol: Ancient Readers at the Limits of their Texts* (Princeton: Princeton University Press).

Swift, L. (2010), *The Hidden Chorus: Echoes of Genre in Tragic Lyric* (Oxford: Oxford University Press).

Taplin, O. (1972), 'Aeschylean Silences and Silences in Aeschylus', *HSPh* 76: 57–97.

—— (1977), *The Stagecraft of Aeschylus* (Oxford: Clarendon).

—— (1978), *Greek Tragedy in Action* (London: Methuen).

Tarrant, R. J. (1976), *Seneca: Agamemnon* (Cambridge: Cambridge University Press).

Thalmann, W. G. (1985), 'Speech and Silence in the *Oresteia* I: *Agamemnon* 1025–1029', *Phoenix* 39: 99–118.

—— (1993), 'Euripides and Aeschylus: The Case of the *Hekabe*', *ClAnt* 12: 126–59.

Thompson, D'A. W. (1936), *A Glossary of Greek Birds*, 2nd edn. (Oxford: Oxford University Press).

Thomson, G. D. (1938), *The Oresteia of Aeschylus* (Cambridge: Cambridge University Press).

Van Keuren, F. D. (1989), *The Frieze from the Hera I Temple at Foce del Sele* (Rome: Bretschneider).

Van Steen, G. A. H. (2008), ' "You Unleash the Tempest of Tragedy": The 1903 Athenian Production of Aeschylus' *Oresteia*', in L. Hardwick and C. Stray, eds., *A Companion to Classical Receptions* (Oxford: Blackwell), 360–72.

Vernant, J-P. (1981), 'The Historical Moment of Greek Tragedy', in J-P. Vernant and P. Vidal-Naquet, *Tragedy and Myth in Ancient Greece*, trans. J. Lloyd (Brighton: Harvester), 1–5.

—— (1991), *Mortals and Immortals: Collected Essays*, ed. F. I. Zeitlin (Princeton: Princeton University Press).

Wallace, R. W. (1989), *The Areopagos Council to 307 BC* (Baltimore: Johns Hopkins University Press).

Wartelle, A. (1971), *Histoire du texte d'Eschyle dans l'antiquité* (Paris: Klincksieck).

West, M. L. (1979), 'Tragica, III', *BICS* 26: 104–17.

—— (1982), *Greek Metre* (Oxford: Clarendon).

—— (1990*a*), *Studies in Aeschylus* (Stuttgart: Teubner).

—— (1990*b*), 'Colloquialism and Naïve Style in Aeschylus', in E. M. Craik, ed., *Owls to Athens: Essays on Classical Subjects Presented to Sir Kenneth Dover* (Oxford: Clarendon), 3–12.

—— (1992), *Ancient Greek Music* (Oxford: Clarendon).

—— (1999), 'Aeschylus, *Agamemnon* 104–59', *Lexis* 17: 41–61.

—— (2003), *Greek Epic Fragments: From the Seventh to the Fifth Centuries BC* (Cambridge, Mass.: Harvard University Press).

West, S. R. (1992), 'Textile Homage: A Note on Aeschylus, *Agamemnon* 895–974', in *Apodosis: Essays Presented to Dr W. W. Cruickshank to Mark his Eightieth Birthday* (London: St Paul's School Publications), 111–18.

—— (2003), 'Aegisthus the Cowardly Lion: A Note on Aeschylus, *Agamemnon* 1224', *Mnemosyne* 56: 480–4.

Wilamowitz-Moellendorff, U. von (1933), *Euripides: Herakles* (2nd edn.; Berlin: Weidmann).

Wiles, D. (1997), *Tragedy in Athens: Performance Space and Theatrical Meaning* (Cambridge: Cambridge University Press).

—— (2000), *Greek Theatre Performance: An Introduction* (Cambridge: Cambridge University Press).

Williams, B. A. O. (1993), *Shame and Necessity* (Berkeley: University of California Press).

Wilson, P. J. (2000), *The Athenian Institution of the Khoregia: The Chorus, the City, and the Stage* (Cambridge: Cambridge University Press).

—— (2006), '*Dikēn* in the *Oresteia* of Aeschylus', in J. F. Davidson, F. Muecke, and P. J. Wilson, eds., *Greek Drama III: Essays in Honour of Kevin Lee* (London: Institute of Classical Studies), 187–201.

—— and Taplin, O. (1993), 'The "Aetiology" of Tragedy in the *Oresteia*', *PCPhS* 39: 169–80.

Winnington-Ingram, R. P. (1983), *Studies in Aeschylus* (Cambridge: Cambridge University Press).

Yarkho, V. N. (1997), 'The Technique of Leitmotivs in the *Oresteia* of Aeschylus', *Philologus* 141: 184–99.

Zeitlin, F. I. (1965), 'The Motif of the Corrupt Sacrifice in Aeschylus' *Oresteia*', *TAPhA* 96: 463–508.

—— (1966), 'Postscript to Sacrificial Imagery in the *Oresteia*: *Ag.* 1235–1237', *TAPhA* 97: 645–53.

—— (1996), *Playing the Other: Gender and Society in Classical Greek Literature* (Chicago: University of Chicago Press).

Index of Other Passages
from the Oresteia

Arabic numerals refer to line-numbers, unless they are italicized and preceded by 'p(p).'.

Index

Arabic numerals refer to line-numbers, unless they are italicized and preceded by 'p(p).'. Emboldened line-ranges indicate that a topic occurs *passim*.